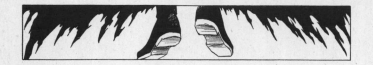

If it rusts, it can never be trusted
If its owner fails to control it, it will cut him
Yes, pride is
Like a blade

BLEACH 8 THE BLADE AND ME

Shonen Jump Manga

STARS AND

Kisuke Urahara

Tessai Tsukabishi

Ichigo Kurosaki

 plot

In a series of strange events, Ichigo Kurosaki encountered Rukia Kuchiki and came to possess her Soul Reaper powers. Now his job is to cleanse fallen souls called Hollows and guide them to the Soul Society. Eventually Ichigo's powers grow strong, enabling him to defeat the colossal Menos Grande.

Now Rukia languishes in a Soul Society jail with a death sentence hanging over her. In order to regain his lost powers and rescue Rukia, Ichigo allows Kisuke Urahara to train him. But Lesson 2, the Shattered Shaft, will either restore Ichigo's powers, or destroy his very soul....

BLEACH 8

THE BLADE AND ME

Contents

BLEACH ALL

夜一
Yoruichi

花刈ジン太
Jinta Hanakari

Ururu Tsumugiya

紬屋雨

STORIES

62. Lesson 2-2: Bad Ending in the Shaft

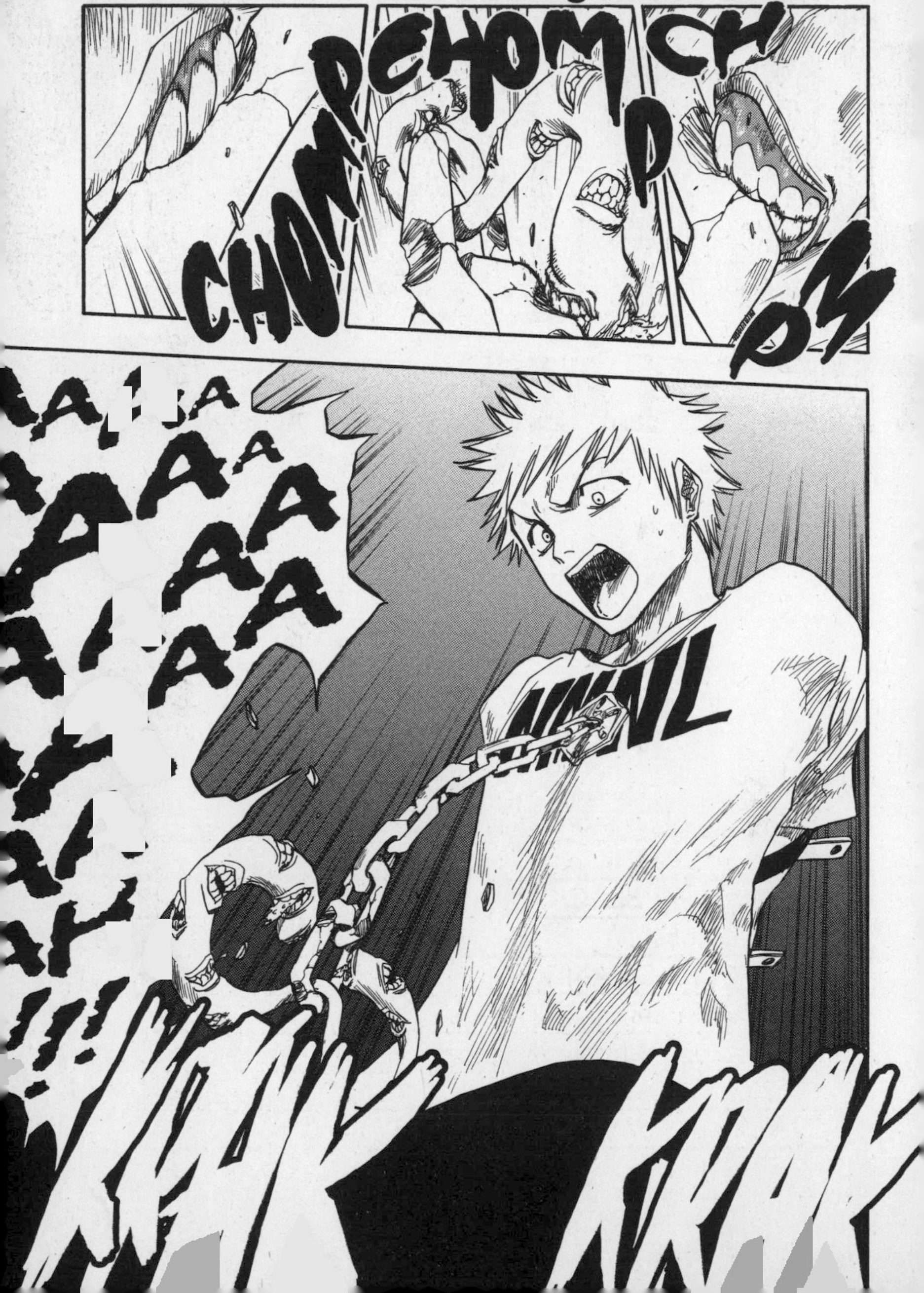
CHOMP
CHOMP
CHOMP
AAAAAA!!!
KRAK

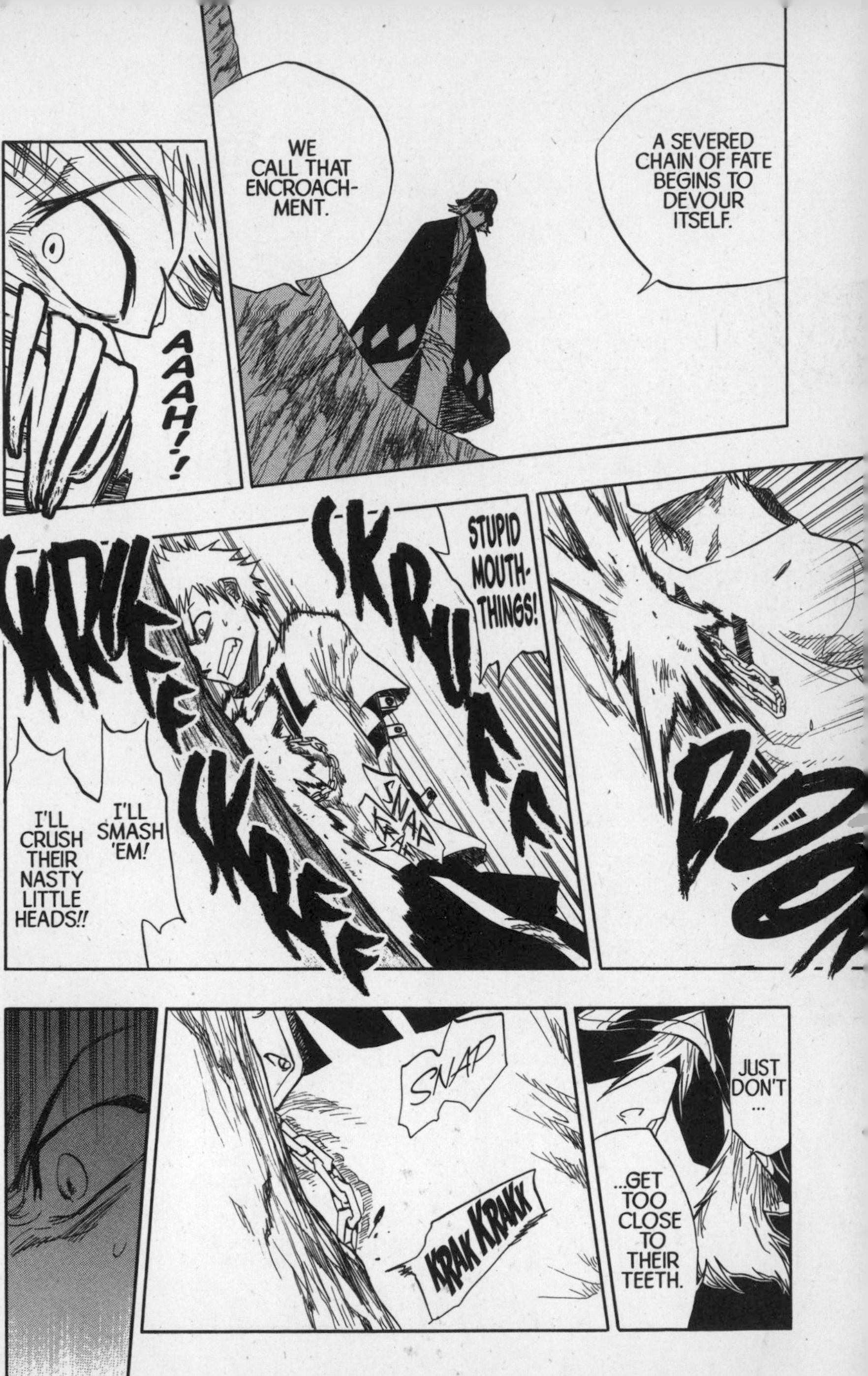
A SEVERED CHAIN OF FATE BEGINS TO DEVOUR ITSELF.
WE CALL THAT ENCROACHMENT.
AAAH!!
STUPID MOUTH-THINGS!
SNAP KRAK
I'LL SMASH 'EM!
I'LL CRUSH THEIR NASTY LITTLE HEADS!!
JUST DON'T ...
...GET TOO CLOSE TO THEIR TEETH.
SNAP
KRAK KRAKK

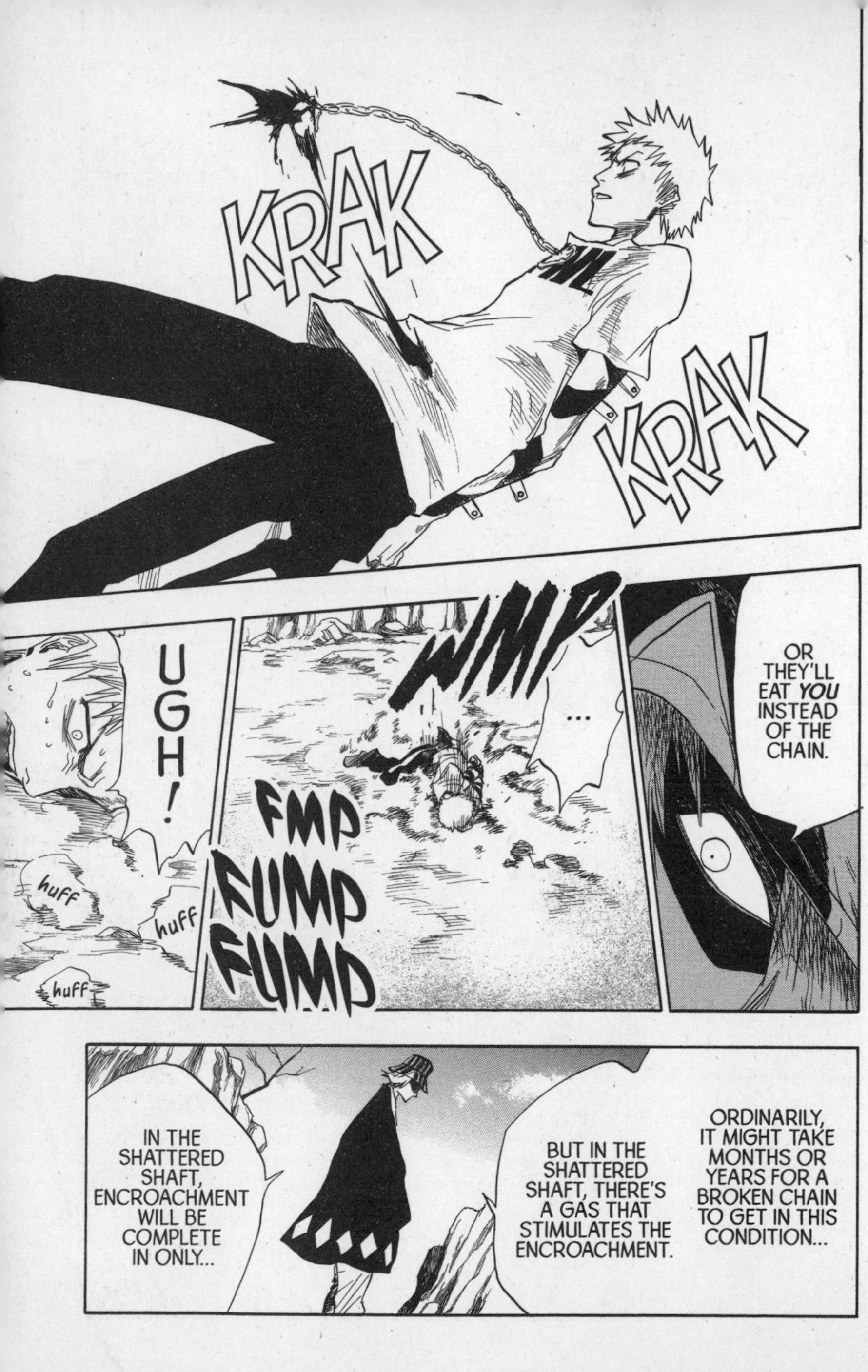
KRAK
KRAK
OR THEY'LL EAT *YOU* INSTEAD OF THE CHAIN.
WMP
...
FMP
FUMP
FUMP
UGH!
huff
huff
huff
ORDINARILY, IT MIGHT TAKE MONTHS OR YEARS FOR A BROKEN CHAIN TO GET IN THIS CONDITION...
BUT IN THE SHATTERED SHAFT, THERE'S A GAS THAT STIMULATES THE ENCROACHMENT.
IN THE SHATTERED SHAFT, ENCROACHMENT WILL BE COMPLETE IN ONLY...

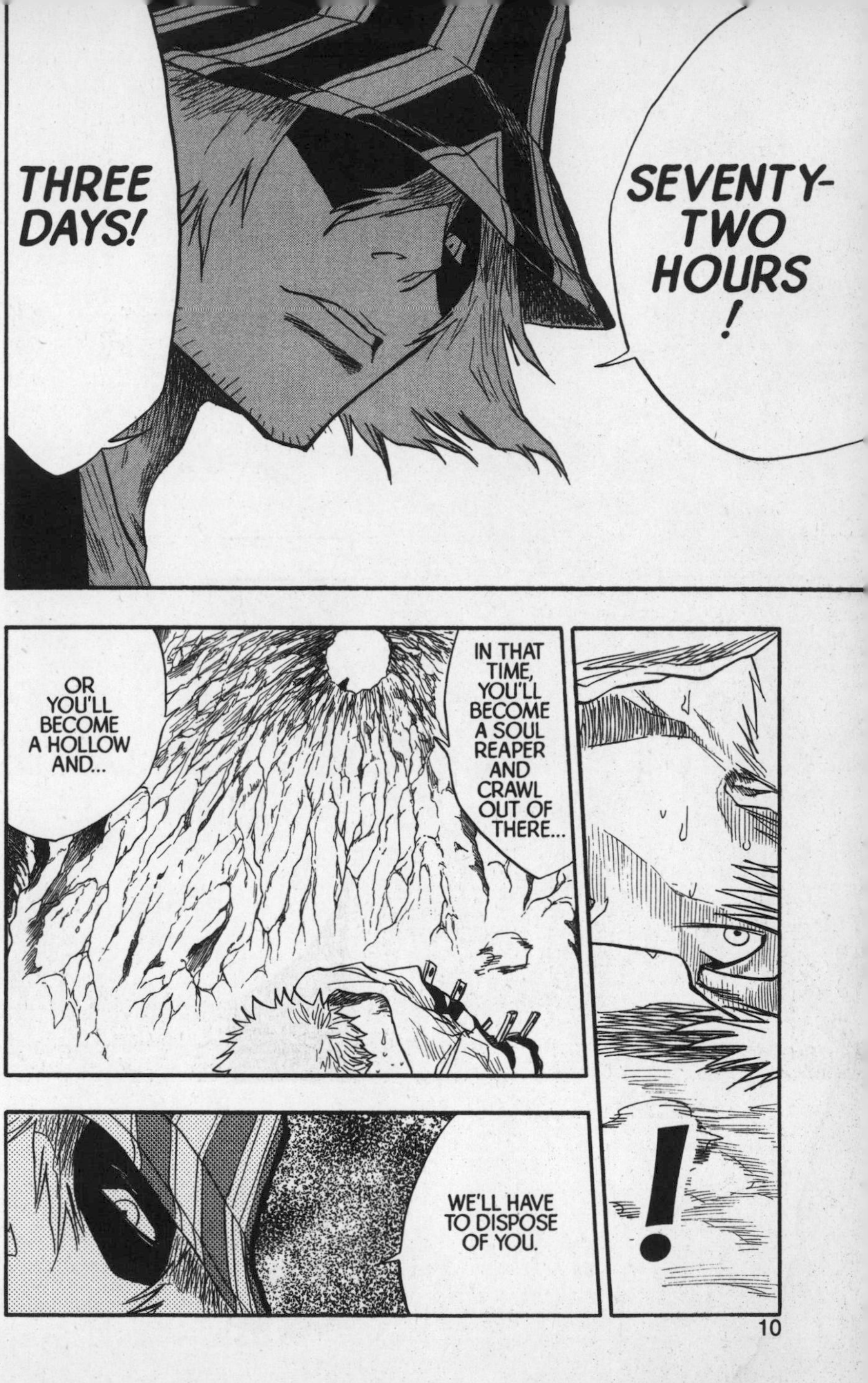
SEVENTY-TWO HOURS!
THREE DAYS!
!
IN THAT TIME, YOU'LL BECOME A SOUL REAPER AND CRAWL OUT OF THERE...
OR YOU'LL BECOME A HOLLOW AND...
WE'LL HAVE TO DISPOSE OF YOU.

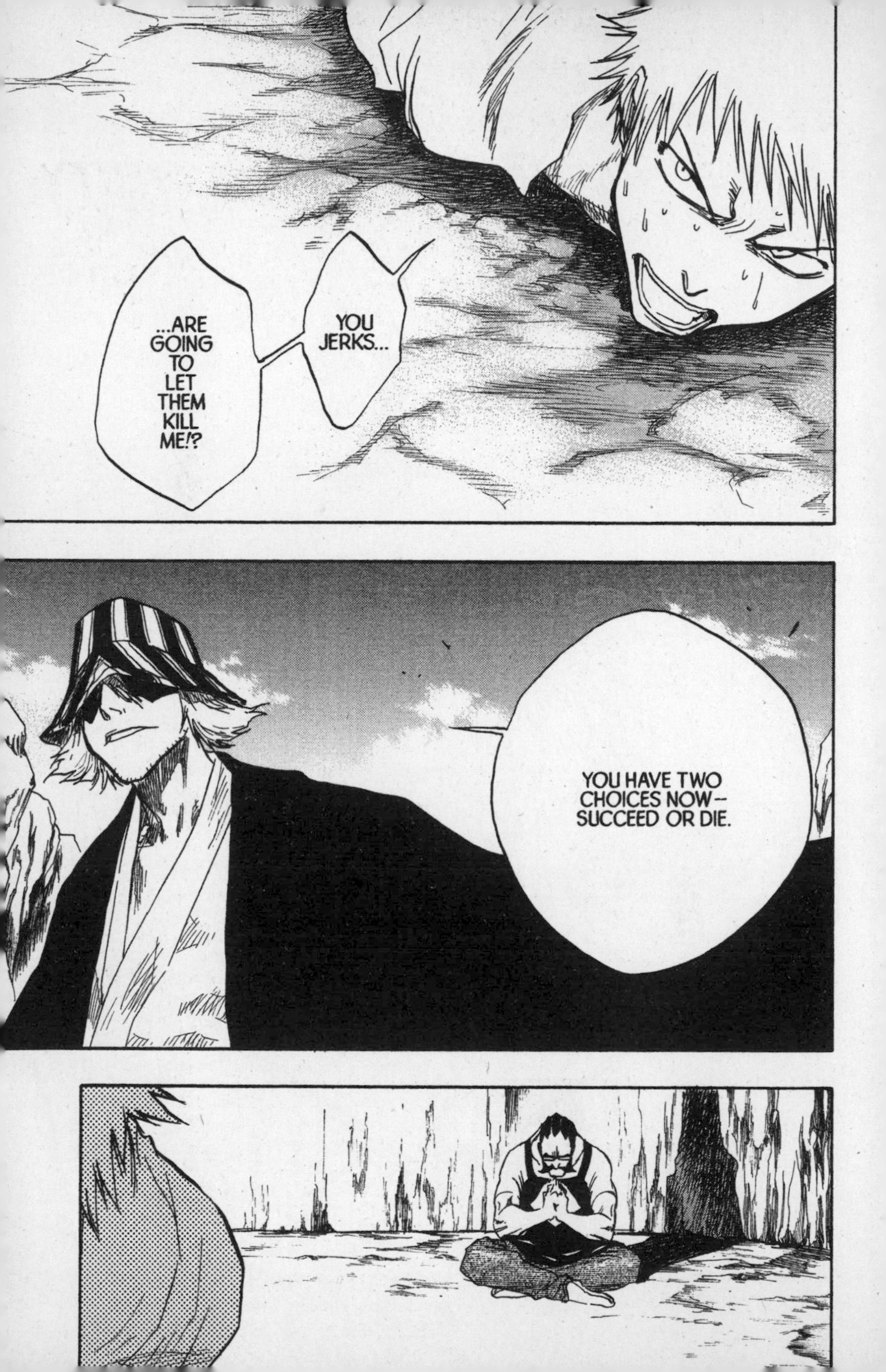
YOU JERKS...
...ARE GOING TO LET THEM KILL ME!?
YOU HAVE TWO CHOICES NOW-- SUCCEED OR DIE.

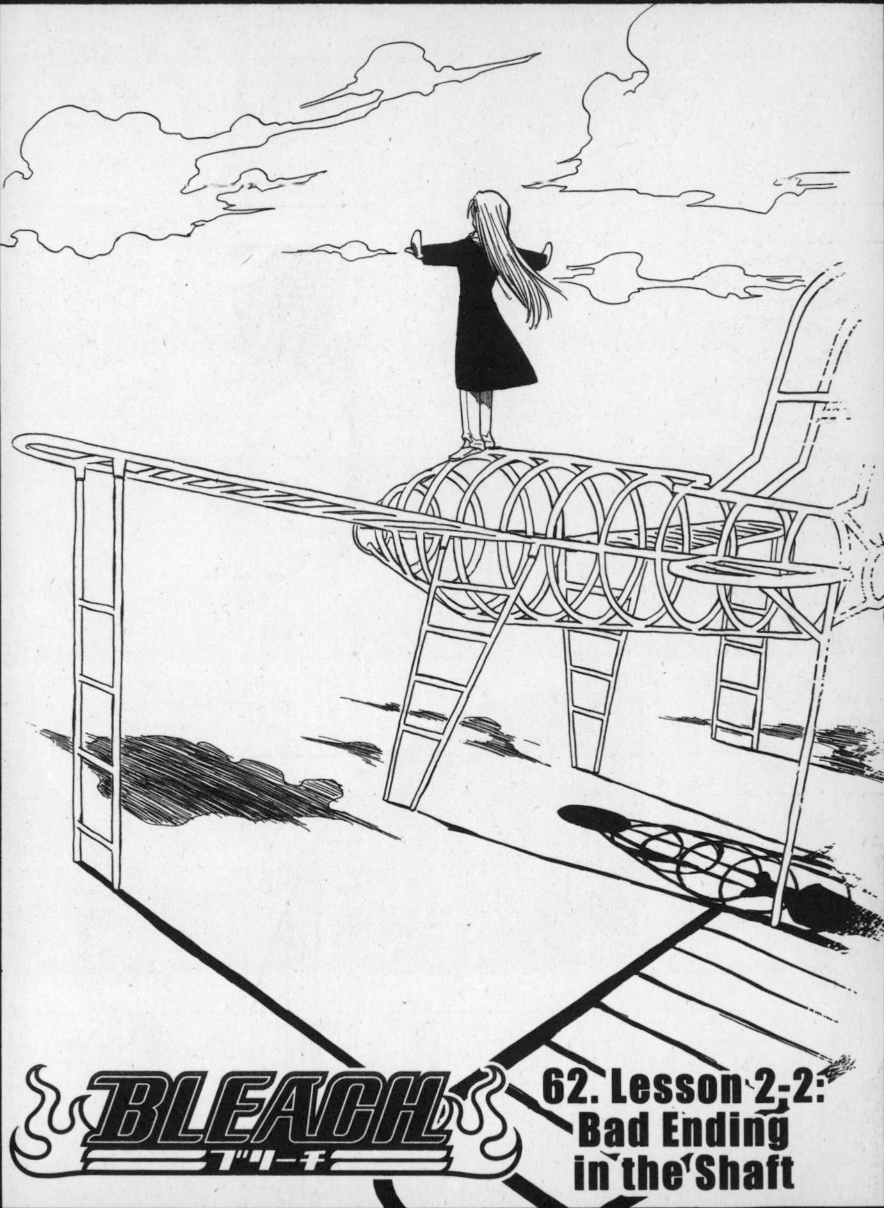
BLEACH
ブリーチ
62. Lesson 2-2:
Bad Ending
in the Shaft

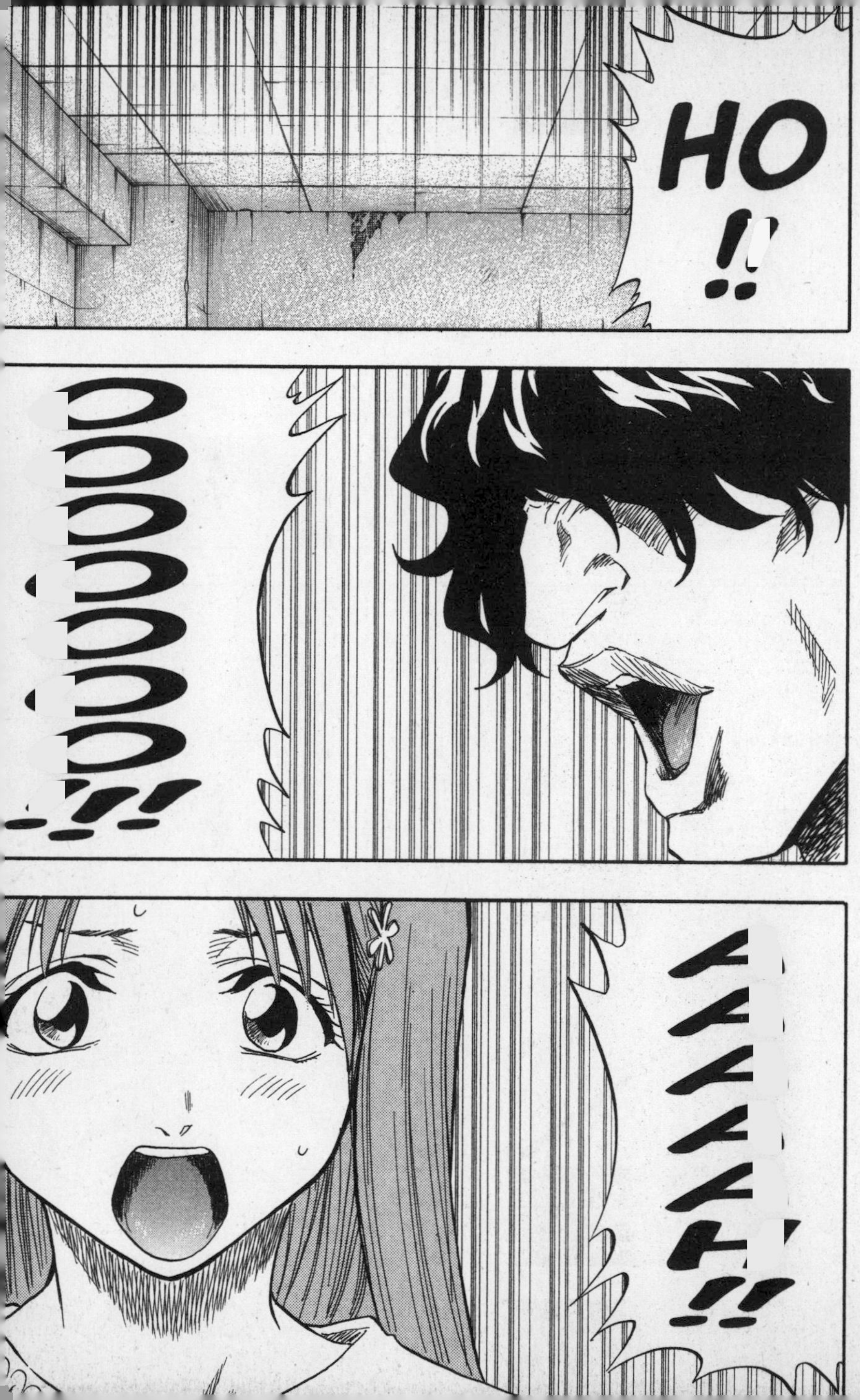
HO!!
OOOOOOO!!
AAAAAH!!

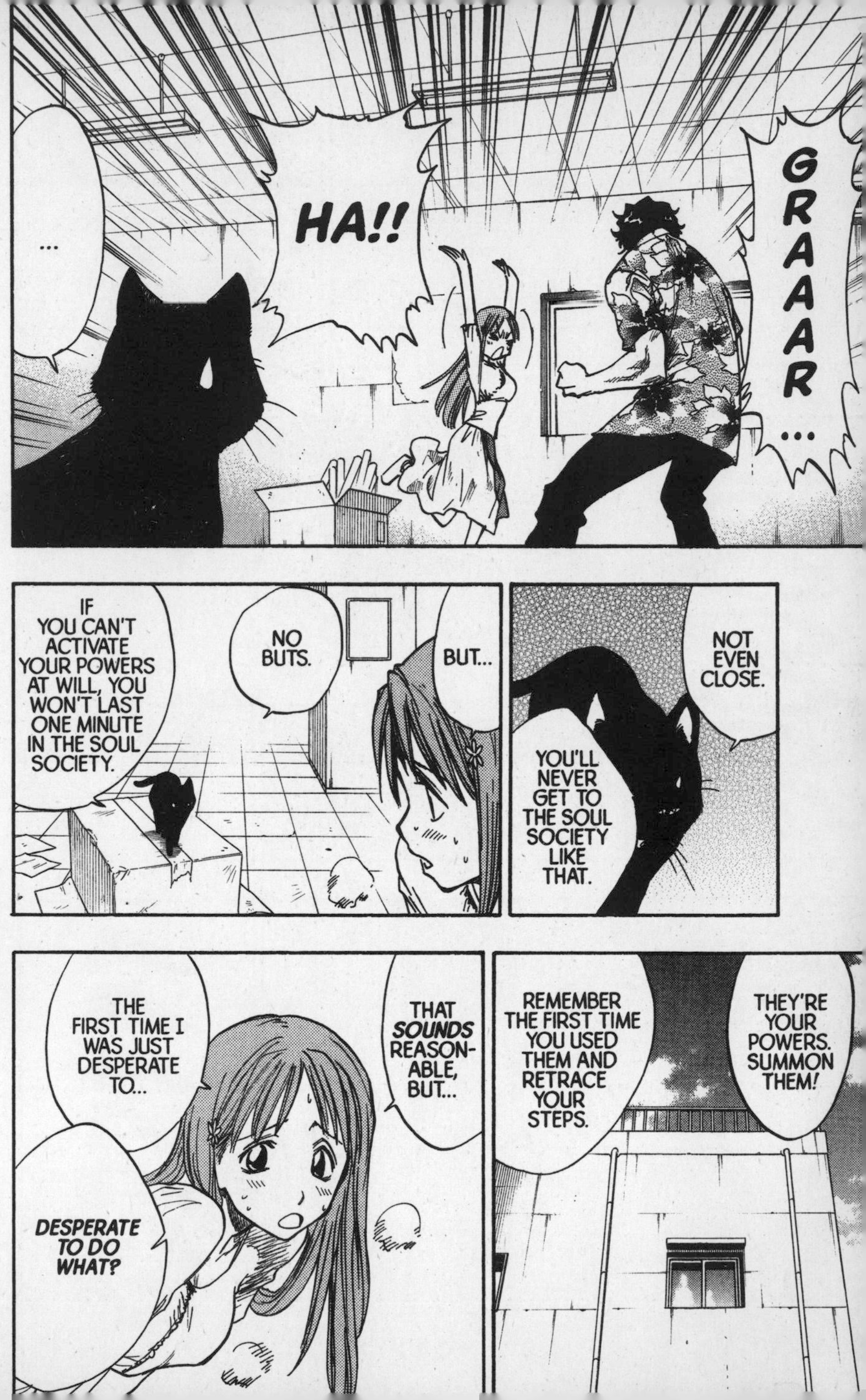
GRAAAR...
HA!!
...
NOT EVEN CLOSE.
YOU'LL NEVER GET TO THE SOUL SOCIETY LIKE THAT.
BUT...
NO BUTS.
IF YOU CAN'T ACTIVATE YOUR POWERS AT WILL, YOU WON'T LAST ONE MINUTE IN THE SOUL SOCIETY.
THEY'RE YOUR POWERS. SUMMON THEM!
REMEMBER THE FIRST TIME YOU USED THEM AND RETRACE YOUR STEPS.
THAT SOUNDS REASONABLE, BUT...
THE FIRST TIME I WAS JUST DESPERATE TO...
DESPERATE TO DO WHAT?

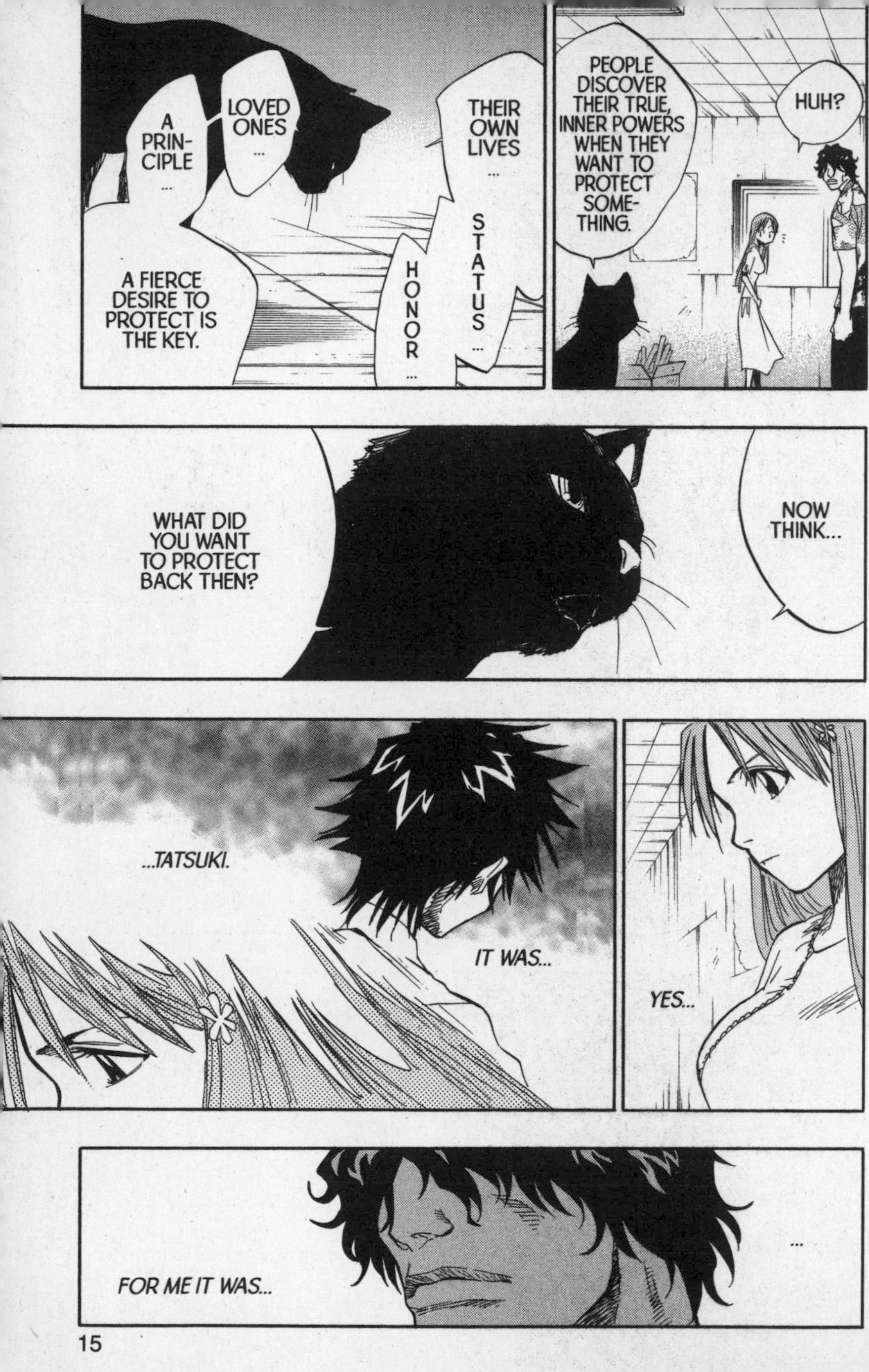
PEOPLE DISCOVER THEIR TRUE, INNER POWERS WHEN THEY WANT TO PROTECT SOME-THING.
HUH?
THEIR OWN LIVES ...
STATUS ...
HONOR ...
LOVED ONES ...
A PRIN-CIPLE ...
A FIERCE DESIRE TO PROTECT IS THE KEY.
NOW THINK...
WHAT DID YOU WANT TO PROTECT BACK THEN?
YES...
IT WAS...
...TATSUKI.
...
FOR ME IT WAS...

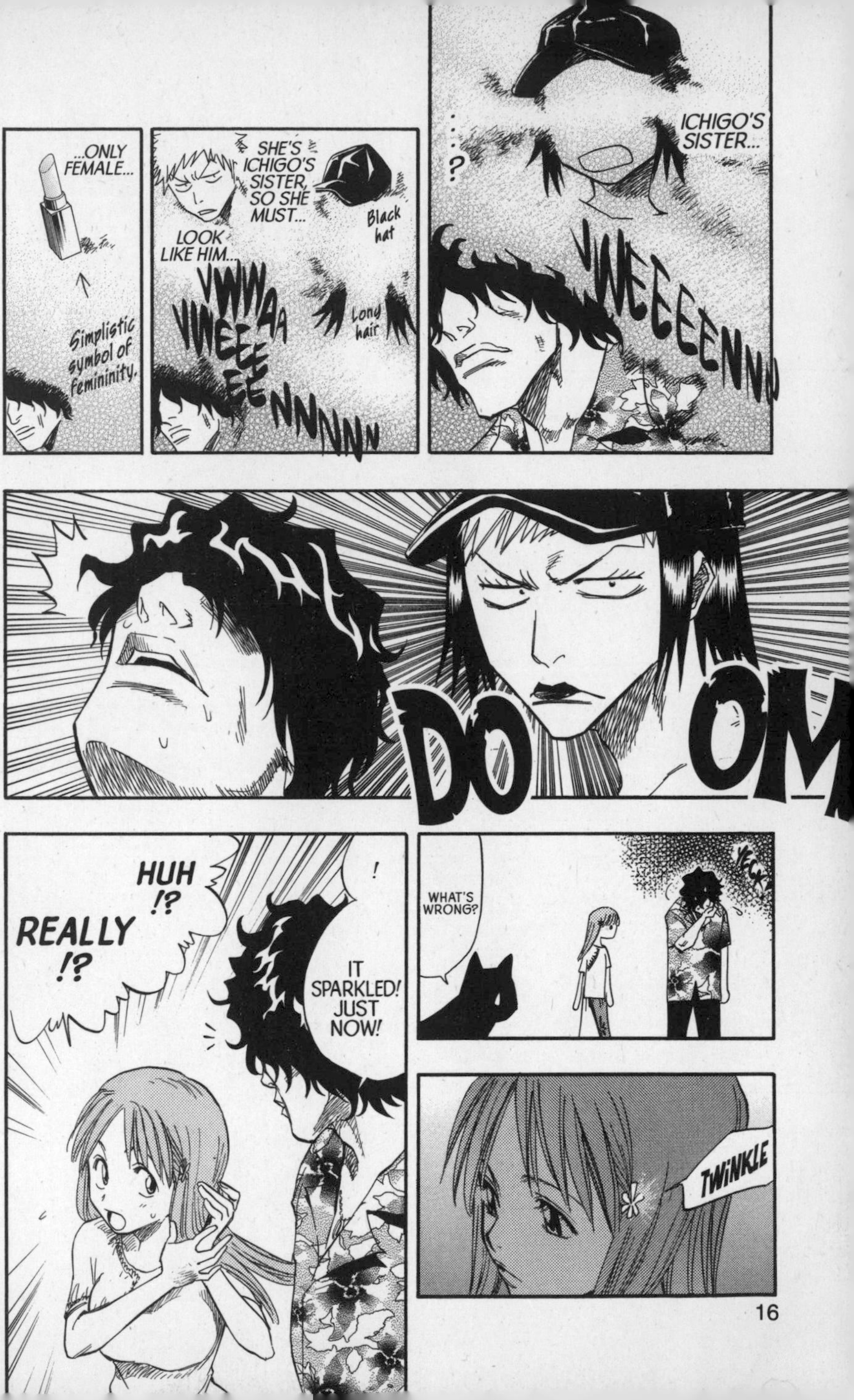
...?
ICHIGO'S SISTER...
VWEEEEENNN
SHE'S ICHIGO'S SISTER, SO SHE MUST...
LOOK LIKE HIM...
Black hat
Long hair
VWWAA VWEEEE EENNNNN
...ONLY FEMALE...
Simplistic symbol of femininity.
DO OM
YECK
WHAT'S WRONG?
TWINKLE
!
IT SPARKLED! JUST NOW!
HUH !?
REALLY !?

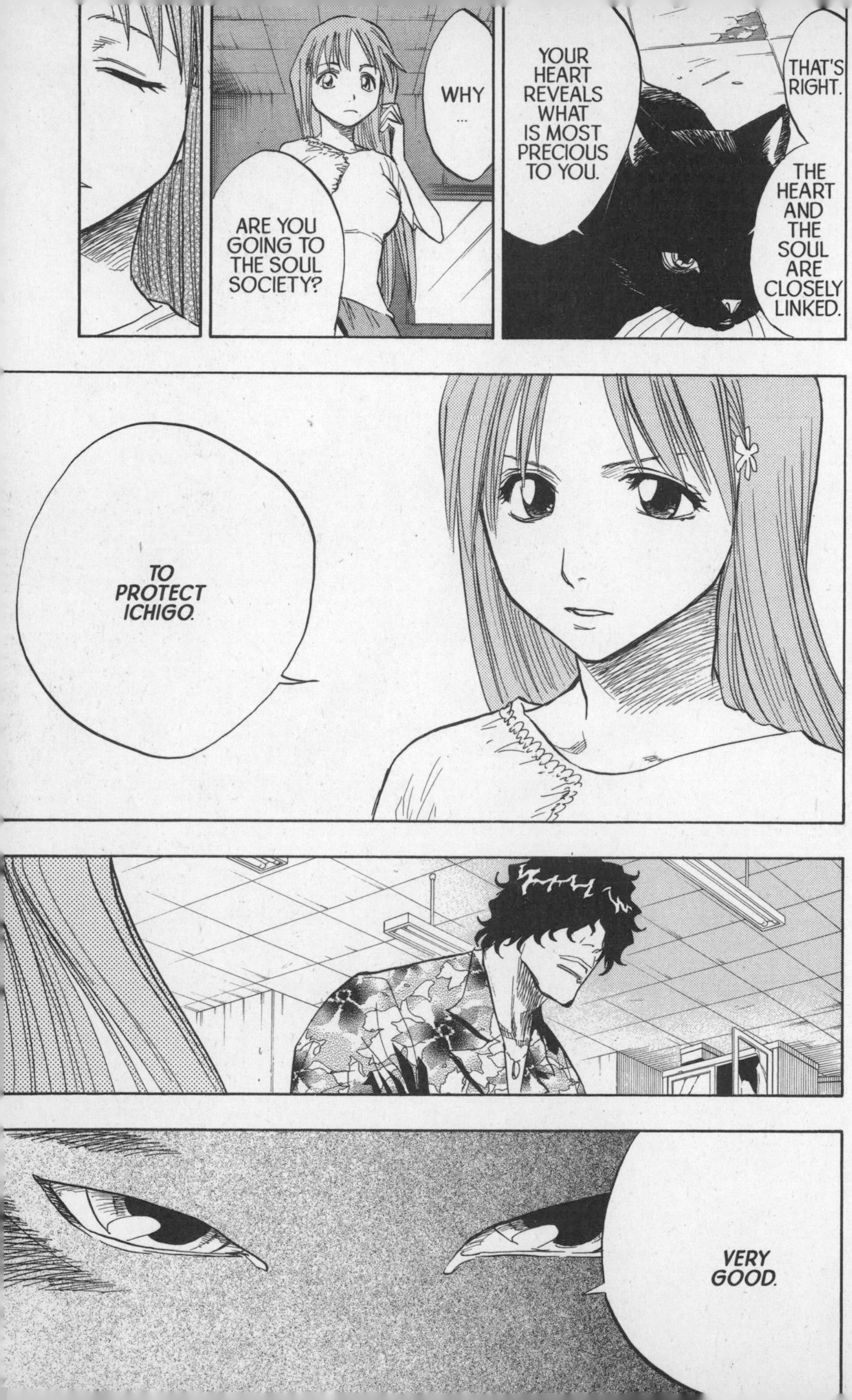
THAT'S RIGHT.
THE HEART AND THE SOUL ARE CLOSELY LINKED.
YOUR HEART REVEALS WHAT IS MOST PRECIOUS TO YOU.
WHY ...
ARE YOU GOING TO THE SOUL SOCIETY?
TO PROTECT ICHIGO.
VERY GOOD.

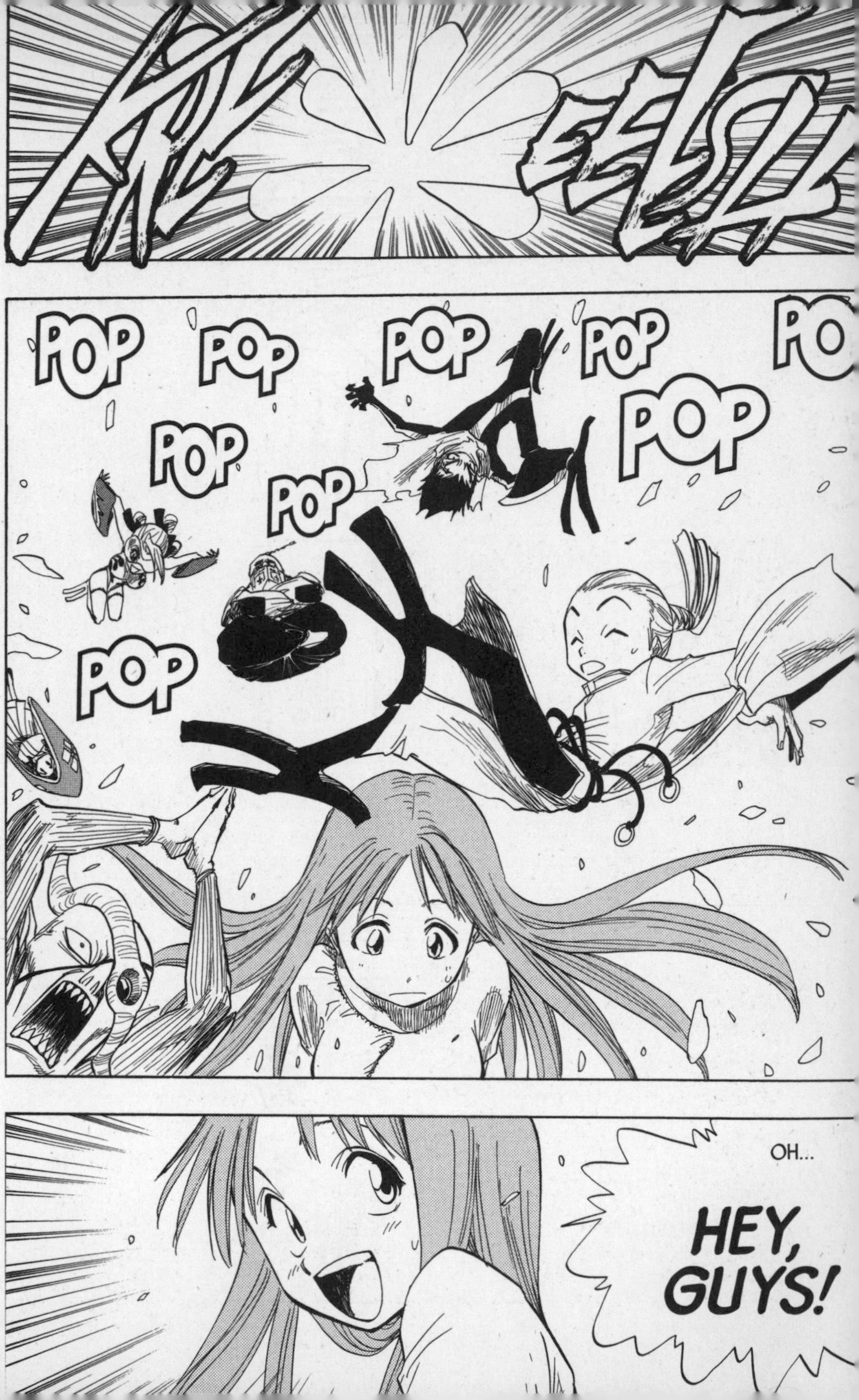
PO
POP
POP
POP
POP
POP
POP
POP
POP
OH...
HEY, GUYS!

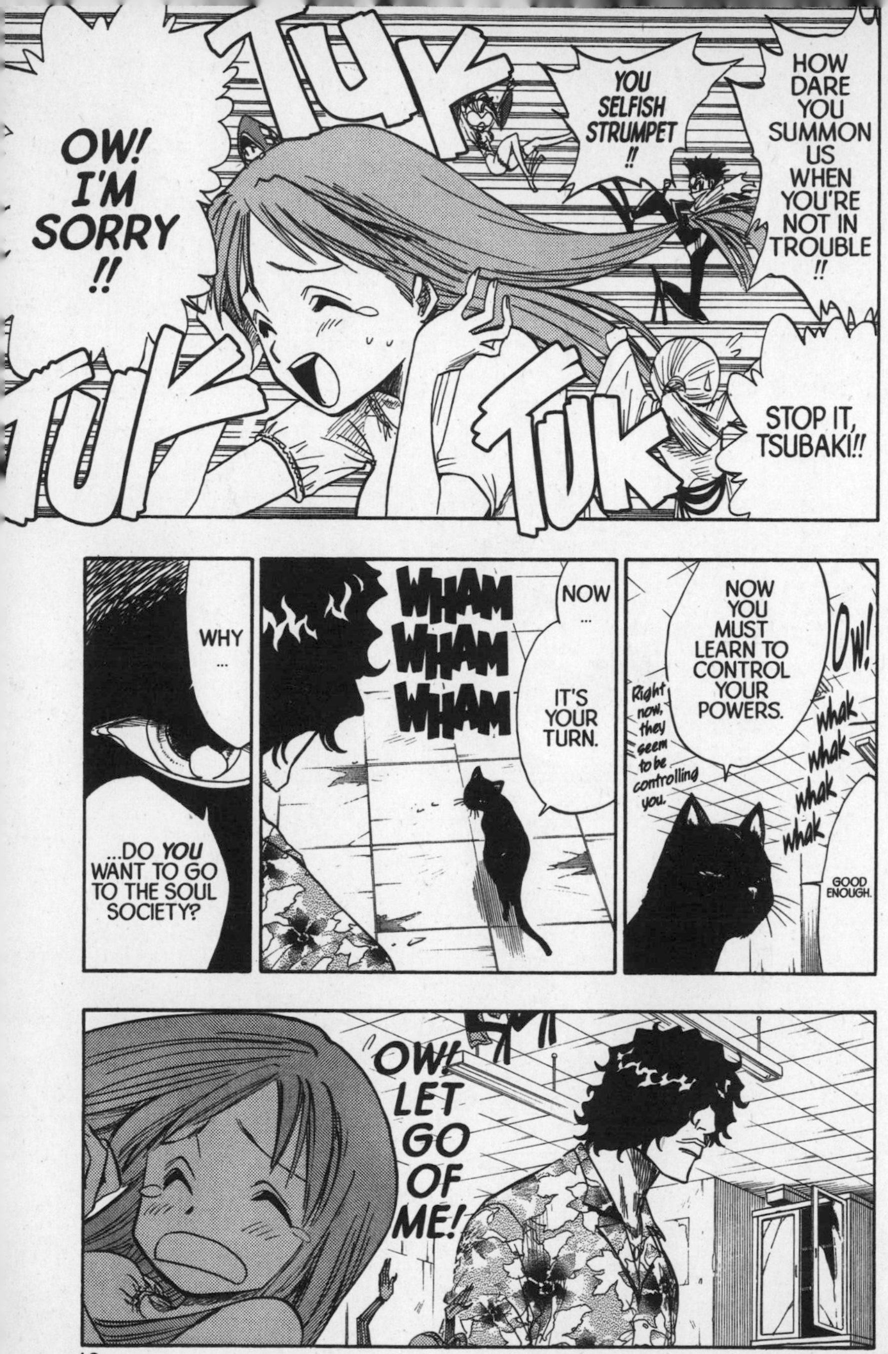
HOW DARE YOU SUMMON US WHEN YOU'RE NOT IN TROUBLE!!
YOU SELFISH STRUMPET!!
TUK
OW! I'M SORRY!!
STOP IT, TSUBAKI!!
TUK
TUK
NOW YOU MUST LEARN TO CONTROL YOUR POWERS.
OW!
Right now, they seem to be controlling you.
whak whak whak whak
GOOD ENOUGH.
NOW ...
IT'S YOUR TURN.
WHAM WHAM WHAM
WHY ...
...DO *YOU* WANT TO GO TO THE SOUL SOCIETY?
OW! LET GO OF ME!

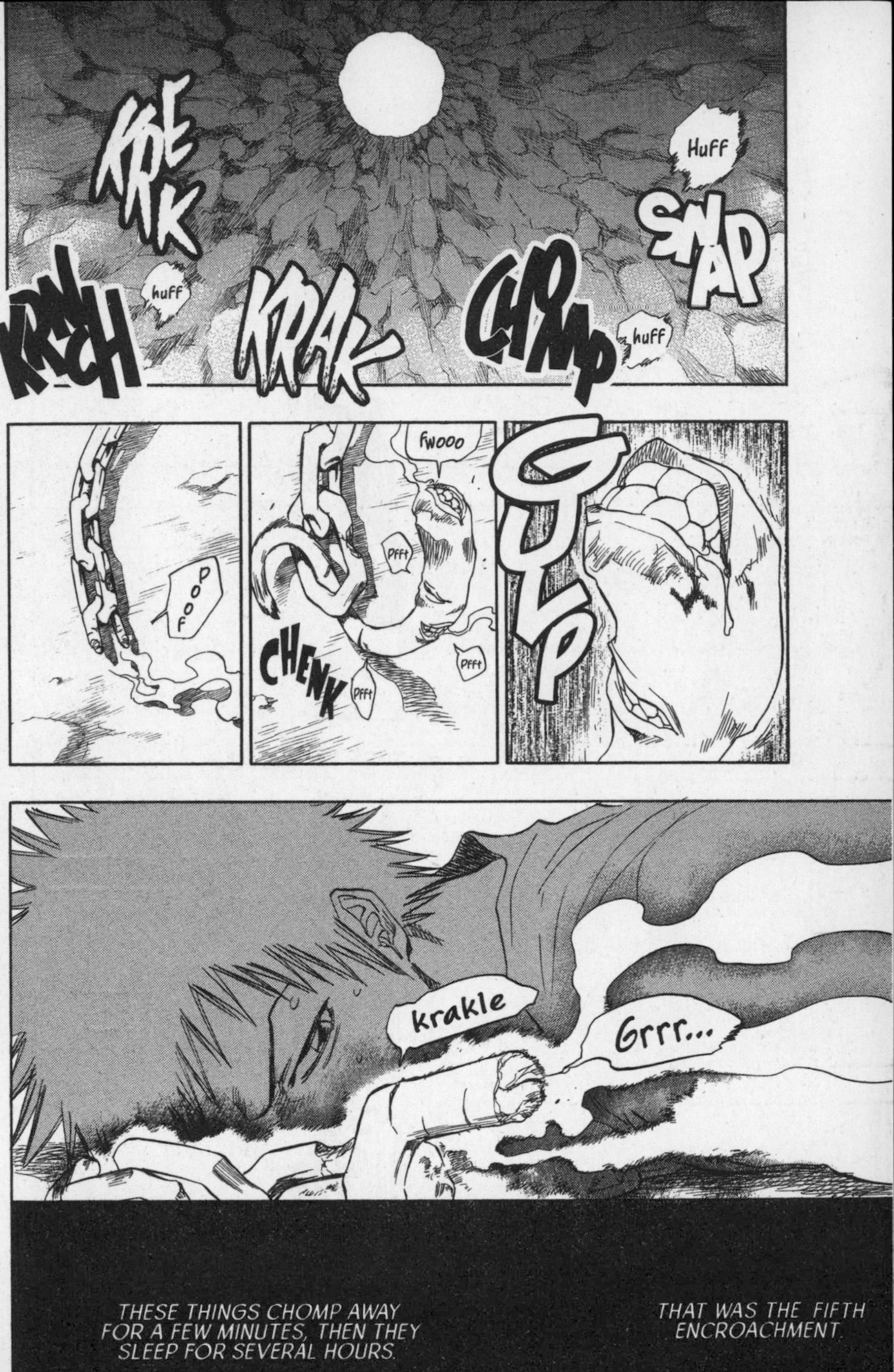
Huff
SNAP
huff
CHOMP
KRAK
huff
KRUNCH
KREAK
GULP
fwooo
pfft
pfft
CHENK
pfft
poof
krakle
Grrr...
THAT WAS THE FIFTH ENCROACHMENT.
THESE THINGS CHOMP AWAY FOR A FEW MINUTES, THEN THEY SLEEP FOR SEVERAL HOURS.

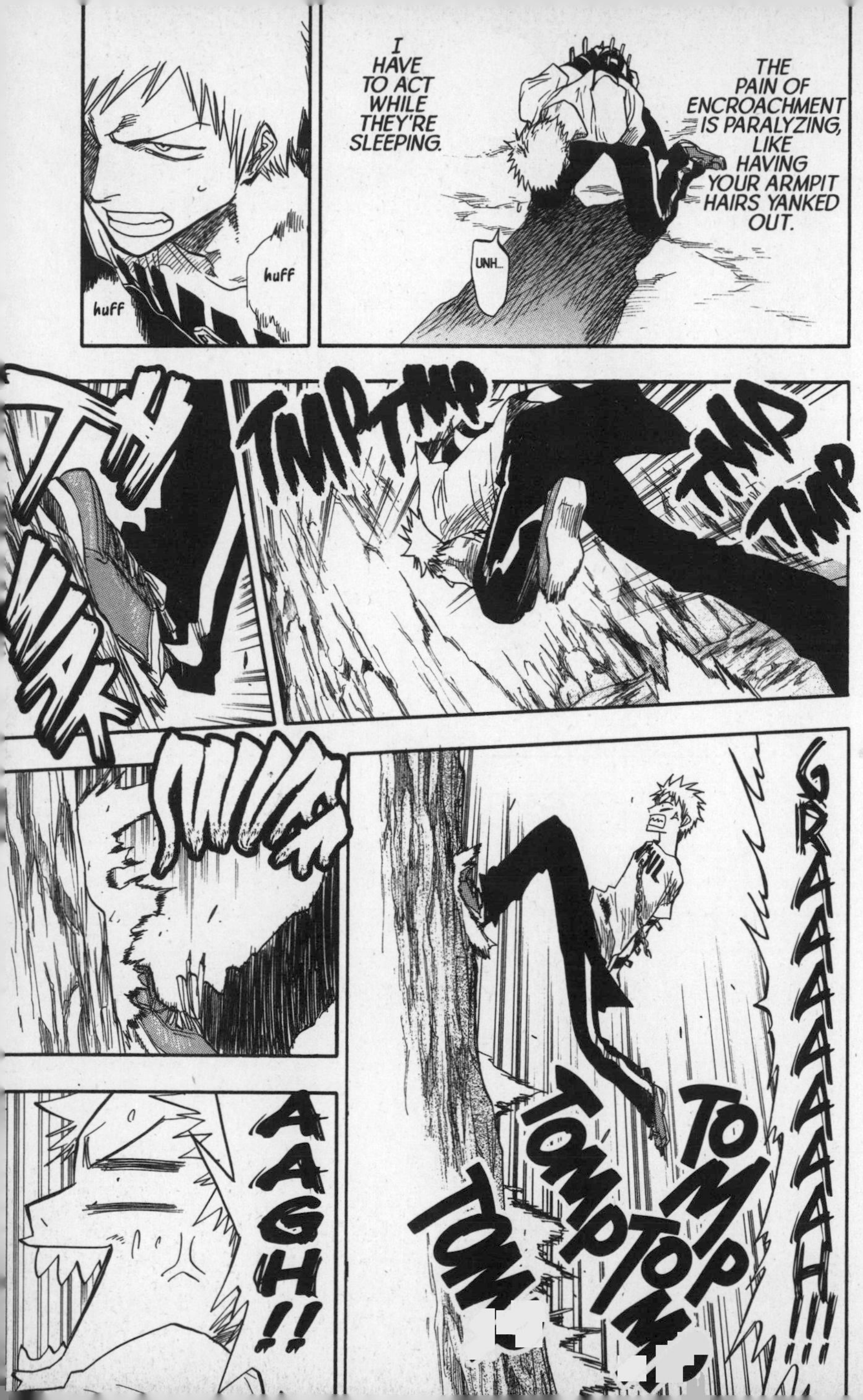
THE PAIN OF ENCROACHMENT IS PARALYZING, LIKE HAVING YOUR ARMPIT HAIRS YANKED OUT.
I HAVE TO ACT WHILE THEY'RE SLEEPING.
UNH...
huff
huff
TMP TMP
TMP TMP
GRAAAAAAAAAH!!!
AAGH!!

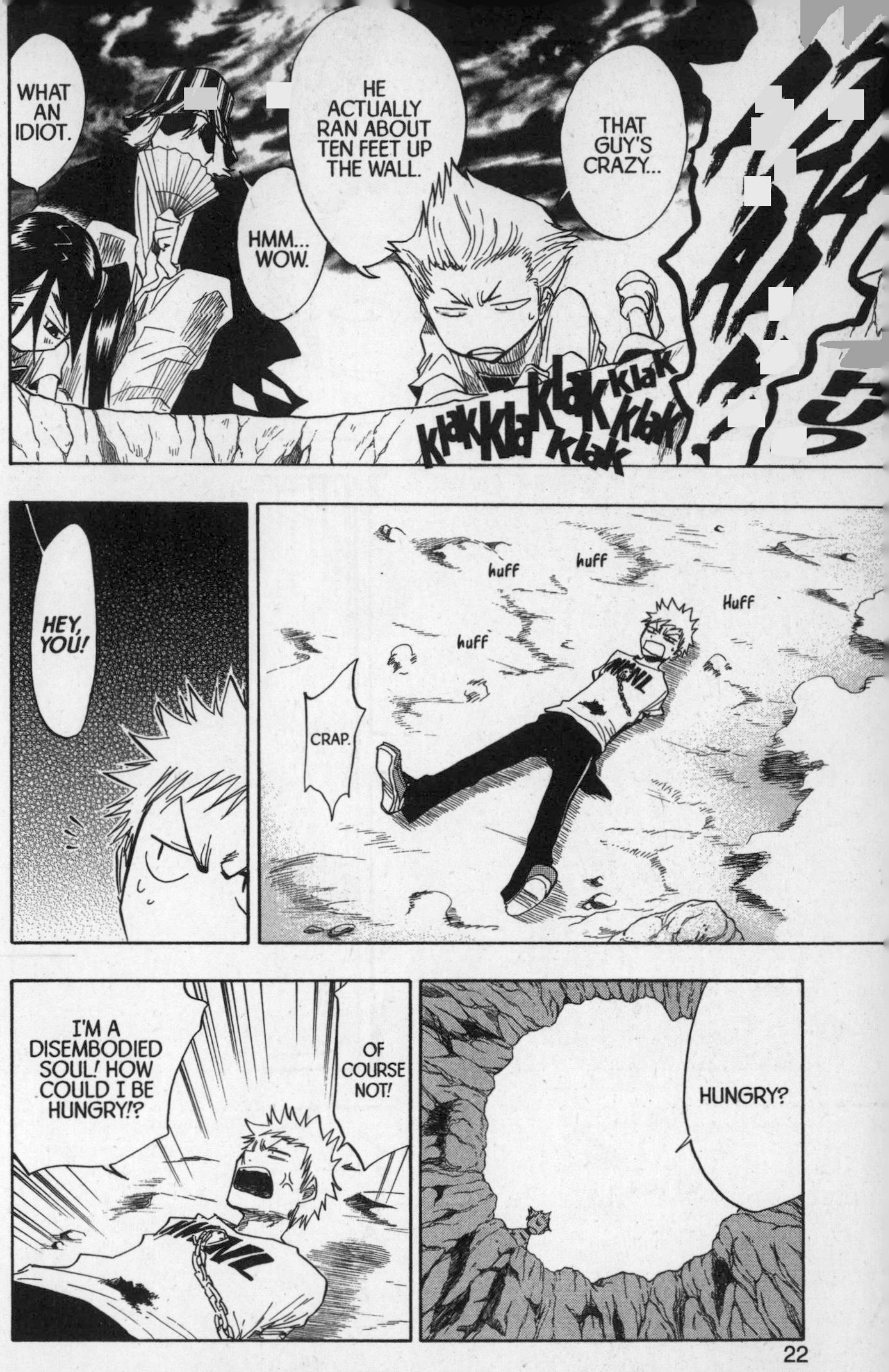
THAT GUY'S CRAZY...
HE ACTUALLY RAN ABOUT TEN FEET UP THE WALL.
HMM... WOW.
WHAT AN IDIOT.
klak klak klak klak klak klak klak
huff
huff
Huff
huff
CRAP.
HEY, YOU!
HUNGRY?
OF COURSE NOT!
I'M A DISEMBODIED SOUL! HOW COULD I BE HUNGRY!?

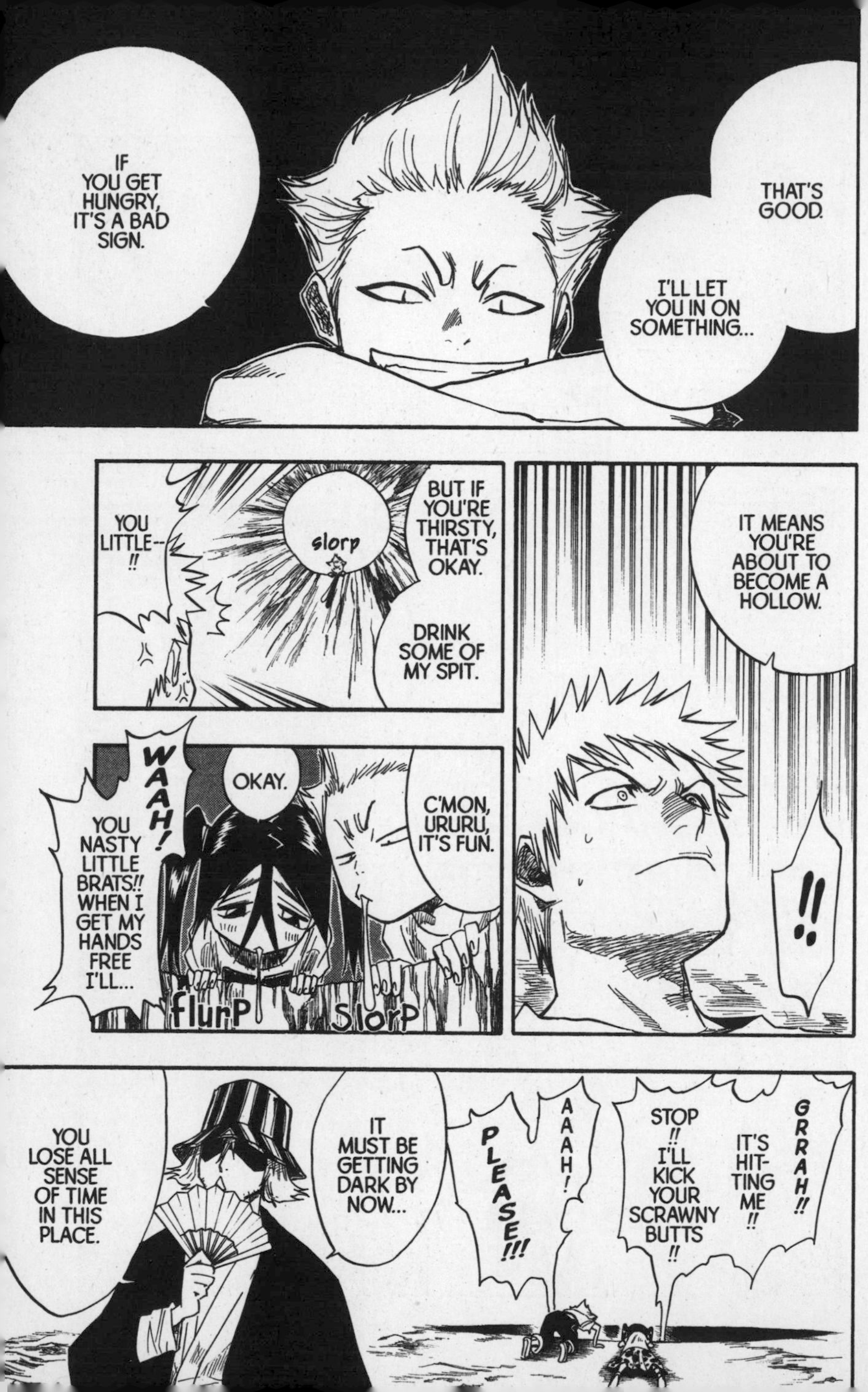
THAT'S GOOD.
I'LL LET YOU IN ON SOMETHING...
IF YOU GET HUNGRY, IT'S A BAD SIGN.
IT MEANS YOU'RE ABOUT TO BECOME A HOLLOW.
!!
BUT IF YOU'RE THIRSTY, THAT'S OKAY.
DRINK SOME OF MY SPIT.
slorp
YOU LITTLE--!!
C'MON, URURU, IT'S FUN.
OKAY.
Slorp
flurP
WAAAH!
YOU NASTY LITTLE BRATS!! WHEN I GET MY HANDS FREE I'LL...
GRRAH!!
IT'S HIT-TING ME!!
STOP!! I'LL KICK YOUR SCRAWNY BUTTS!!
AAAH!
PLEASE!!!
IT MUST BE GETTING DARK BY NOW...
YOU LOSE ALL SENSE OF TIME IN THIS PLACE.

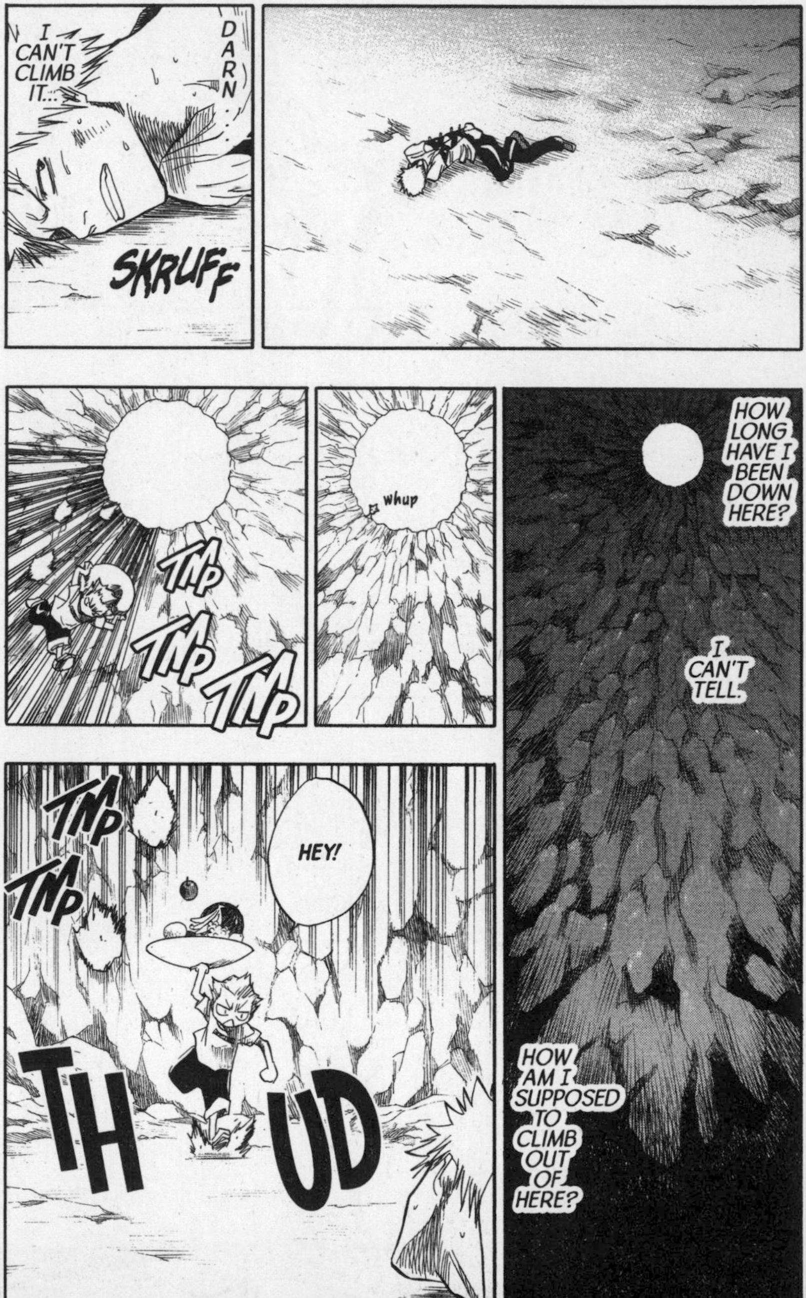
DARN...
I CAN'T CLIMB IT...
SKRUFF
HOW LONG HAVE I BEEN DOWN HERE?
I CAN'T TELL.
HOW AM I SUPPOSED TO CLIMB OUT OF HERE?
whup
TMP
TMP
TMP
TMP
TMP
HEY!
THUD

READ THIS WAY

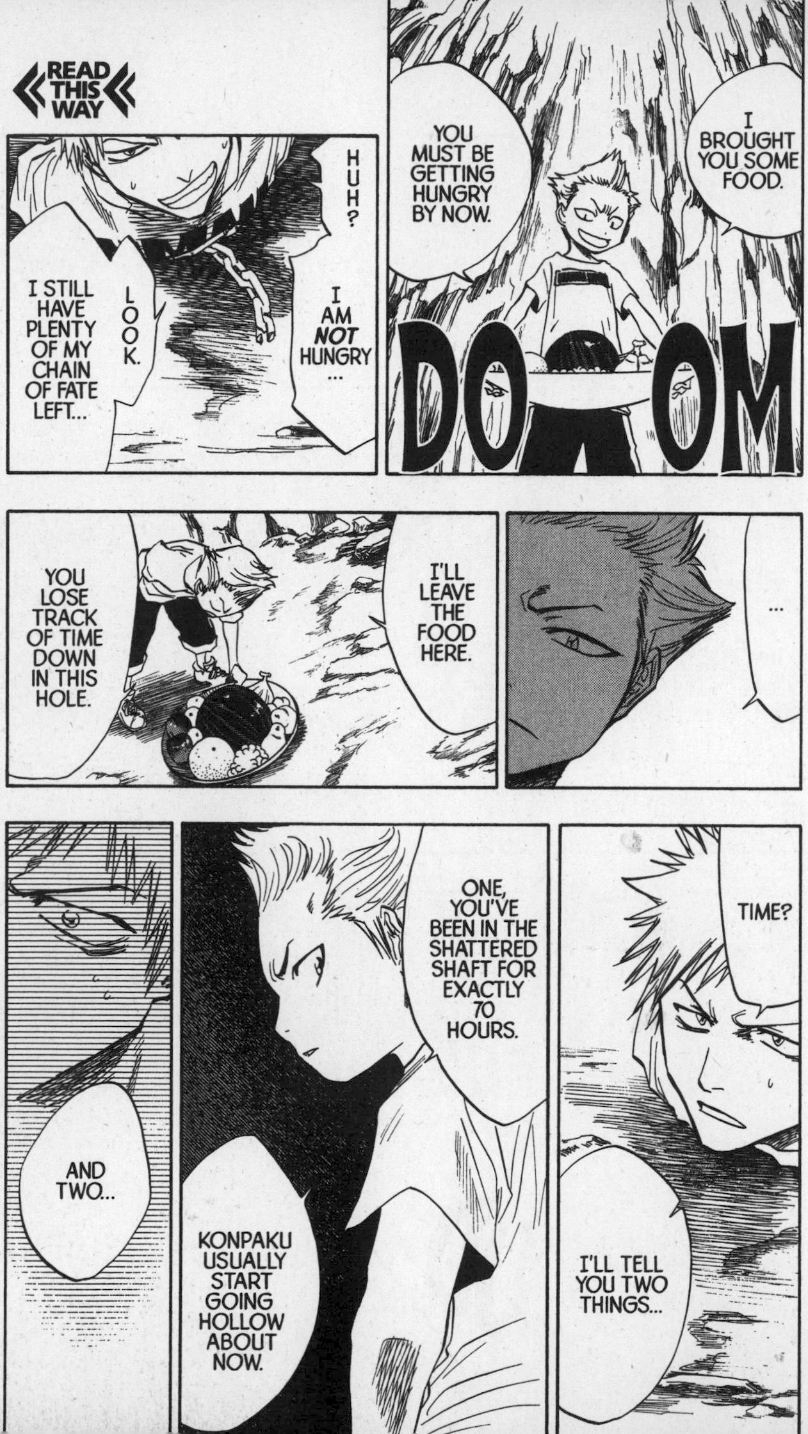
I BROUGHT YOU SOME FOOD.
YOU MUST BE GETTING HUNGRY BY NOW.
DOOM
HUH?
I AM *NOT* HUNGRY...
LOOK.
I STILL HAVE PLENTY OF MY CHAIN OF FATE LEFT...
...
I'LL LEAVE THE FOOD HERE.
YOU LOSE TRACK OF TIME DOWN IN THIS HOLE.
TIME?
I'LL TELL YOU TWO THINGS...
ONE, YOU'VE BEEN IN THE SHATTERED SHAFT FOR EXACTLY 70 HOURS.
KONPAKU USUALLY START GOING HOLLOW ABOUT NOW.
AND TWO...

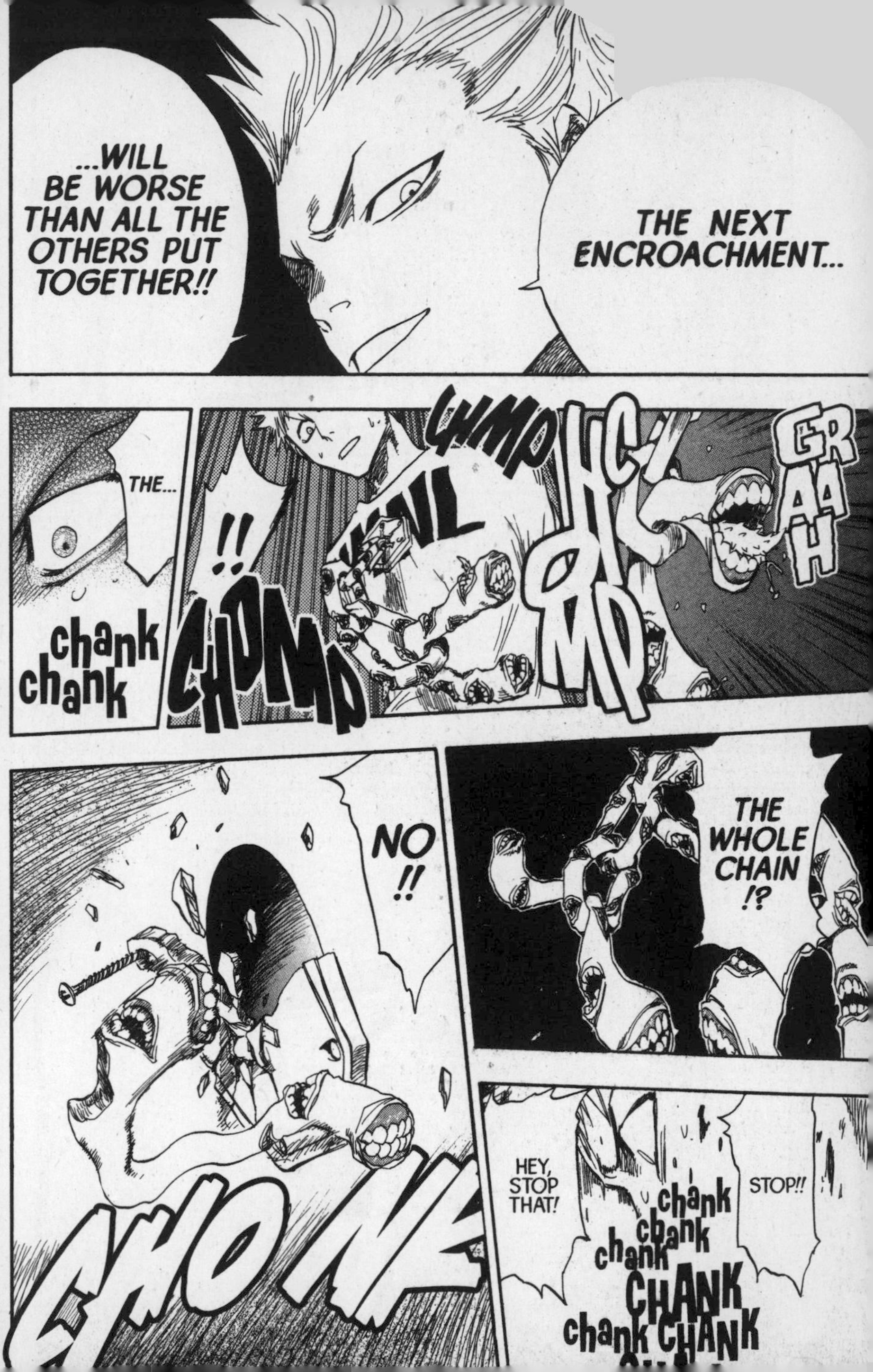
THE NEXT ENCROACHMENT...
...WILL BE WORSE THAN ALL THE OTHERS PUT TOGETHER!!
GRAAH
CHOMP
!!
THE...
chank chank
THE WHOLE CHAIN !?
STOP!!
HEY, STOP THAT!
chank chank chank CHANK chank CHANK
NO !!

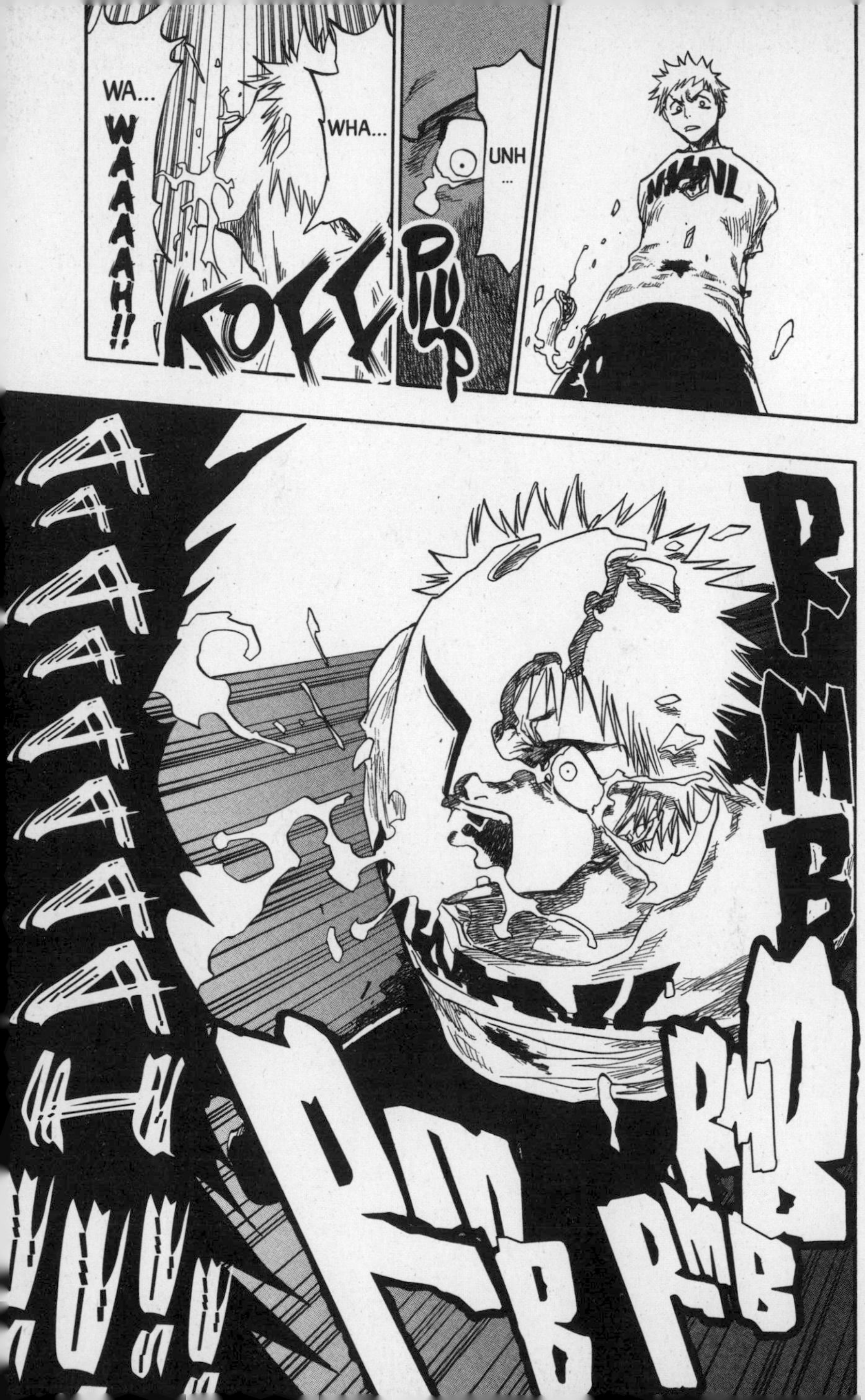
UNH ...
WHA...
WA... WAAAAAH!!
KOFF

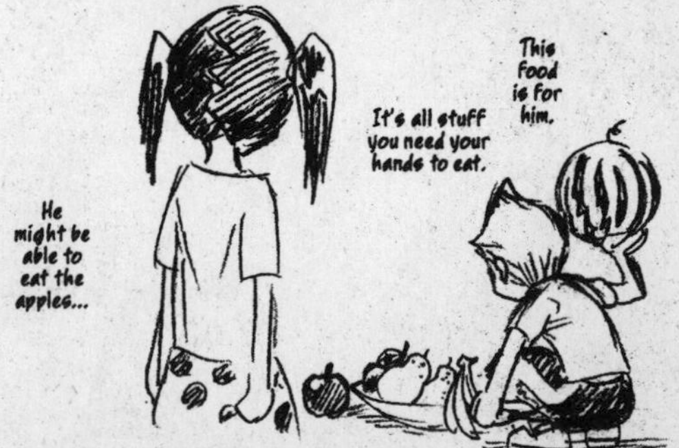
This food is for him.
It's all stuff you need your hands to eat.
He might be able to eat the apples...

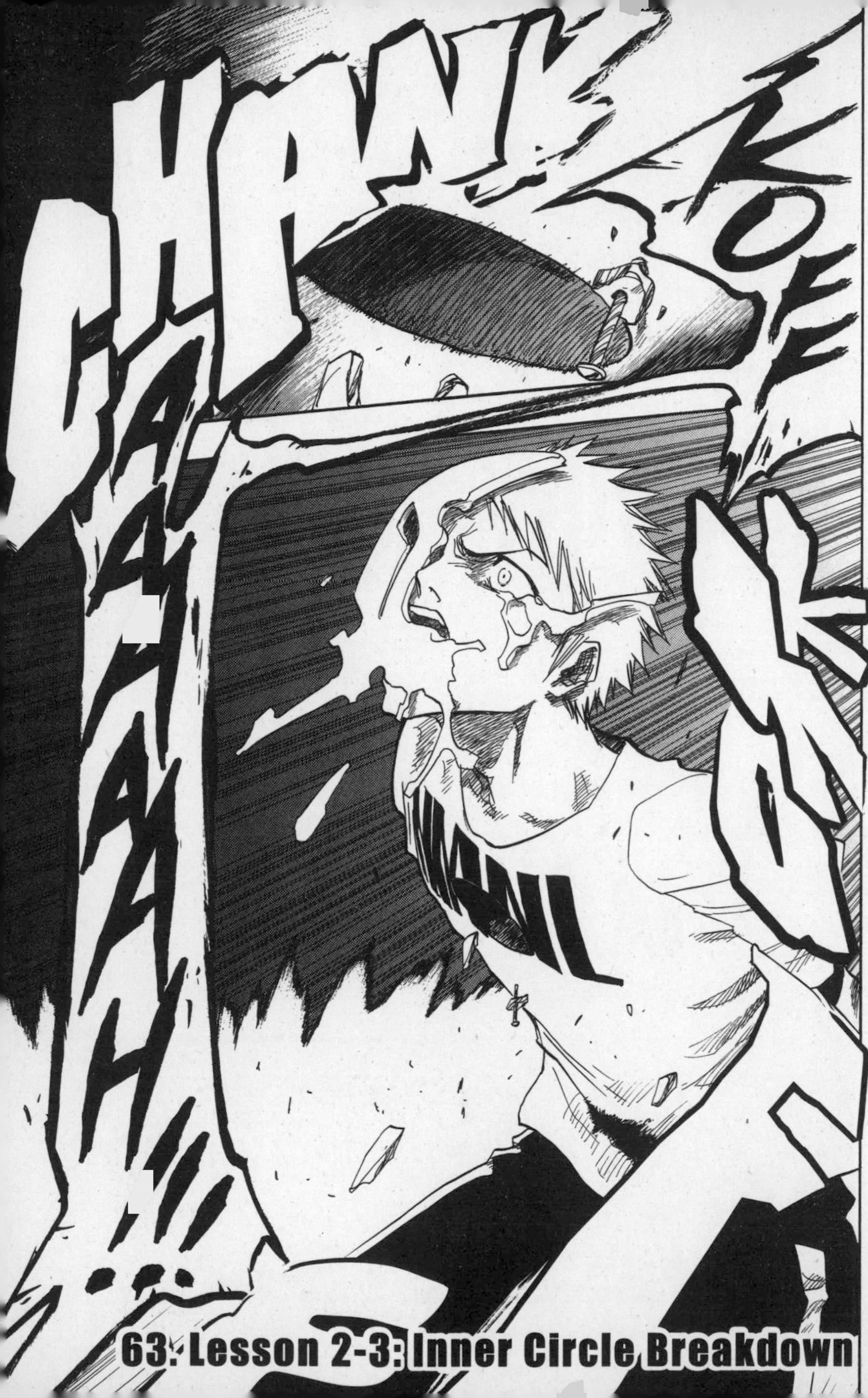

63: Lesson 2-3: Inner Circle Breakdown

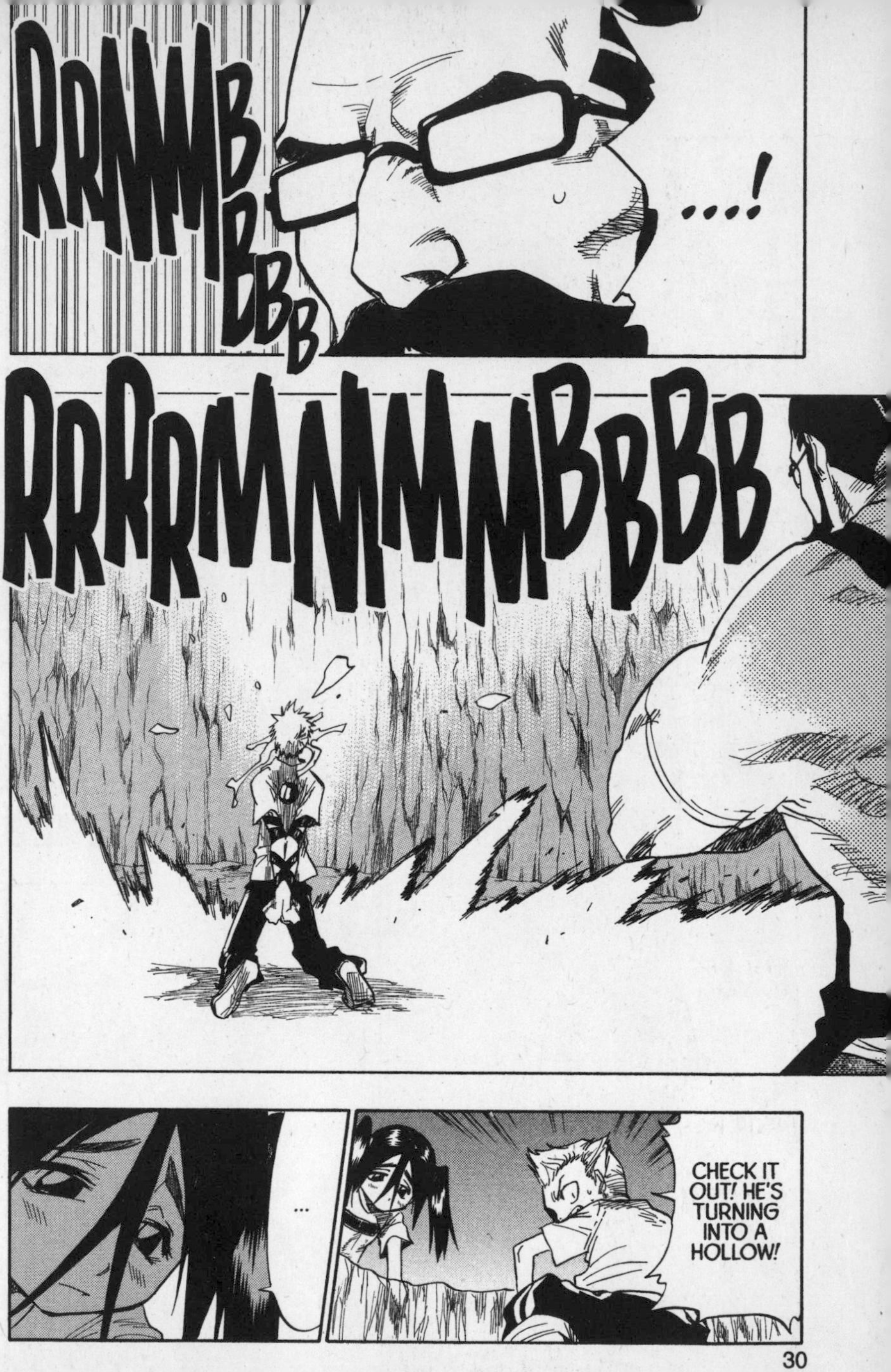

...!
RRAMMBBDBB
RRRRMMMMMBBBB
CHECK IT OUT! HE'S TURNING INTO A HOLLOW!
...

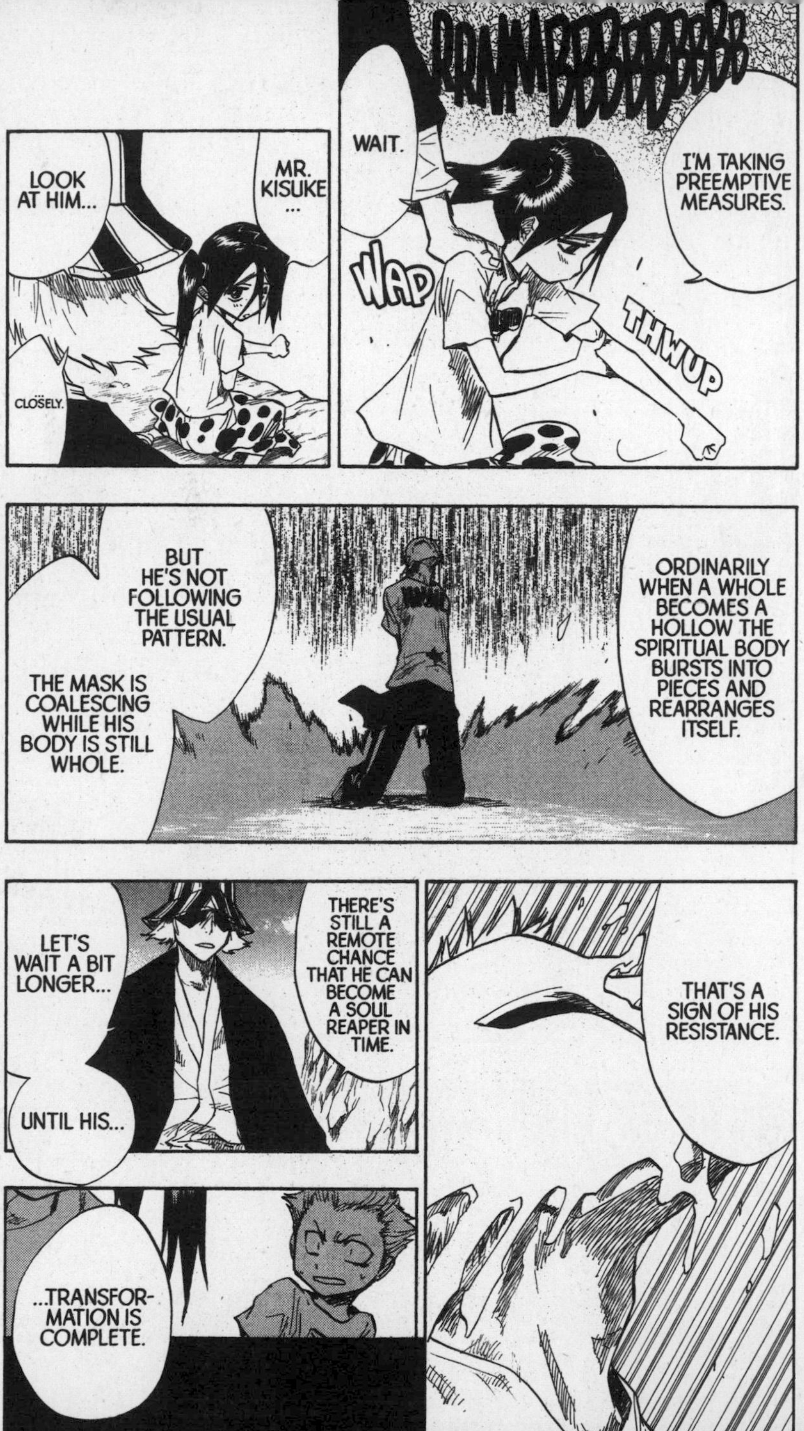
I'M TAKING PREEMPTIVE MEASURES.
WAIT.
WAP
THWUP
MR. KISUKE...
LOOK AT HIM...
CLOSELY.
ORDINARILY WHEN A WHOLE BECOMES A HOLLOW THE SPIRITUAL BODY BURSTS INTO PIECES AND REARRANGES ITSELF.
BUT HE'S NOT FOLLOWING THE USUAL PATTERN.
THE MASK IS COALESCING WHILE HIS BODY IS STILL WHOLE.
THAT'S A SIGN OF HIS RESISTANCE.
THERE'S STILL A REMOTE CHANCE THAT HE CAN BECOME A SOUL REAPER IN TIME.
LET'S WAIT A BIT LONGER...
UNTIL HIS...
...TRANSFORMATION IS COMPLETE.

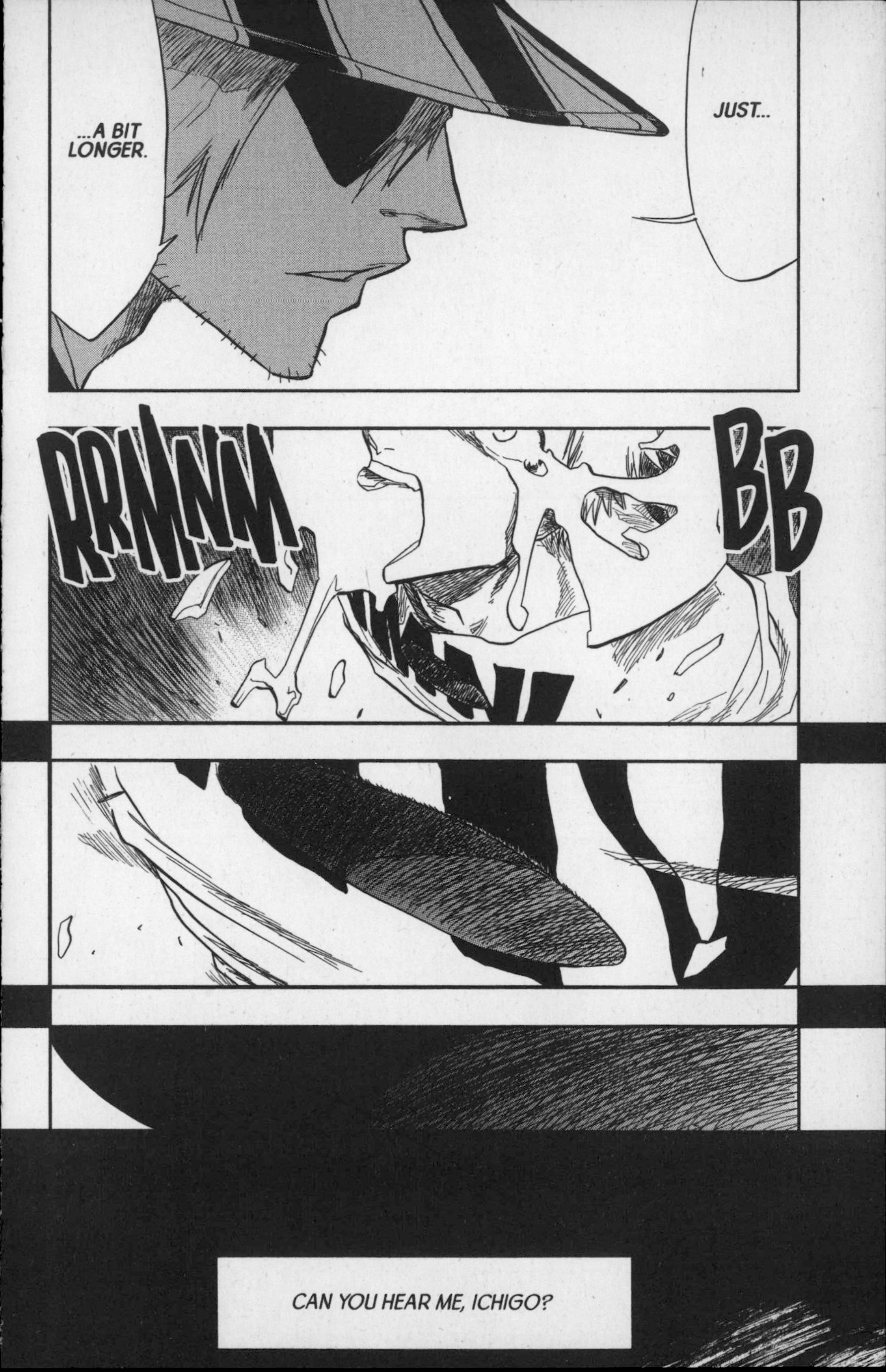
JUST...
...A BIT LONGER.
BB
RRMNNM
CAN YOU HEAR ME, ICHIGO?

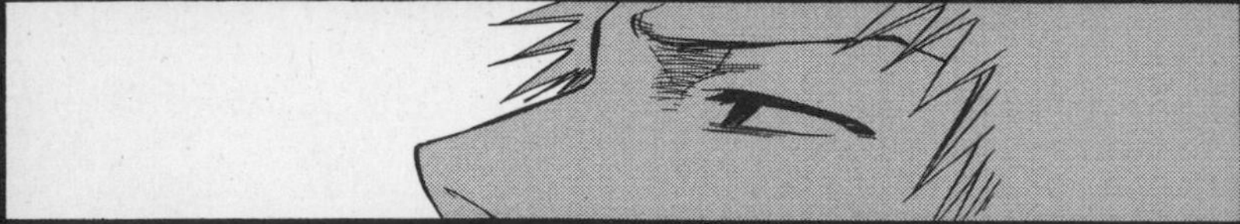

BLEACH ブリーチ

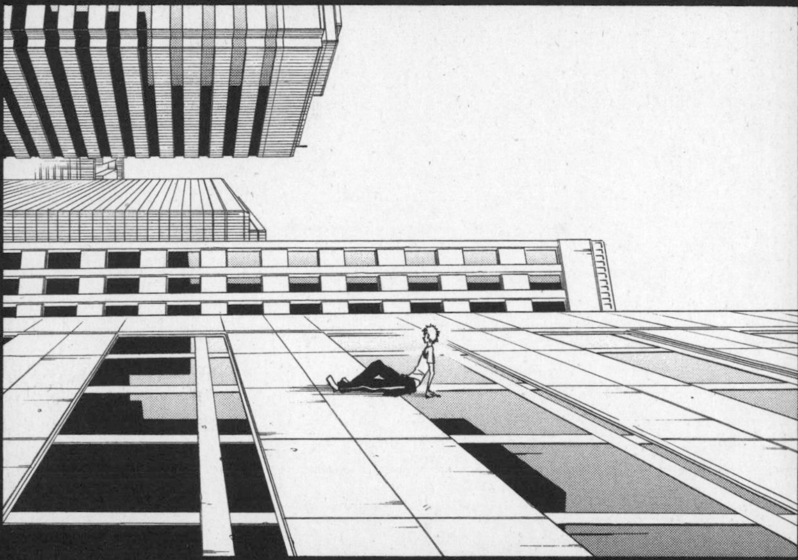

63. Lesson 2-3: Inner Circle Breakdown

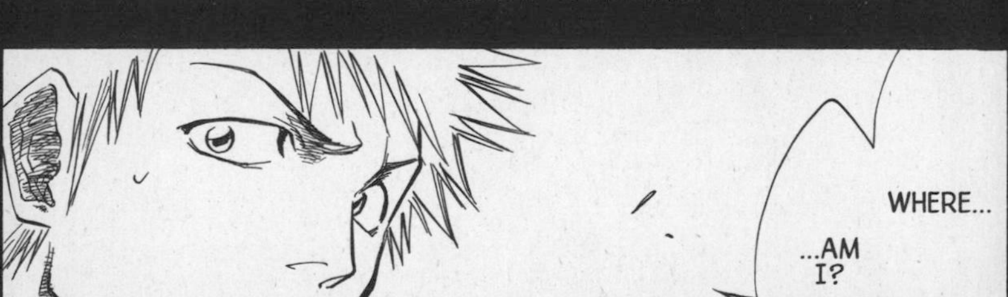
WHERE...
...AM I?

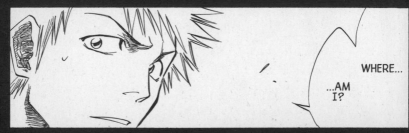

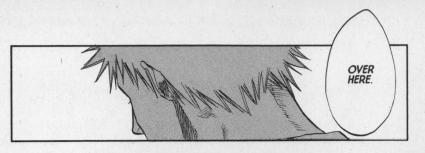

OVER HERE.

IT'S ME.

WHO AM I?

DON'T YOU KNOW?

WHO...

...ARE YOU?

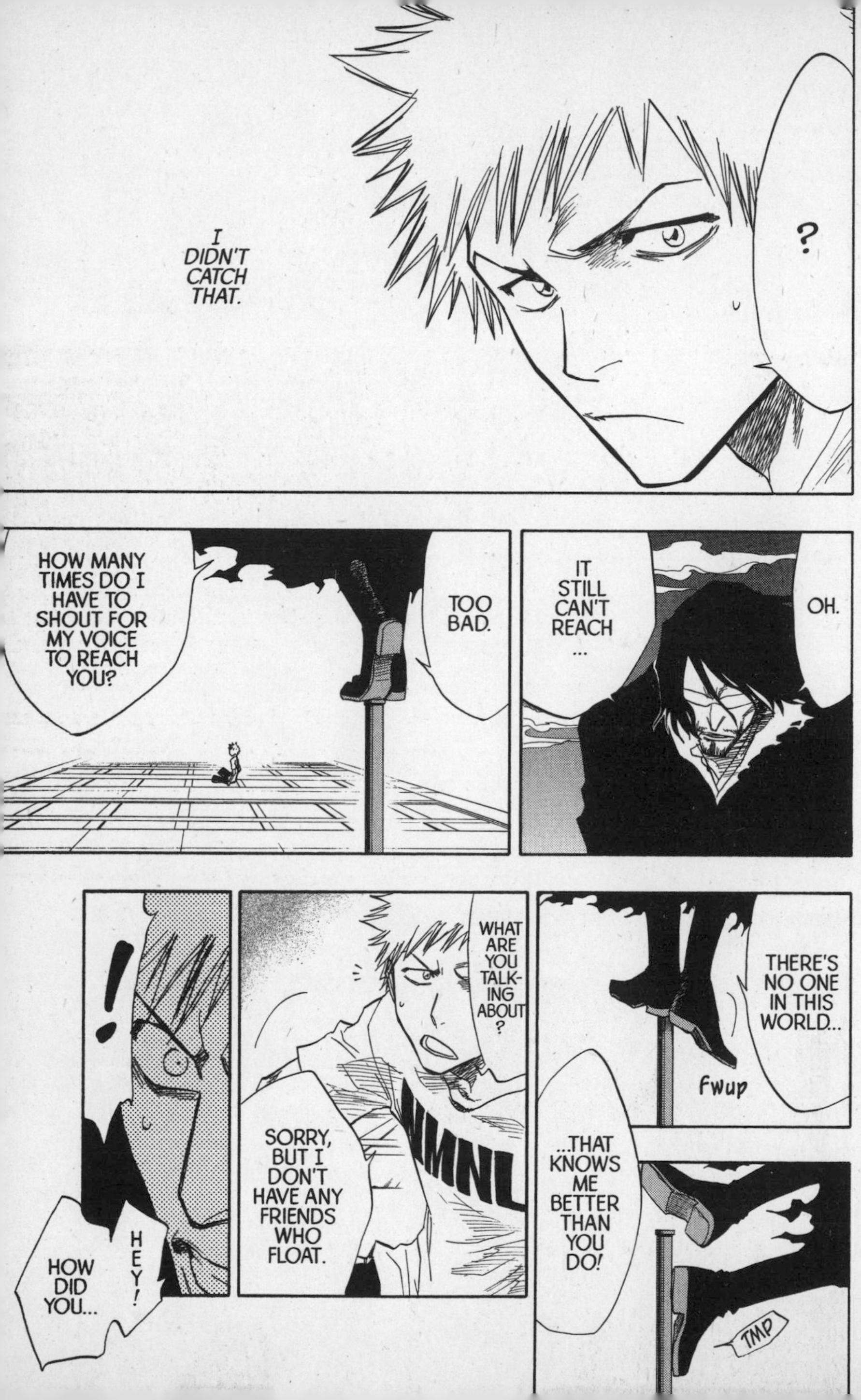
?
I DIDN'T CATCH THAT.
OH.
IT STILL CAN'T REACH ...
TOO BAD.
HOW MANY TIMES DO I HAVE TO SHOUT FOR MY VOICE TO REACH YOU?
THERE'S NO ONE IN THIS WORLD...
fwup
...THAT KNOWS ME BETTER THAN YOU DO!
TMP
WHAT ARE YOU TALKING ABOUT?
MMNL
SORRY, BUT I DON'T HAVE ANY FRIENDS WHO FLOAT.
!
HEY!
HOW DID YOU...

HOW CAN YOU SIT IN A PLACE LIKE THAT?

HOW STRANGE.

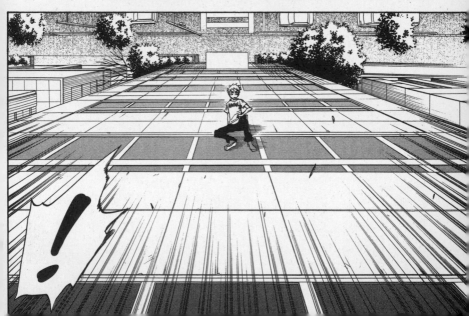

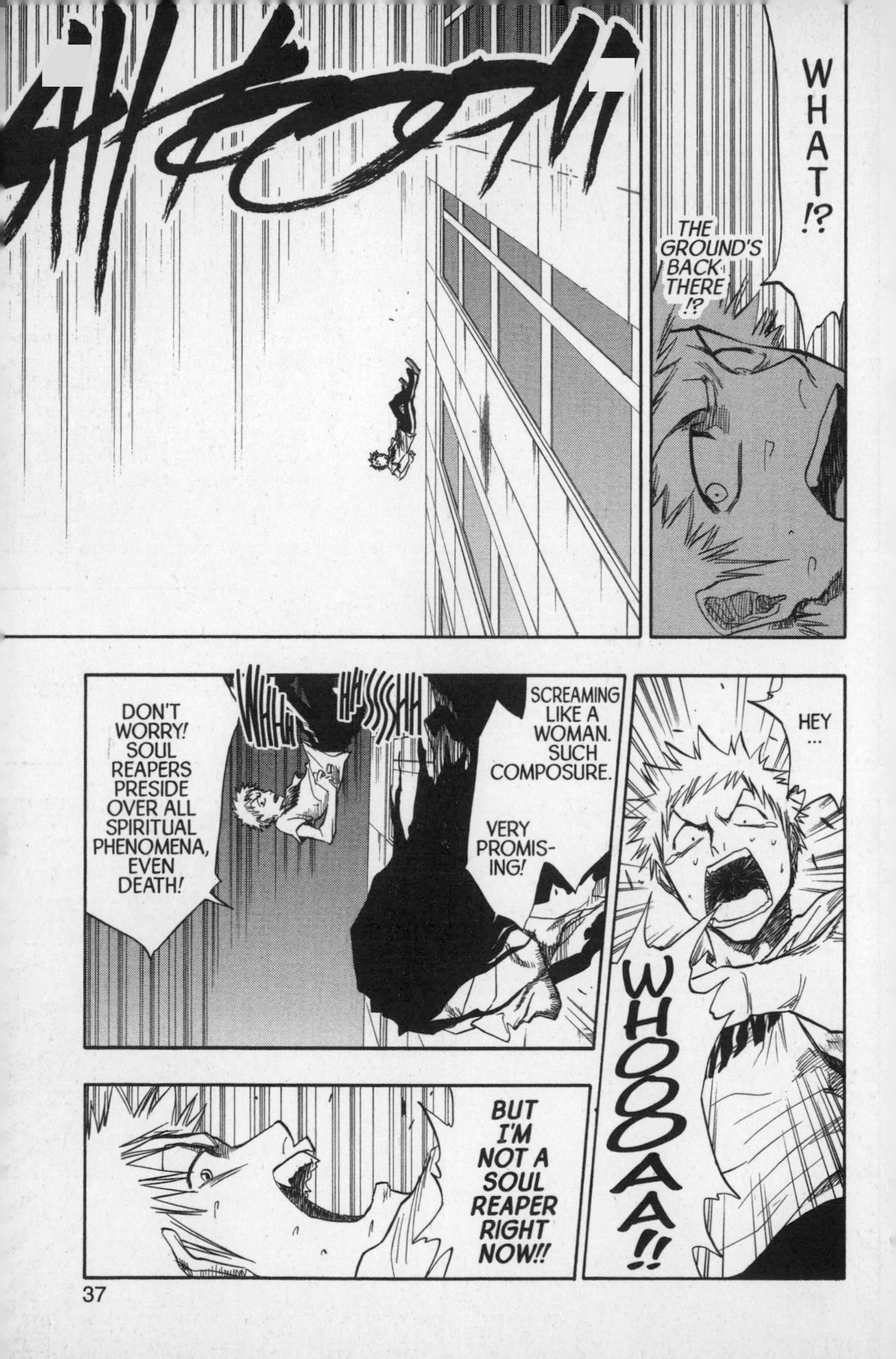
WHAT!?
THE GROUND'S BACK THERE!?
HEY...
WHOOOOAA!!
SCREAMING LIKE A WOMAN. SUCH COMPOSURE.
VERY PROMISING!
DON'T WORRY! SOUL REAPERS PRESIDE OVER ALL SPIRITUAL PHENOMENA, EVEN DEATH!
BUT I'M NOT A SOUL REAPER RIGHT NOW!!

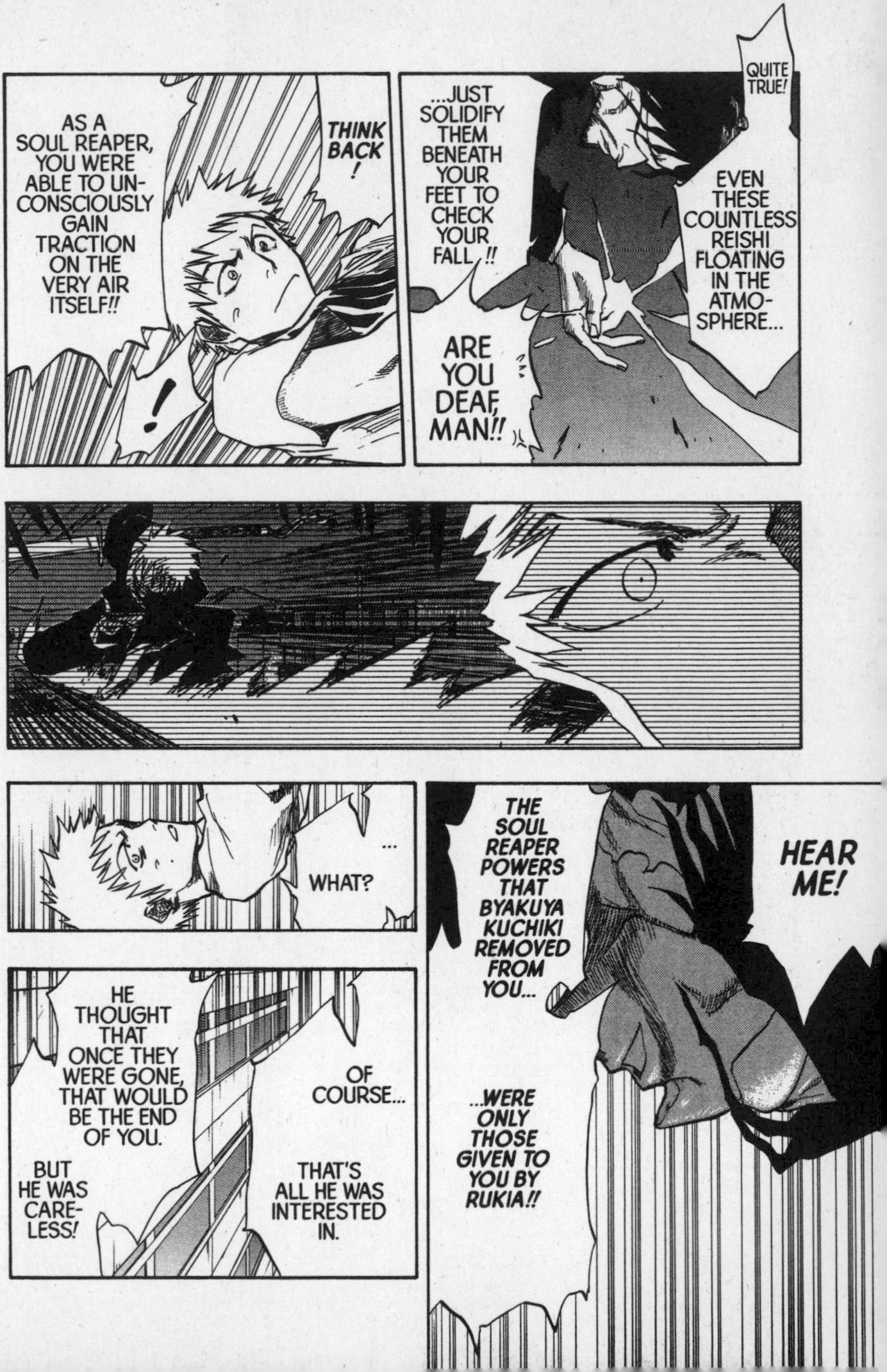
QUITE TRUE!
EVEN THESE COUNTLESS REISHI FLOATING IN THE ATMOSPHERE...
...JUST SOLIDIFY THEM BENEATH YOUR FEET TO CHECK YOUR FALL!!
ARE YOU DEAF, MAN!!
THINK BACK!
AS A SOUL REAPER, YOU WERE ABLE TO UNCONSCIOUSLY GAIN TRACTION ON THE VERY AIR ITSELF!!
!
HEAR ME!
THE SOUL REAPER POWERS THAT BYAKUYA KUCHIKI REMOVED FROM YOU...
...WERE ONLY THOSE GIVEN TO YOU BY RUKIA!!
...
WHAT?
OF COURSE...
HE THOUGHT THAT ONCE THEY WERE GONE, THAT WOULD BE THE END OF YOU.
THAT'S ALL HE WAS INTERESTED IN.
BUT HE WAS CARELESS!

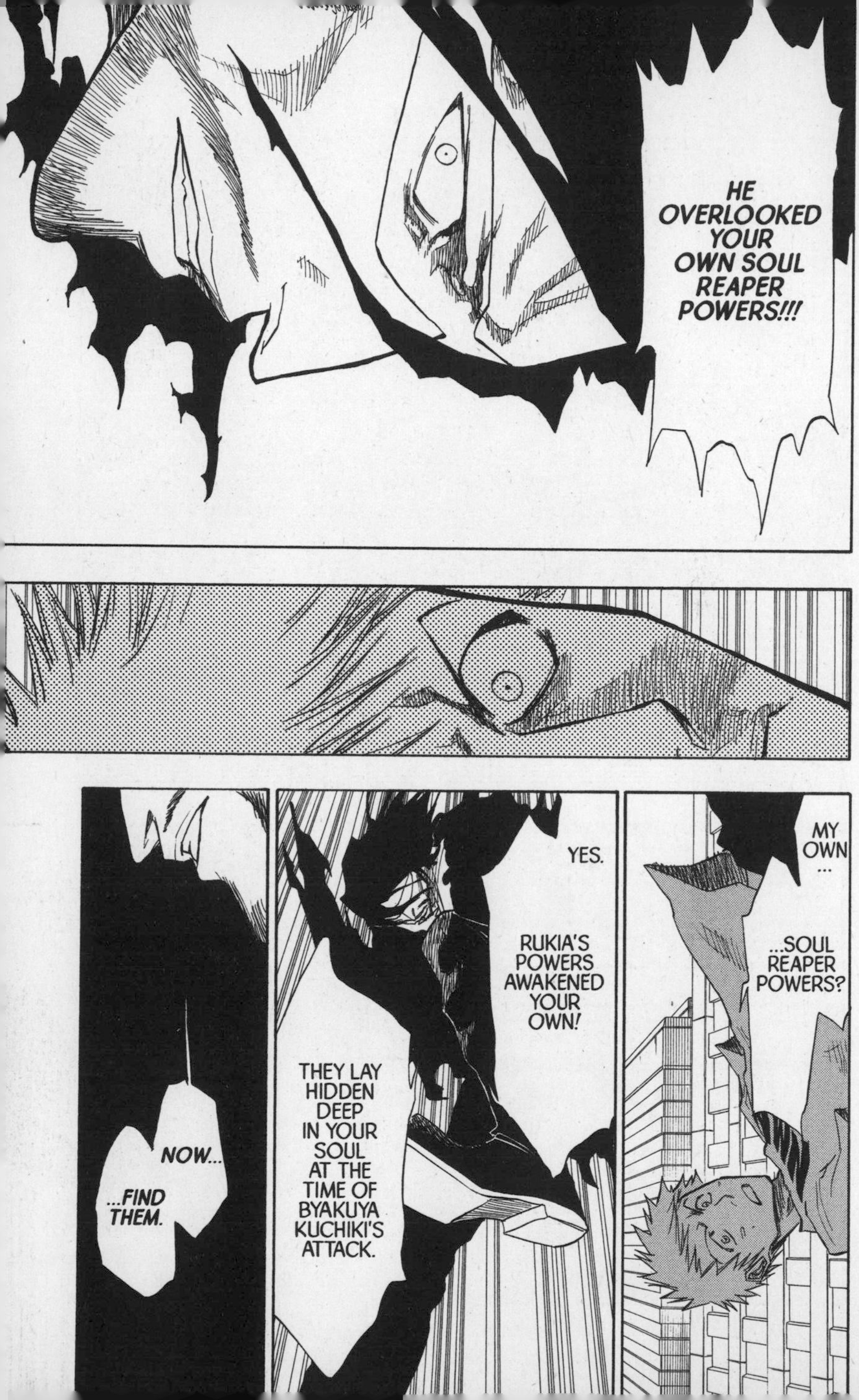
HE OVERLOOKED YOUR OWN SOUL REAPER POWERS!!!
MY OWN...
...SOUL REAPER POWERS?
YES.
RUKIA'S POWERS AWAKENED YOUR OWN!
THEY LAY HIDDEN DEEP IN YOUR SOUL AT THE TIME OF BYAKUYA KUCHIKI'S ATTACK.
NOW...
...FIND THEM.

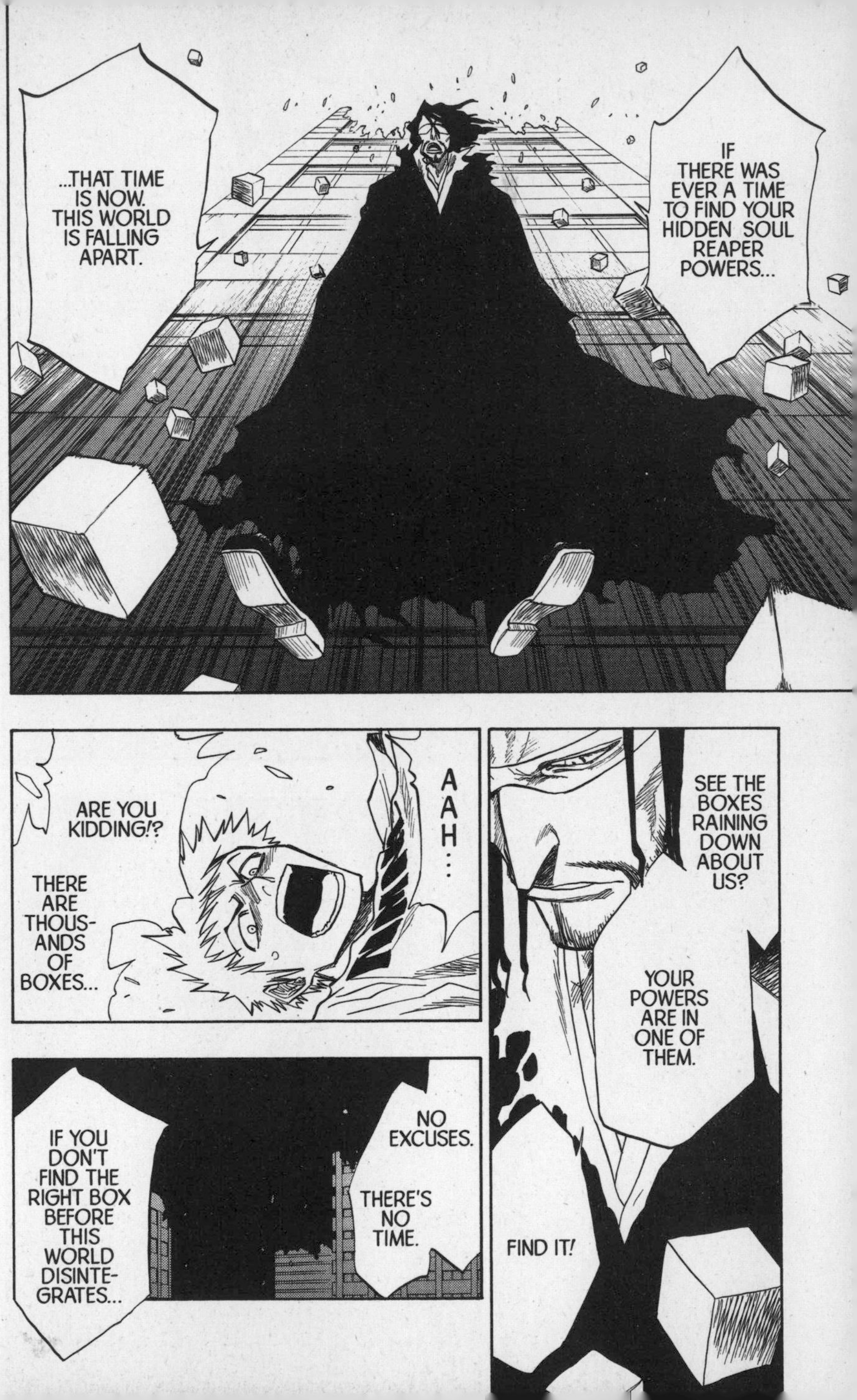
IF THERE WAS EVER A TIME TO FIND YOUR HIDDEN SOUL REAPER POWERS...
...THAT TIME IS NOW. THIS WORLD IS FALLING APART.
SEE THE BOXES RAINING DOWN ABOUT US?
YOUR POWERS ARE IN ONE OF THEM.
FIND IT!
AAH...
ARE YOU KIDDING!?
THERE ARE THOUSANDS OF BOXES...
NO EXCUSES.
THERE'S NO TIME.
IF YOU DON'T FIND THE RIGHT BOX BEFORE THIS WORLD DISINTEGRATES...

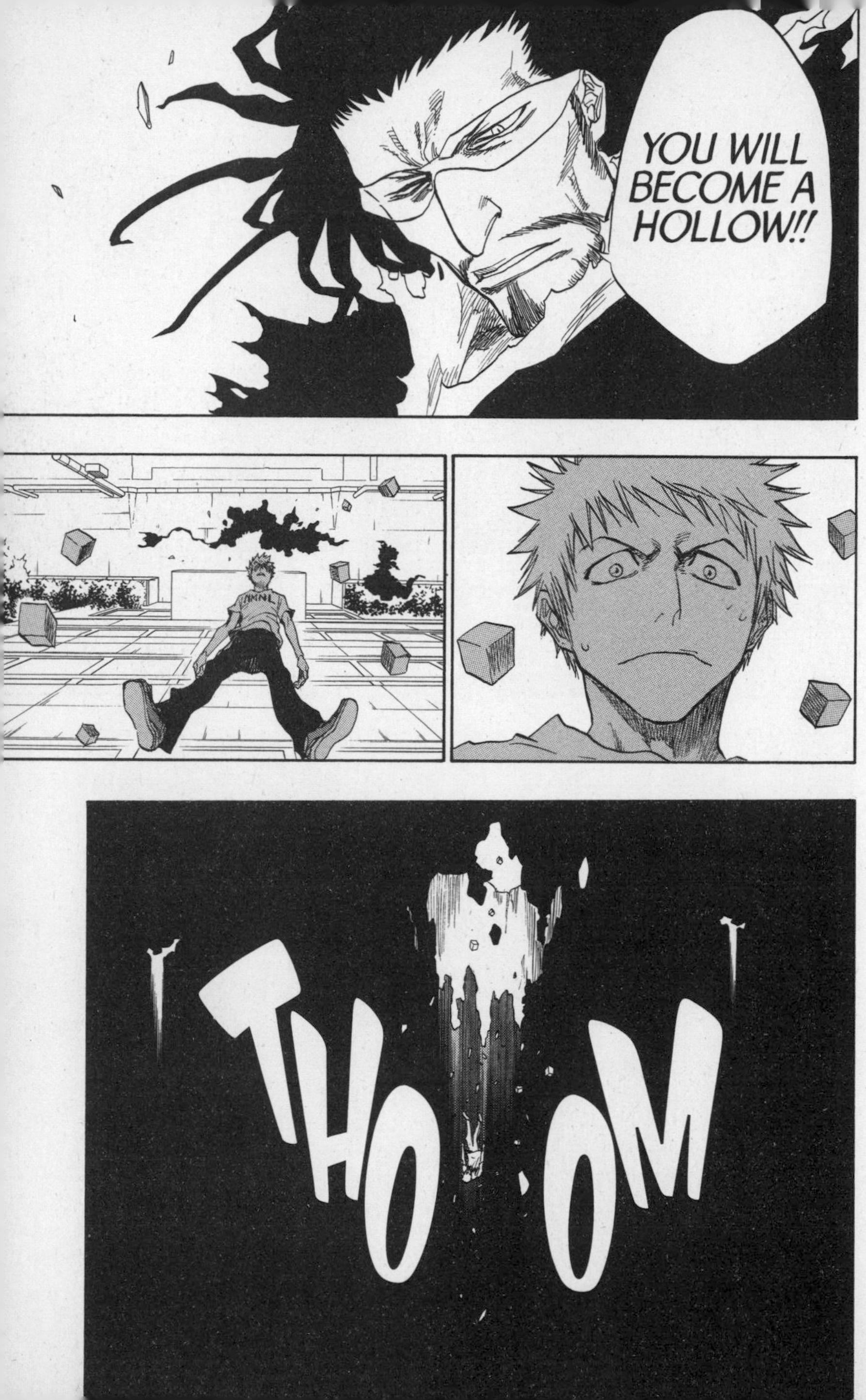
YOU WILL BECOME A HOLLOW!!
THO OM

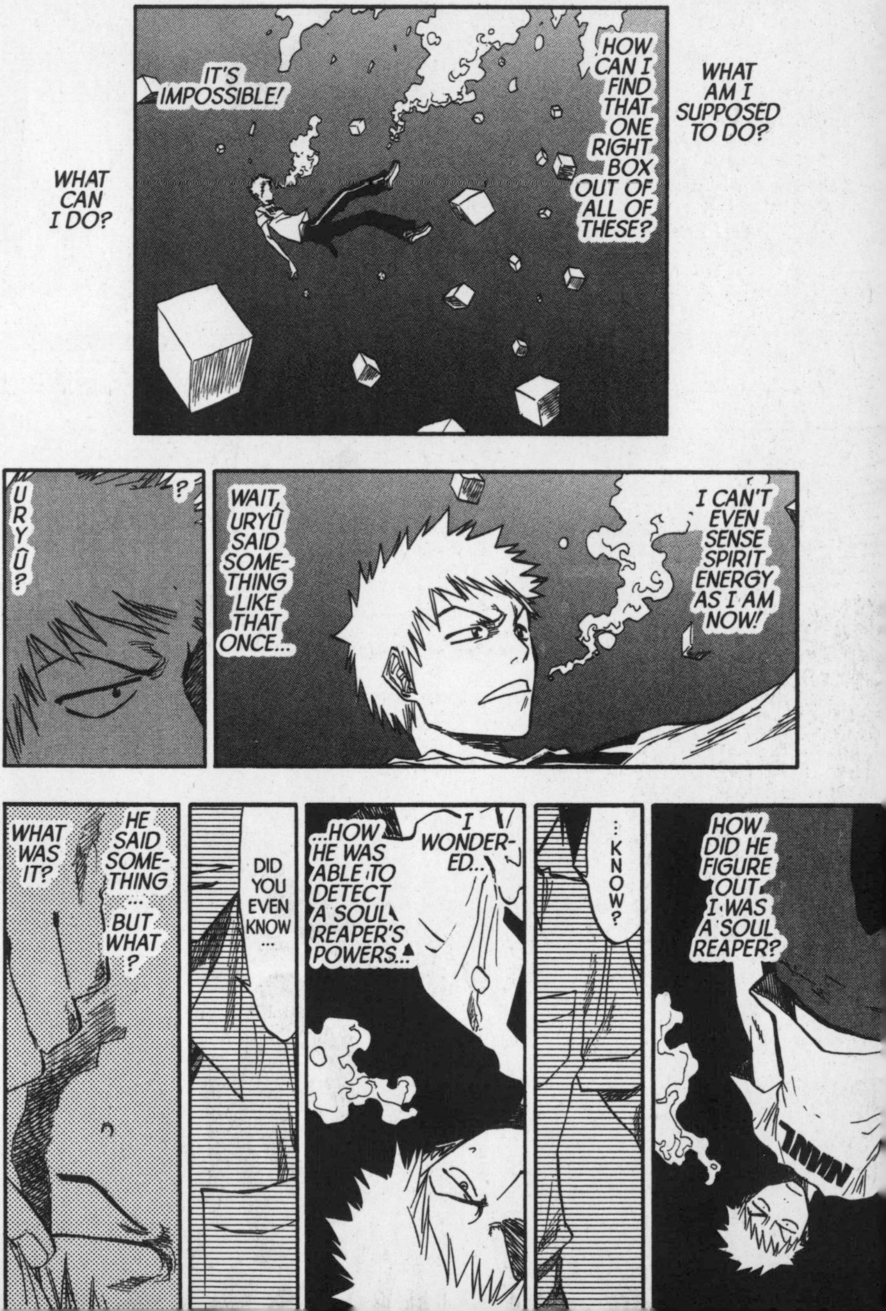
WHAT AM I SUPPOSED TO DO?
HOW CAN I FIND THAT ONE RIGHT BOX OUT OF ALL OF THESE?
IT'S IMPOSSIBLE!
WHAT CAN I DO?
I CAN'T EVEN SENSE SPIRIT ENERGY AS I AM NOW!
WAIT, URYŪ SAID SOMETHING LIKE THAT ONCE...
?
URYŪ?
HOW DID HE FIGURE OUT I WAS A SOUL REAPER?
...KNOW?
I WONDERED...
...HOW HE WAS ABLE TO DETECT A SOUL REAPER'S POWERS...
DID YOU EVEN KNOW ...
HE SAID SOMETHING ... BUT WHAT?
WHAT WAS IT?

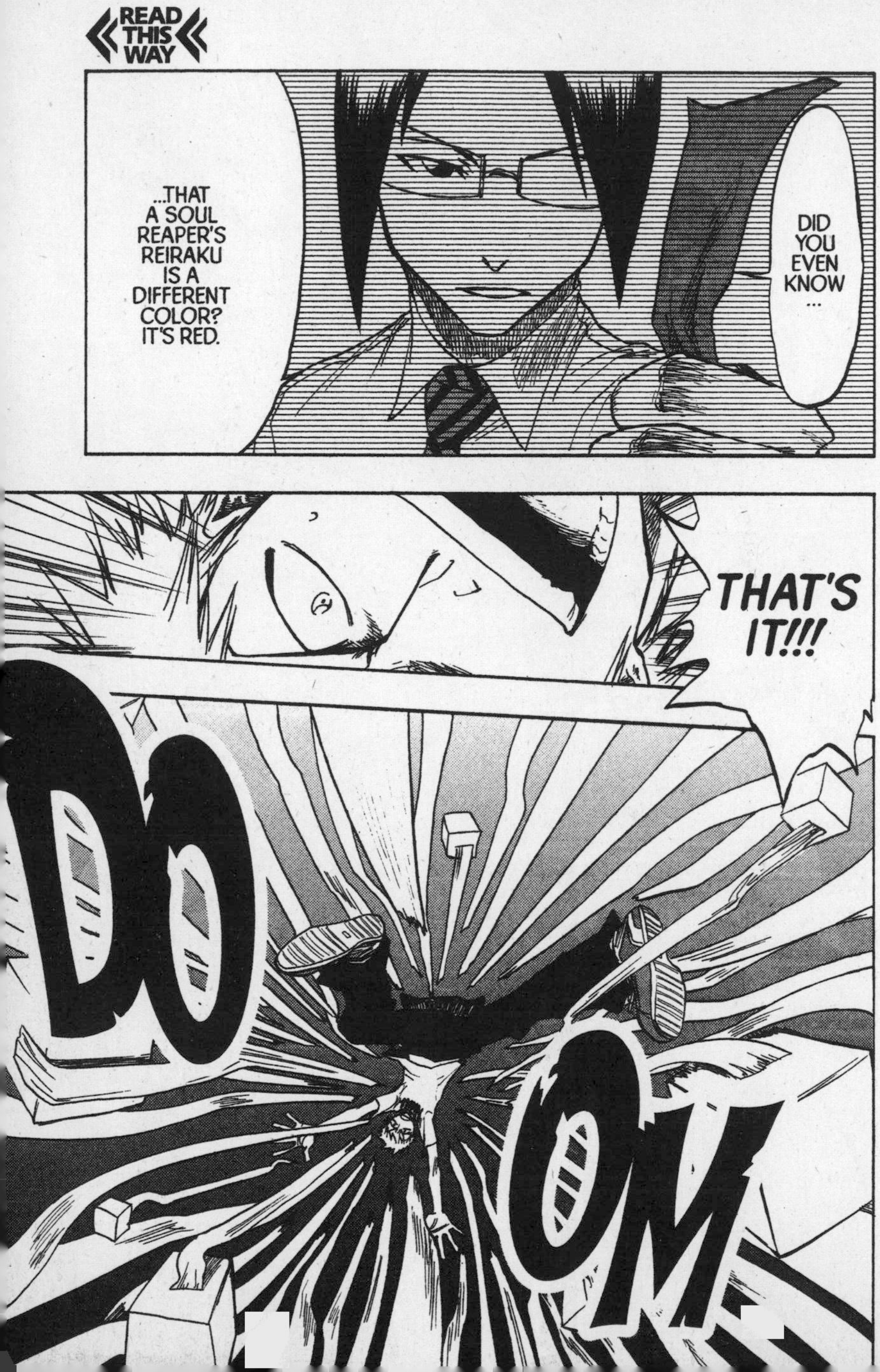
READ THIS WAY
DID YOU EVEN KNOW ...
...THAT A SOUL REAPER'S REIRAKU IS A DIFFERENT COLOR? IT'S RED.
THAT'S IT!!!
DOOOM

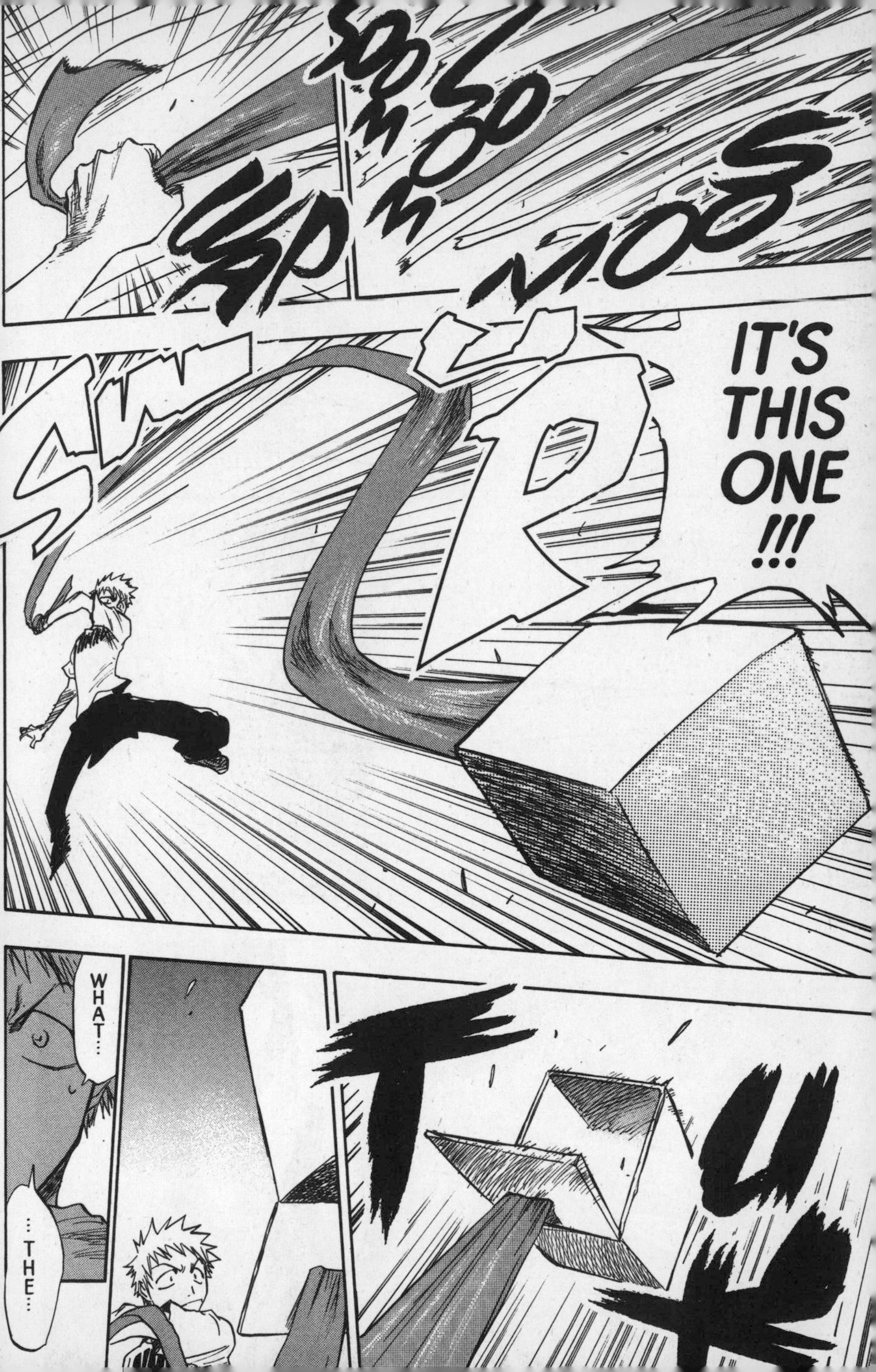
IT'S THIS ONE !!!
WHAT...
...THE...

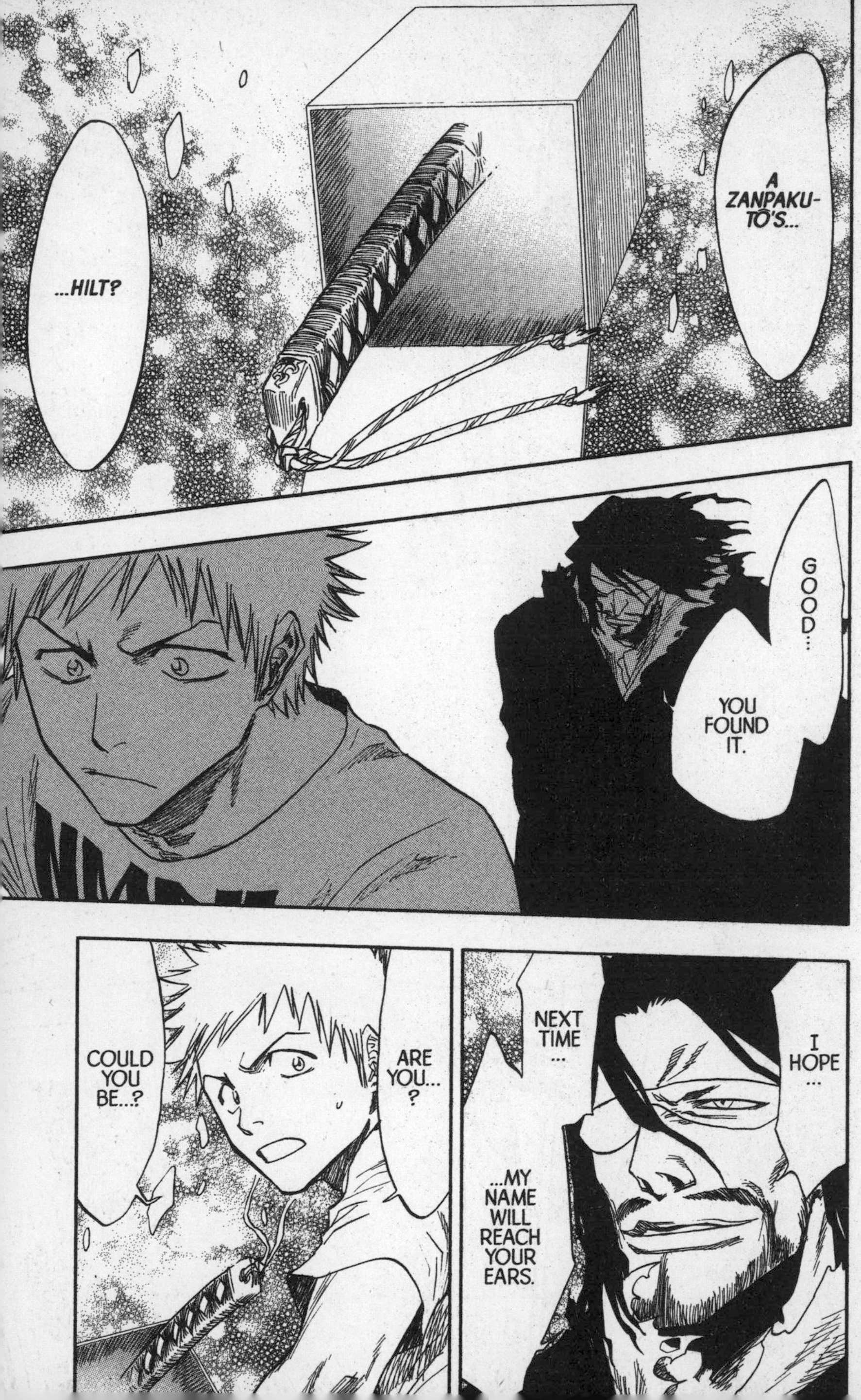
A ZANPAKU-TŌ'S...
...HILT?
GOOD...
YOU FOUND IT.
I HOPE...
NEXT TIME...
...MY NAME WILL REACH YOUR EARS.
ARE YOU...?
COULD YOU BE...?

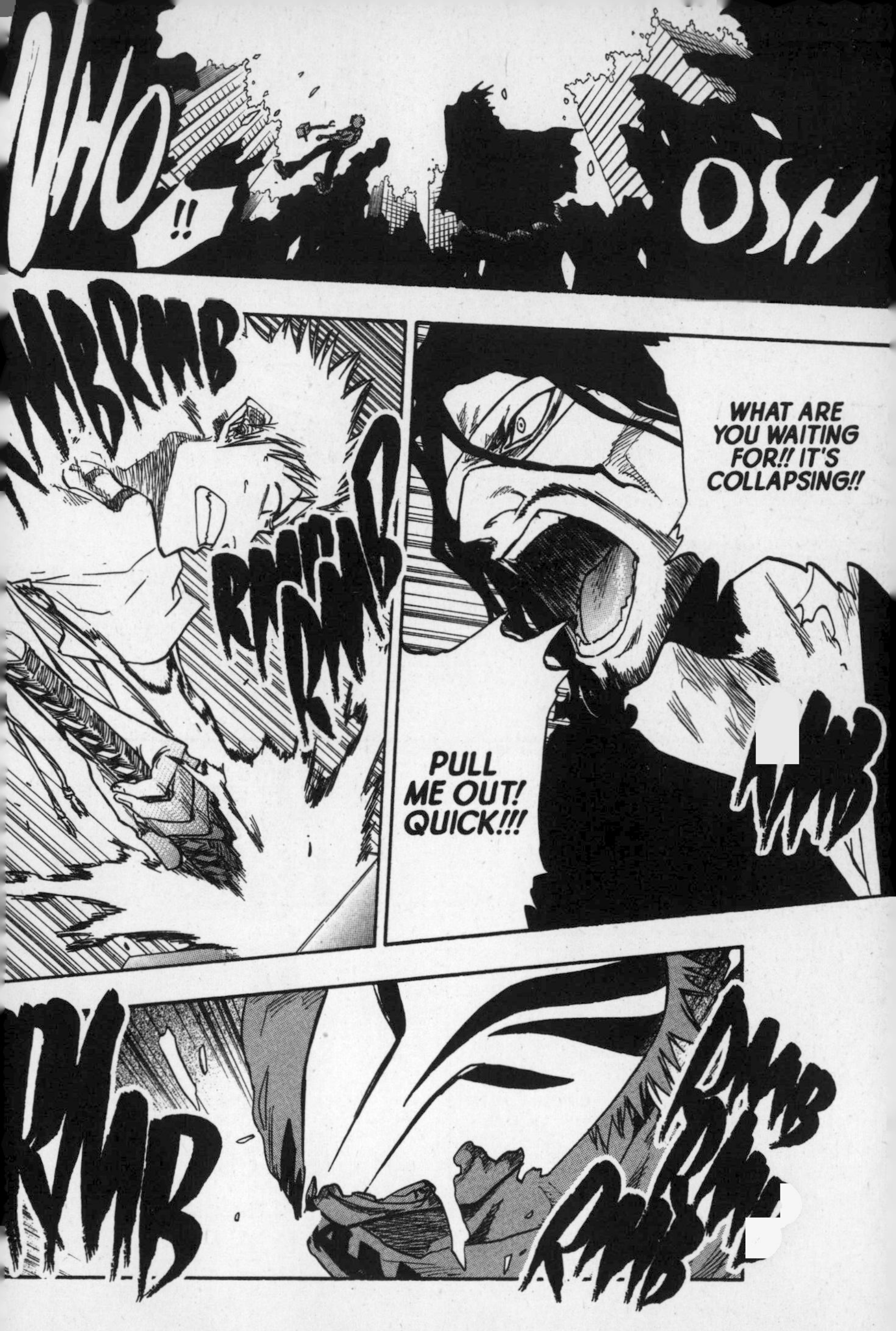
WHAT ARE YOU WAITING FOR!! IT'S COLLAPSING!!
PULL ME OUT! QUICK!!!

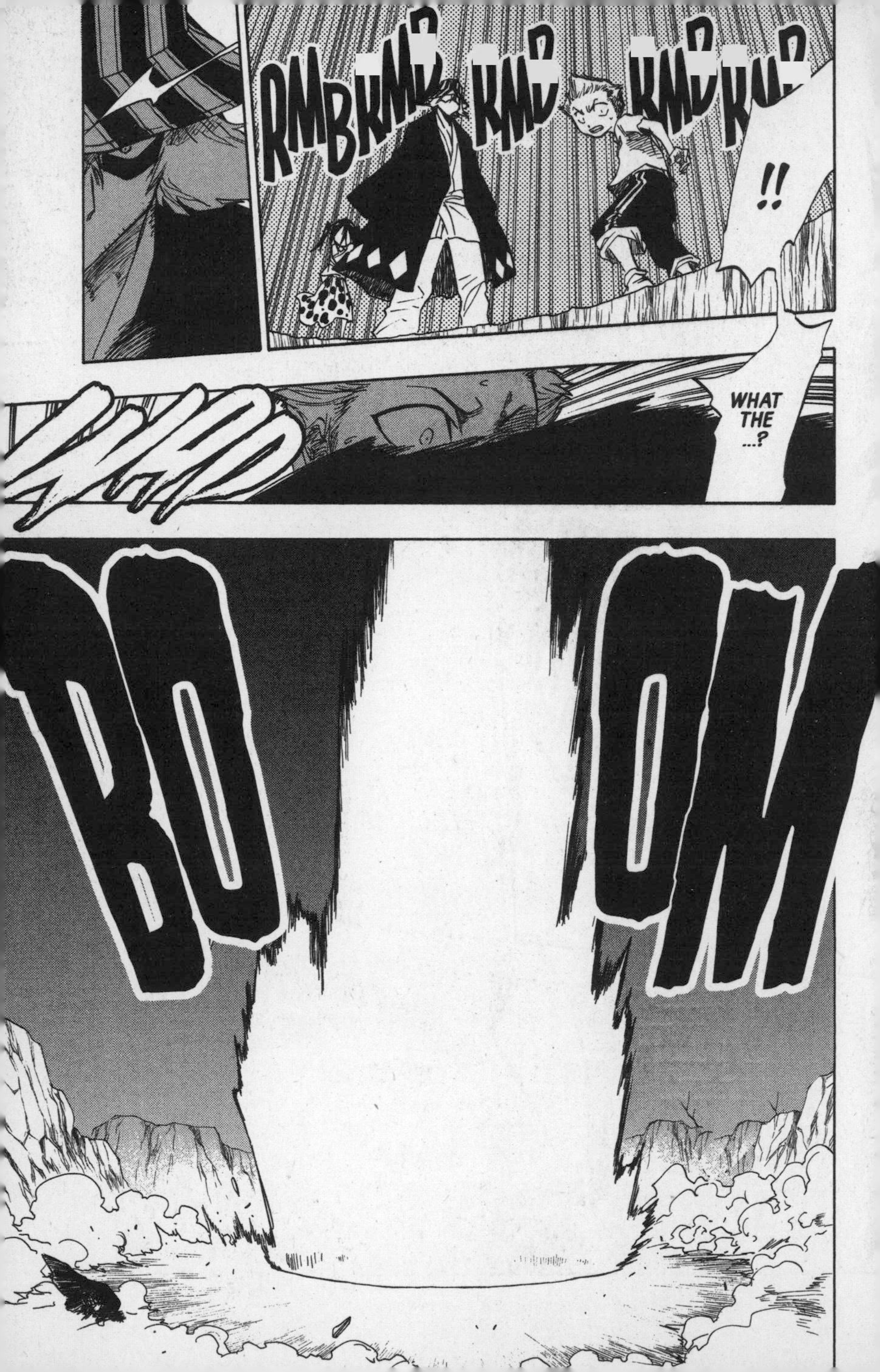
RMB RMB
!!
RMB RMB RMB
WHAT THE ...?

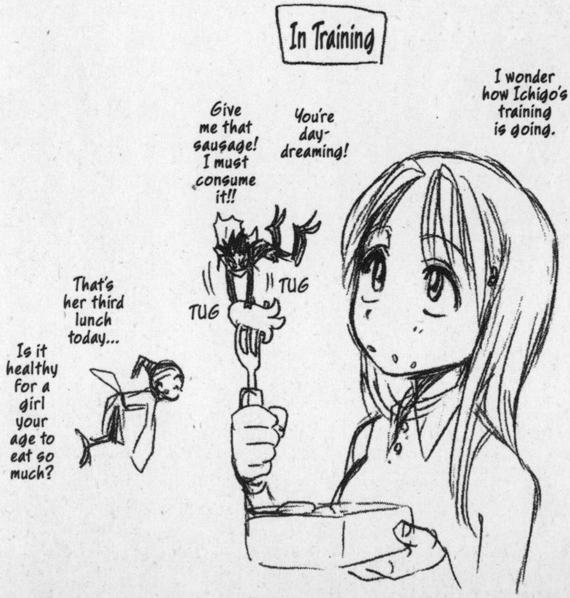
In Training
I wonder how Ichigo's training is going.
You're day-dreaming!
Give me that sausage! I must consume it!!
TUG
TUG
That's her third lunch today...
Is it healthy for a girl your age to eat so much?

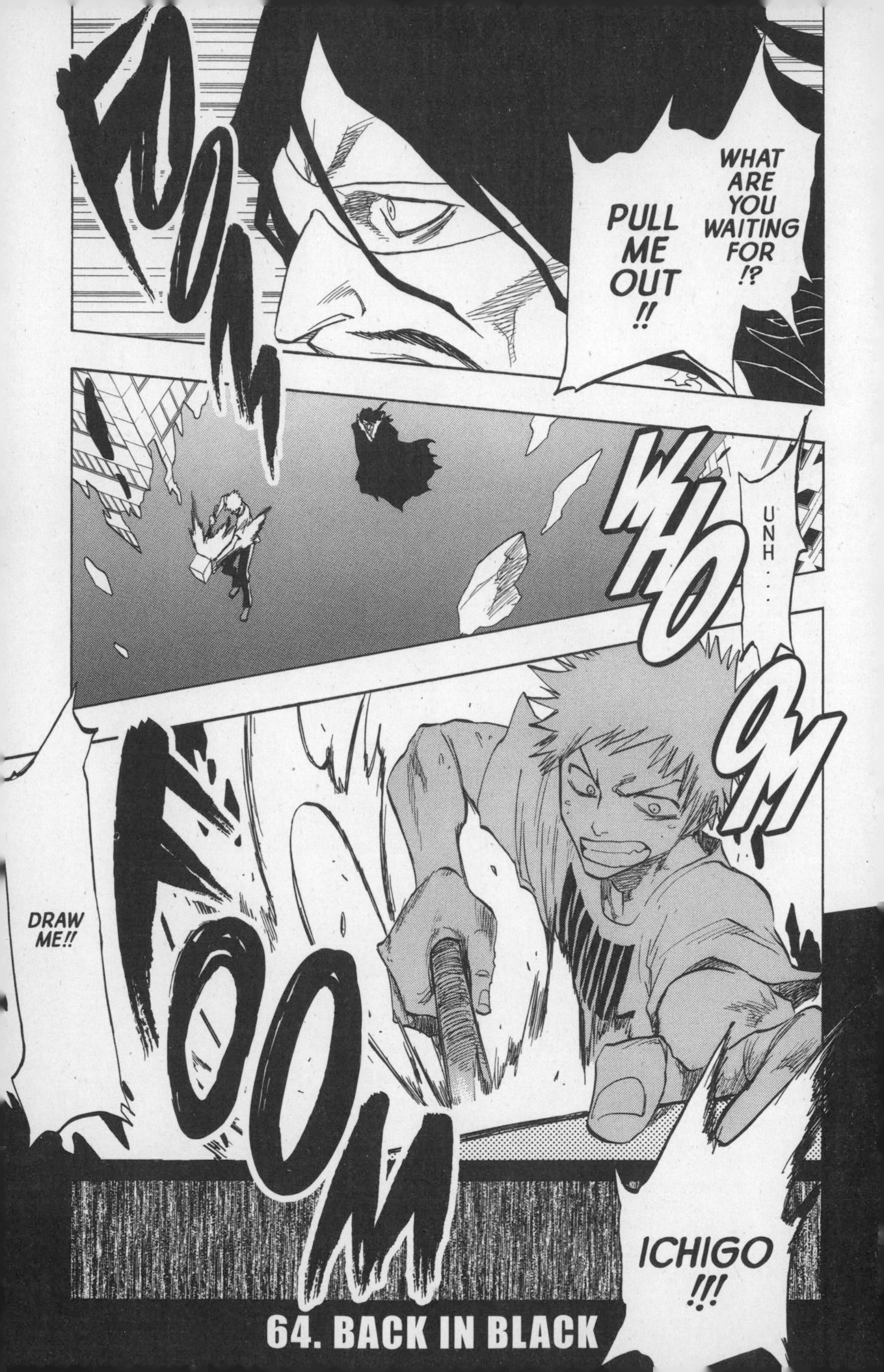
WHAT ARE YOU WAITING FOR !?
PULL ME OUT !!
WHOOM
UNH...
FOOOM
DRAW ME!!
ICHIGO !!!

64. BACK IN BLACK

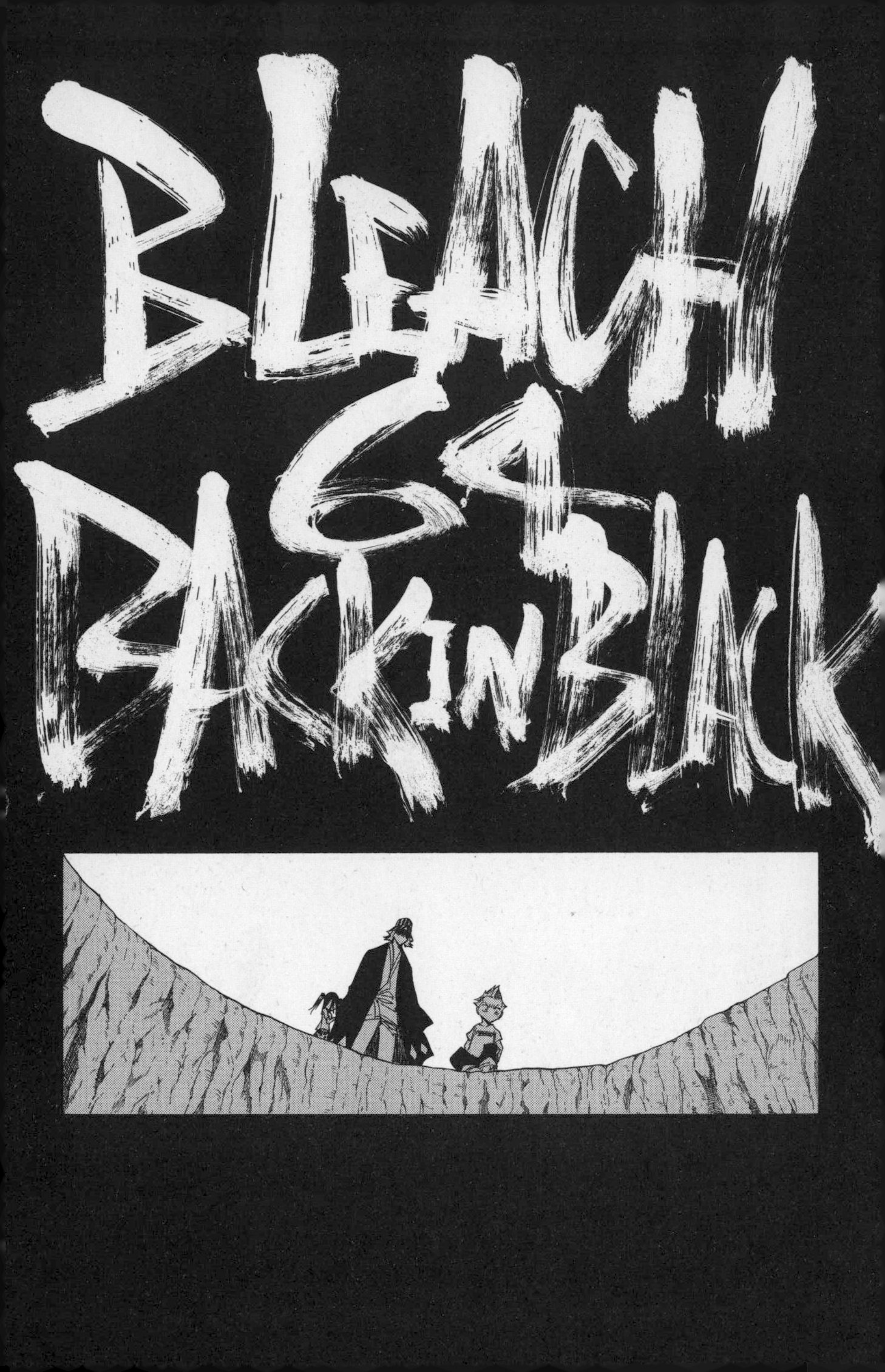
BLEACH 64
BACK IN BLACK

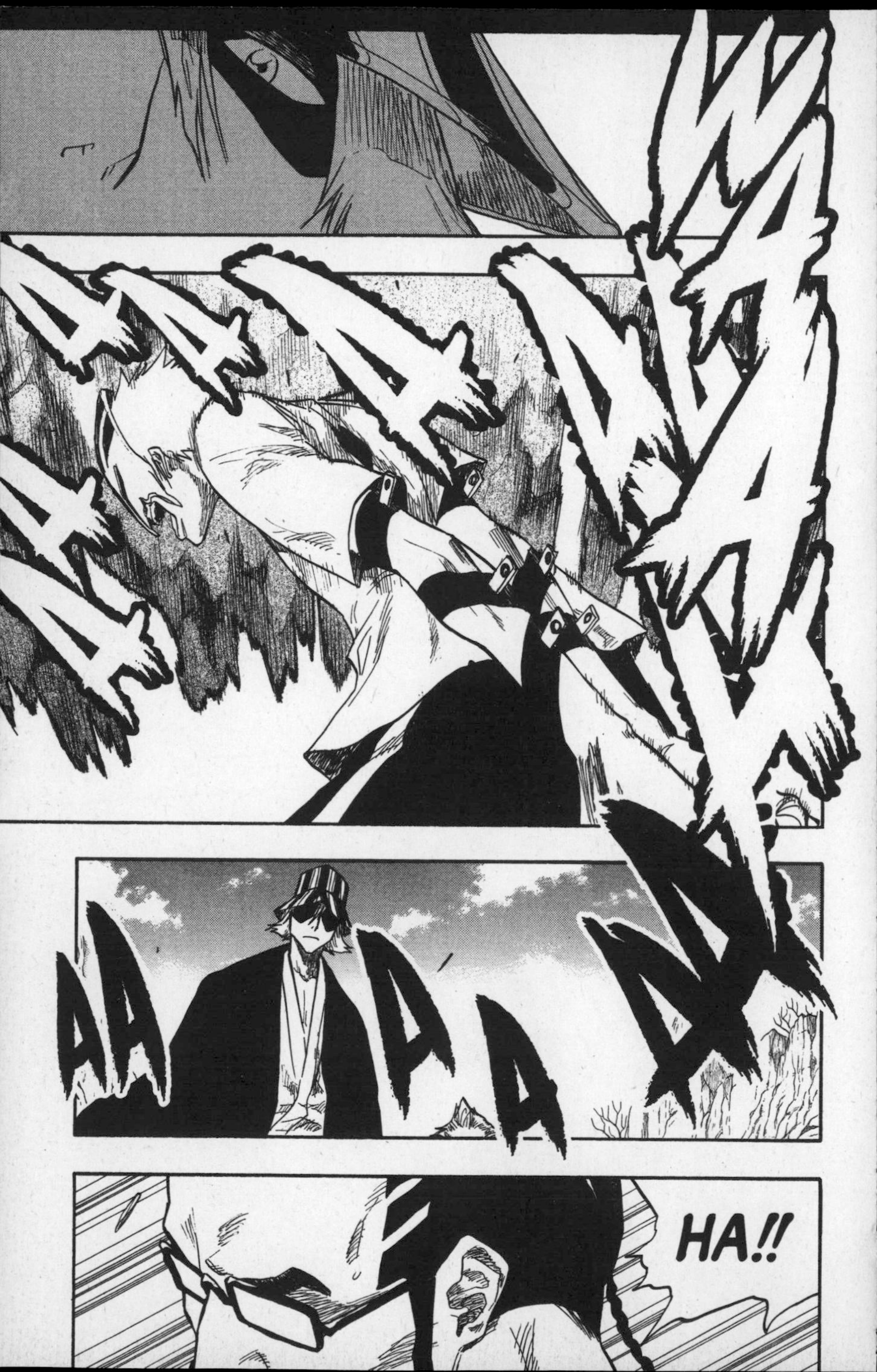
HA!!

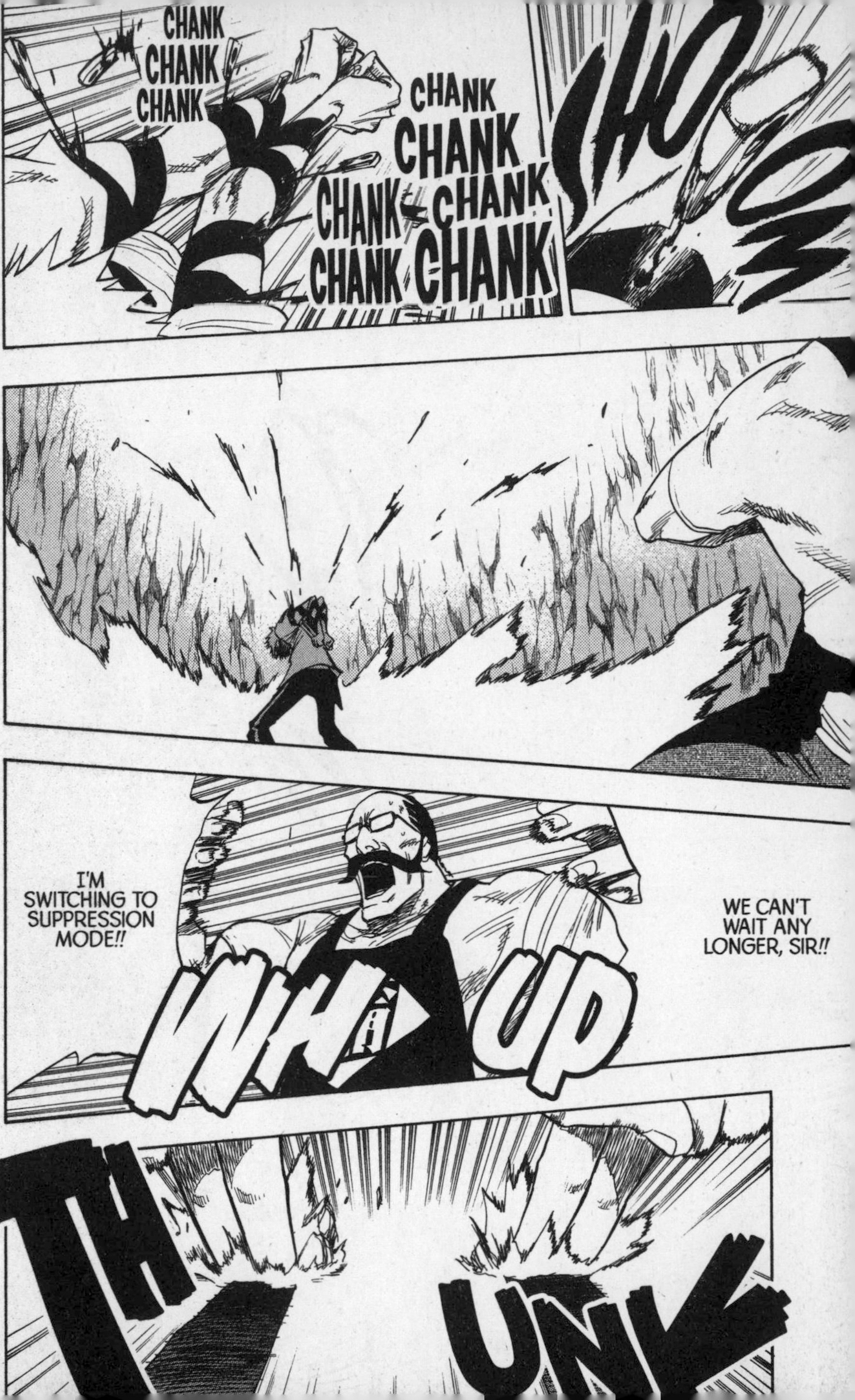

SHOOOM
CHANK
CHANK
CHANK
CHANK
CHANK
CHANK
CHANK
CHANK
CHANK
WE CAN'T WAIT ANY LONGER, SIR!!
I'M SWITCHING TO SUPPRESSION MODE!!
WH UP
TH UNK

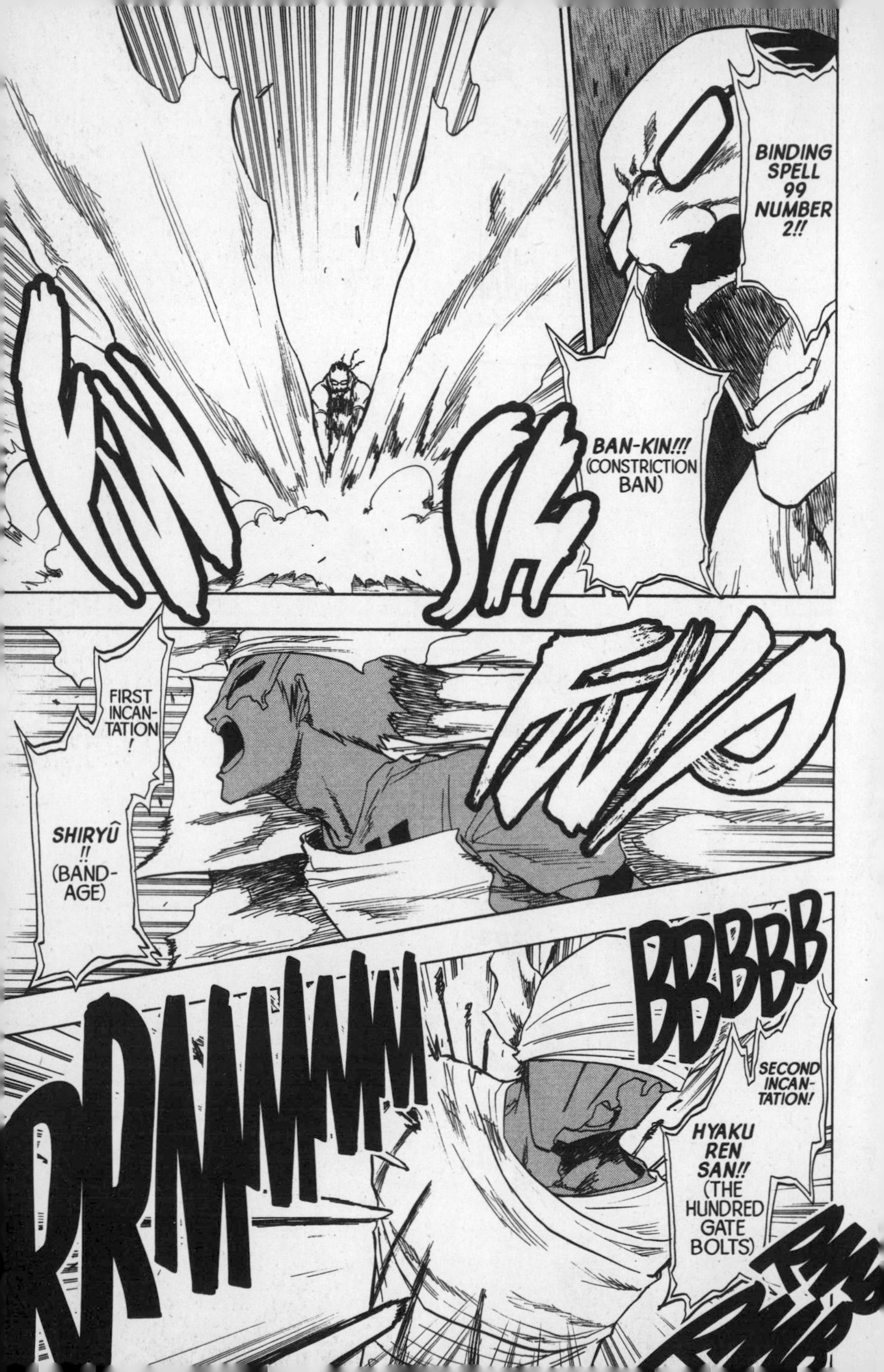
BINDING SPELL 99 NUMBER 2!!
BAN-KIN!!! (CONSTRICTION BAN)
FIRST INCAN-TATION!
SHIRYÛ!! (BAND-AGE)
BBBBB
SECOND INCAN-TATION!
HYAKU REN SAN!! (THE HUNDRED GATE BOLTS)

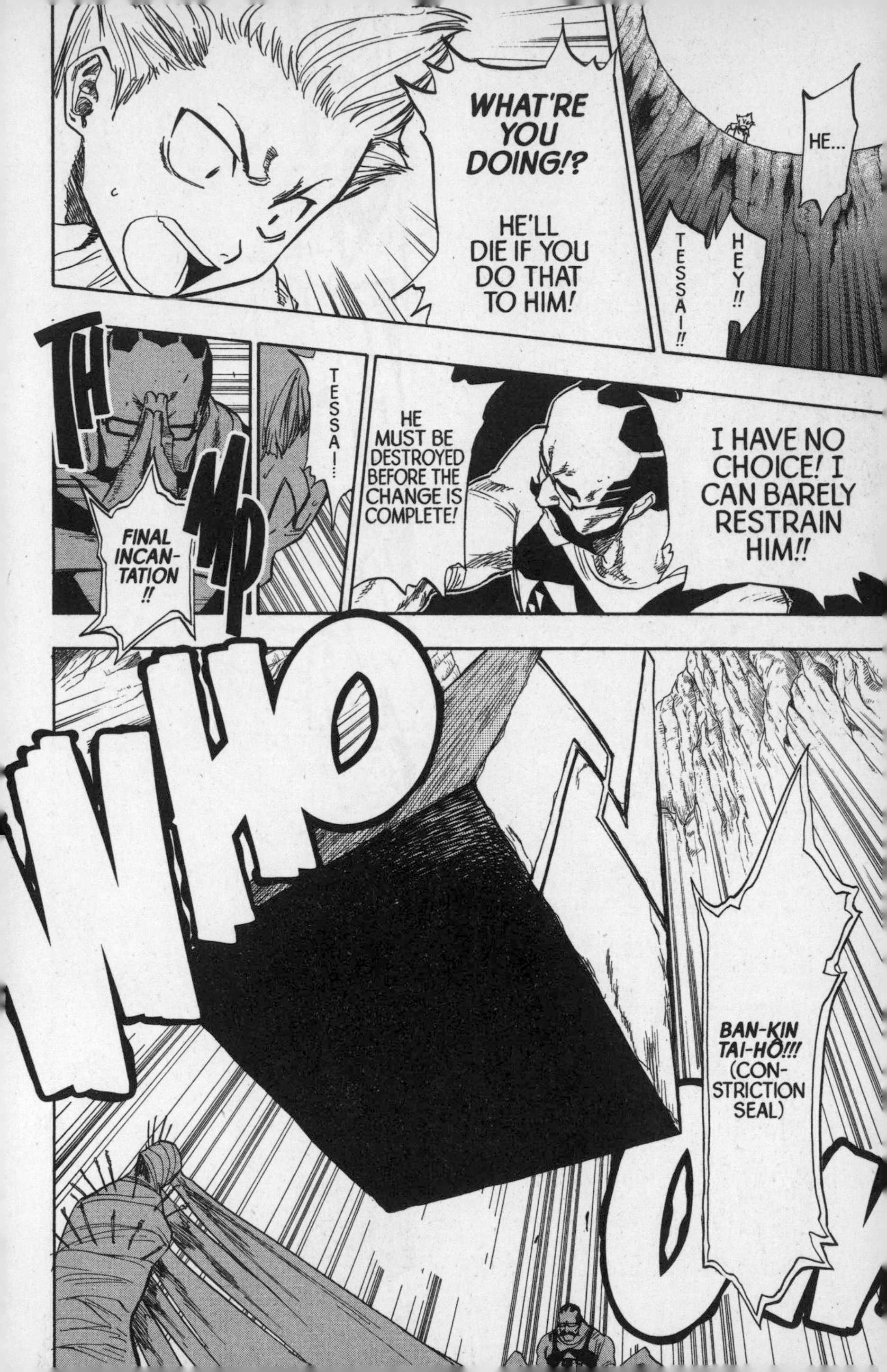
HE...
HEY!!
TESSAI!!
WHAT'RE YOU DOING!?
HE'LL DIE IF YOU DO THAT TO HIM!
I HAVE NO CHOICE! I CAN BARELY RESTRAIN HIM!!
HE MUST BE DESTROYED BEFORE THE CHANGE IS COMPLETE!
TESSAI!...
THMP
FINAL INCANTATION!!
BAN-KIN TAI-HŌ!!! (CONSTRICTION SEAL)
WHO

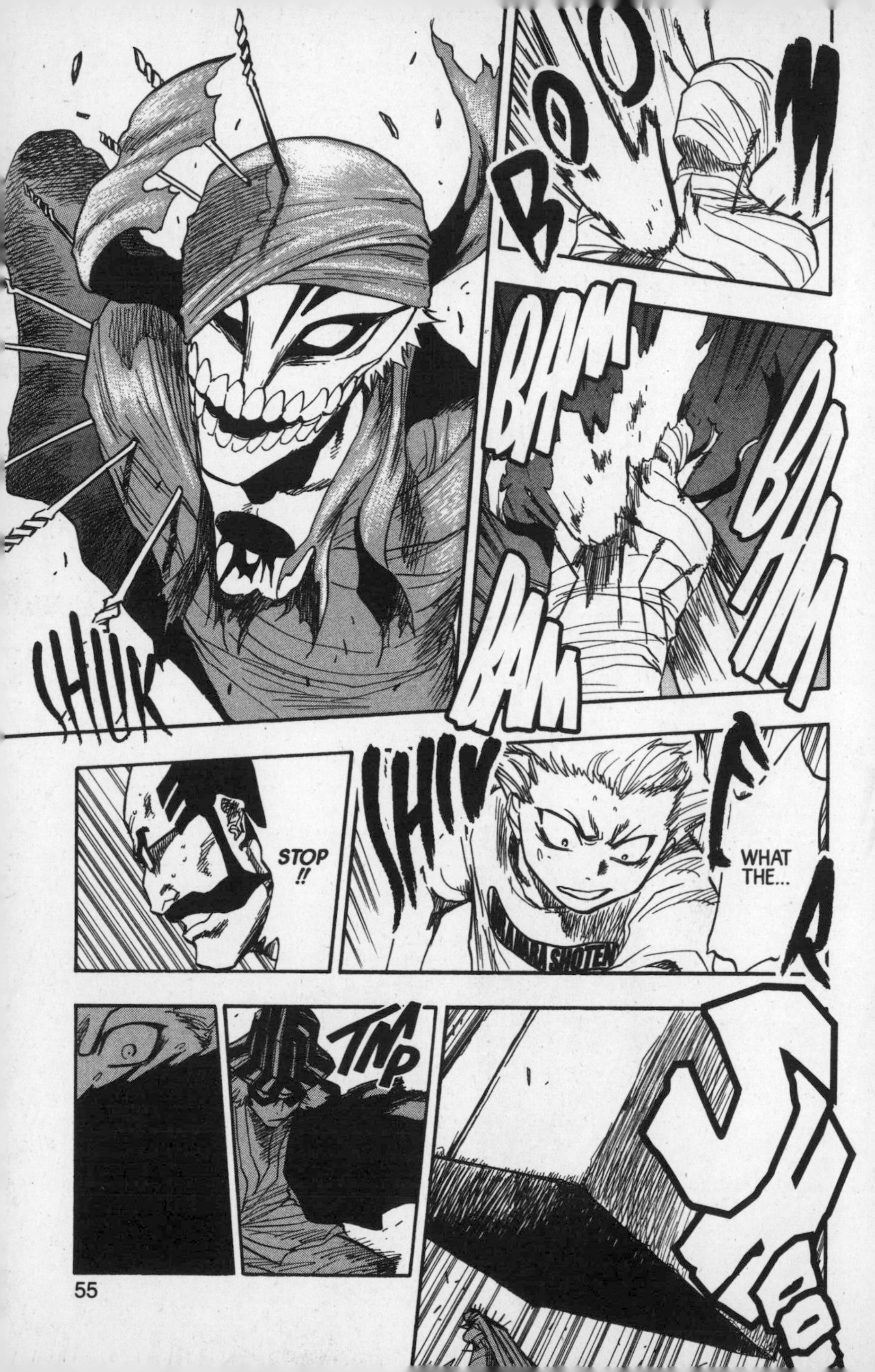

BOOM
BAM
BAM
BAM
CHUK
WHAT THE...
SHIV
STOP !!
TMP

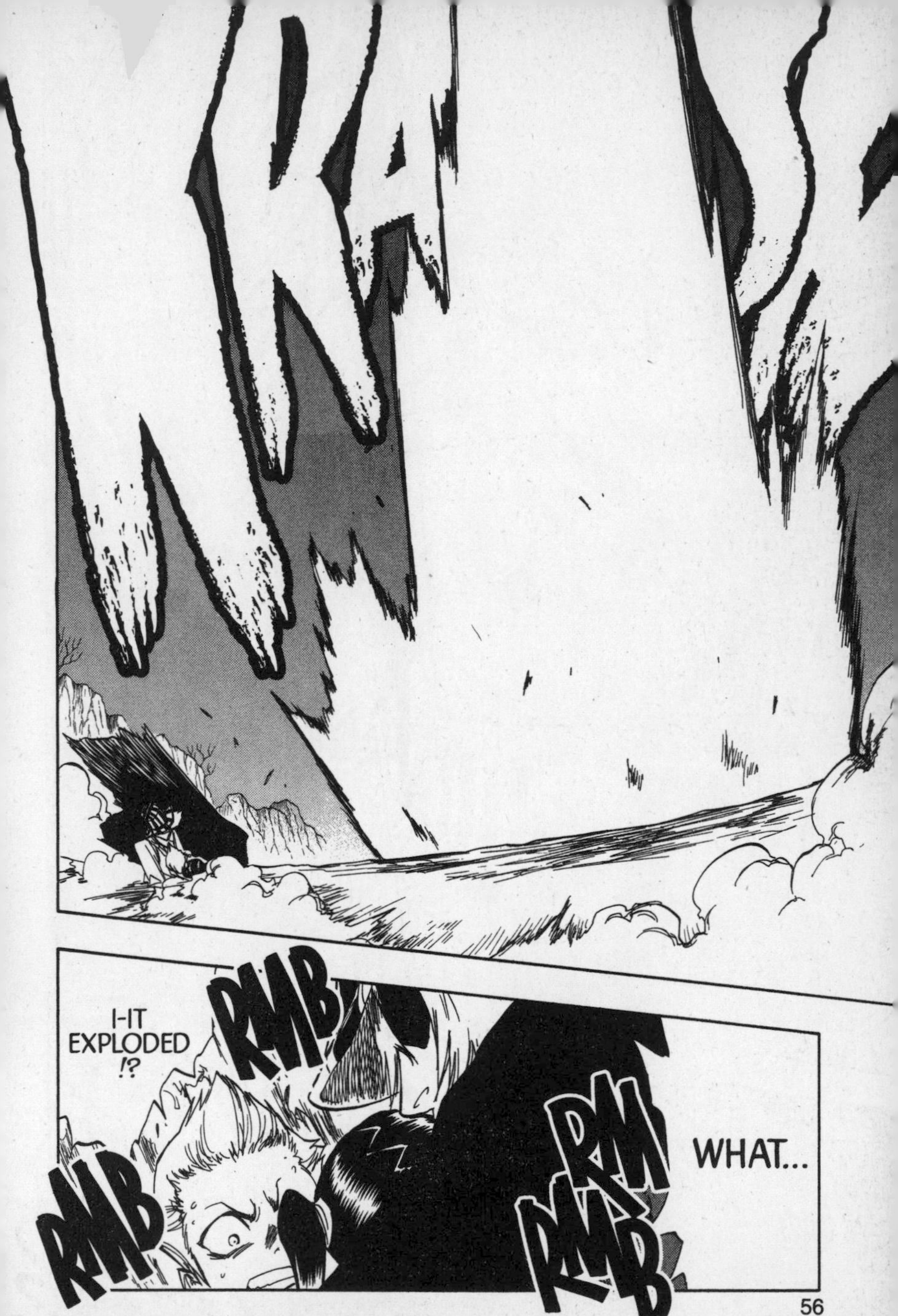
WHAT...
RM
RMB
RMB
I-IT EXPLODED !?
RMB

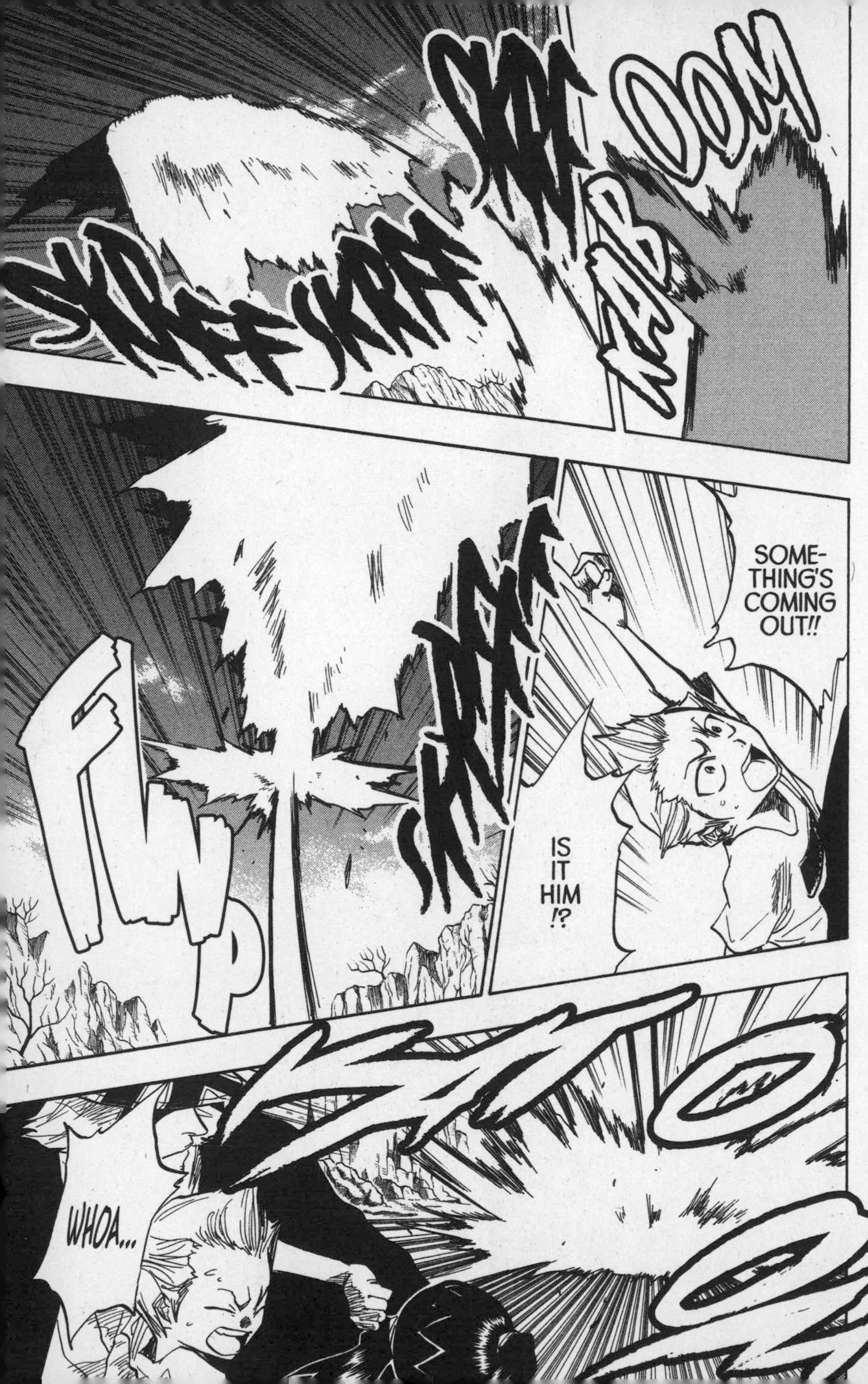
SOME-THING'S COMING OUT!!
IS IT HIM!?
WHOA...

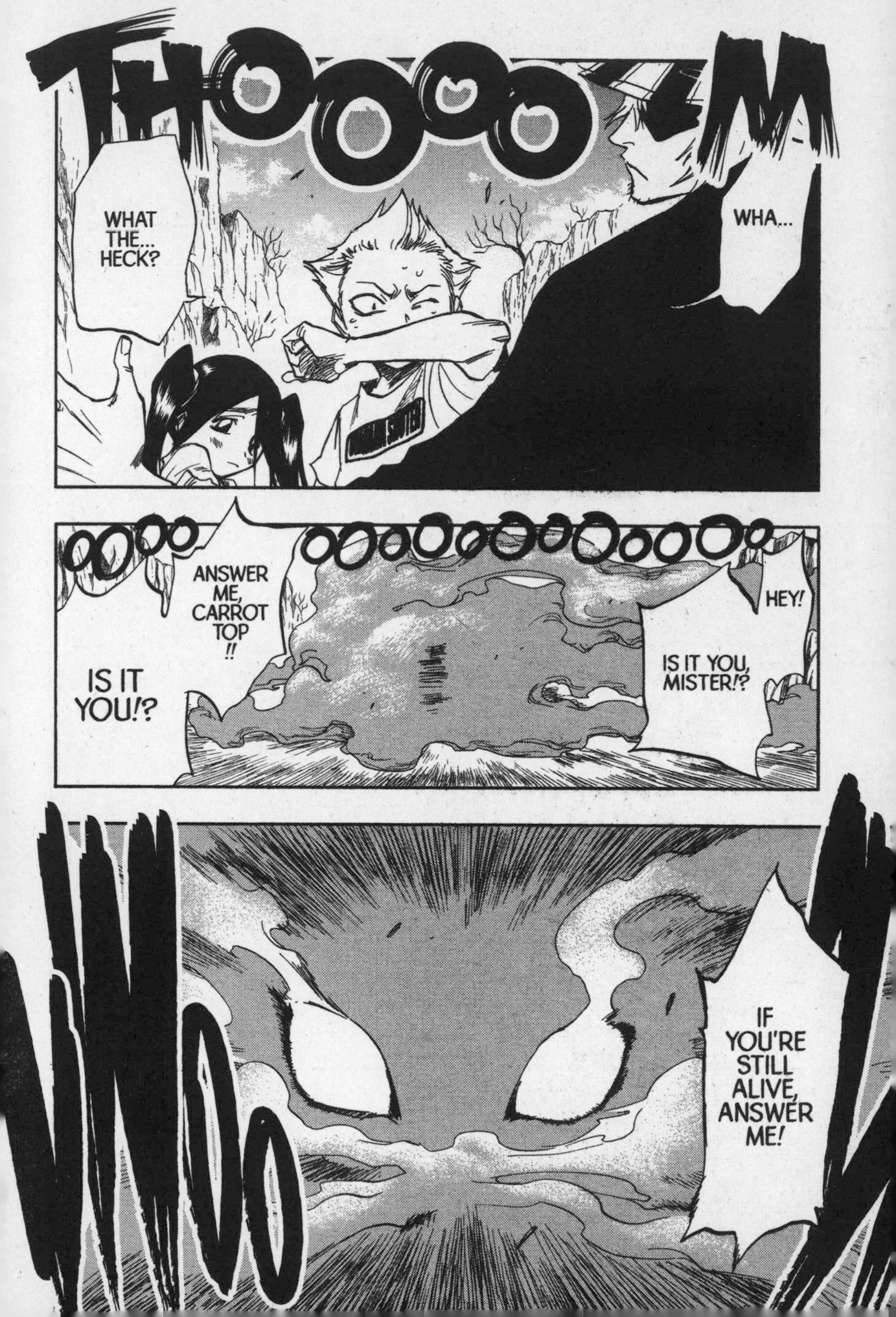
WHA...
WHAT THE... HECK?
HEY!
IS IT YOU, MISTER!?
ANSWER ME, CARROT TOP!!
IS IT YOU!?
IF YOU'RE STILL ALIVE, ANSWER ME!

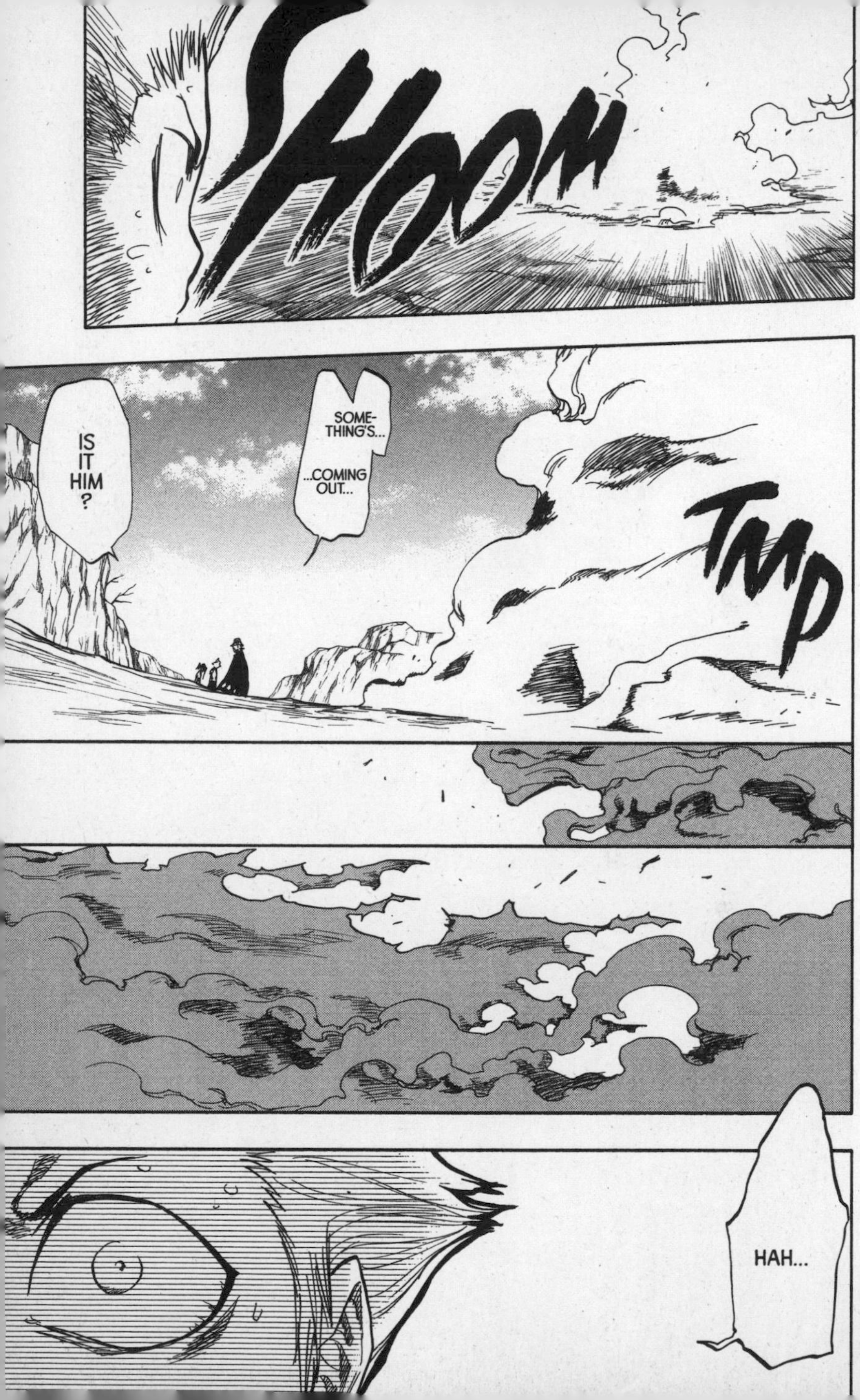
SHOOM
TMP
SOME-THING'S...
...COMING OUT...
IS IT HIM?
HAH...

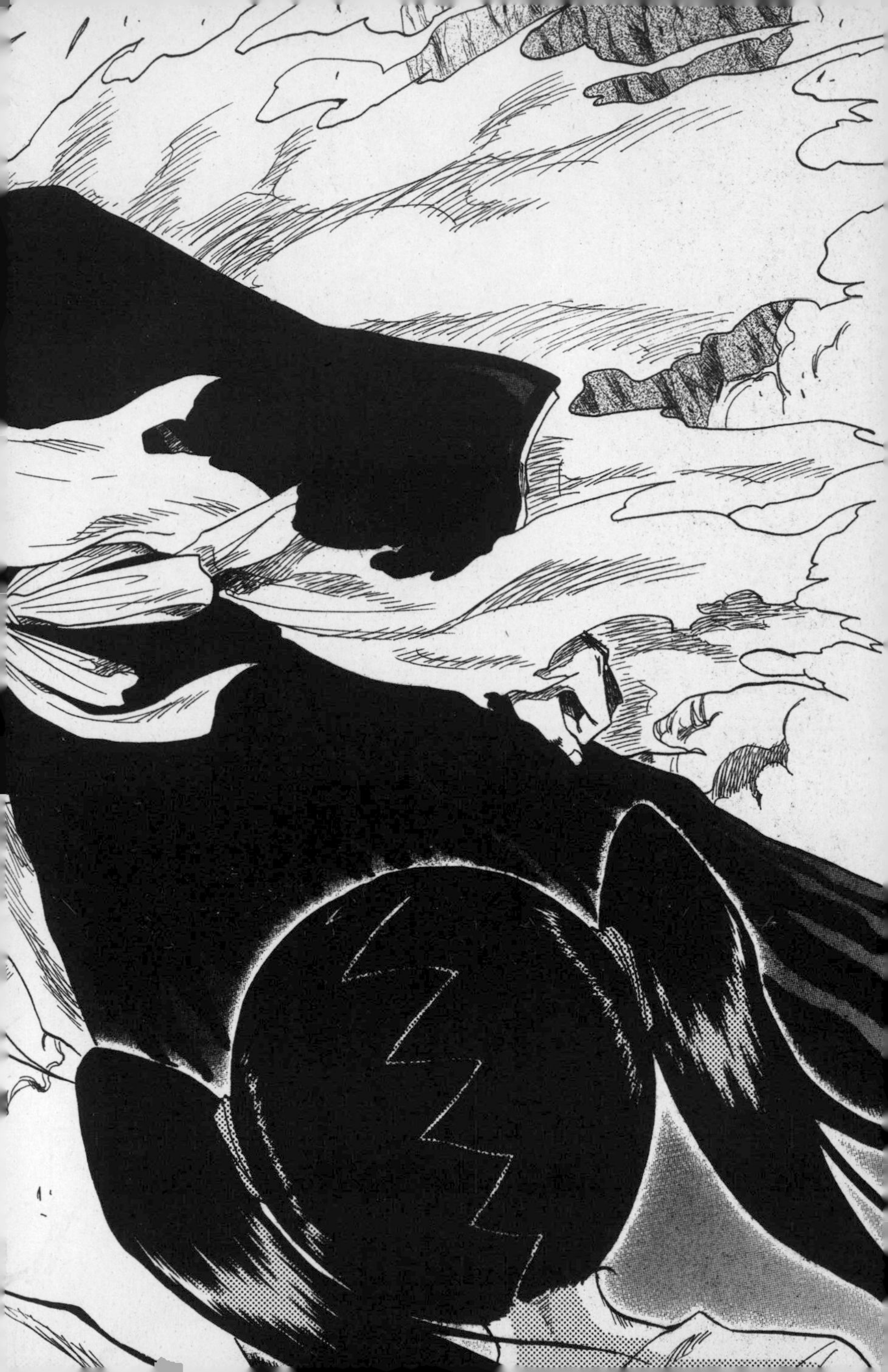

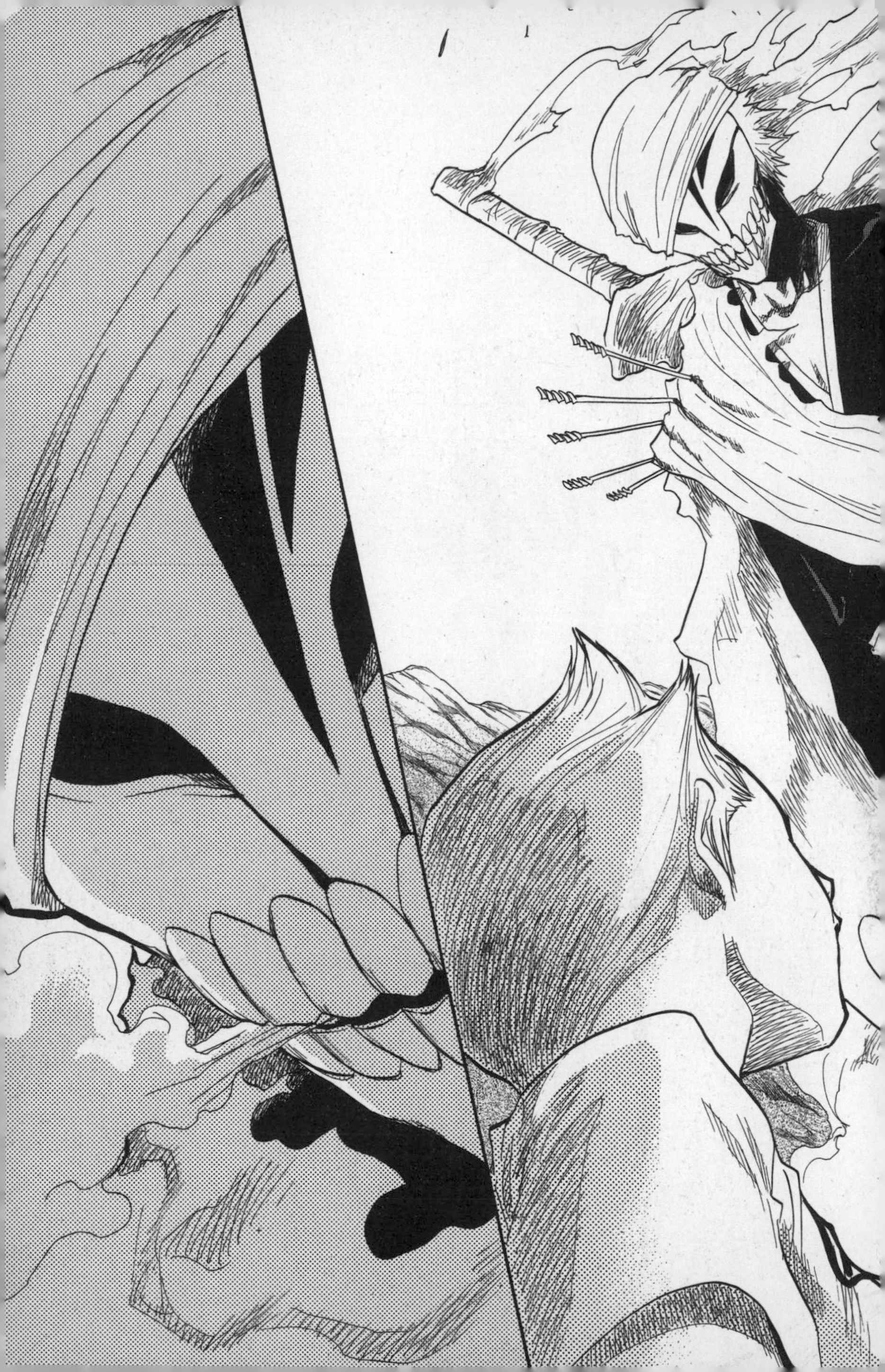

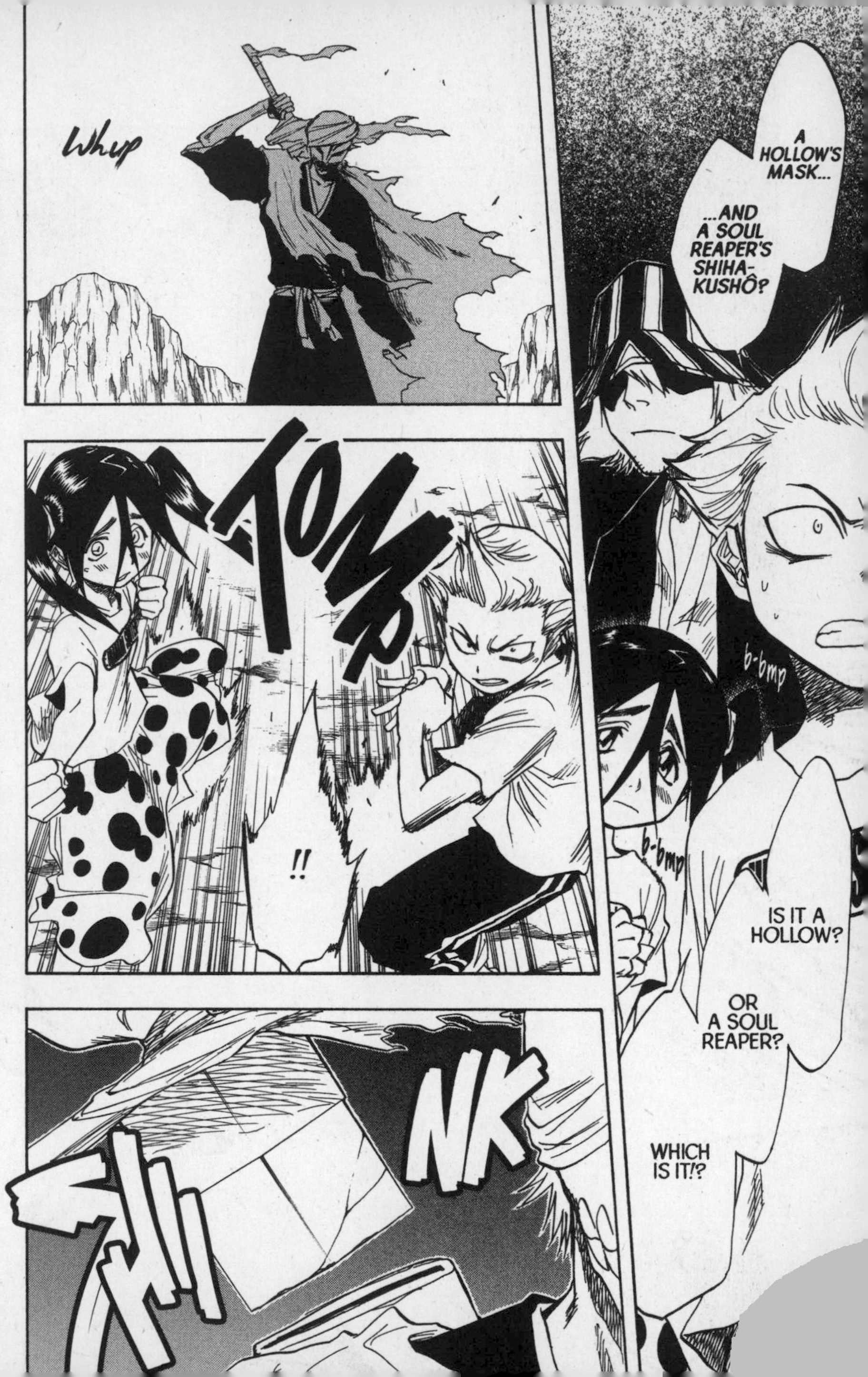
A HOLLOW'S MASK...
...AND A SOUL REAPER'S SHIHA-KUSHÔ?
b-bmp
b-bmp
IS IT A HOLLOW?
OR A SOUL REAPER?
WHICH IS IT!?
Whup
TOMP
!!
NK

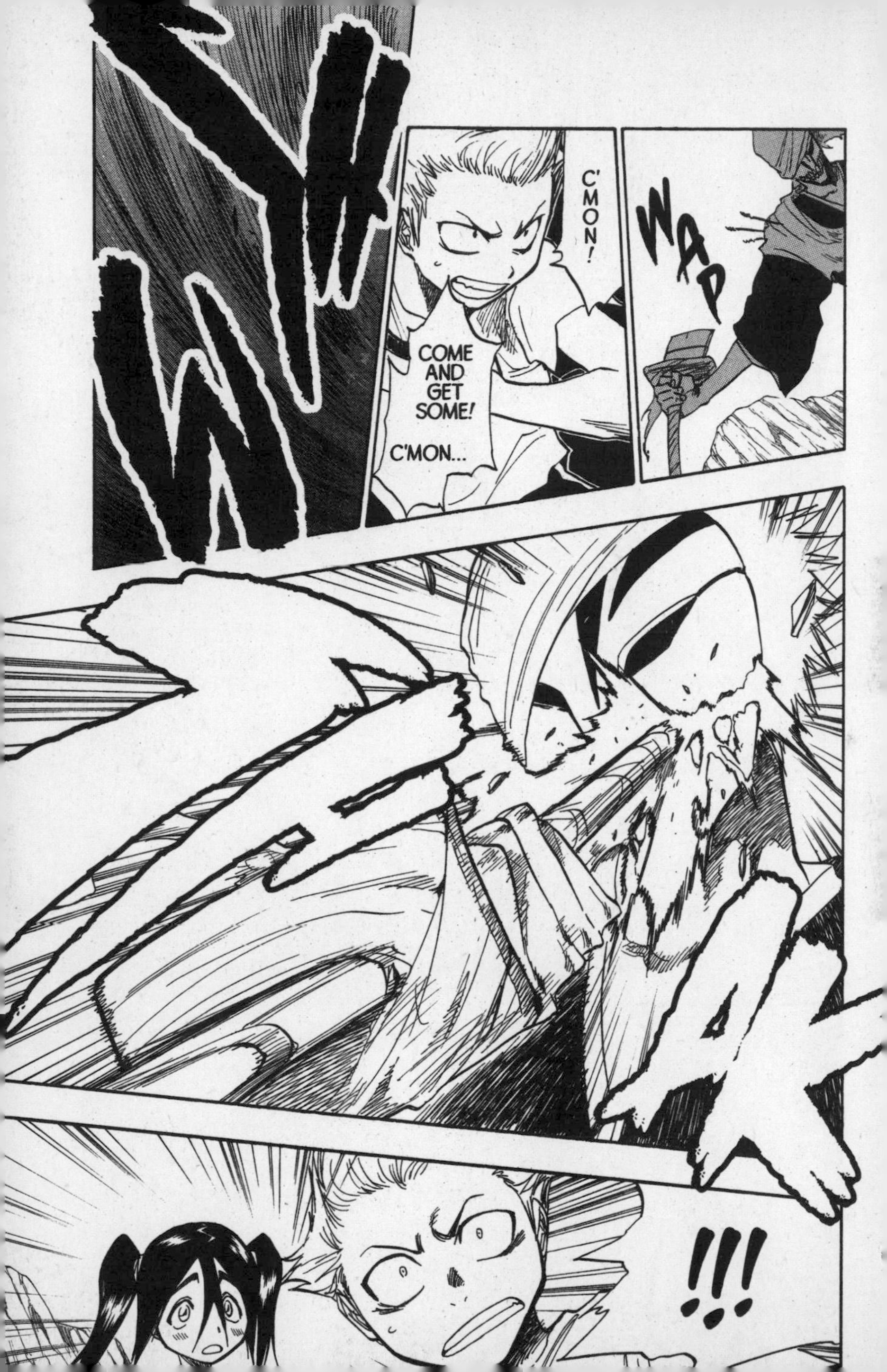
WAP
C'MON!
COME AND GET SOME!
C'MON...
!!!

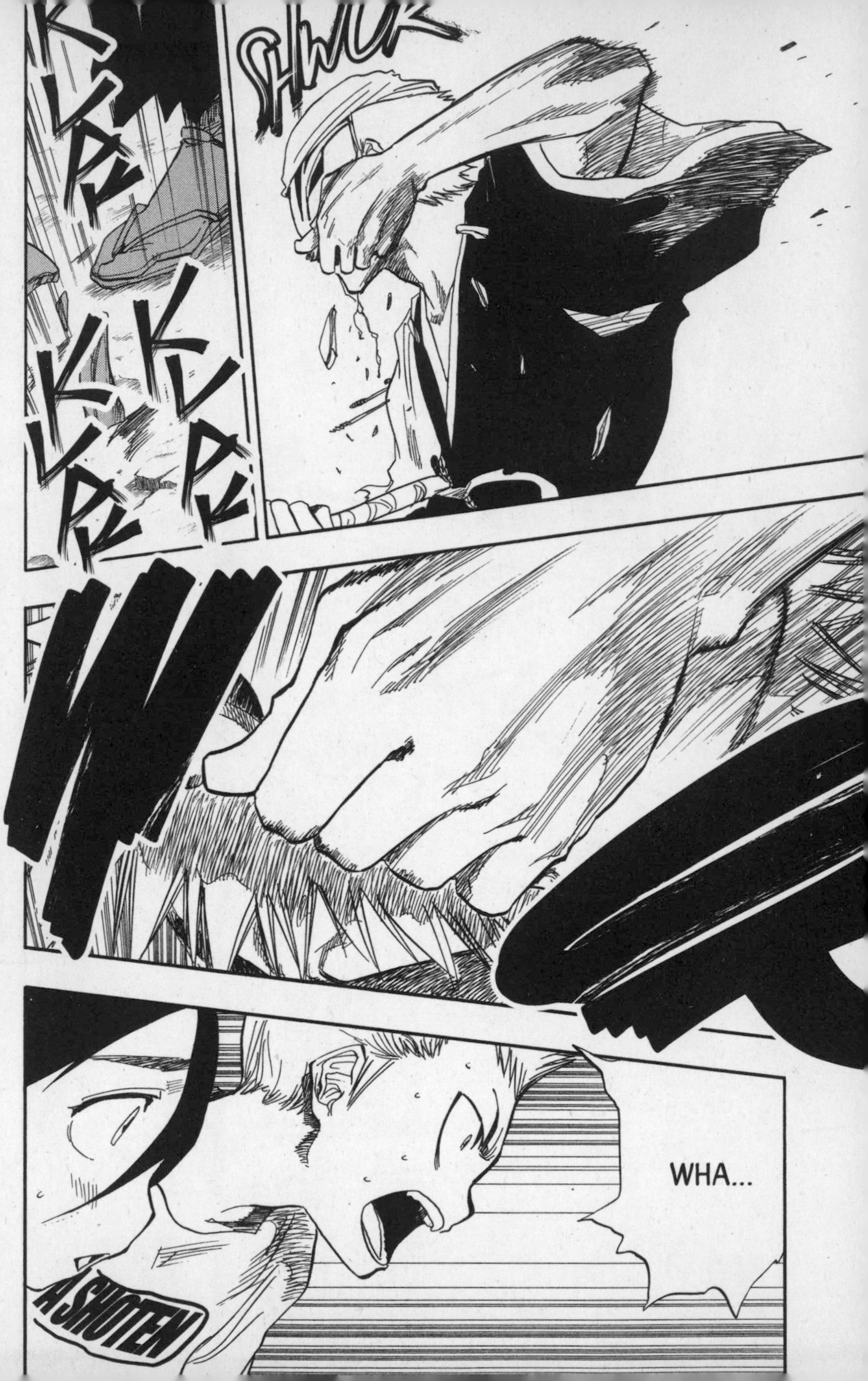
SHWUK
WHA...

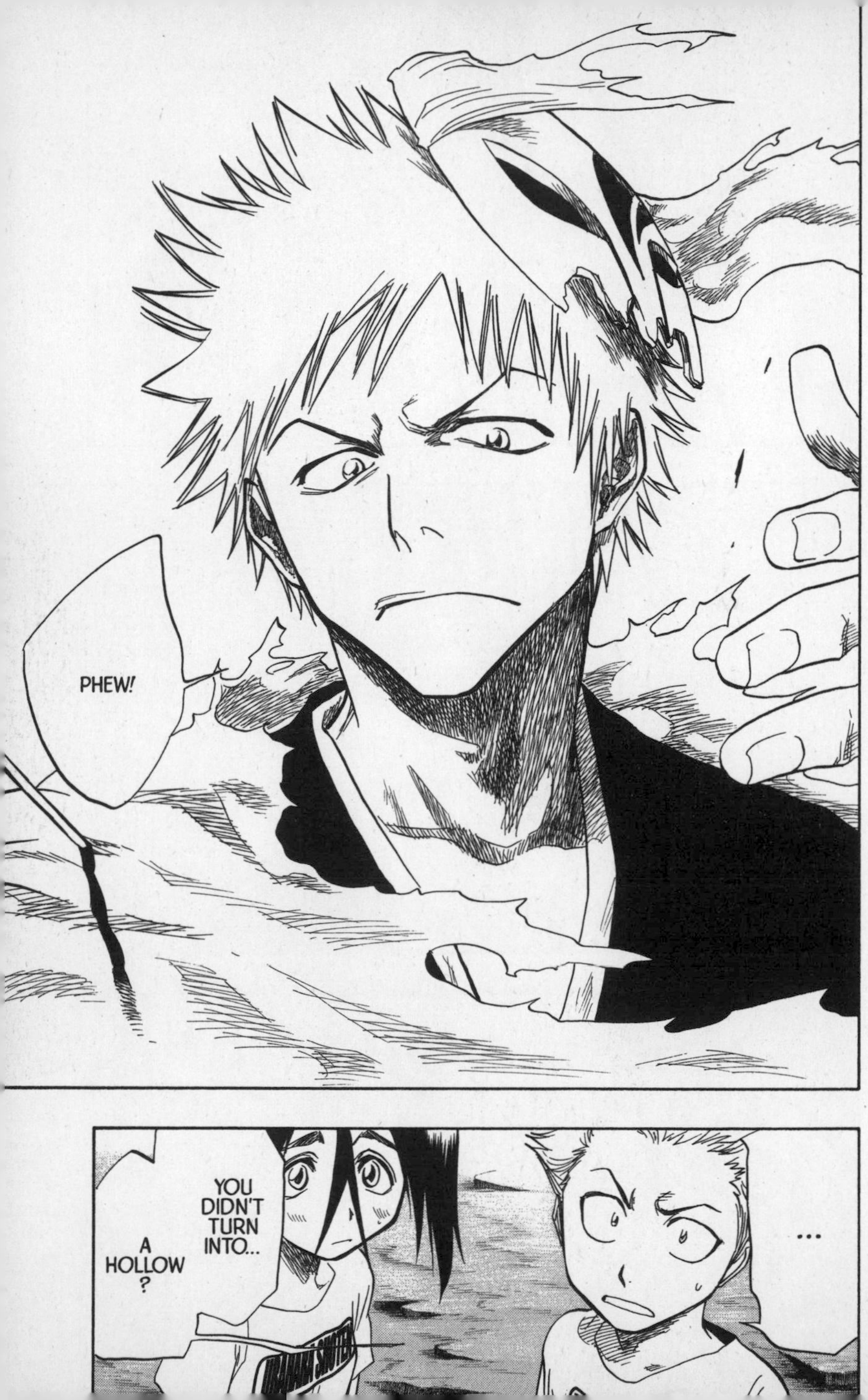
PHEW!
...
YOU DIDN'T TURN INTO...
A HOLLOW?
URAHARA SHOTEN

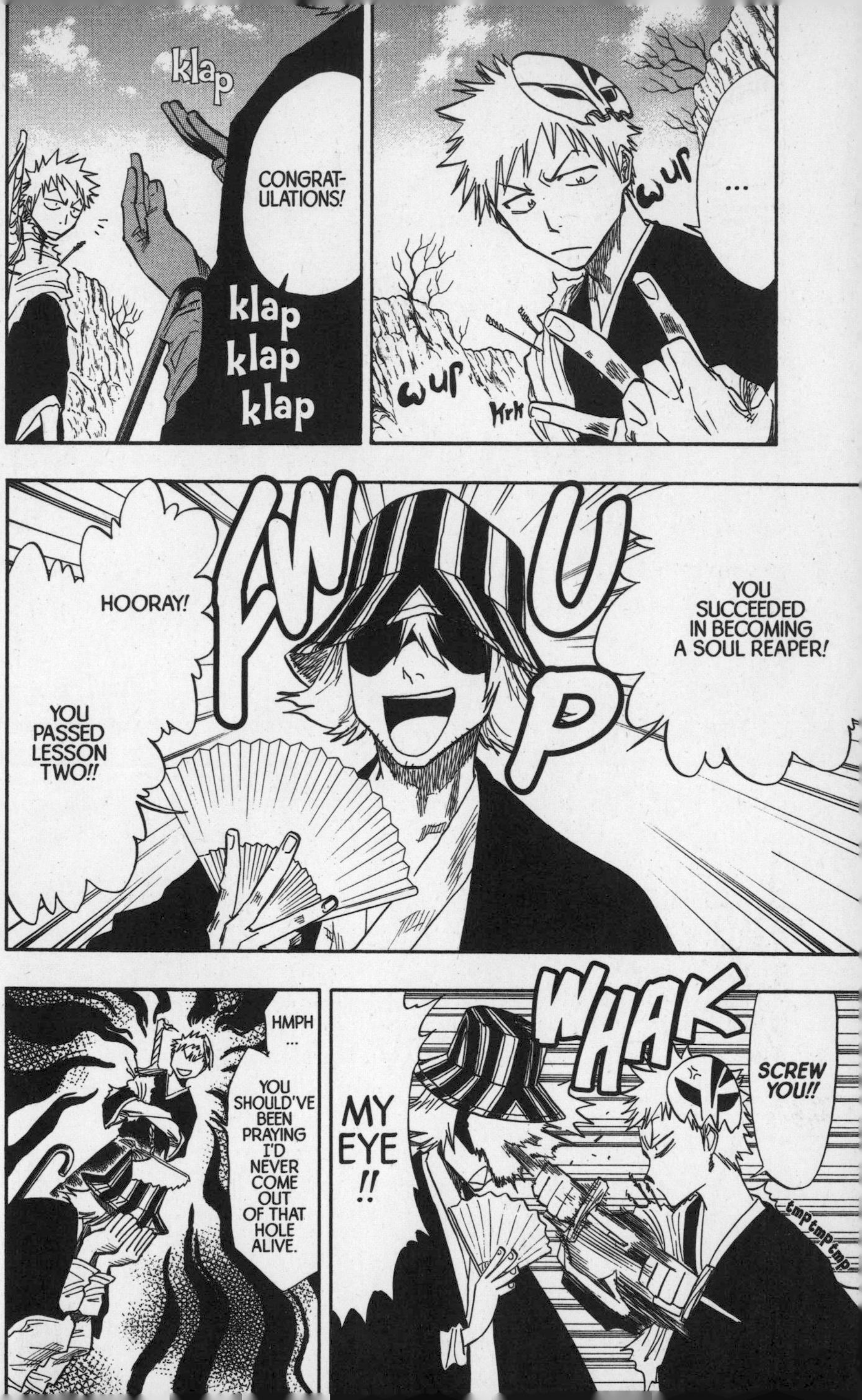
...
wur
wur
Krk
klap
CONGRAT-ULATIONS!
klap klap klap
FWUP
YOU SUCCEEDED IN BECOMING A SOUL REAPER!
HOORAY!
YOU PASSED LESSON TWO!!
SCREW YOU!!
WHAK
MY EYE!!
tmptmptmp
HMPH...
YOU SHOULD'VE BEEN PRAYING I'D NEVER COME OUT OF THAT HOLE ALIVE.

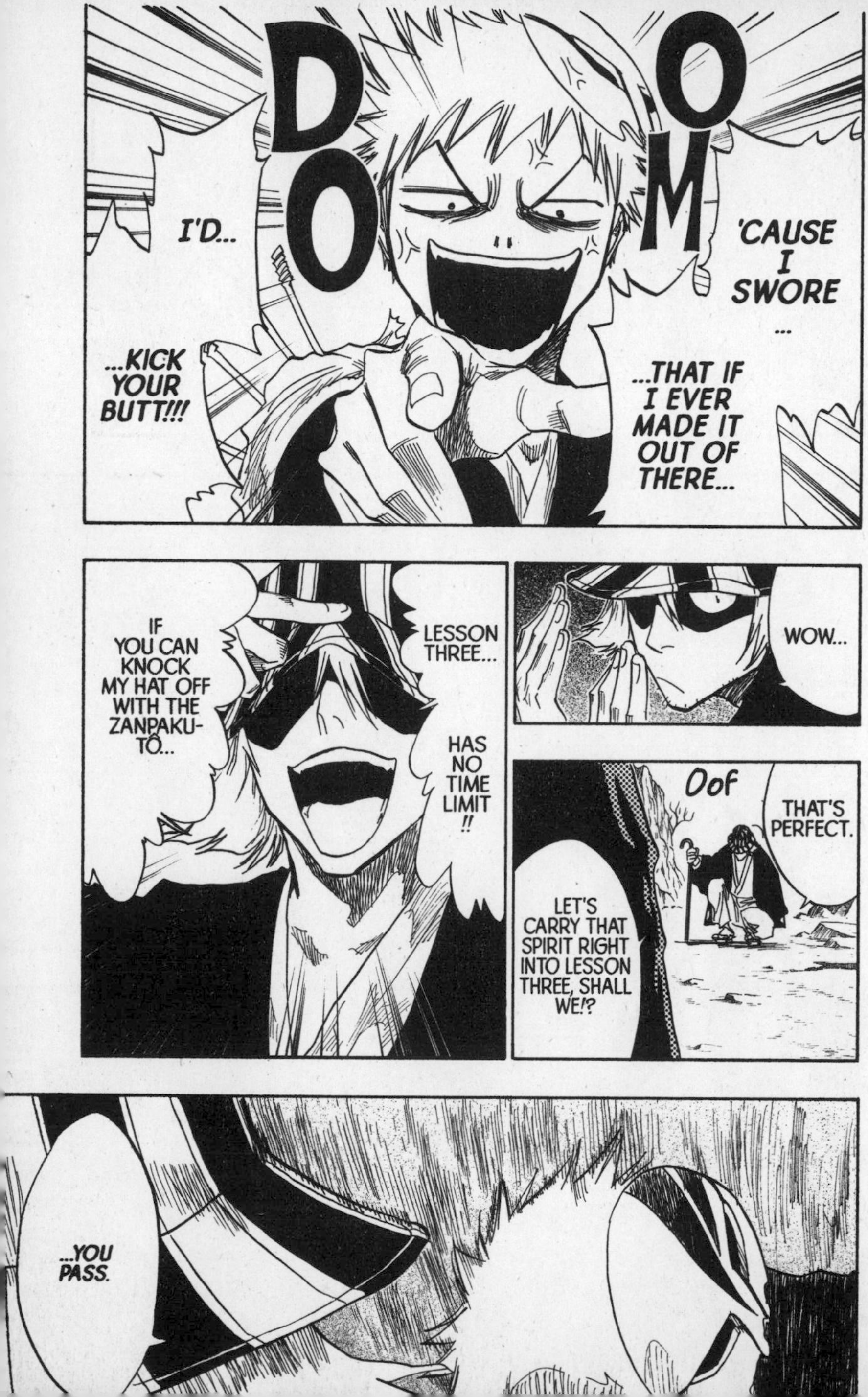
'CAUSE I SWORE...
...THAT IF I EVER MADE IT OUT OF THERE...
DOOM
I'D...
...KICK YOUR BUTT!!!
WOW...
Oof
THAT'S PERFECT.
LET'S CARRY THAT SPIRIT RIGHT INTO LESSON THREE, SHALL WE!?
LESSON THREE...
HAS NO TIME LIMIT!!
IF YOU CAN KNOCK MY HAT OFF WITH THE ZANPAKU-TÔ...
...YOU PASS.

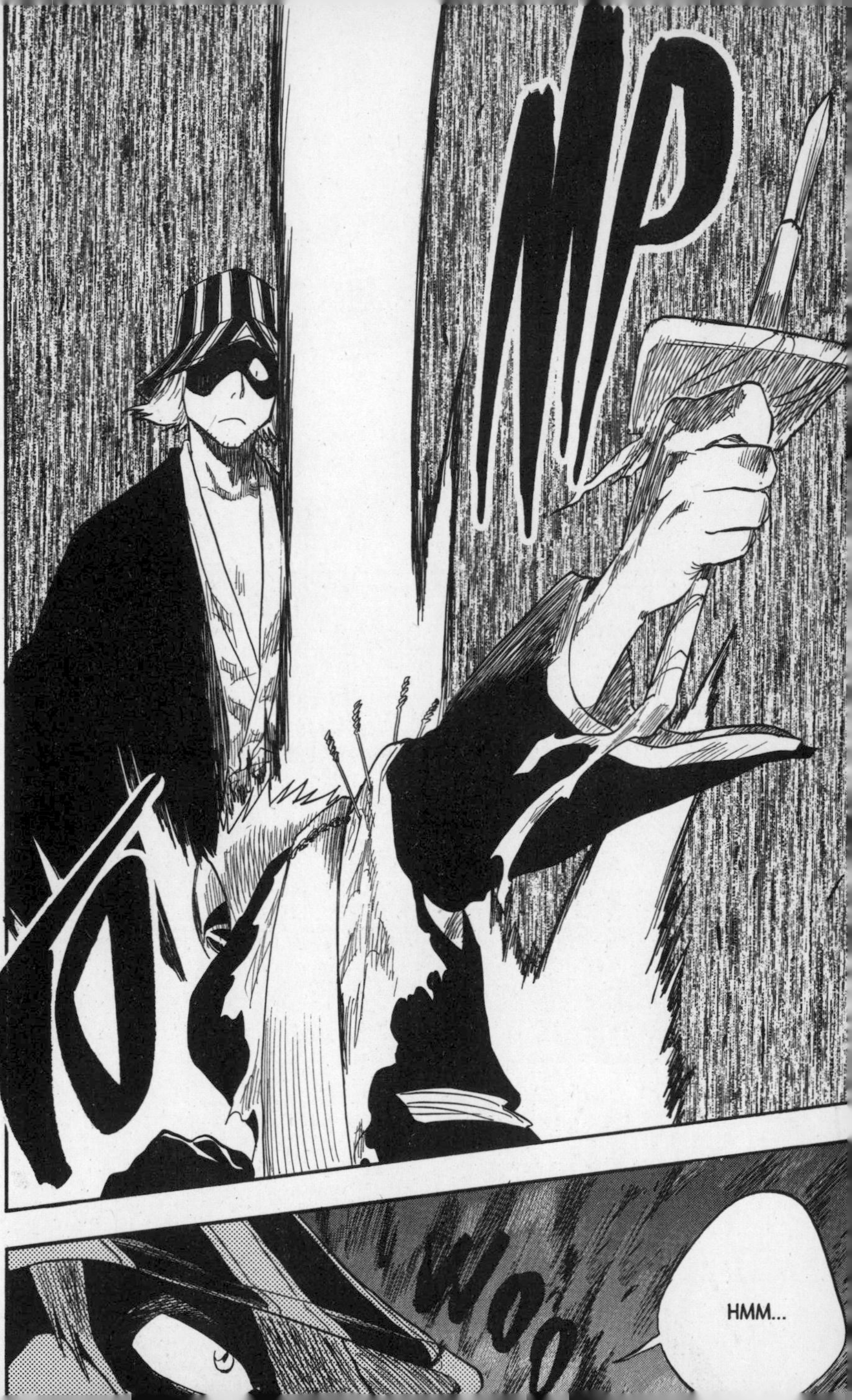
MP
TO
HMM...
WOO

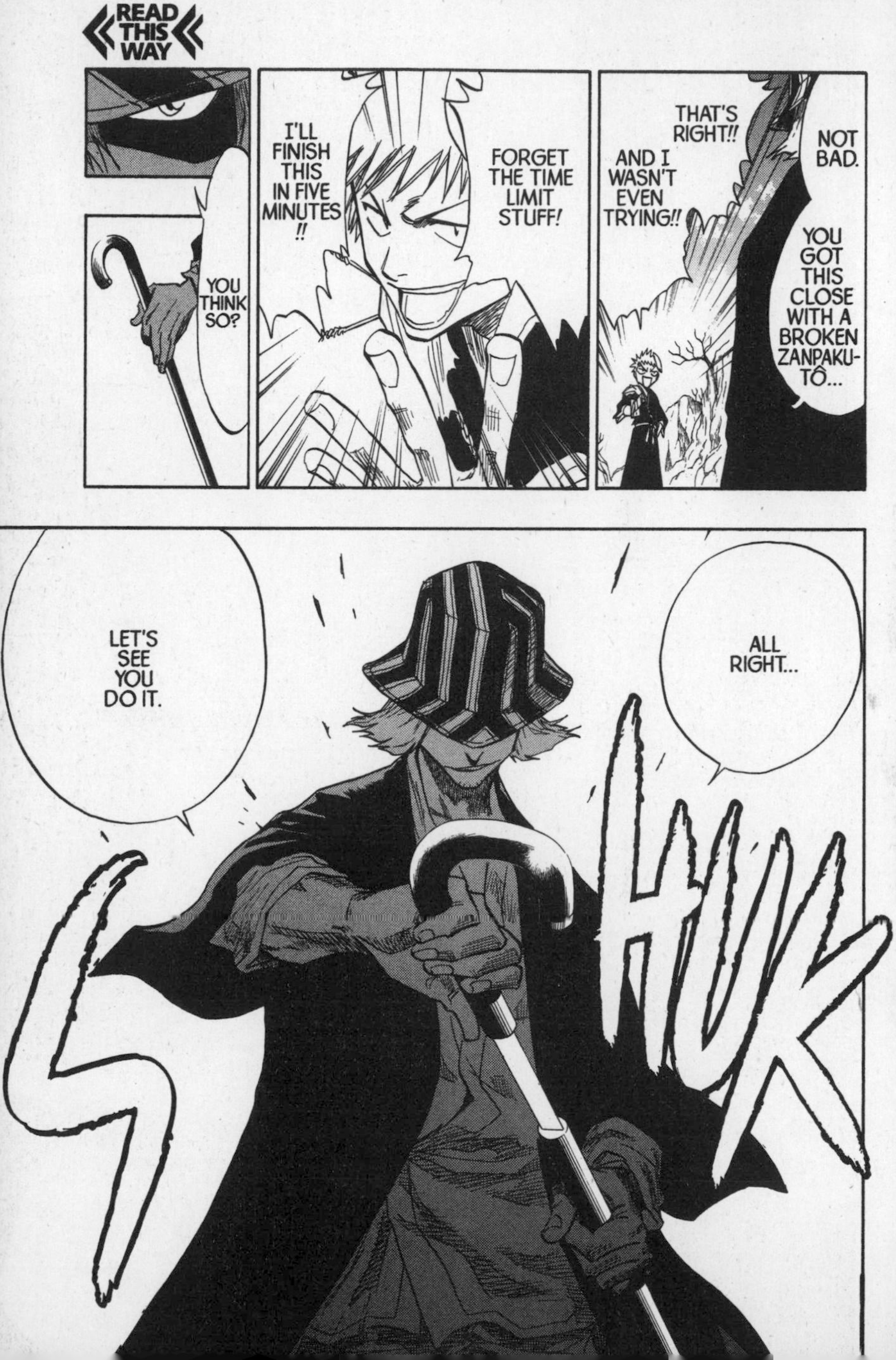
READ THIS WAY
NOT BAD.
YOU GOT THIS CLOSE WITH A BROKEN ZANPAKU-TÔ...
THAT'S RIGHT!!
AND I WASN'T EVEN TRYING!!
FORGET THE TIME LIMIT STUFF!
I'LL FINISH THIS IN FIVE MINUTES!!
YOU THINK SO?
ALL RIGHT...
LET'S SEE YOU DO IT.
SHUK

PEOPLE WHO MISS ICHIGO

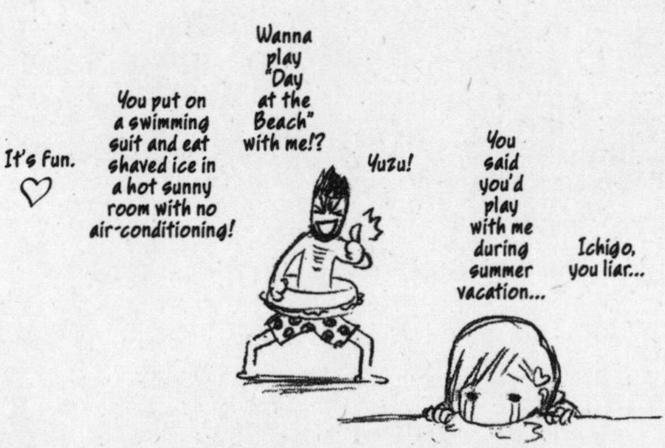
Ichigo, you liar...
You said you'd play with me during summer vacation...
Yuzu!
Wanna play "Day at the Beach" with me!?
You put on a swimming suit and eat shaved ice in a hot sunny room with no air-conditioning!
It's fun. ♡

65. Collisions

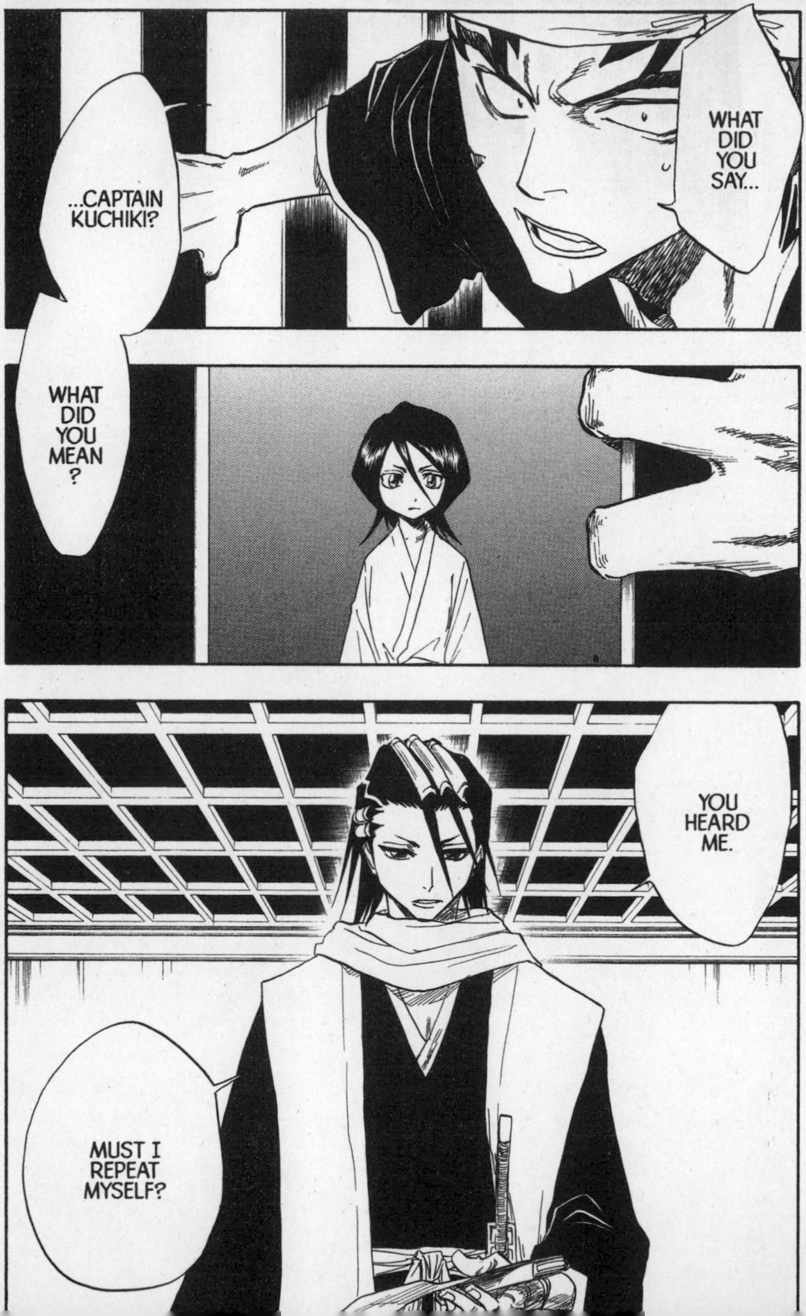
WHAT DID YOU SAY...
...CAPTAIN KUCHIKI?
WHAT DID YOU MEAN?
YOU HEARD ME.
MUST I REPEAT MYSELF?

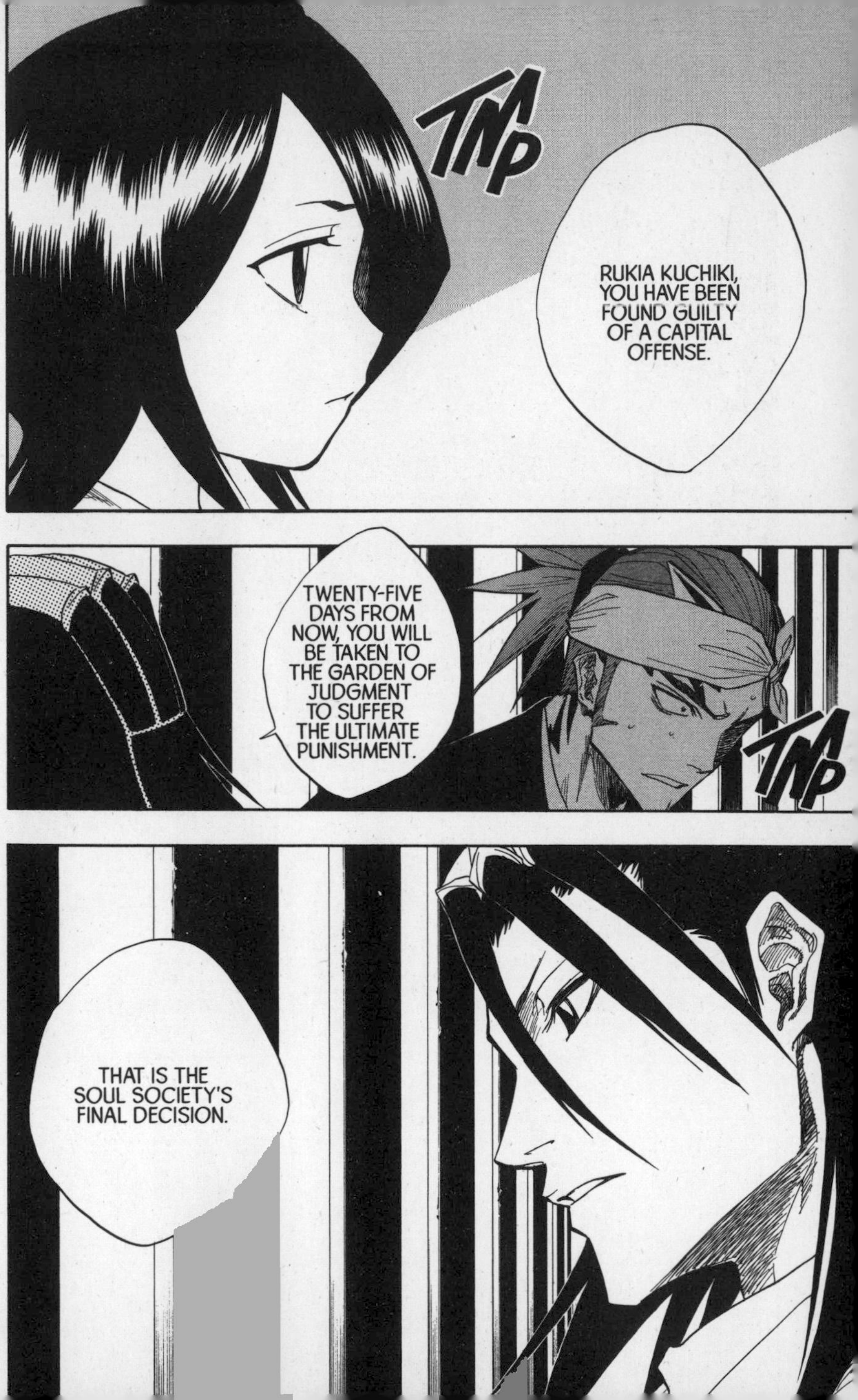
TMP
RUKIA KUCHIKI, YOU HAVE BEEN FOUND GUILTY OF A CAPITAL OFFENSE.
TMP
TWENTY-FIVE DAYS FROM NOW, YOU WILL BE TAKEN TO THE GARDEN OF JUDGMENT TO SUFFER THE ULTIMATE PUNISHMENT.
THAT IS THE SOUL SOCIETY'S FINAL DECISION.

READ THIS WAY

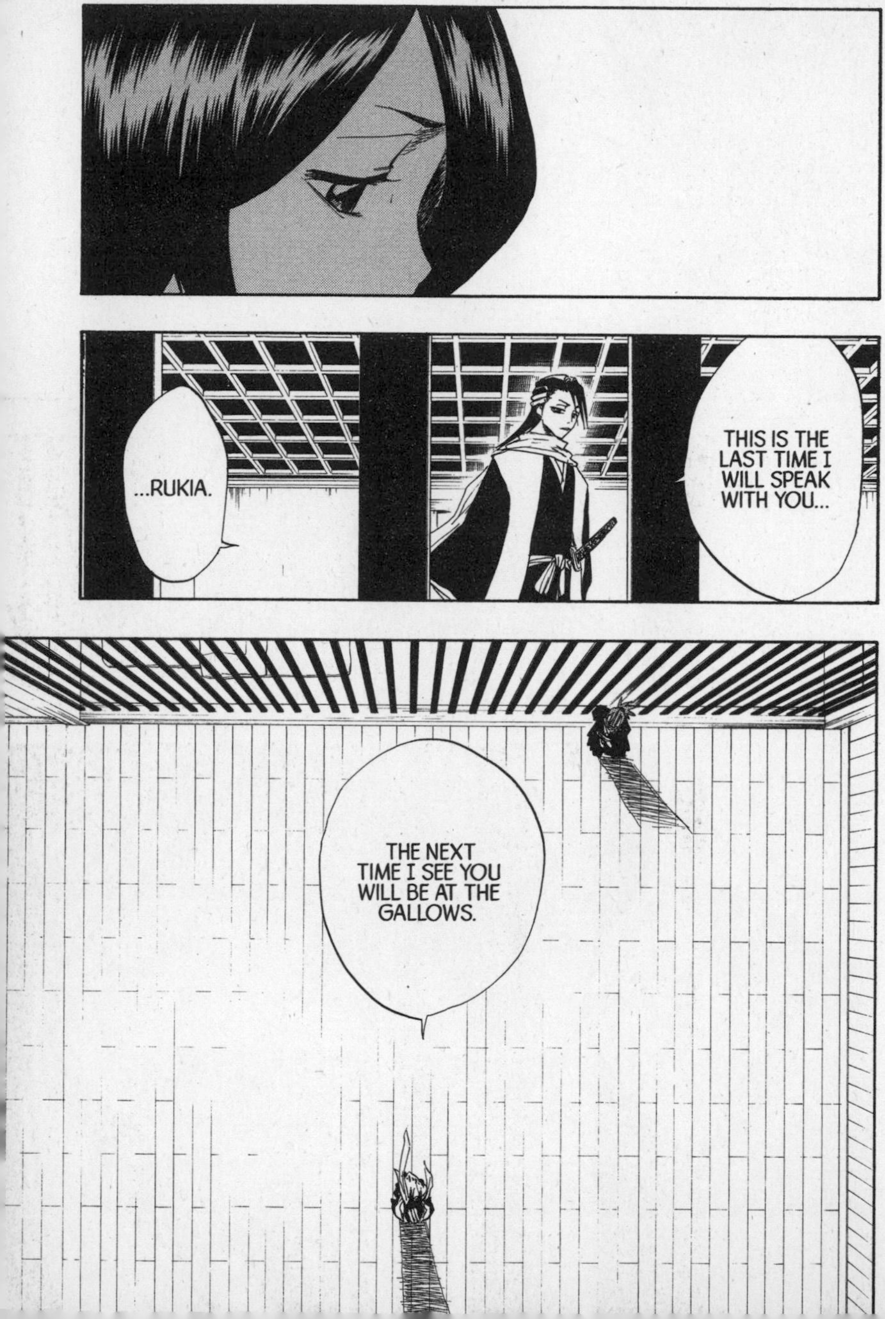
THIS IS THE LAST TIME I WILL SPEAK WITH YOU...
...RUKIA.
THE NEXT TIME I SEE YOU WILL BE AT THE GALLOWS.

65. Collisions

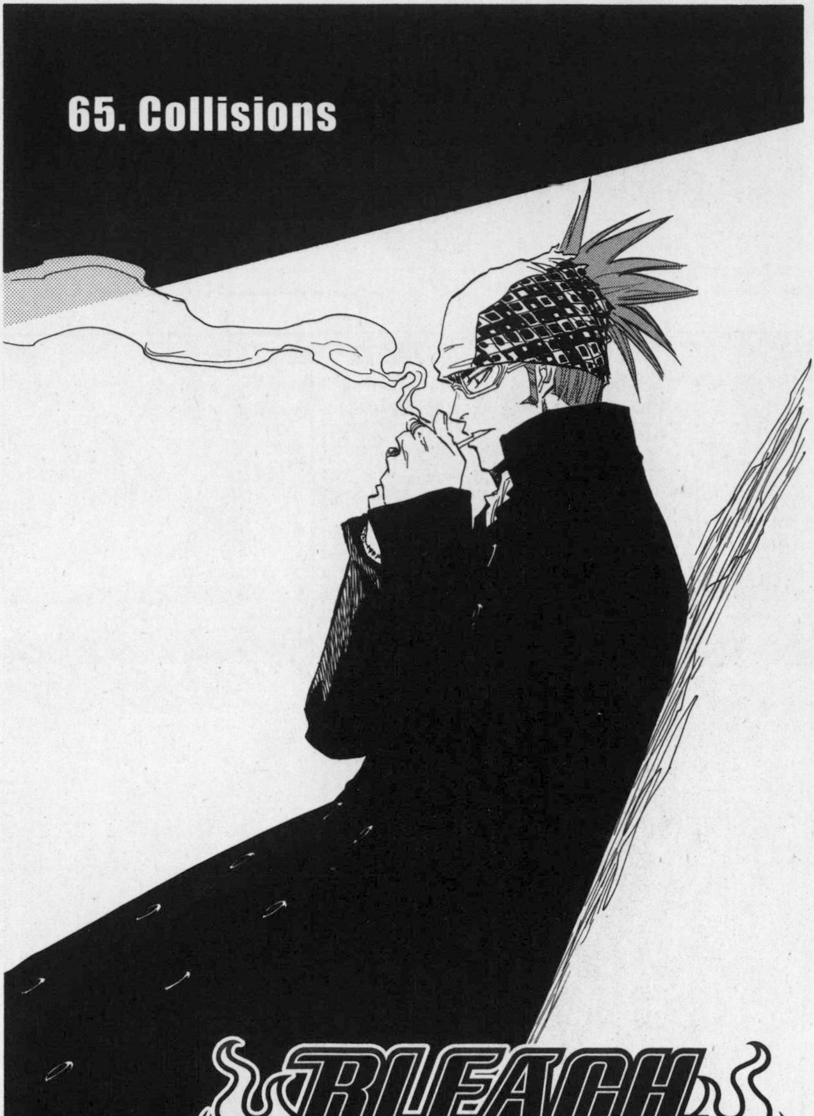
BLEACH
ブリーチ

READ THIS WAY

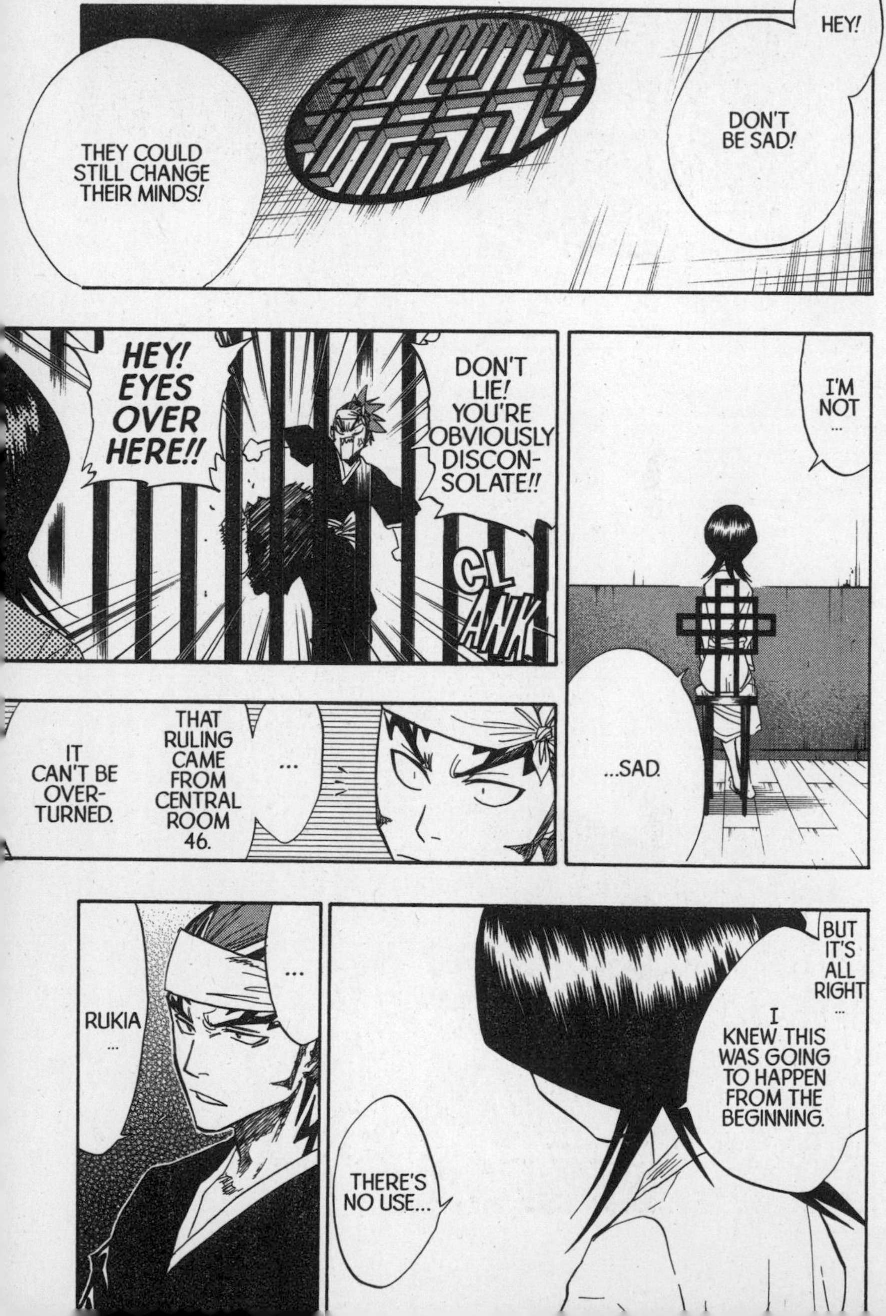
HEY!
DON'T BE SAD!
THEY COULD STILL CHANGE THEIR MINDS!
I'M NOT ...
...SAD.
DON'T LIE! YOU'RE OBVIOUSLY DISCON-SOLATE!!
HEY! EYES OVER HERE!!
CLANK
...
THAT RULING CAME FROM CENTRAL ROOM 46.
IT CAN'T BE OVER-TURNED.
BUT IT'S ALL RIGHT ...
I KNEW THIS WAS GOING TO HAPPEN FROM THE BEGINNING.
THERE'S NO USE...
...
RUKIA ...

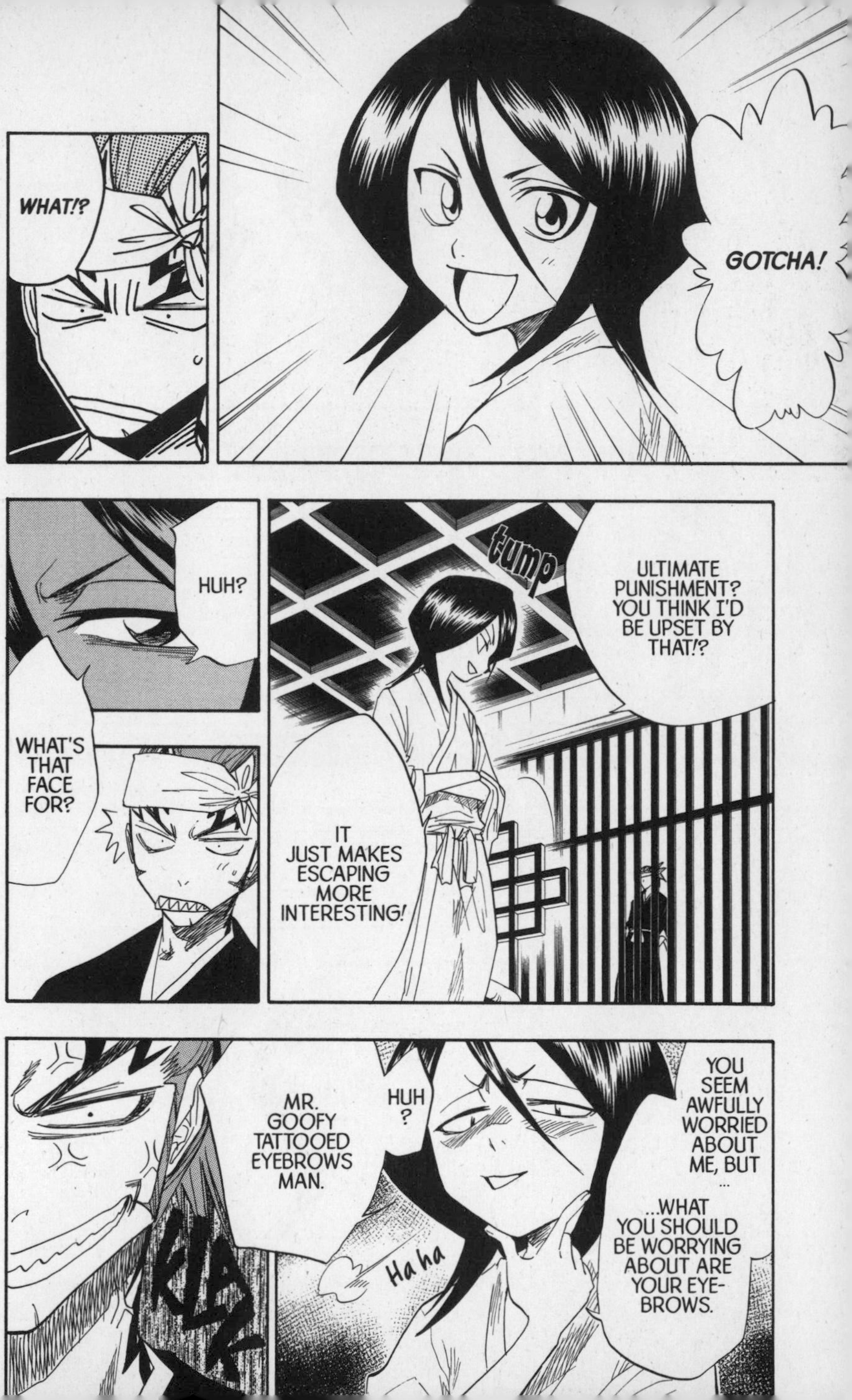
GOTCHA!
WHAT!?
tump
ULTIMATE PUNISHMENT? YOU THINK I'D BE UPSET BY THAT!?
IT JUST MAKES ESCAPING MORE INTERESTING!
HUH?
WHAT'S THAT FACE FOR?
YOU SEEM AWFULLY WORRIED ABOUT ME, BUT ...
...WHAT YOU SHOULD BE WORRYING ABOUT ARE YOUR EYE-BROWS.
Ha ha
HUH?
MR. GOOFY TATTOOED EYEBROWS MAN.

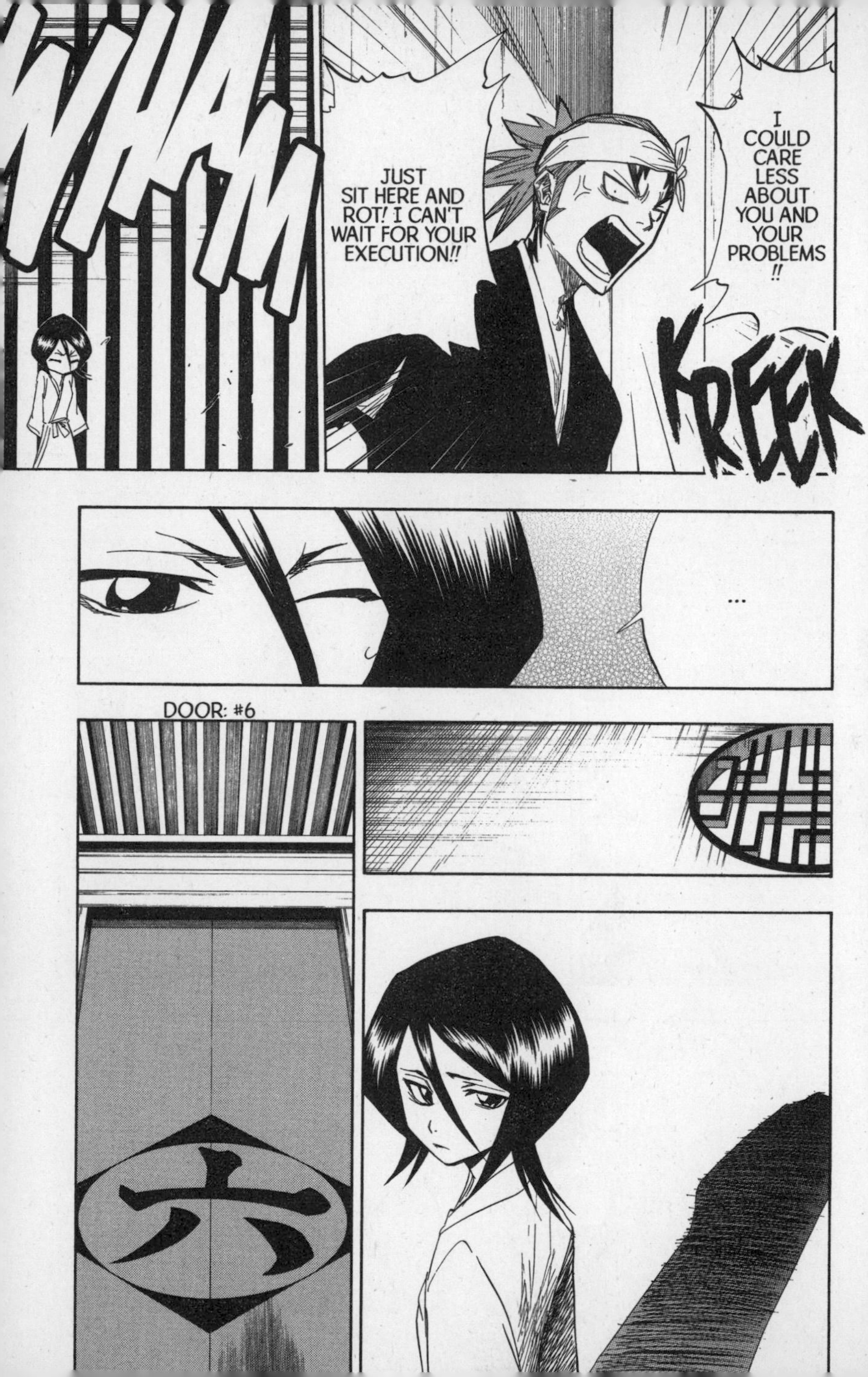
I COULD CARE LESS ABOUT YOU AND YOUR PROBLEMS!!
JUST SIT HERE AND ROT! I CAN'T WAIT FOR YOUR EXECUTION!!
KREEK
WHAM
...
DOOR: #6

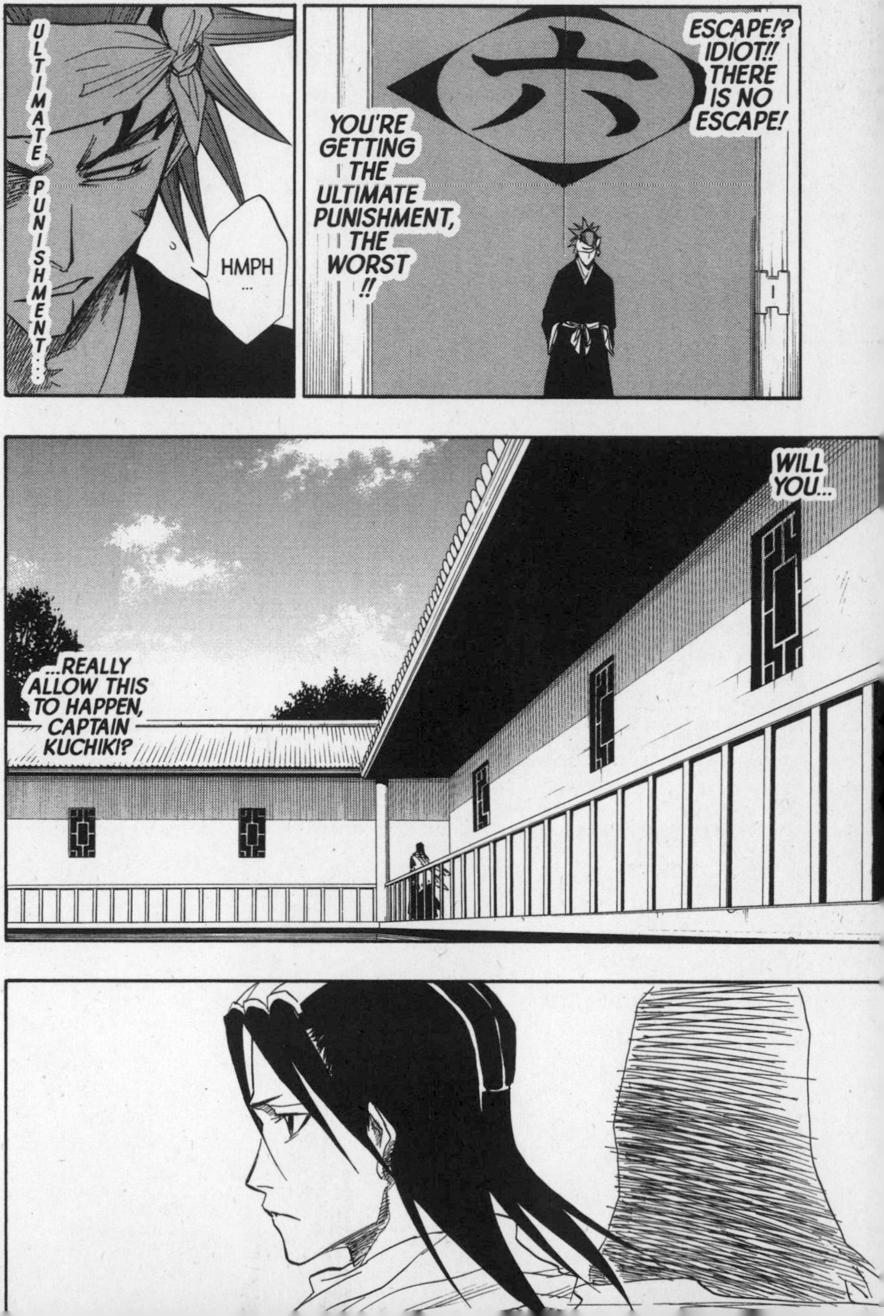
ESCAPE!? IDIOT!! THERE IS NO ESCAPE!
六
YOU'RE GETTING THE ULTIMATE PUNISHMENT, THE WORST !!
HMPH ...
ULTIMATE PUNISHMENT...
WILL YOU...
...REALLY ALLOW THIS TO HAPPEN, CAPTAIN KUCHIKI!?

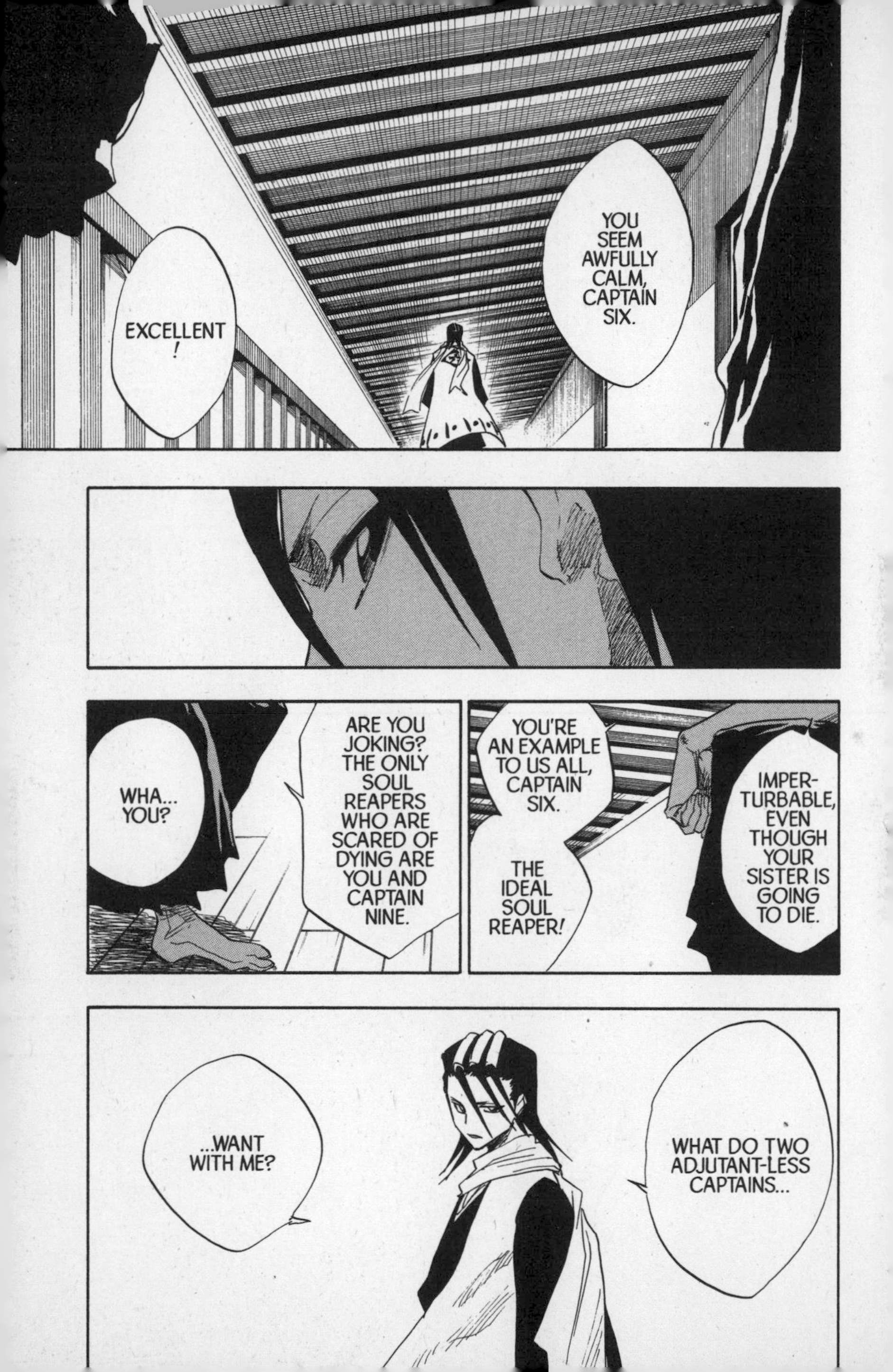
YOU SEEM AWFULLY CALM, CAPTAIN SIX.
EXCELLENT!
IMPER-TURBABLE, EVEN THOUGH YOUR SISTER IS GOING TO DIE.
YOU'RE AN EXAMPLE TO US ALL, CAPTAIN SIX.
THE IDEAL SOUL REAPER!
ARE YOU JOKING? THE ONLY SOUL REAPERS WHO ARE SCARED OF DYING ARE YOU AND CAPTAIN NINE.
WHA... YOU?
WHAT DO TWO ADJUTANT-LESS CAPTAINS...
...WANT WITH ME?

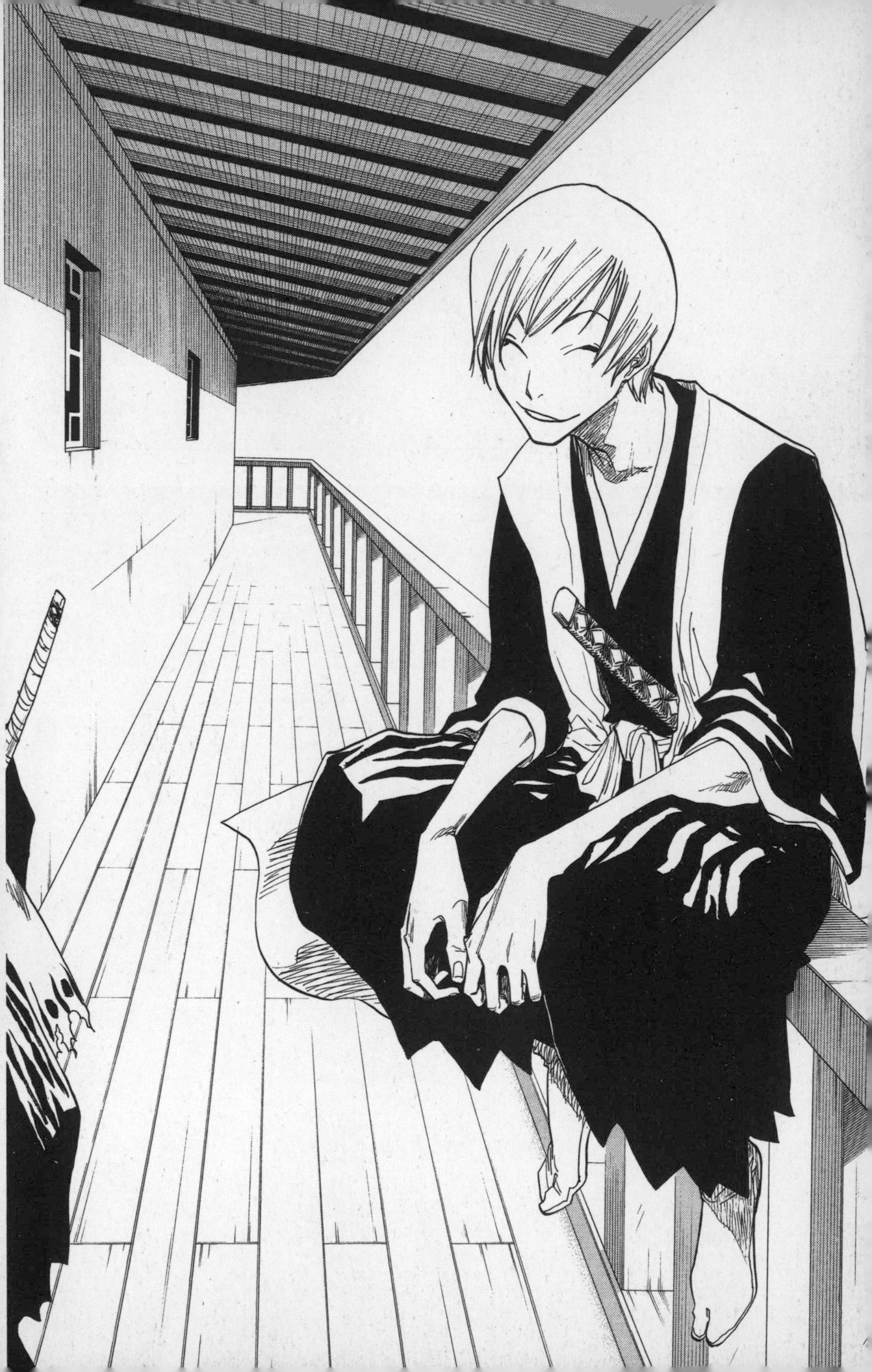

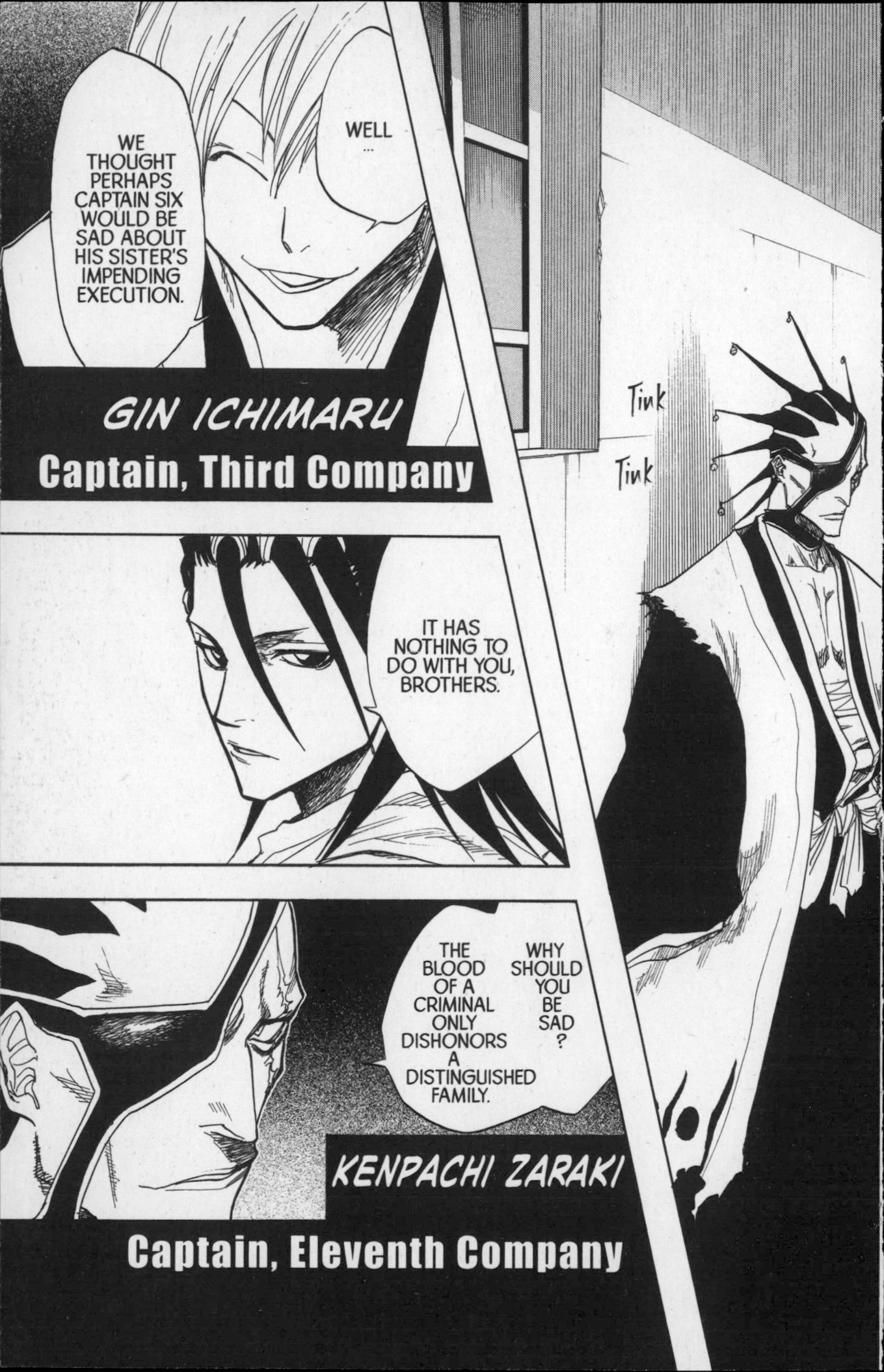
Tink
Tink
WELL ...
WE THOUGHT PERHAPS CAPTAIN SIX WOULD BE SAD ABOUT HIS SISTER'S IMPENDING EXECUTION.
GIN ICHIMARU
Captain, Third Company
IT HAS NOTHING TO DO WITH YOU, BROTHERS.
WHY SHOULD YOU BE SAD ?
THE BLOOD OF A CRIMINAL ONLY DISHONORS A DISTINGUISHED FAMILY.
KENPACHI ZARAKI
Captain, Eleventh Company

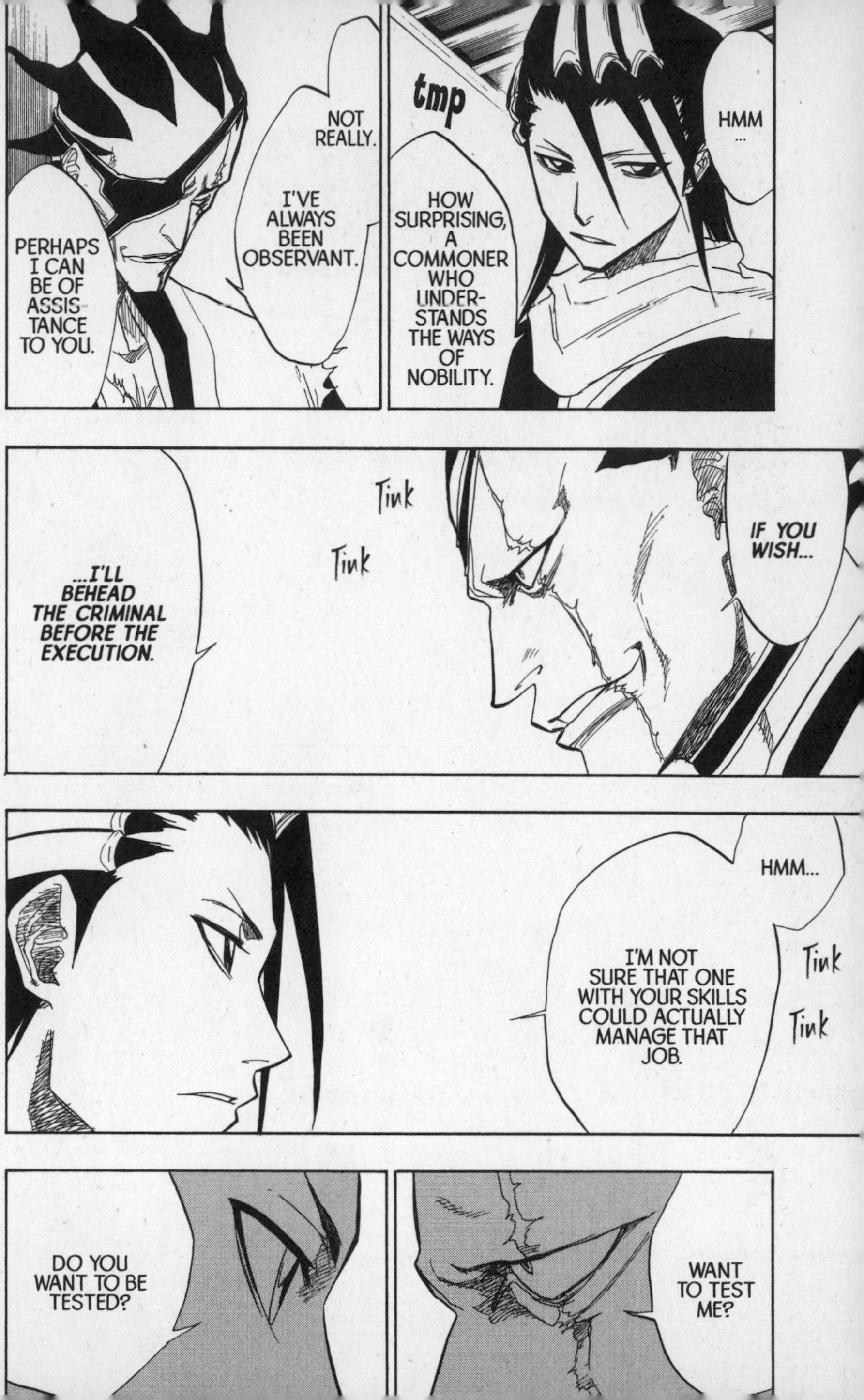
HMM ...
tmp
HOW SURPRISING, A COMMONER WHO UNDERSTANDS THE WAYS OF NOBILITY.
NOT REALLY.
I'VE ALWAYS BEEN OBSERVANT.
PERHAPS I CAN BE OF ASSISTANCE TO YOU.
IF YOU WISH...
Tink
Tink
...I'LL BEHEAD THE CRIMINAL BEFORE THE EXECUTION.
HMM...
Tink
Tink
I'M NOT SURE THAT ONE WITH YOUR SKILLS COULD ACTUALLY MANAGE THAT JOB.
WANT TO TEST ME?
DO YOU WANT TO BE TESTED?

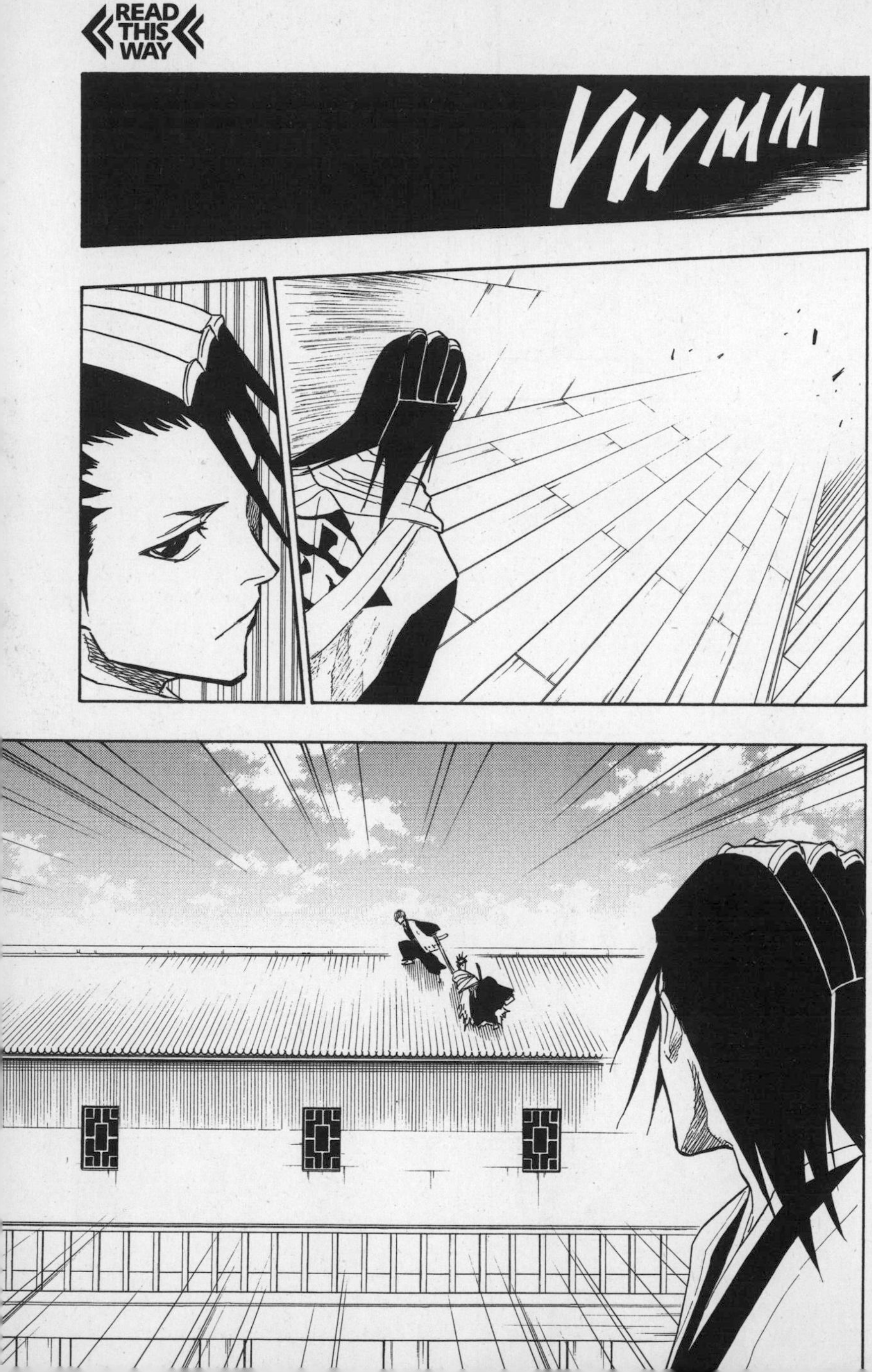
READ THIS WAY
VWMM

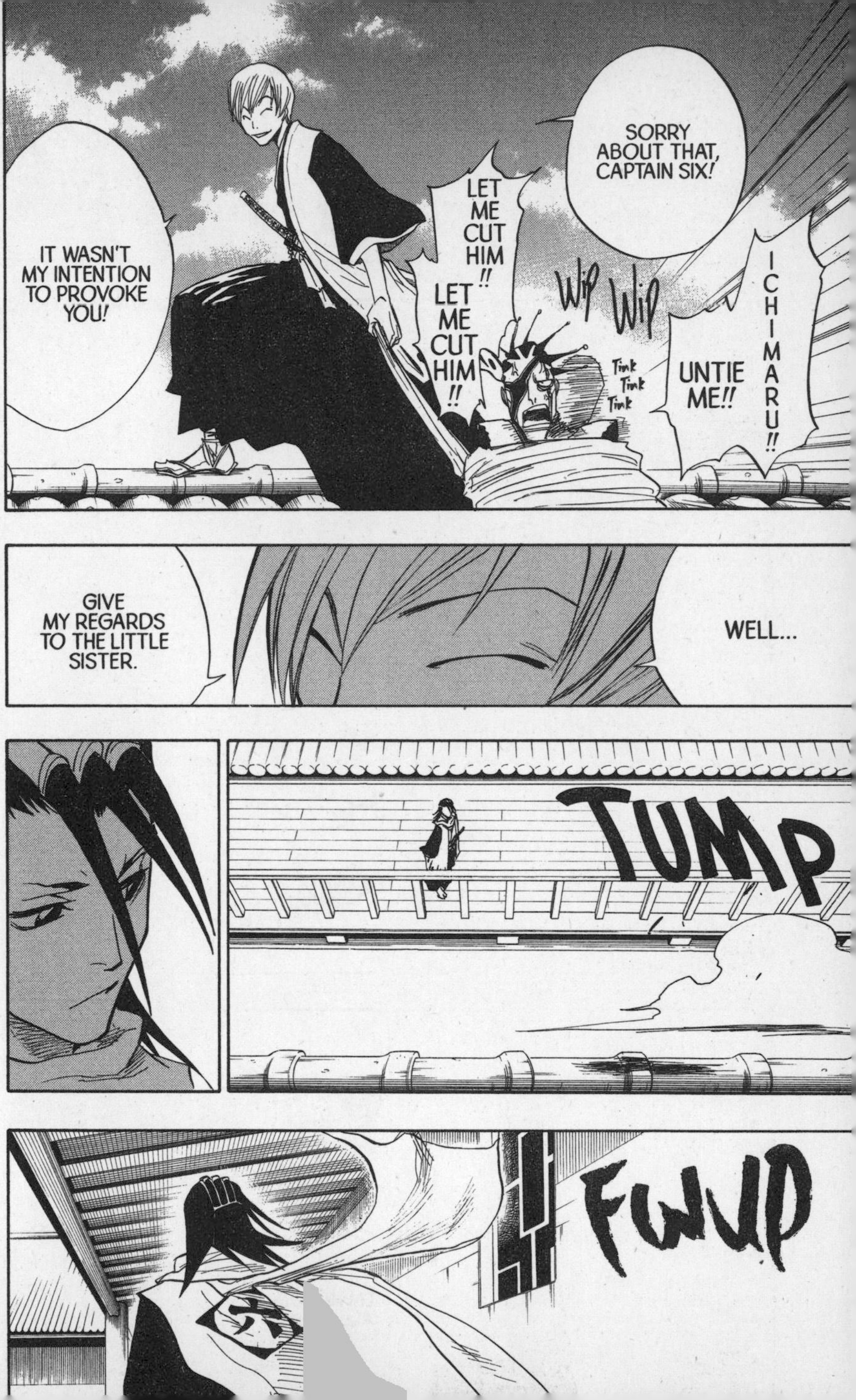
ICHIMARU!!
UNTIE ME!!
Tink Tink Tink
Wip Wip
LET ME CUT HIM!!
LET ME CUT HIM!!
SORRY ABOUT THAT, CAPTAIN SIX!
IT WASN'T MY INTENTION TO PROVOKE YOU!
WELL...
GIVE MY REGARDS TO THE LITTLE SISTER.
TUMP
FWUP

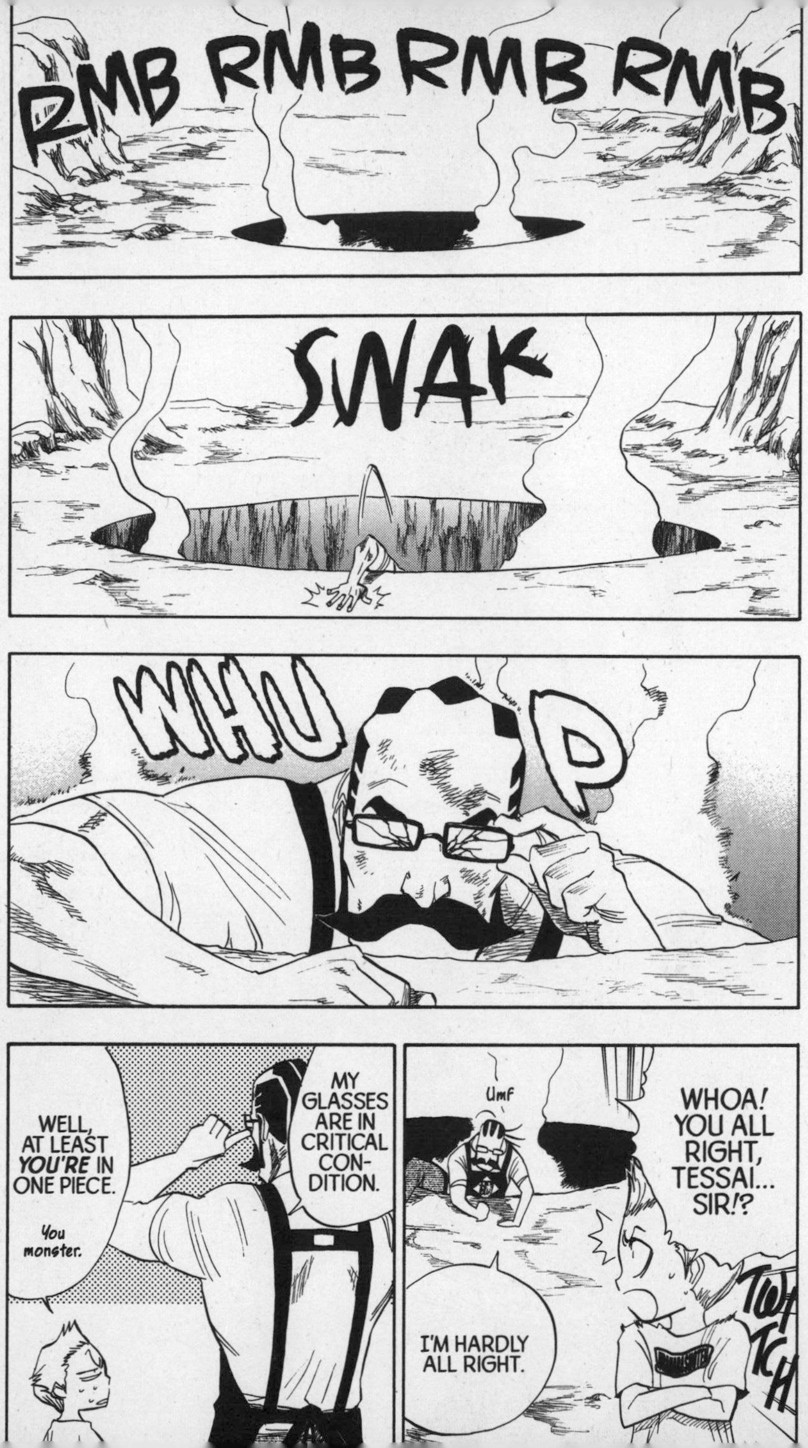
RMB RMB RMB RMB
SWAK
WHUP
WHOA! YOU ALL RIGHT, TESSAI... SIR!?
Umf
TWITCH
I'M HARDLY ALL RIGHT.
MY GLASSES ARE IN CRITICAL CON-DITION.
WELL, AT LEAST *YOU'RE* IN ONE PIECE.
You monster.

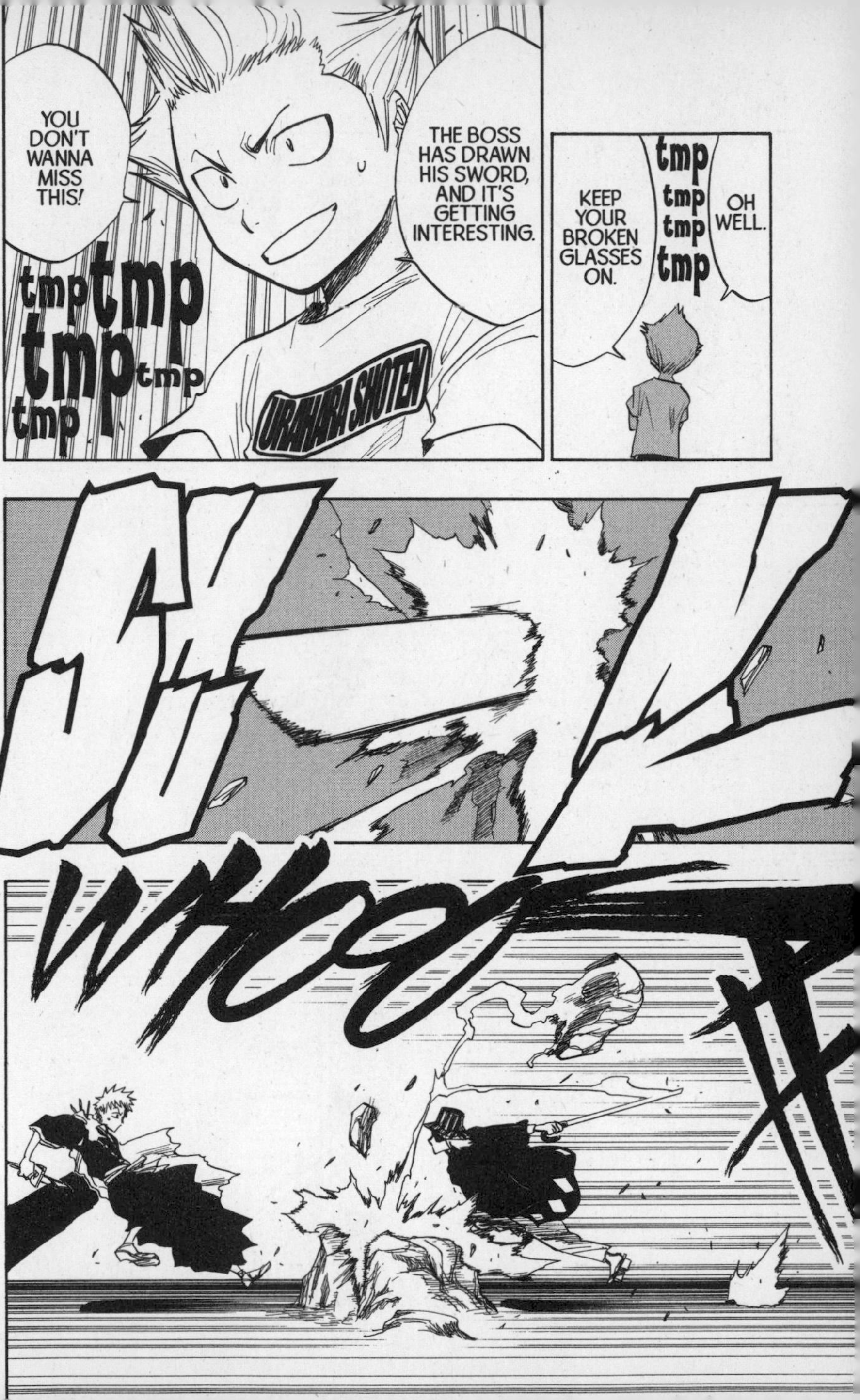
OH WELL.
tmp tmp tmp tmp
KEEP YOUR BROKEN GLASSES ON.
THE BOSS HAS DRAWN HIS SWORD, AND IT'S GETTING INTERESTING.
YOU DON'T WANNA MISS THIS!
tmp tmp tmp tmp tmp
URAHARA SHOTEN

READ THIS WAY

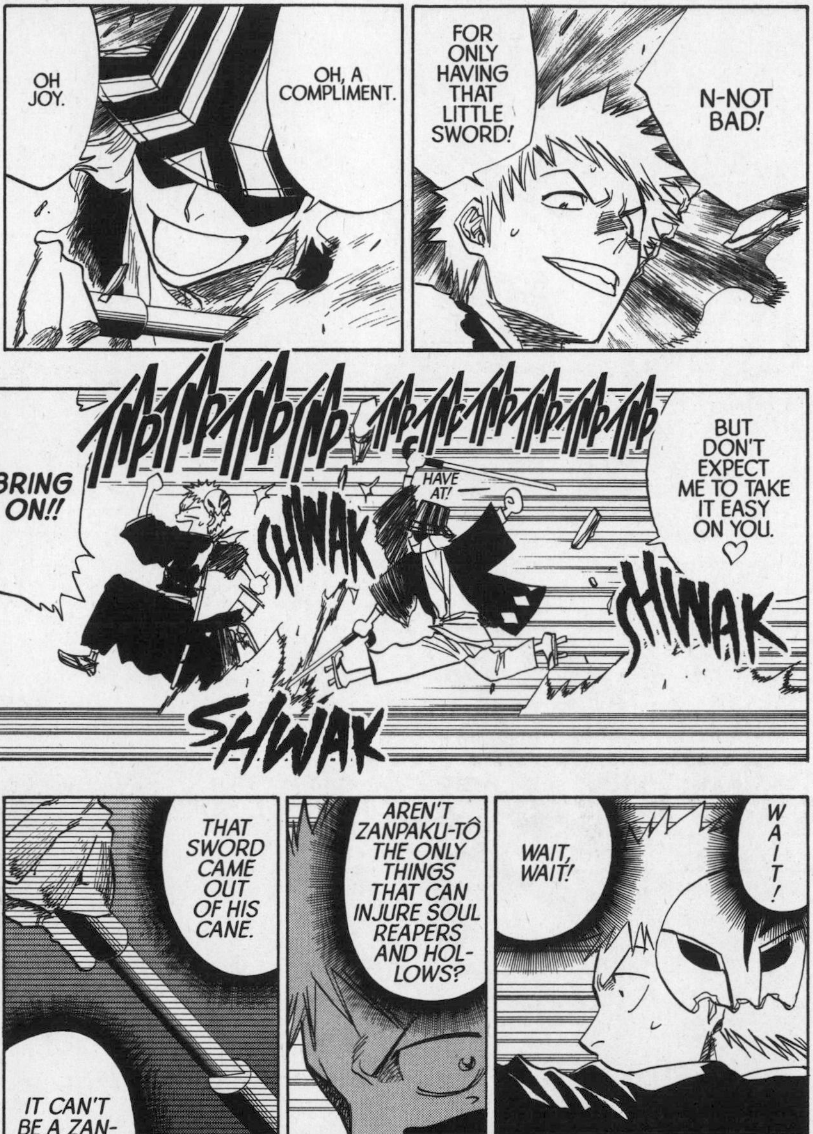
N-NOT BAD!
FOR ONLY HAVING THAT LITTLE SWORD!
OH, A COMPLIMENT.
OH JOY.
BUT DON'T EXPECT ME TO TAKE IT EASY ON YOU. ♡
SHWAK
HAVE AT!
SHWAK
SHWAK
B-BRING IT ON!!
WAIT!
WAIT, WAIT!
AREN'T ZANPAKU-TÔ THE ONLY THINGS THAT CAN INJURE SOUL REAPERS AND HOLLOWS?
THAT SWORD CAME OUT OF HIS CANE.
IT CAN'T BE A ZANPAKU-TÔ!!

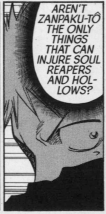

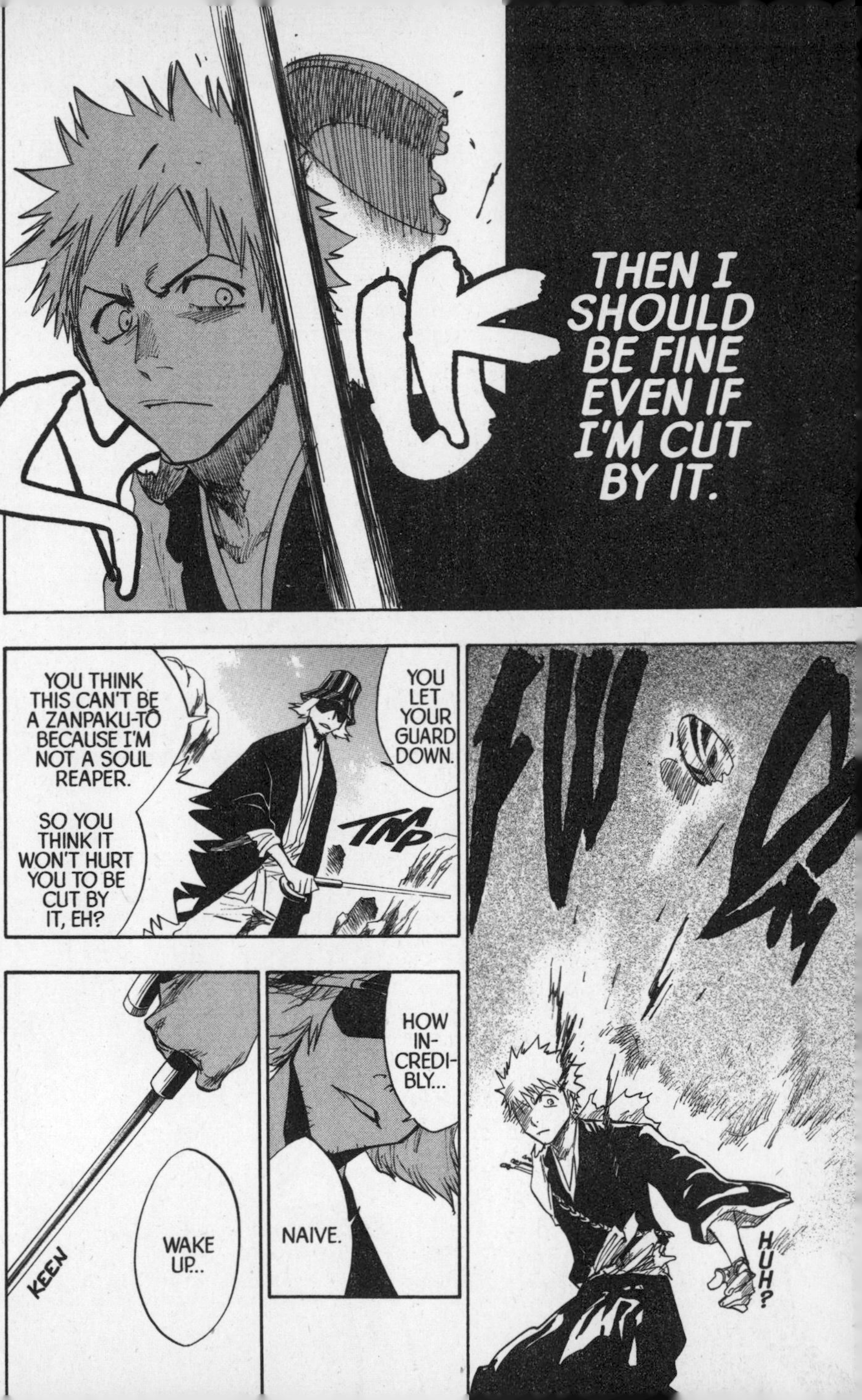
THEN I SHOULD BE FINE EVEN IF I'M CUT BY IT.
HUH?
YOU LET YOUR GUARD DOWN.
YOU THINK THIS CAN'T BE A ZANPAKU-TŌ BECAUSE I'M NOT A SOUL REAPER.
TMP
SO YOU THINK IT WON'T HURT YOU TO BE CUT BY IT, EH?
HOW IN-CREDI-BLY...
NAIVE.
WAKE UP...
KEEN

....!

krak

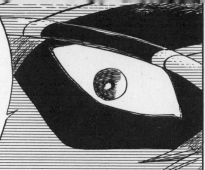

...BENIHIME,
THE RED
PRINCESS.

THIS
BLADE
IS VERY
MUCH A...

...ZANPAKU-TÔ.

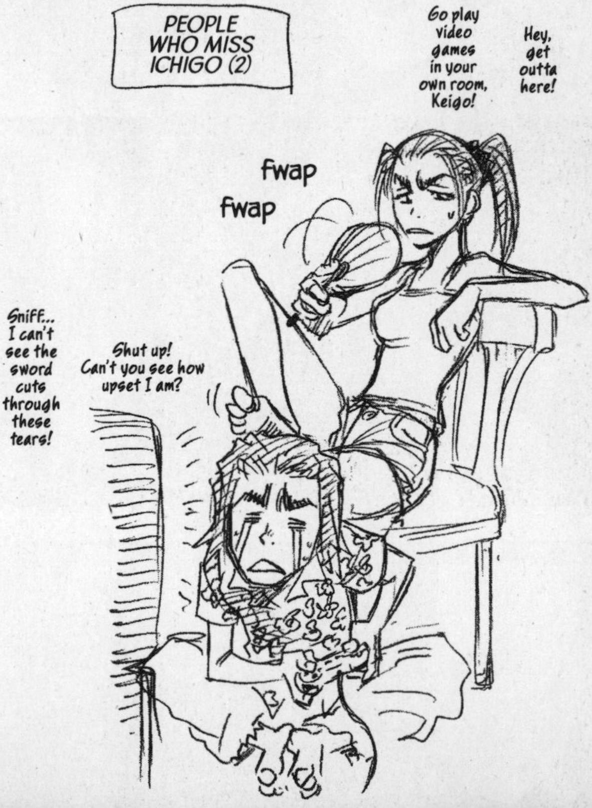
PEOPLE WHO MISS ICHIGO (2)
Hey, get outta here!
Go play video games in your own room, Keigo!
fwap
fwap
Shut up! Can't you see how upset I am?
Sniff... I can't see the sword cuts through these tears!

66. THE BLADE AND ME

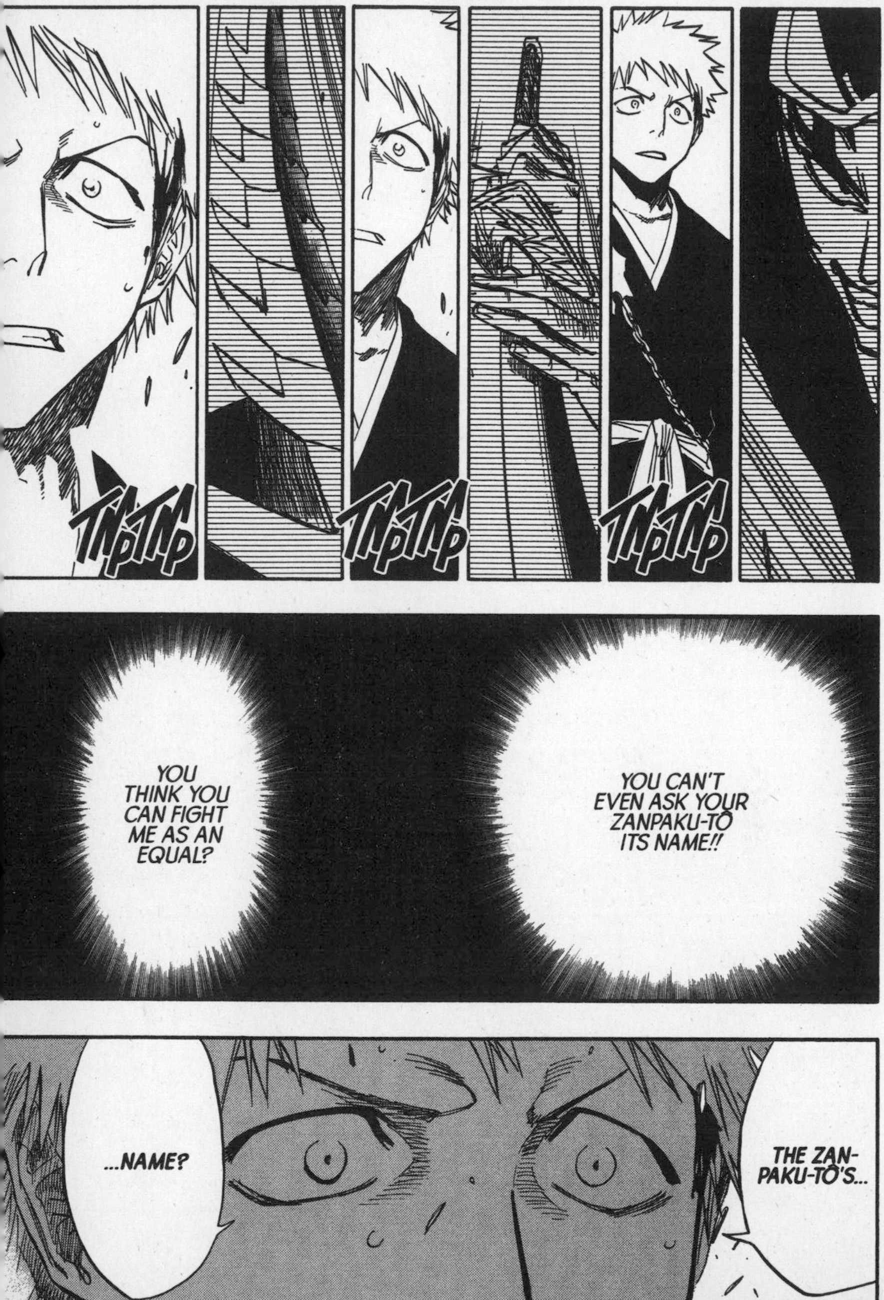
TMP TMP
TMP TMP
TMP TMP
YOU CAN'T EVEN ASK YOUR ZANPAKU-TŌ ITS NAME!!
YOU THINK YOU CAN FIGHT ME AS AN EQUAL?
THE ZAN-PAKU-TŌ'S...
...NAME?

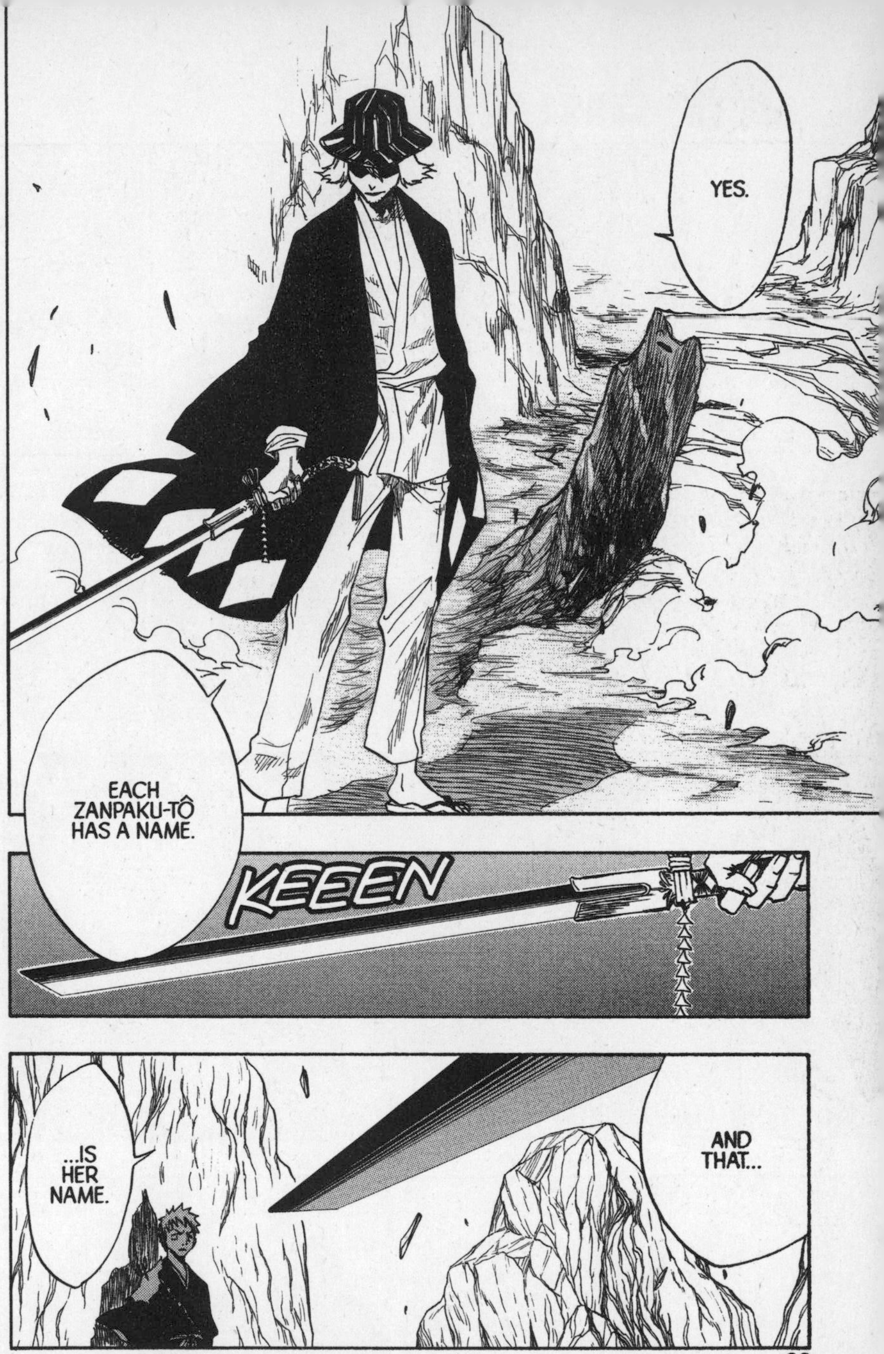
YES.
EACH ZANPAKU-TÔ HAS A NAME.
KEEEN
AND THAT...
...IS HER NAME.

READ THIS WAY

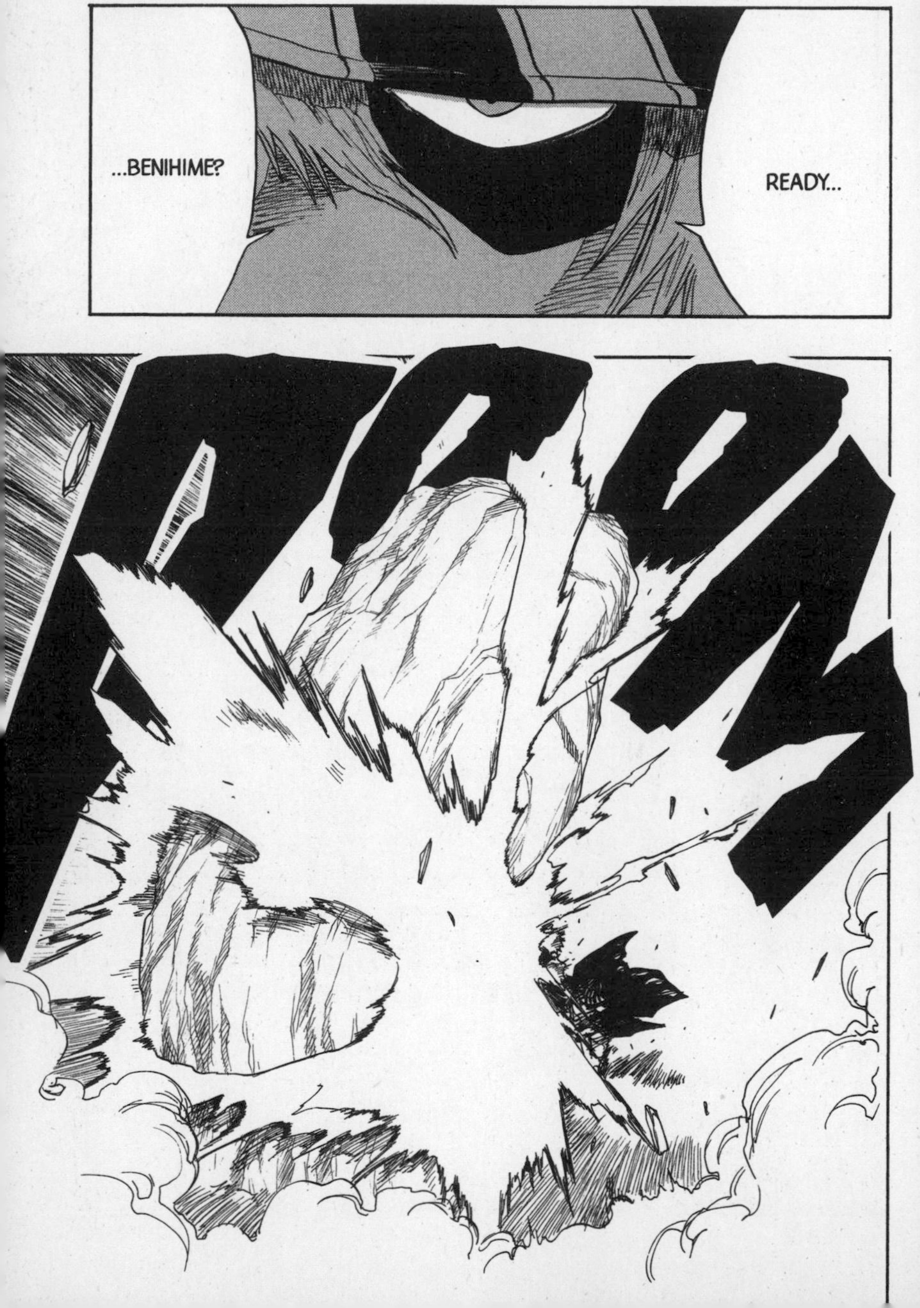
READY...
...BENIHIME?

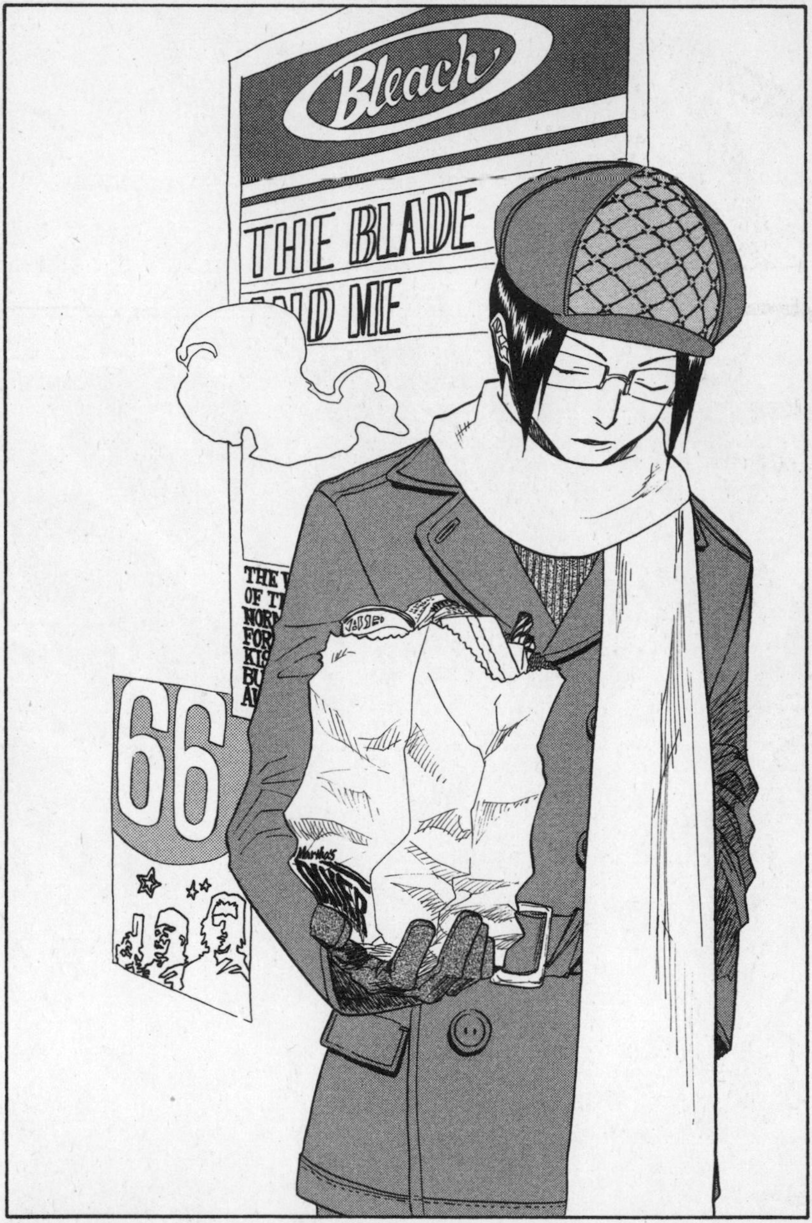
Bleach
THE BLADE
ME
66

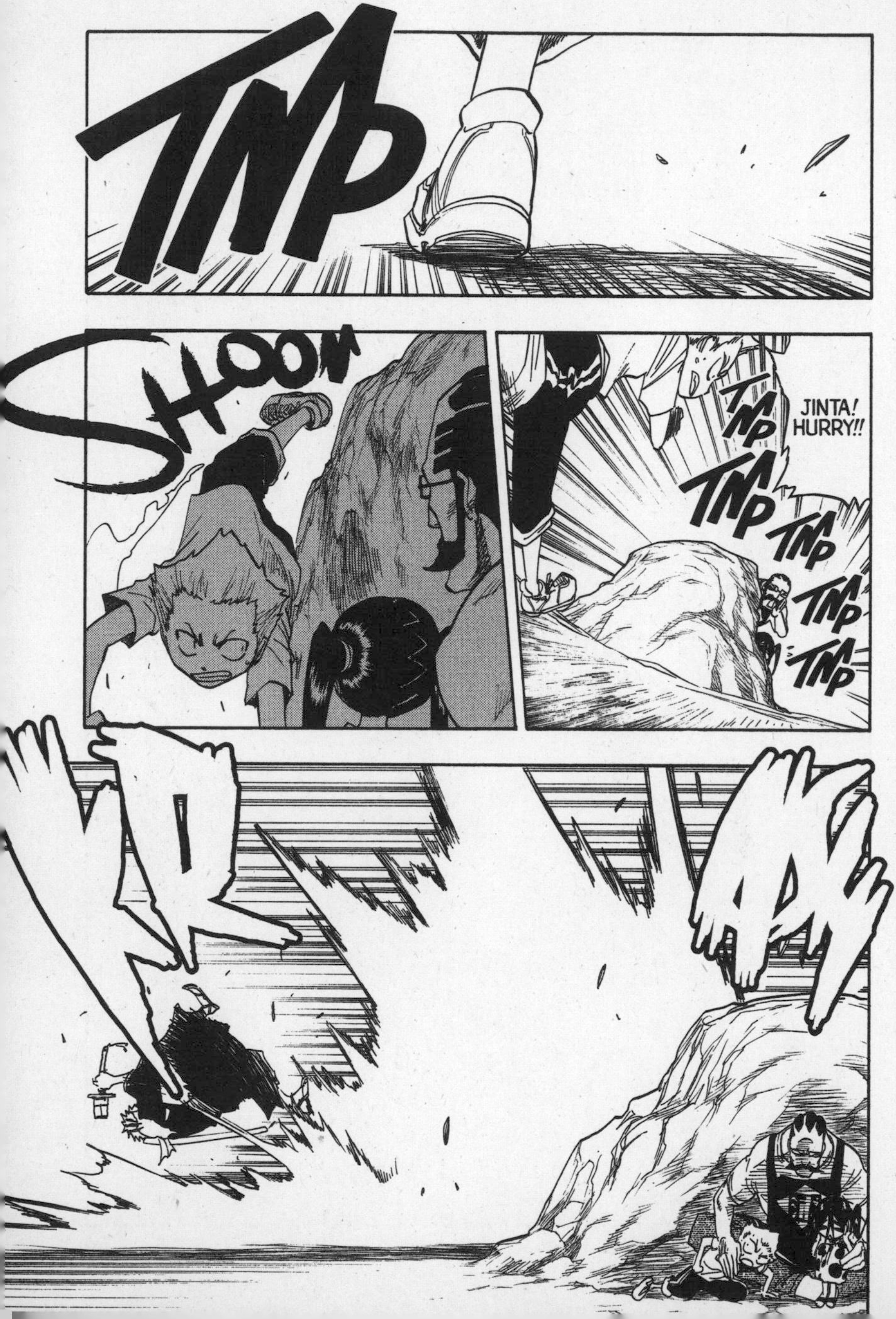
TMP
JINTA! HURRY!!
TMP
TMP
TMP
TMP
TMP
SHOOM

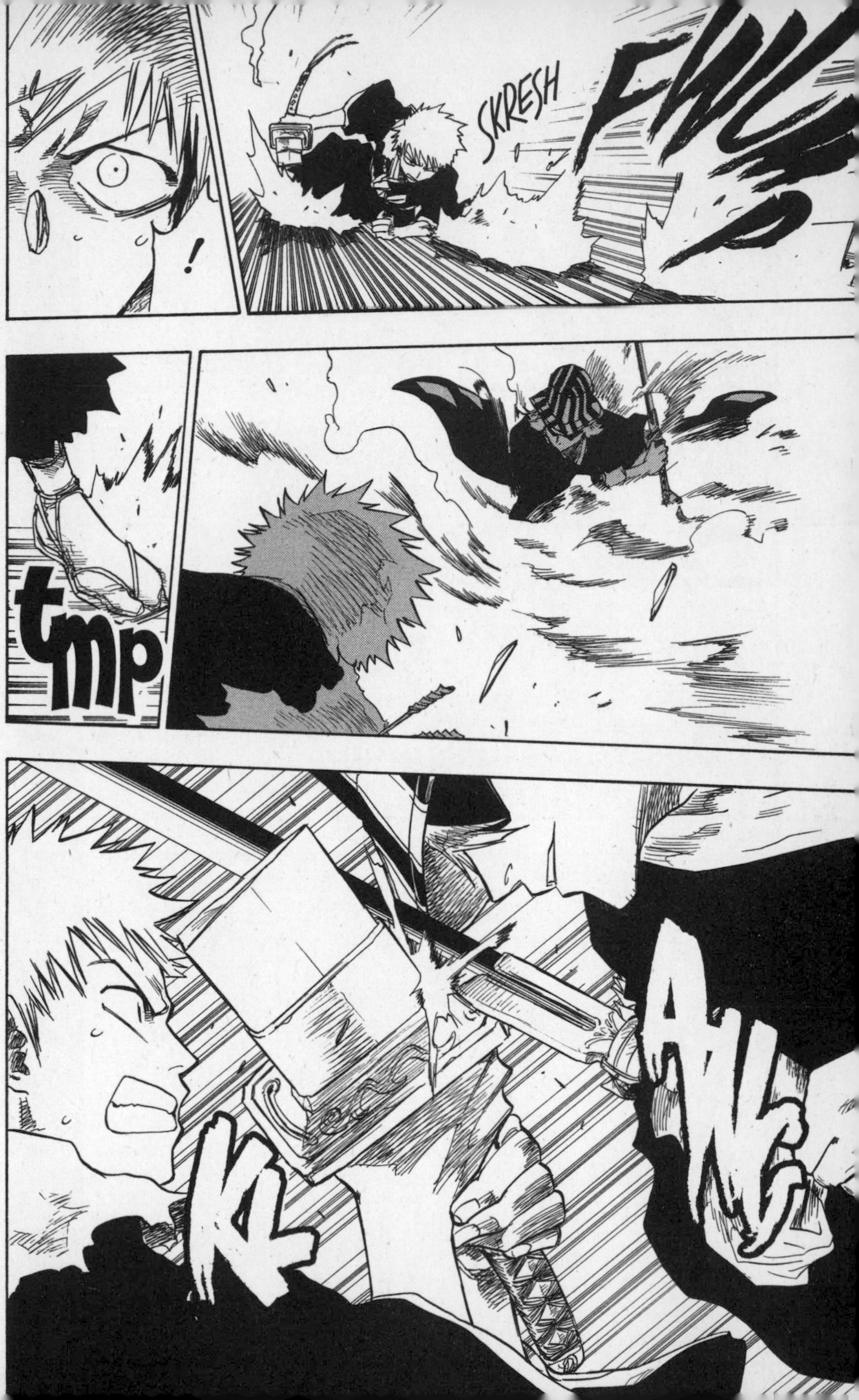
SKRESH
FWUMP
!
tmp
KLANG

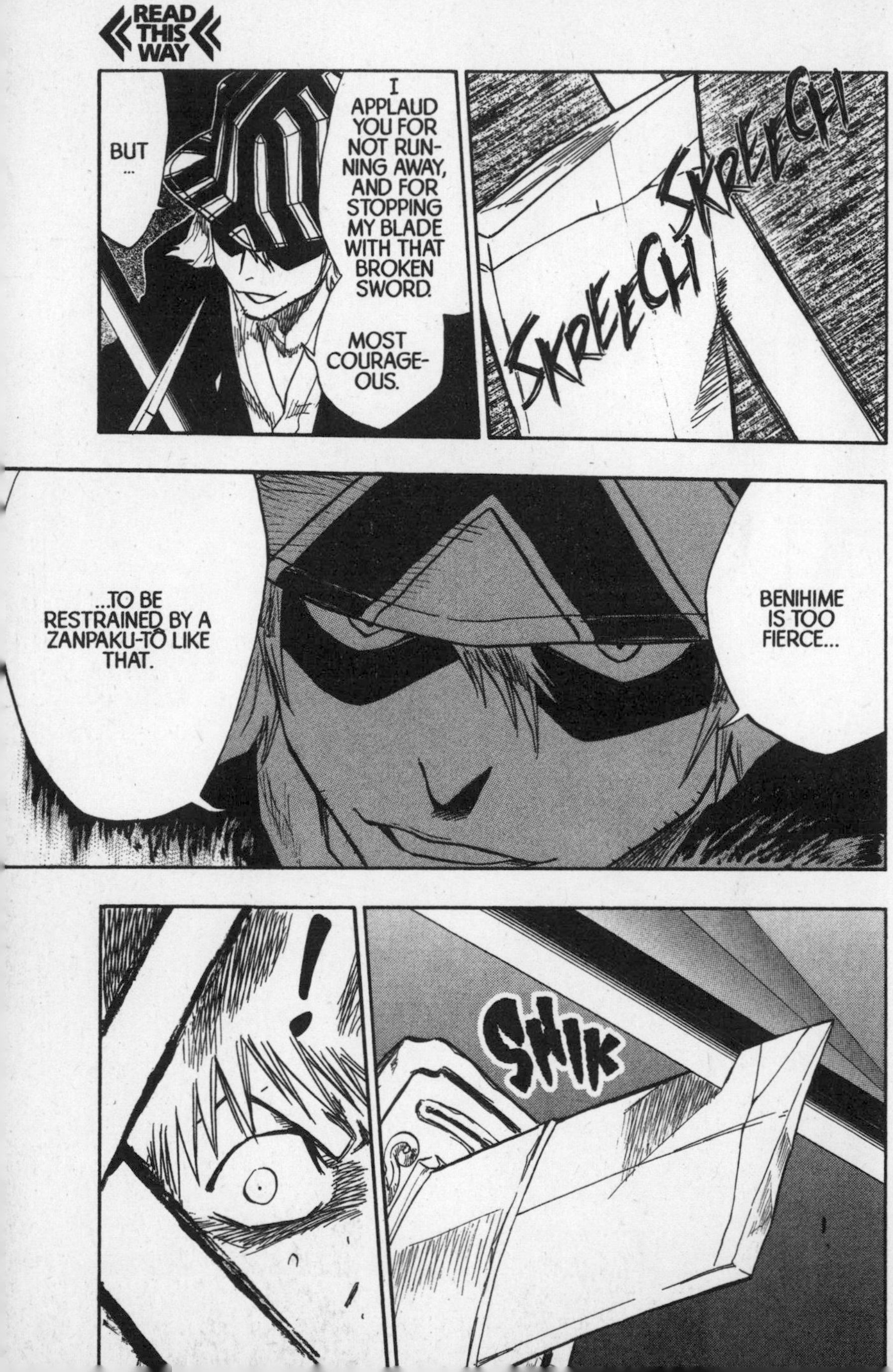
READ THIS WAY
SKREECH SKREECH
I APPLAUD YOU FOR NOT RUN-NING AWAY, AND FOR STOPPING MY BLADE WITH THAT BROKEN SWORD.
MOST COURAGE-OUS.
BUT ...
BENIHIME IS TOO FIERCE...
...TO BE RESTRAINED BY A ZANPAKU-TŌ LIKE THAT.
SHIK
!

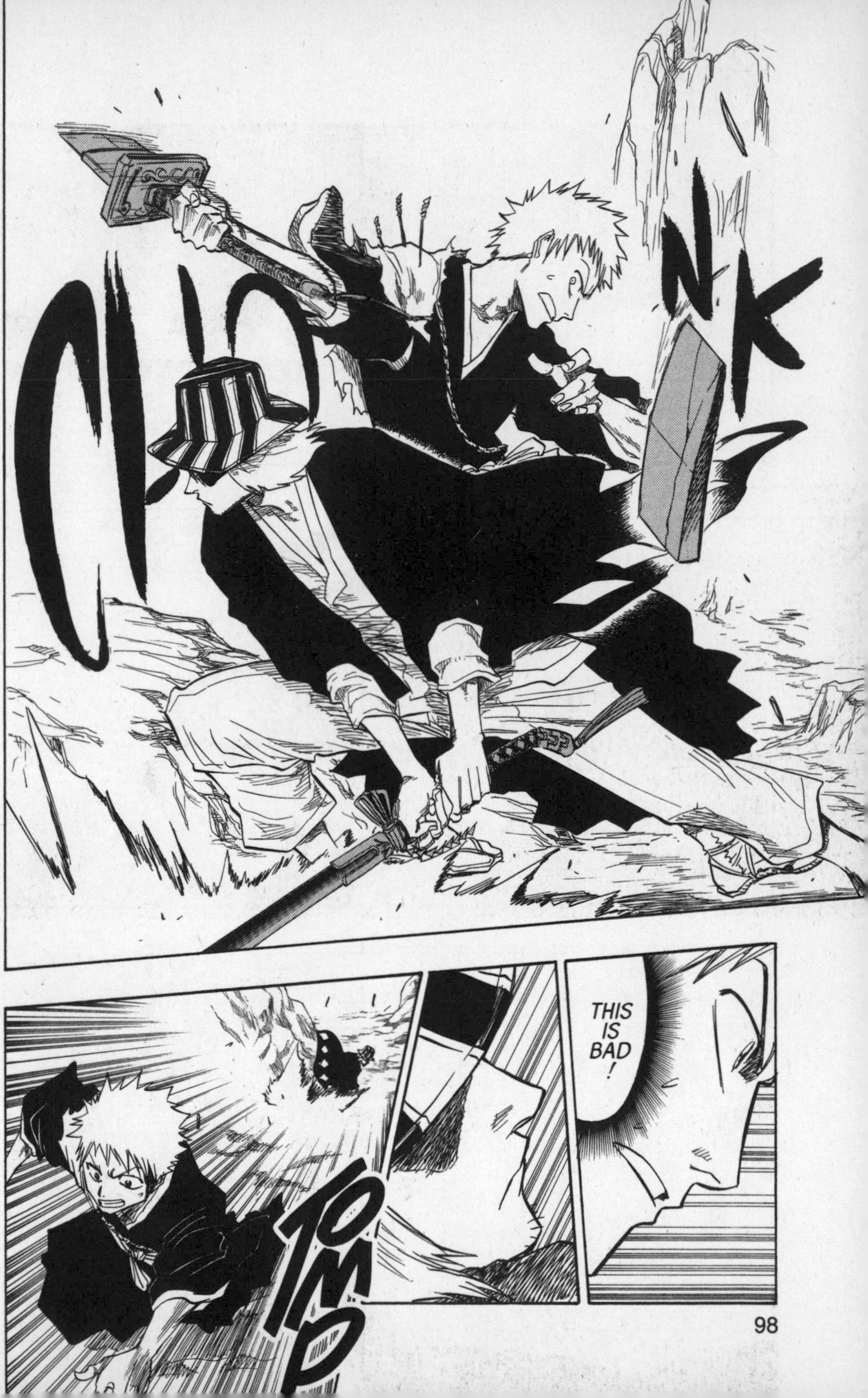
CLINK
THIS IS BAD!

READ THIS WAY

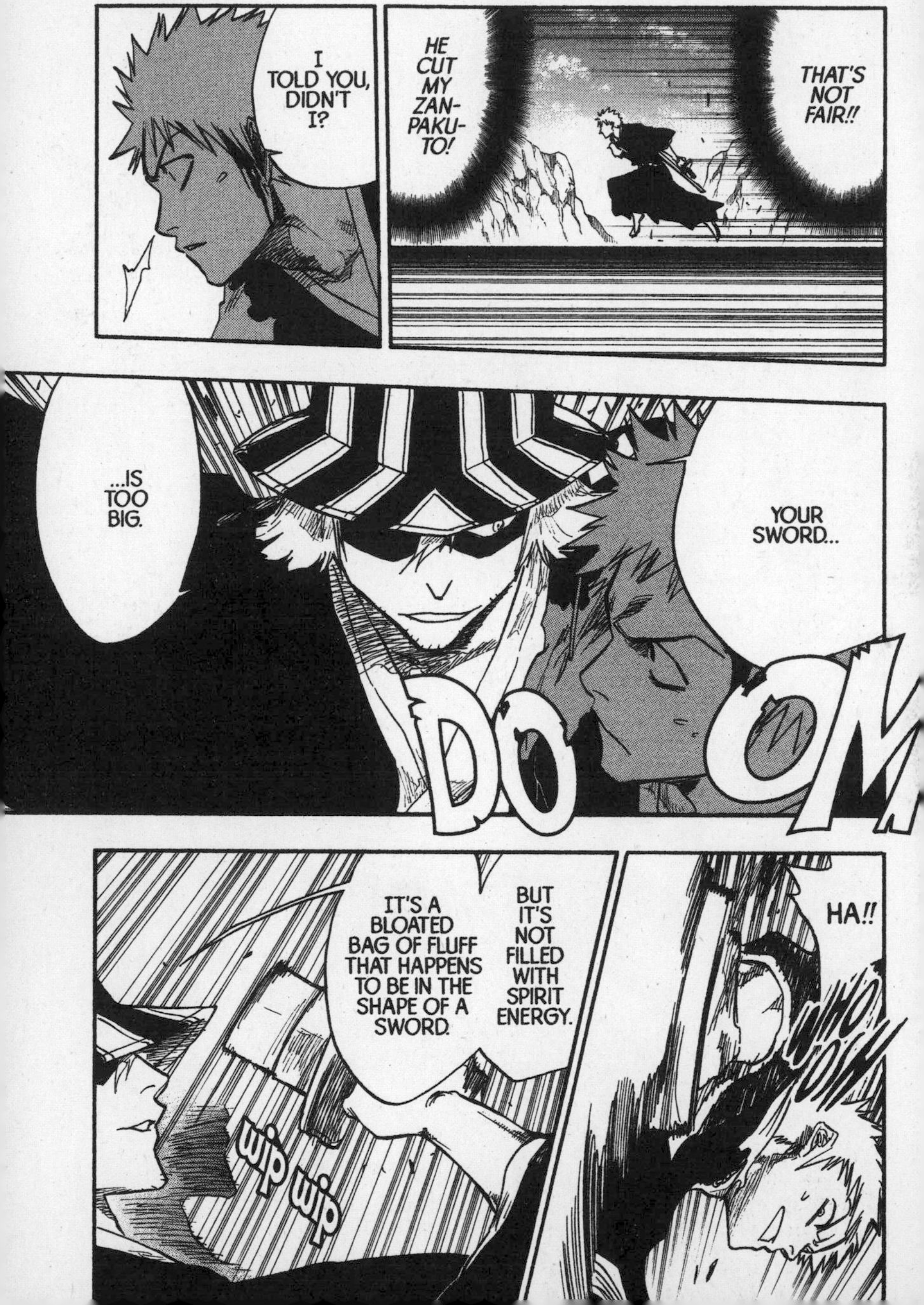

THAT'S NOT FAIR!!
HE CUT MY ZAN-PAKU-TO!
I TOLD YOU, DIDN'T I?
YOUR SWORD...
...IS TOO BIG.
DOOM
HA!!
BUT IT'S NOT FILLED WITH SPIRIT ENERGY.
IT'S A BLOATED BAG OF FLUFF THAT HAPPENS TO BE IN THE SHAPE OF A SWORD.
wip wip

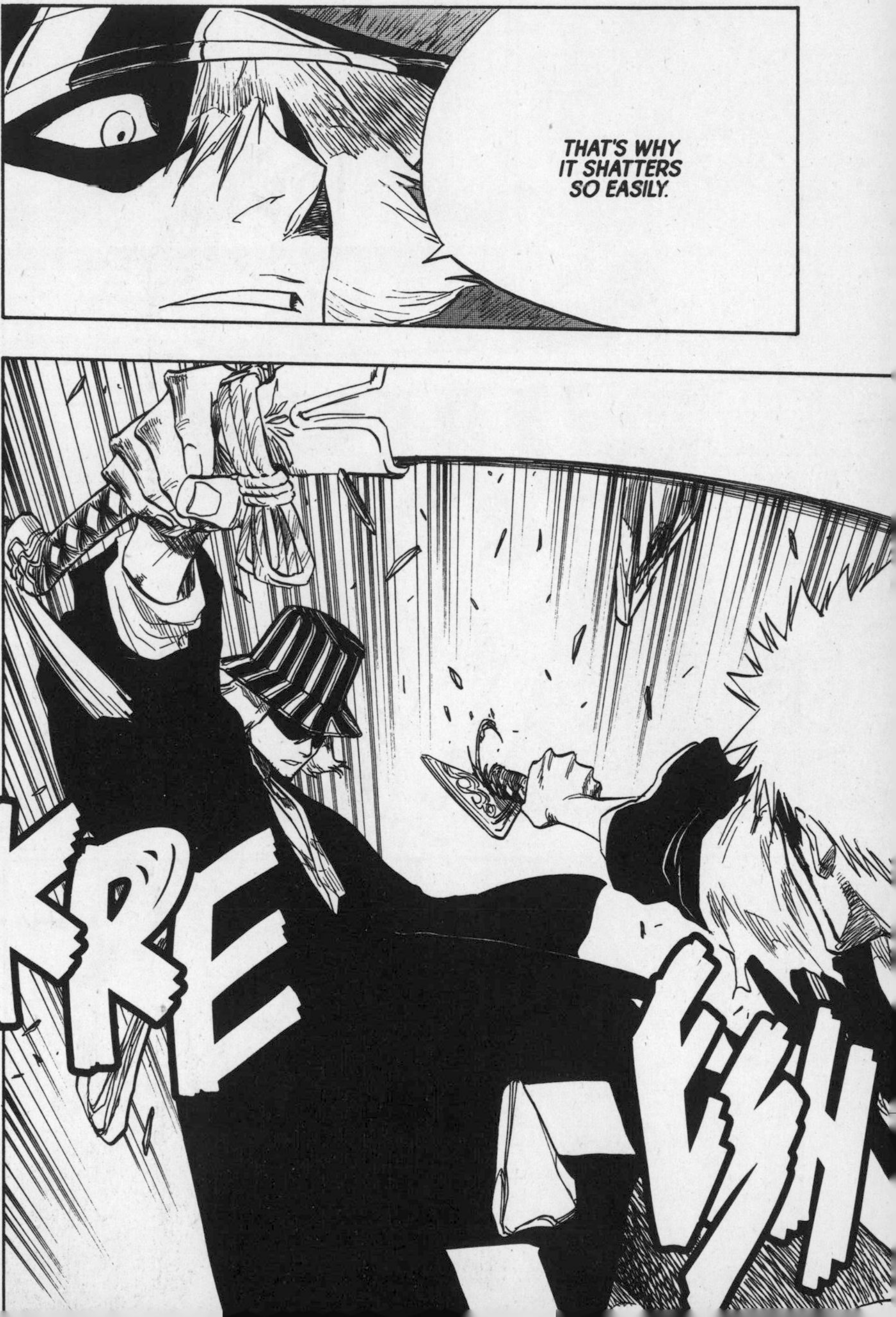
THAT'S WHY IT SHATTERS SO EASILY.
KRE
ESH

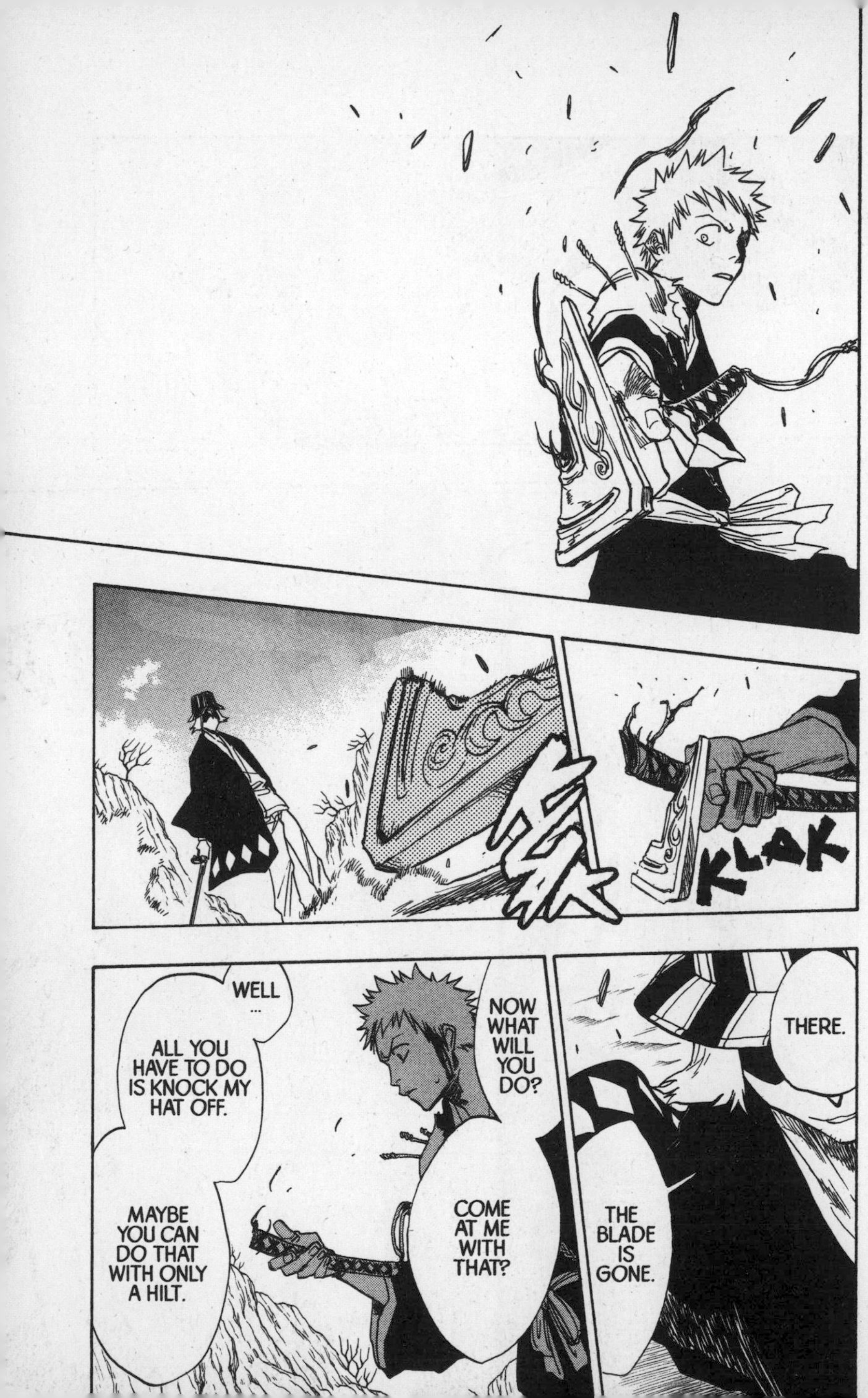
KLAK
THERE.
THE BLADE IS GONE.
NOW WHAT WILL YOU DO?
COME AT ME WITH THAT?
WELL ...
ALL YOU HAVE TO DO IS KNOCK MY HAT OFF.
MAYBE YOU CAN DO THAT WITH ONLY A HILT.

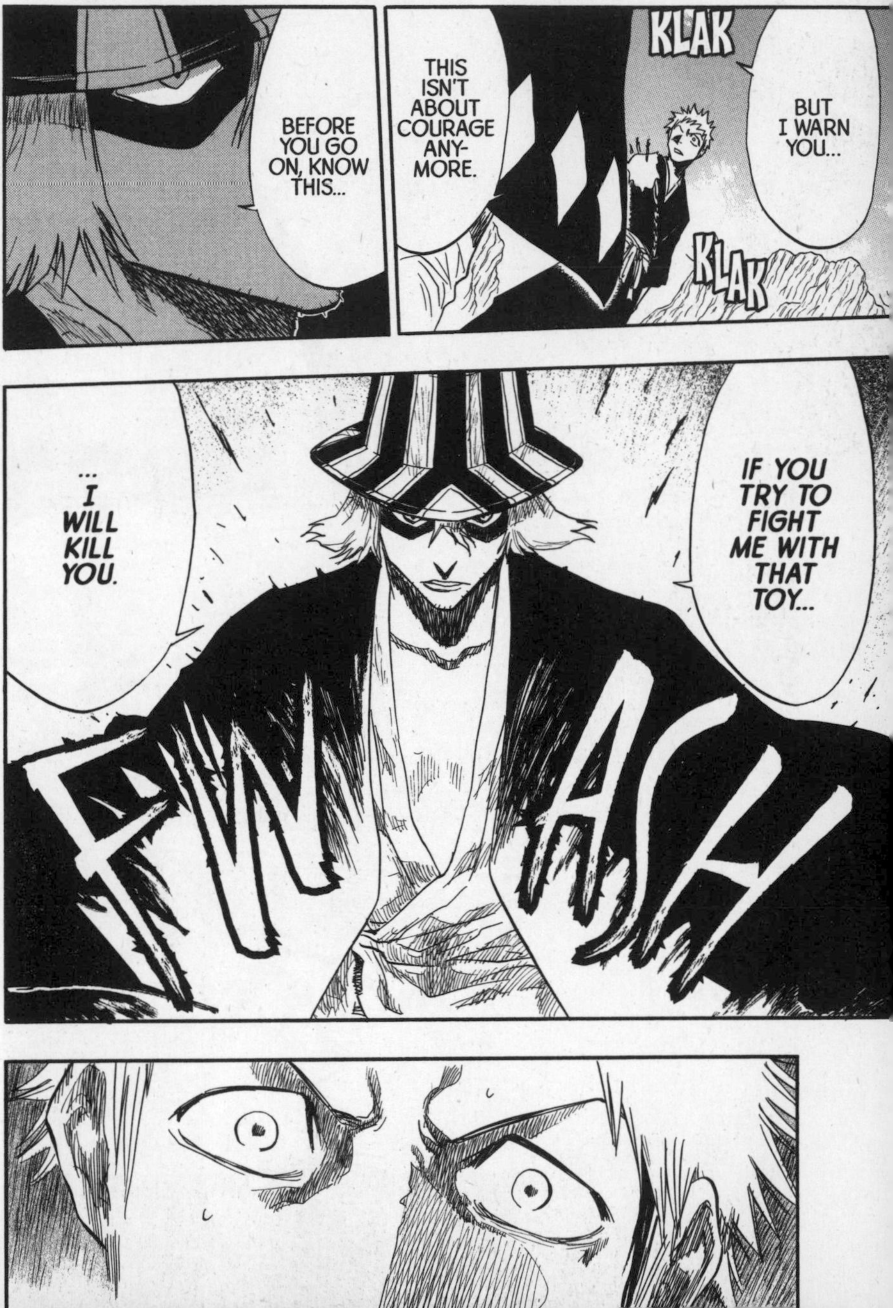
KLAK
BUT I WARN YOU...
KLAK
THIS ISN'T ABOUT COURAGE ANY-MORE.
BEFORE YOU GO ON, KNOW THIS...
IF YOU TRY TO FIGHT ME WITH THAT TOY...
... I WILL KILL YOU.
FWASH

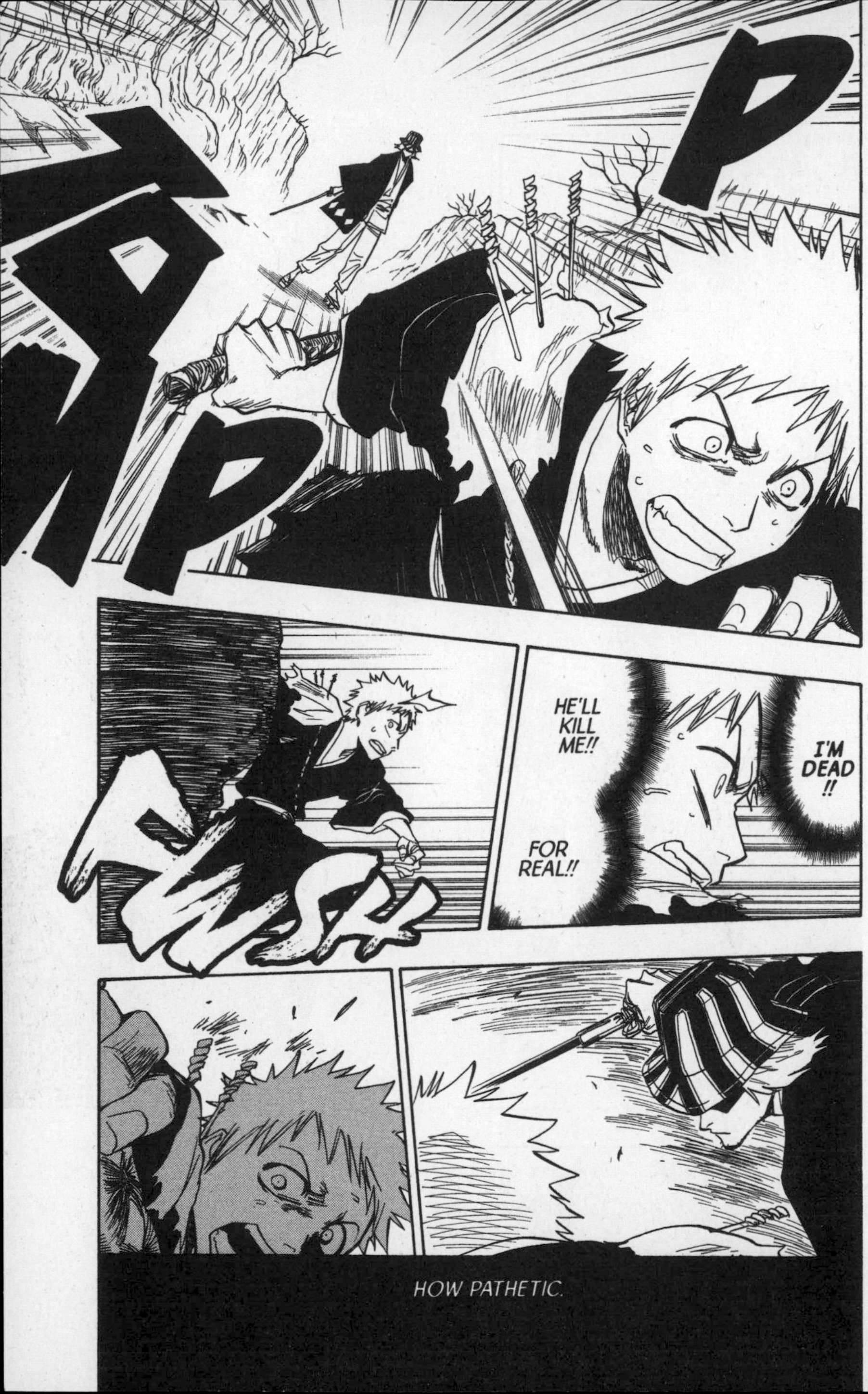
HE'LL KILL ME!!
FOR REAL!!
I'M DEAD!!
HOW PATHETIC.

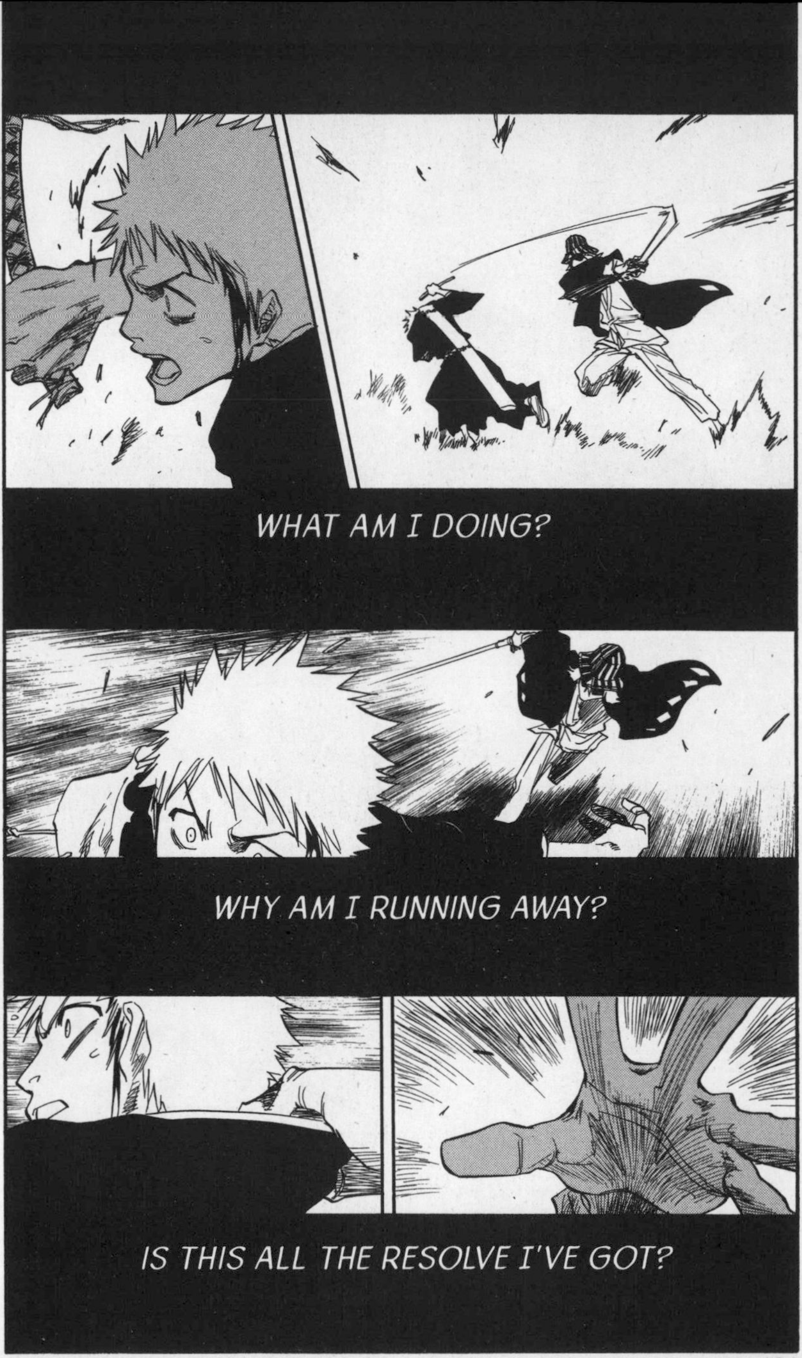
WHAT AM I DOING?
WHY AM I RUNNING AWAY?
IS THIS ALL THE RESOLVE I'VE GOT?

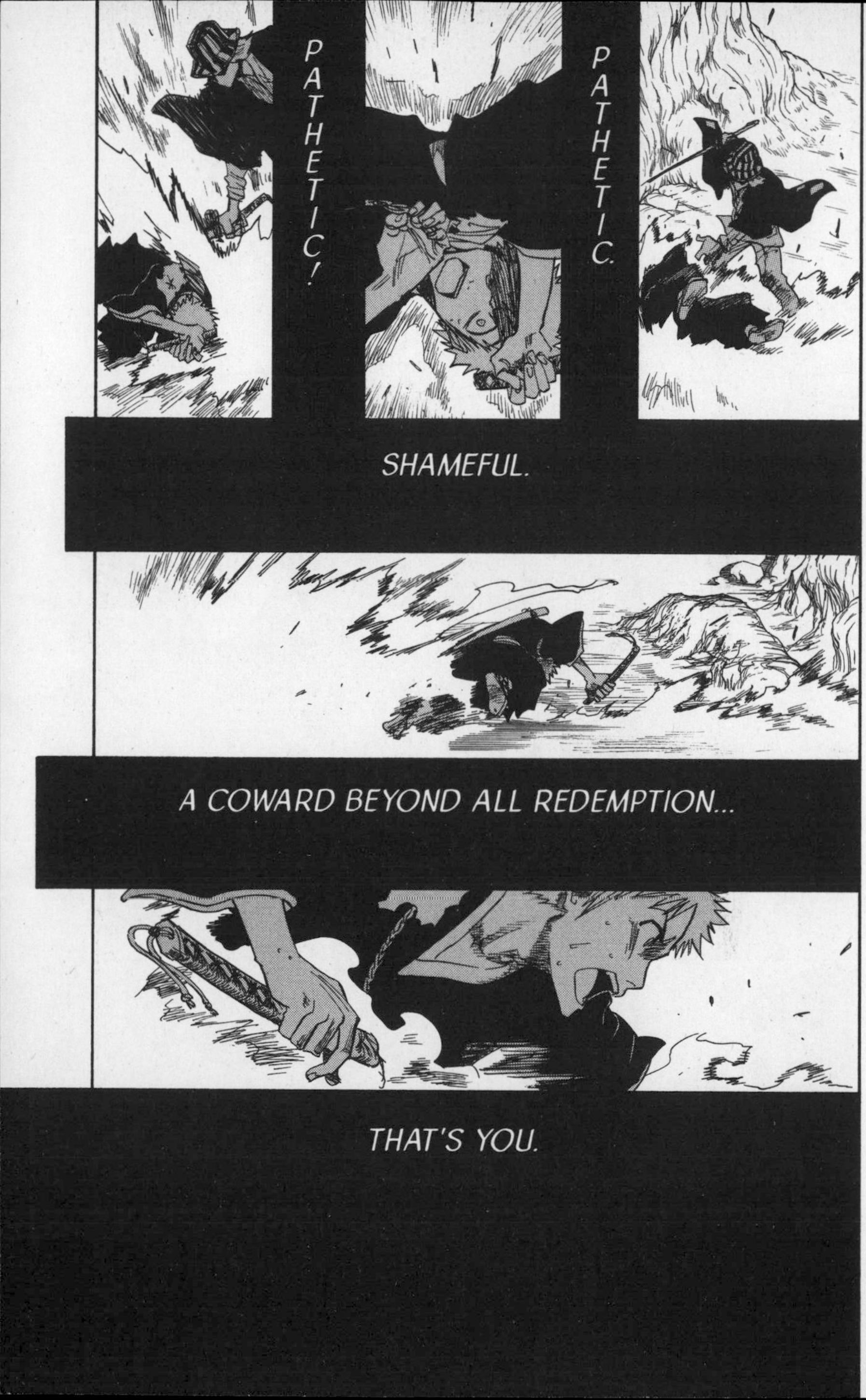
PATHETIC.
PATHETIC!
SHAMEFUL.
A COWARD BEYOND ALL REDEMPTION...
THAT'S YOU.

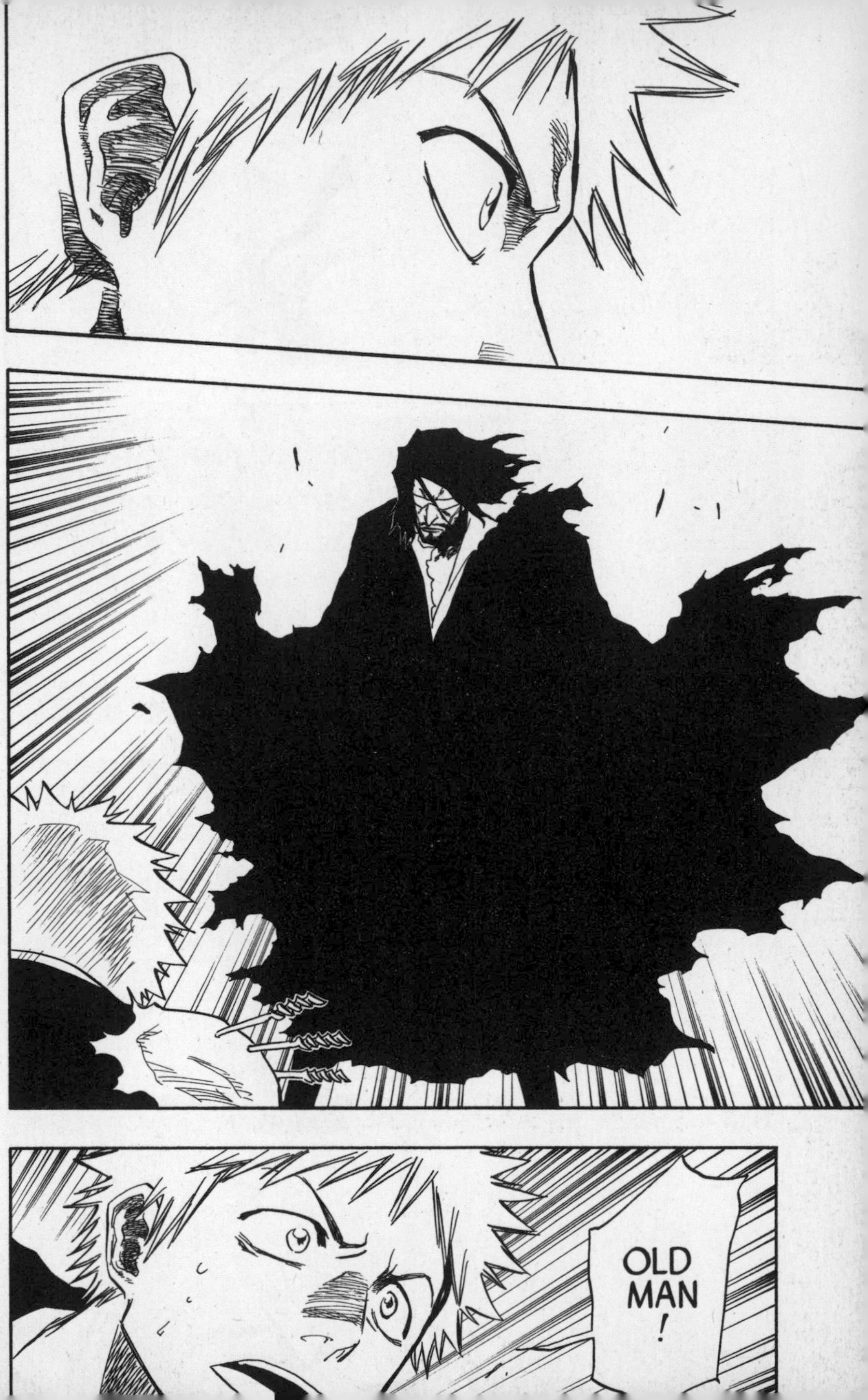
OLD MAN!

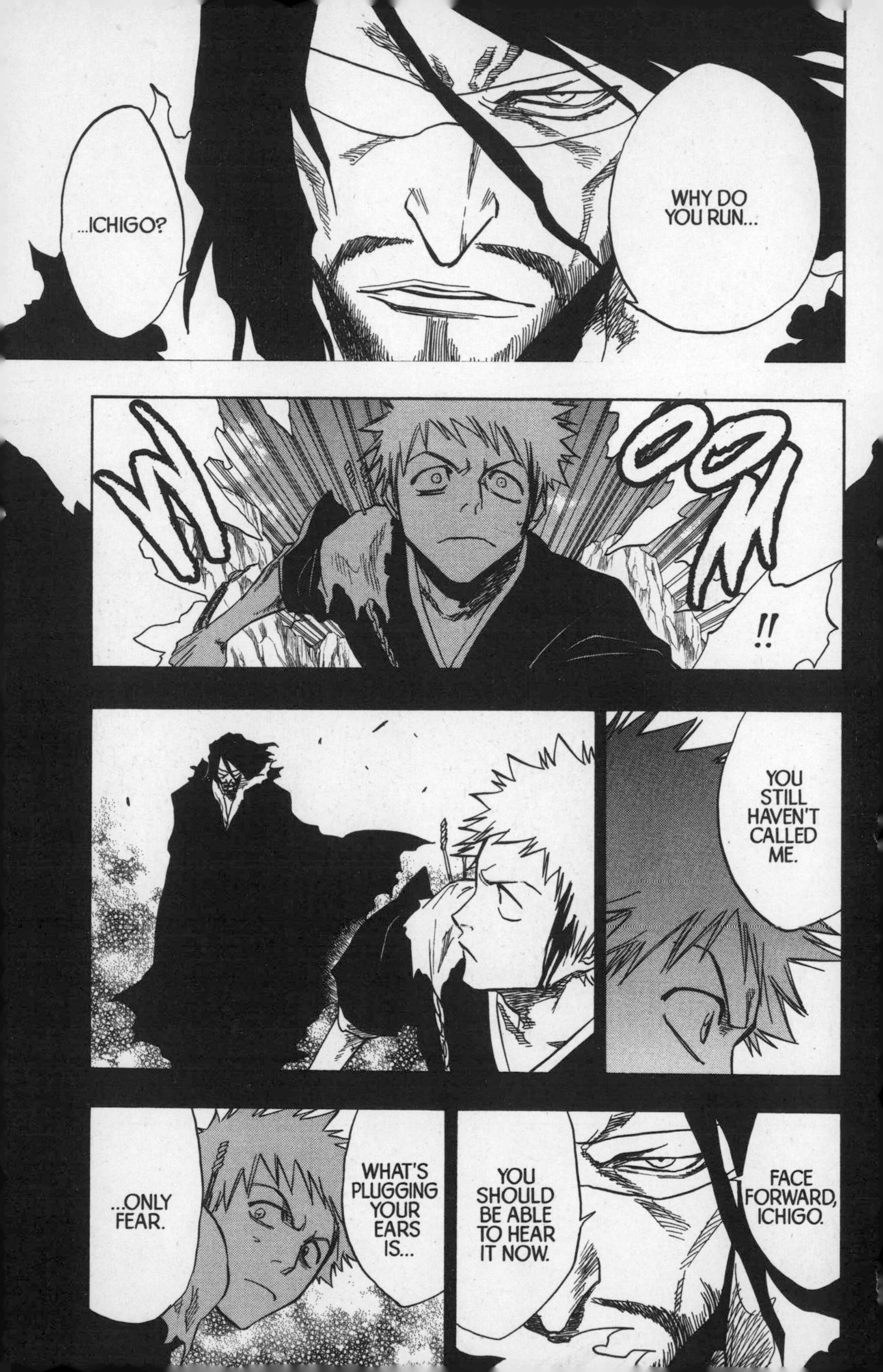
WHY DO YOU RUN...
...ICHIGO?
!!
YOU STILL HAVEN'T CALLED ME.
FACE FORWARD, ICHIGO.
YOU SHOULD BE ABLE TO HEAR IT NOW.
WHAT'S PLUGGING YOUR EARS IS...
...ONLY FEAR.

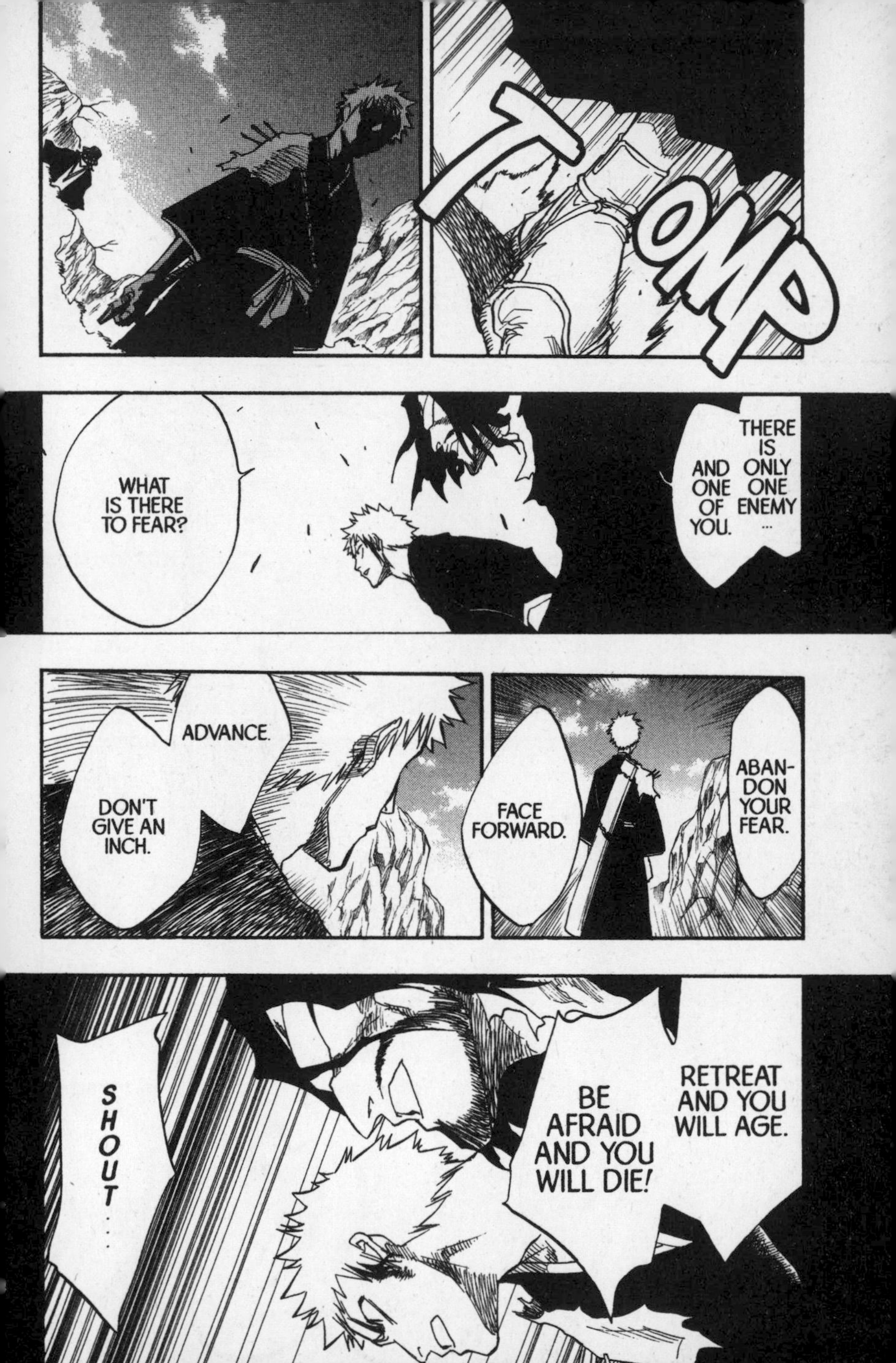
TOMP
THERE IS ONLY ONE ENEMY...
AND ONE OF YOU.
WHAT IS THERE TO FEAR?
ABANDON YOUR FEAR.
FACE FORWARD.
ADVANCE.
DON'T GIVE AN INCH.
RETREAT AND YOU WILL AGE.
BE AFRAID AND YOU WILL DIE!
SHOUT...

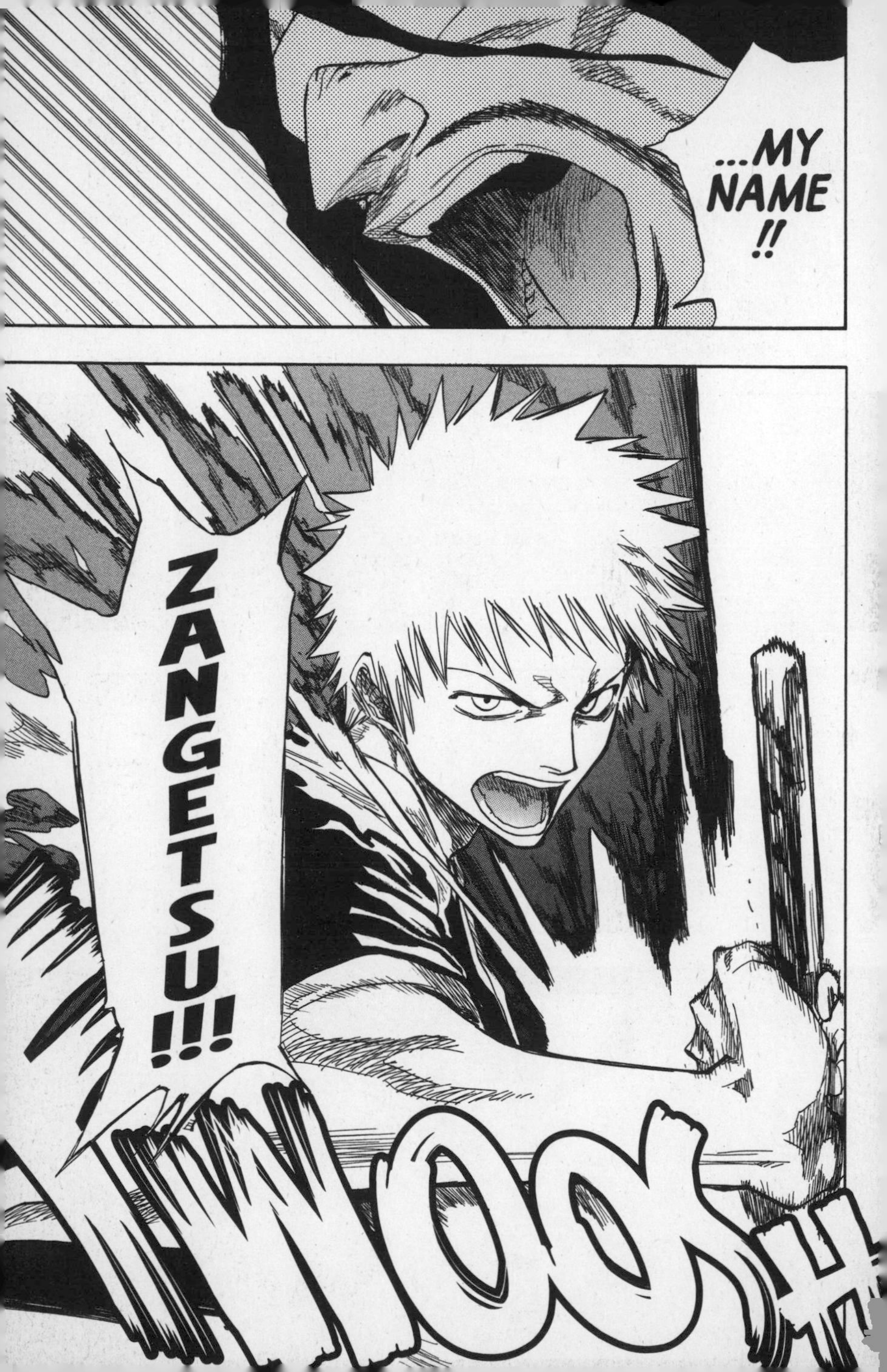
...MY NAME !!
ZANGETSU!!!
WHOOSH

67. End of Lessons

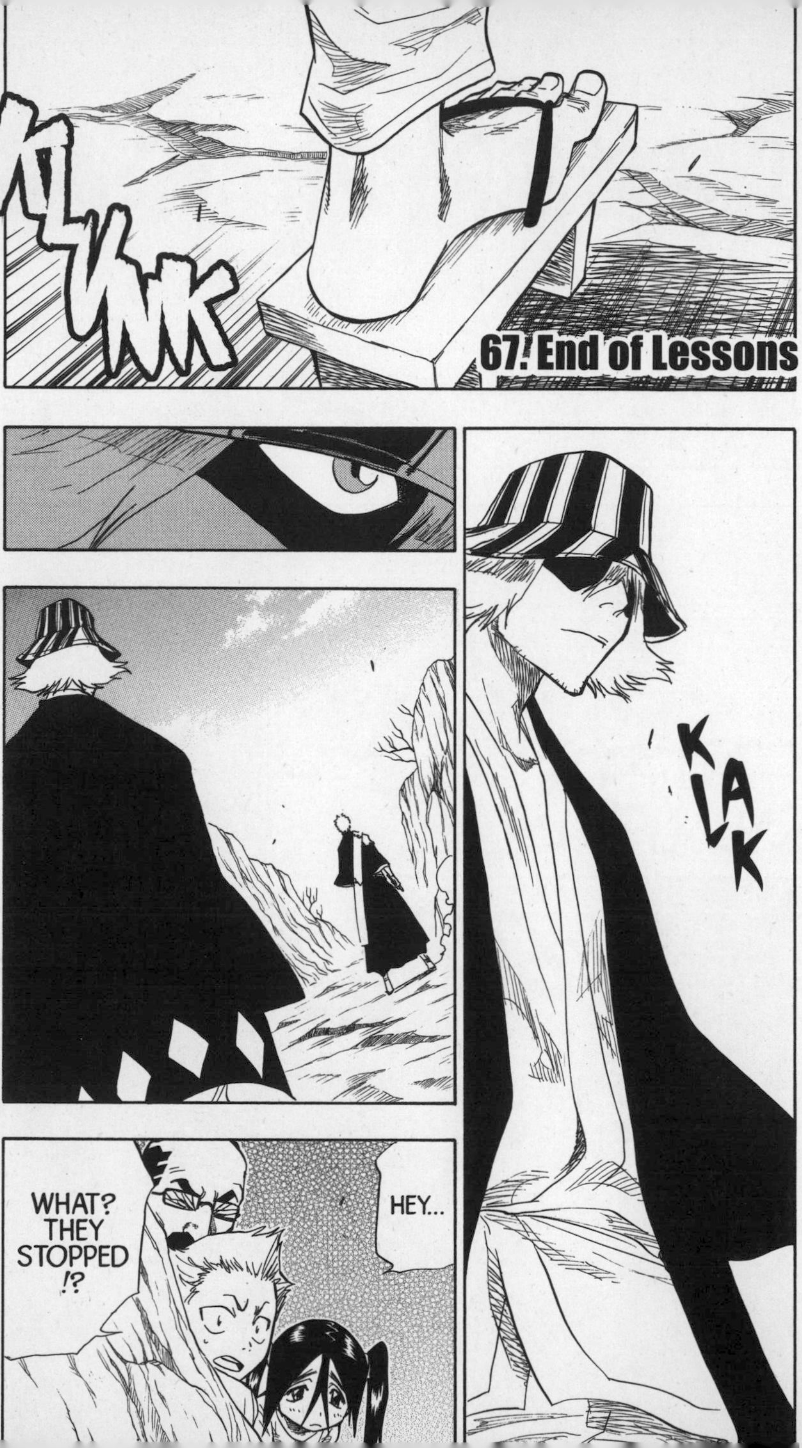
KLUNK
KLAK
HEY...
WHAT? THEY STOPPED!?

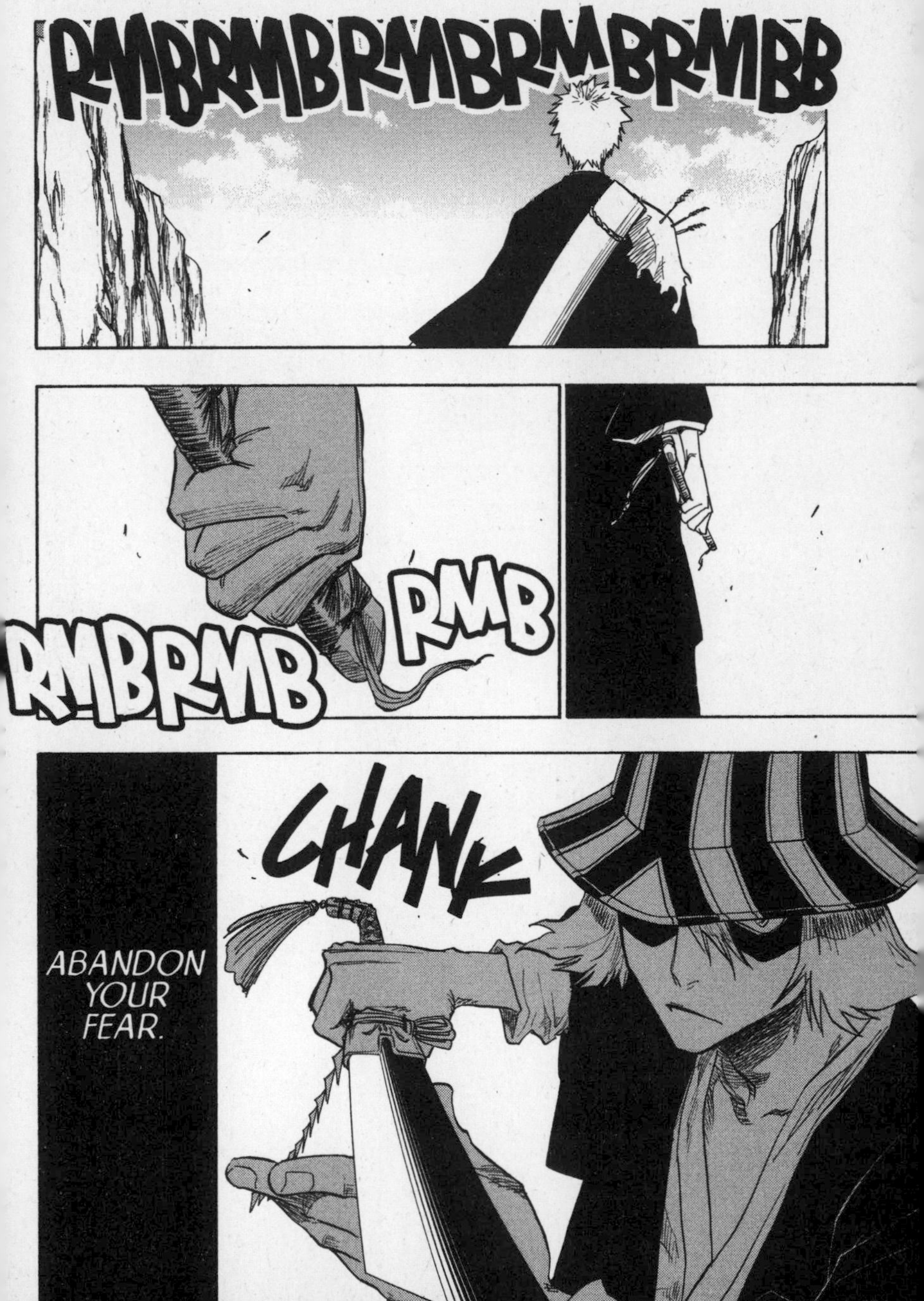
RMBRMBRMBRMBRMBB
RMB
RMBRMB
CHANK
ABANDON YOUR FEAR.

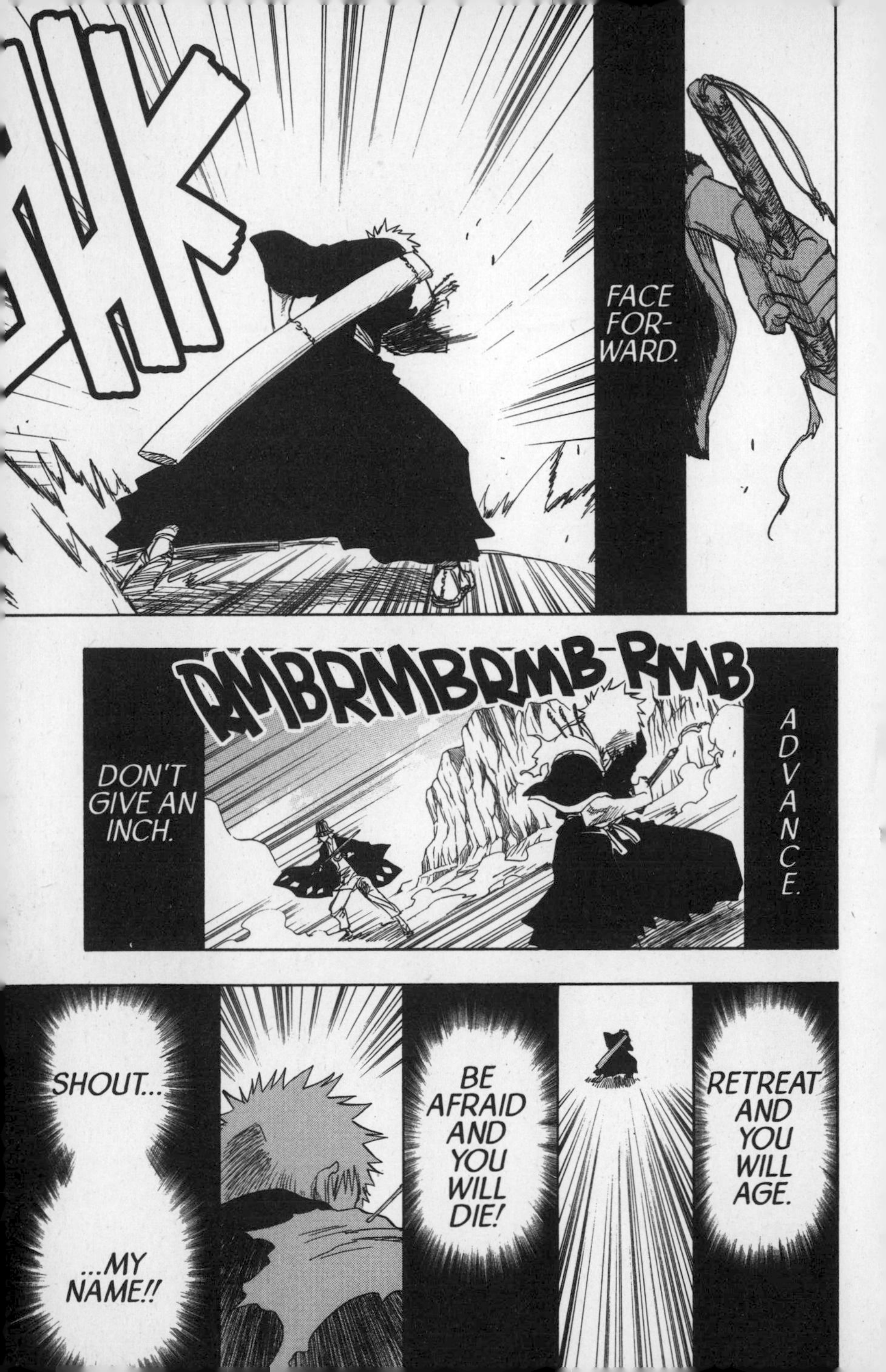
FACE FOR-WARD.
ADVANCE.
RMBRMBRMB RMB
DON'T GIVE AN INCH.
RETREAT AND YOU WILL AGE.
BE AFRAID AND YOU WILL DIE!
SHOUT...
...MY NAME!!

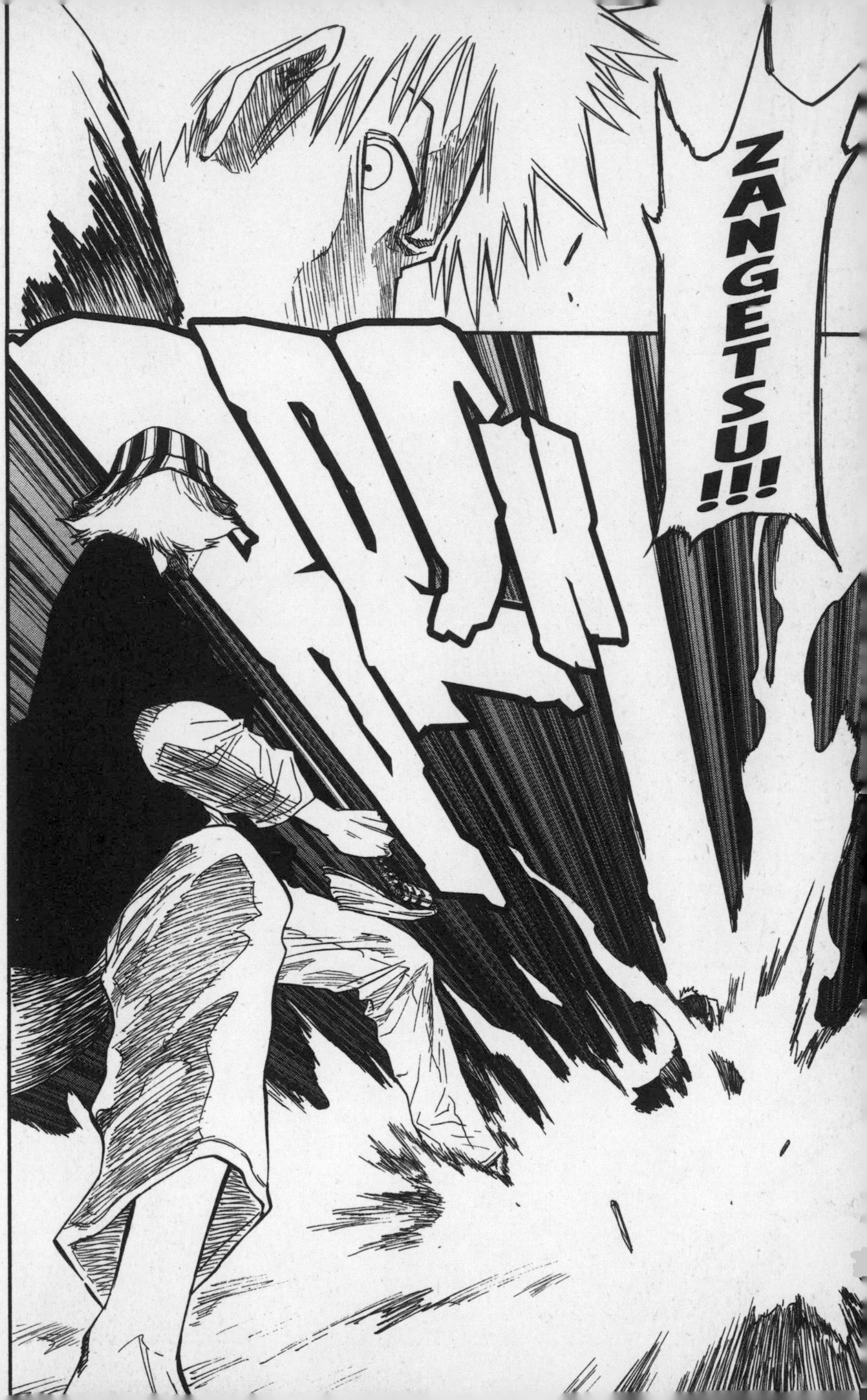
ZANGETSU!!!

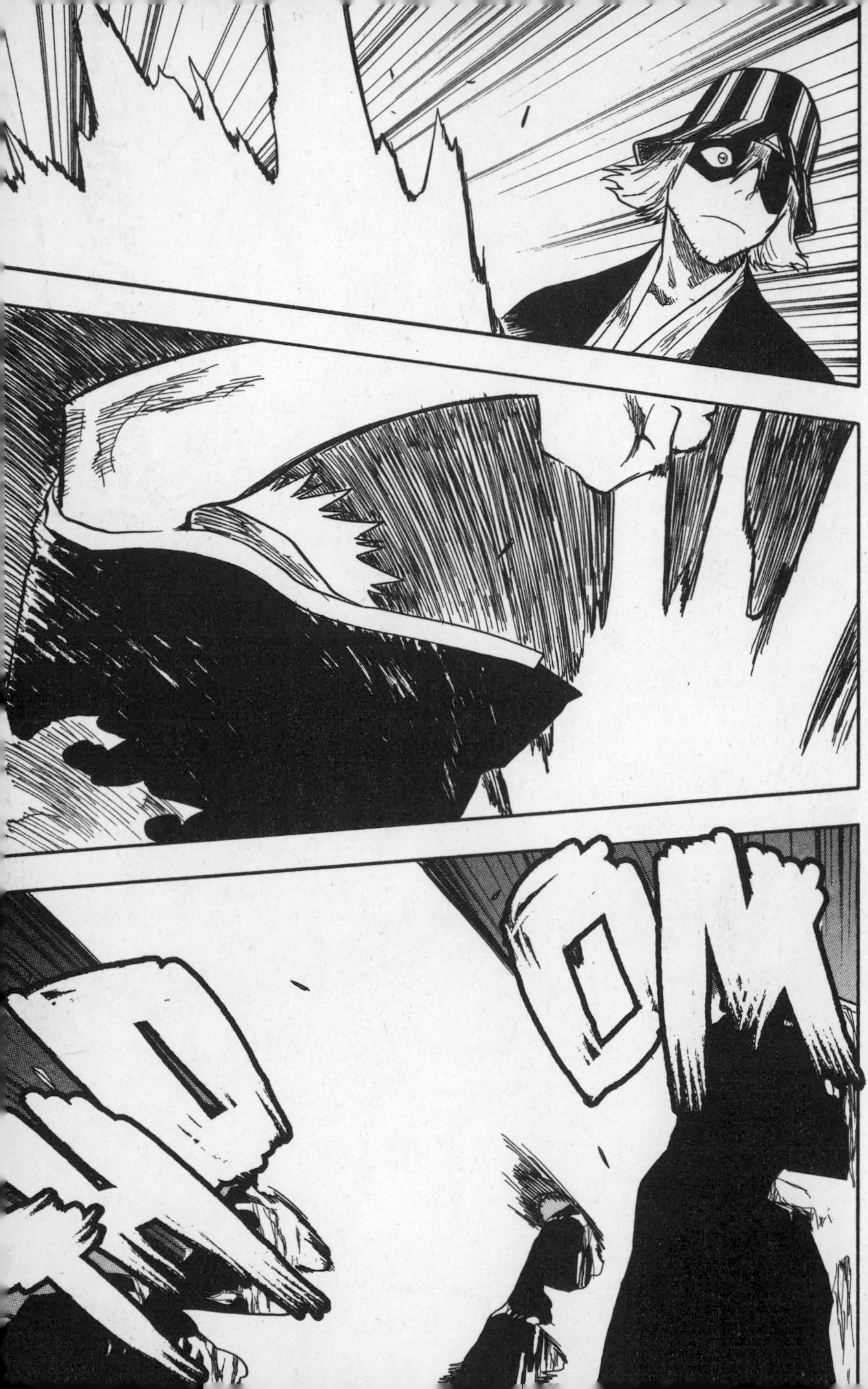
DON

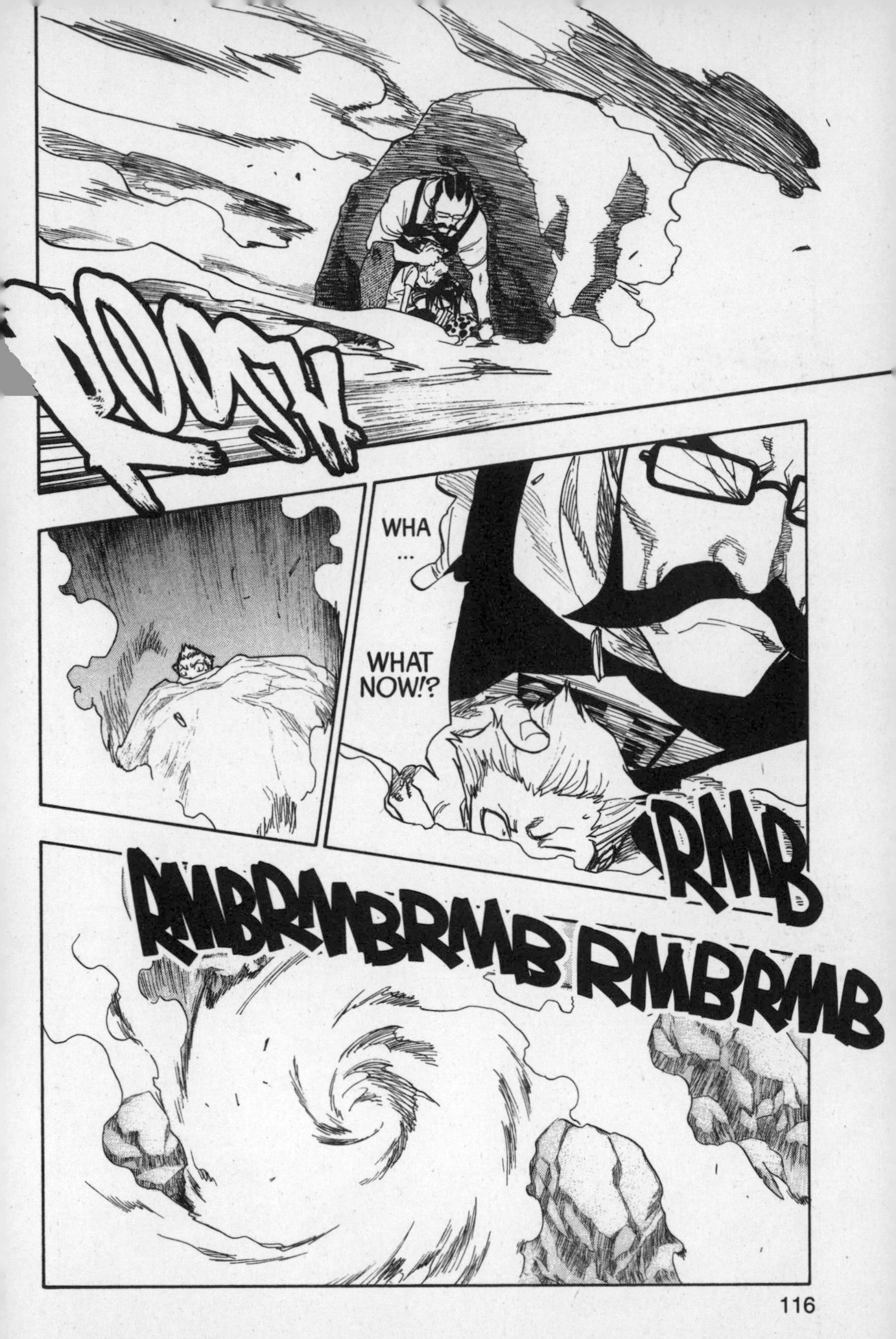
BOOOSH
WHA ...
WHAT NOW!?
RMB
RMBRMBRMB RMBRMB

RRMMBB

RRMMBB

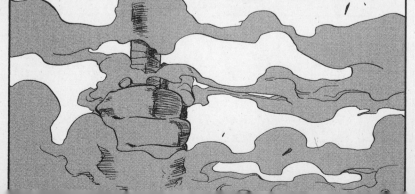

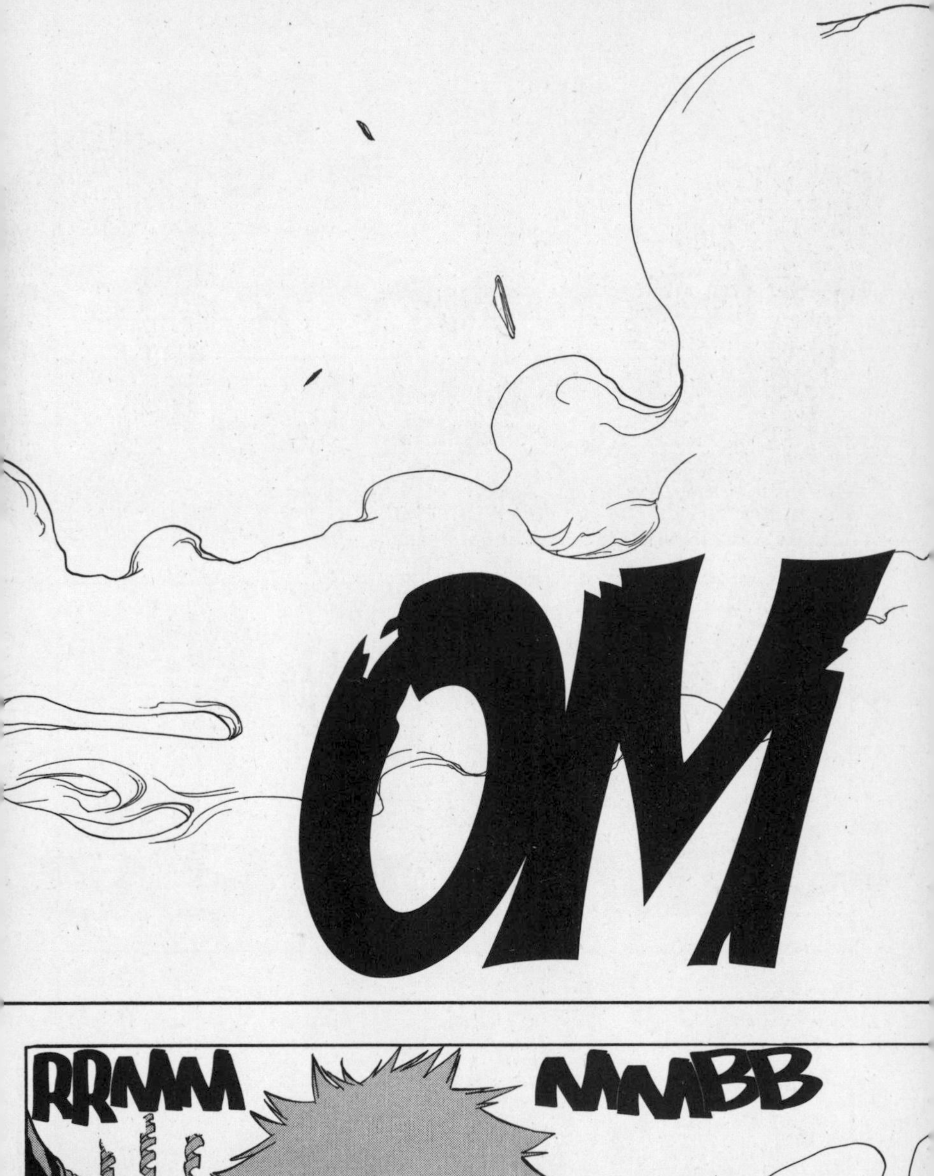
OM
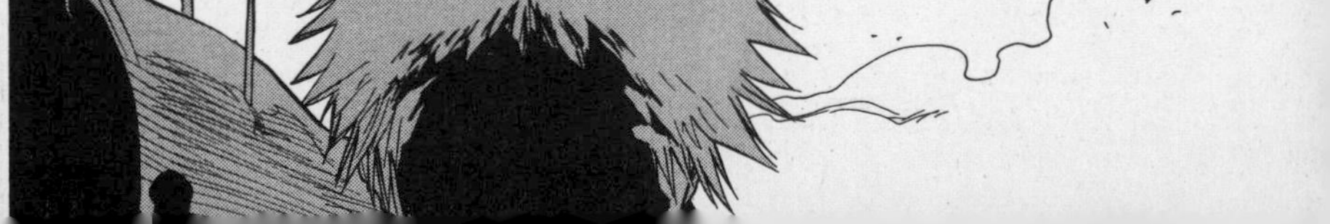
RRMM
MMBB

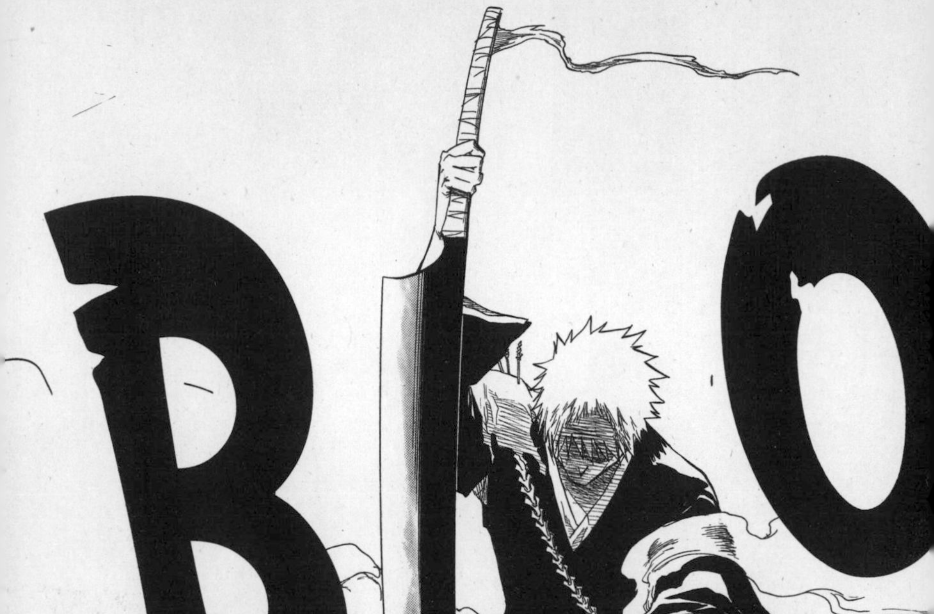
BO
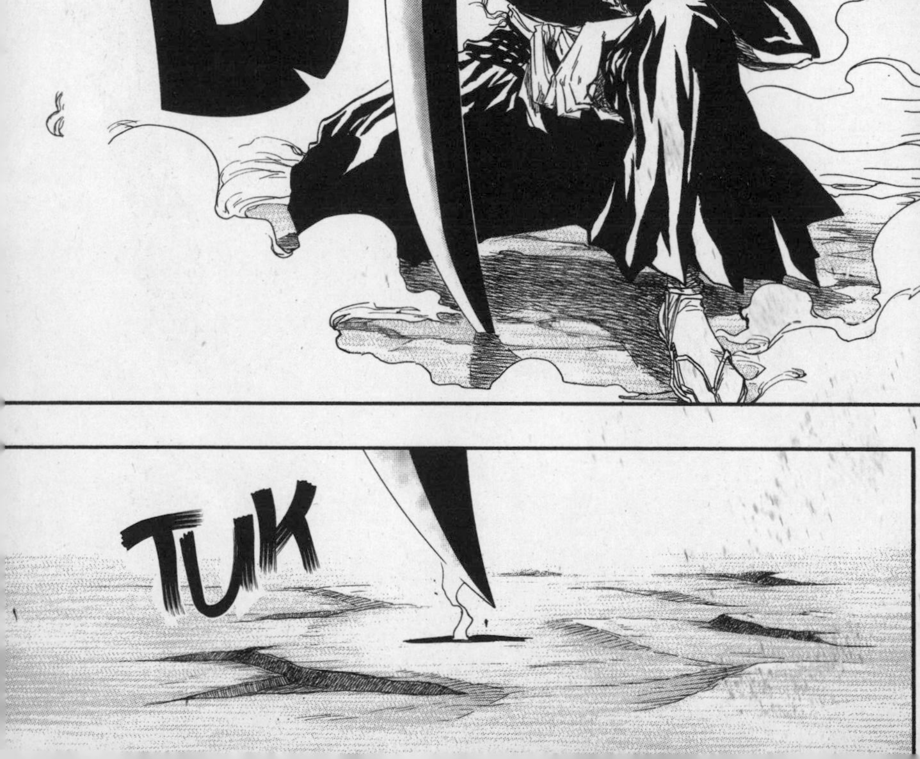
TUK

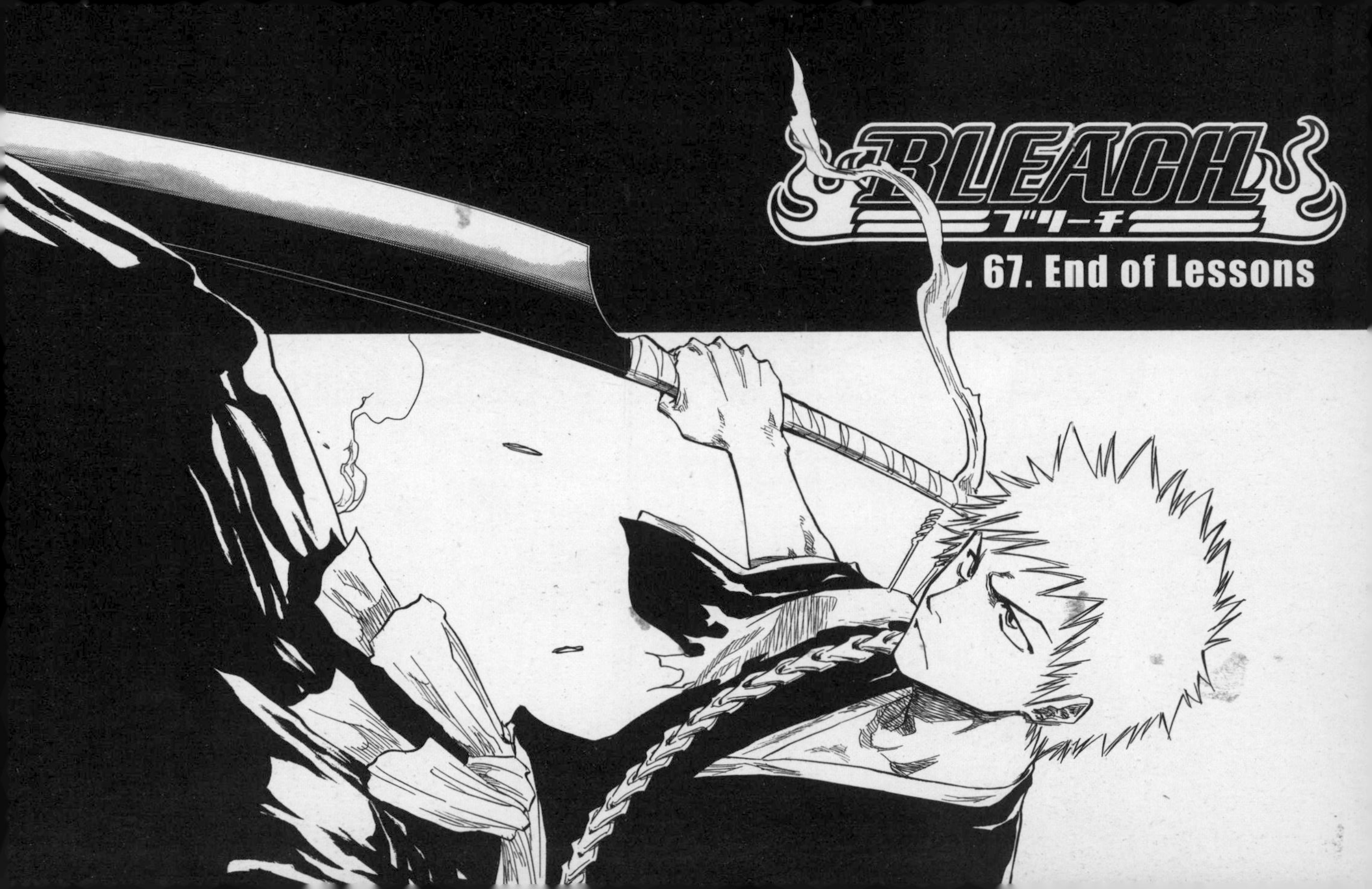
BLEACH
ブリーチ
67. End of Lessons

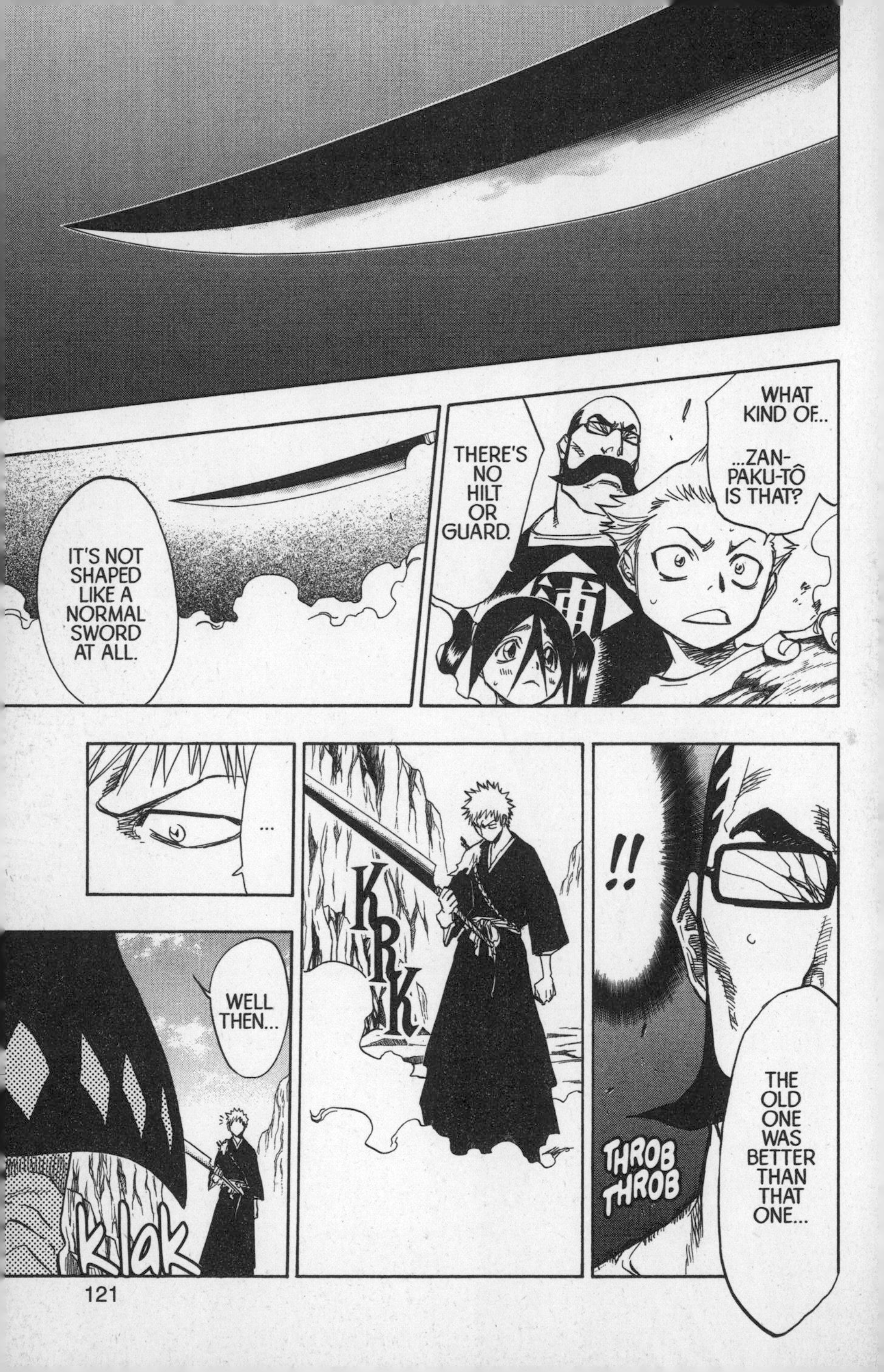
WHAT KIND OF...
...ZAN-PAKU-TÔ IS THAT?
THERE'S NO HILT OR GUARD.
IT'S NOT SHAPED LIKE A NORMAL SWORD AT ALL.
!!
THROB THROB
THE OLD ONE WAS BETTER THAN THAT ONE...
KRK
...
WELL THEN...
klak

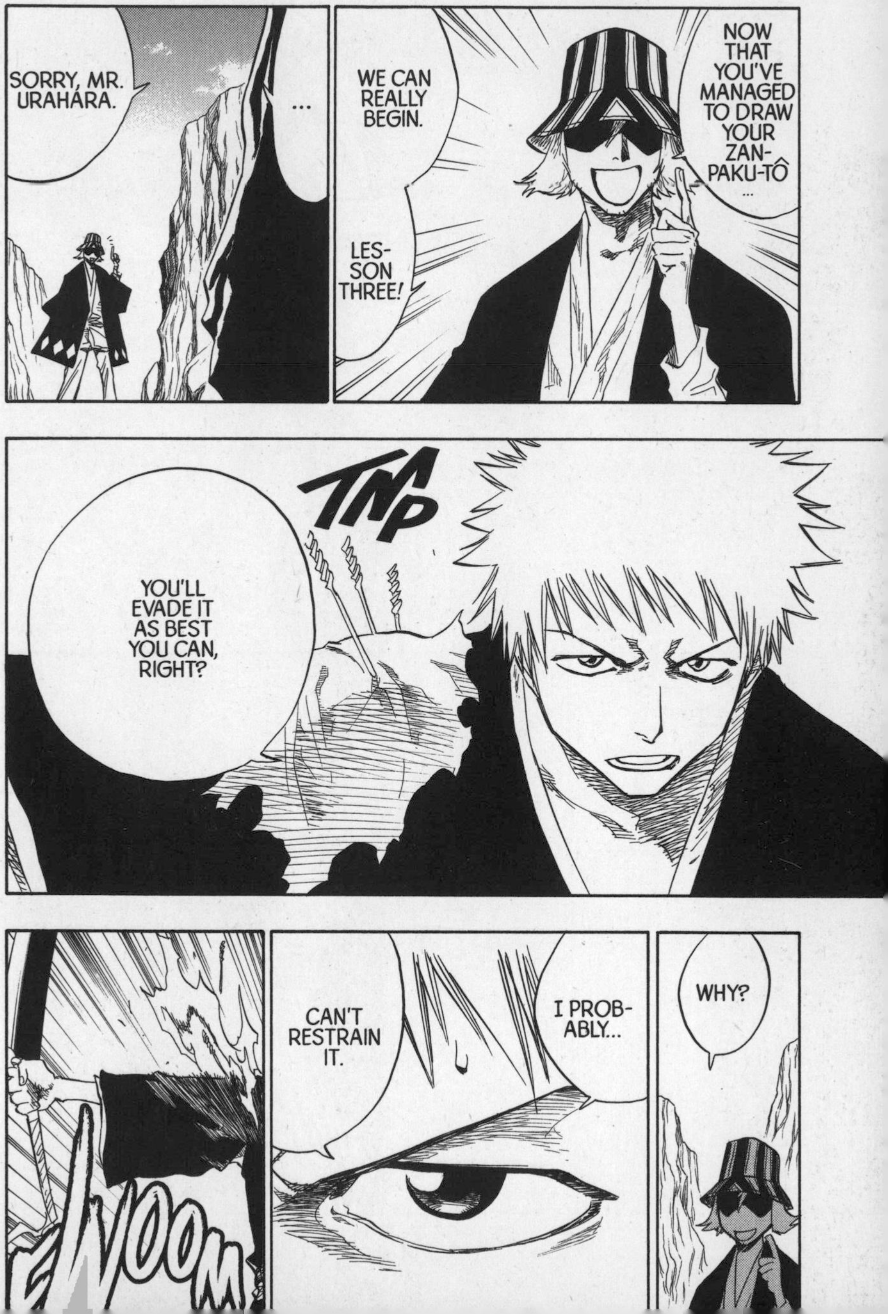
NOW THAT YOU'VE MANAGED TO DRAW YOUR ZAN-PAKU-TÔ ...
WE CAN REALLY BEGIN.
LES-SON THREE!
...
SORRY, MR. URAHARA.
TMP
YOU'LL EVADE IT AS BEST YOU CAN, RIGHT?
WHY?
I PROB-ABLY...
CAN'T RESTRAIN IT.
VOOM

READ THIS WAY

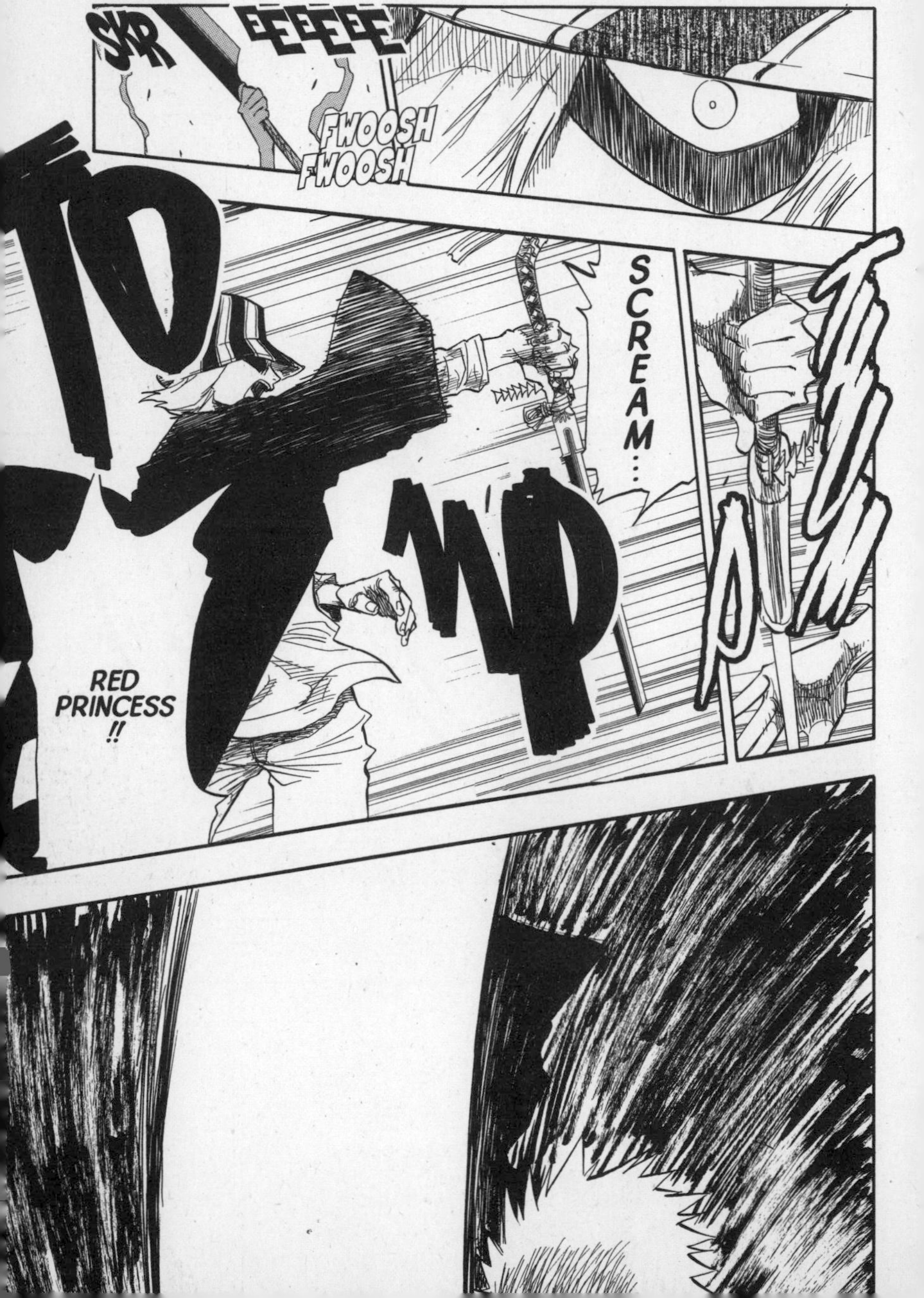
SKREEEEEE
FWOOSH FWOOSH
SCREAM...
RED PRINCESS !!

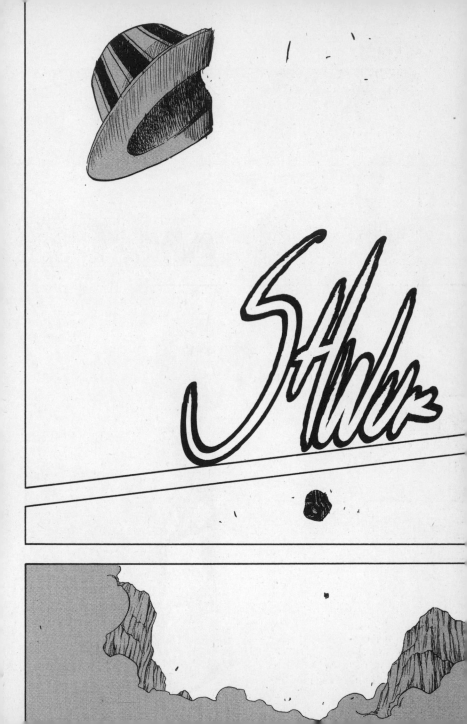

READ THIS WAY

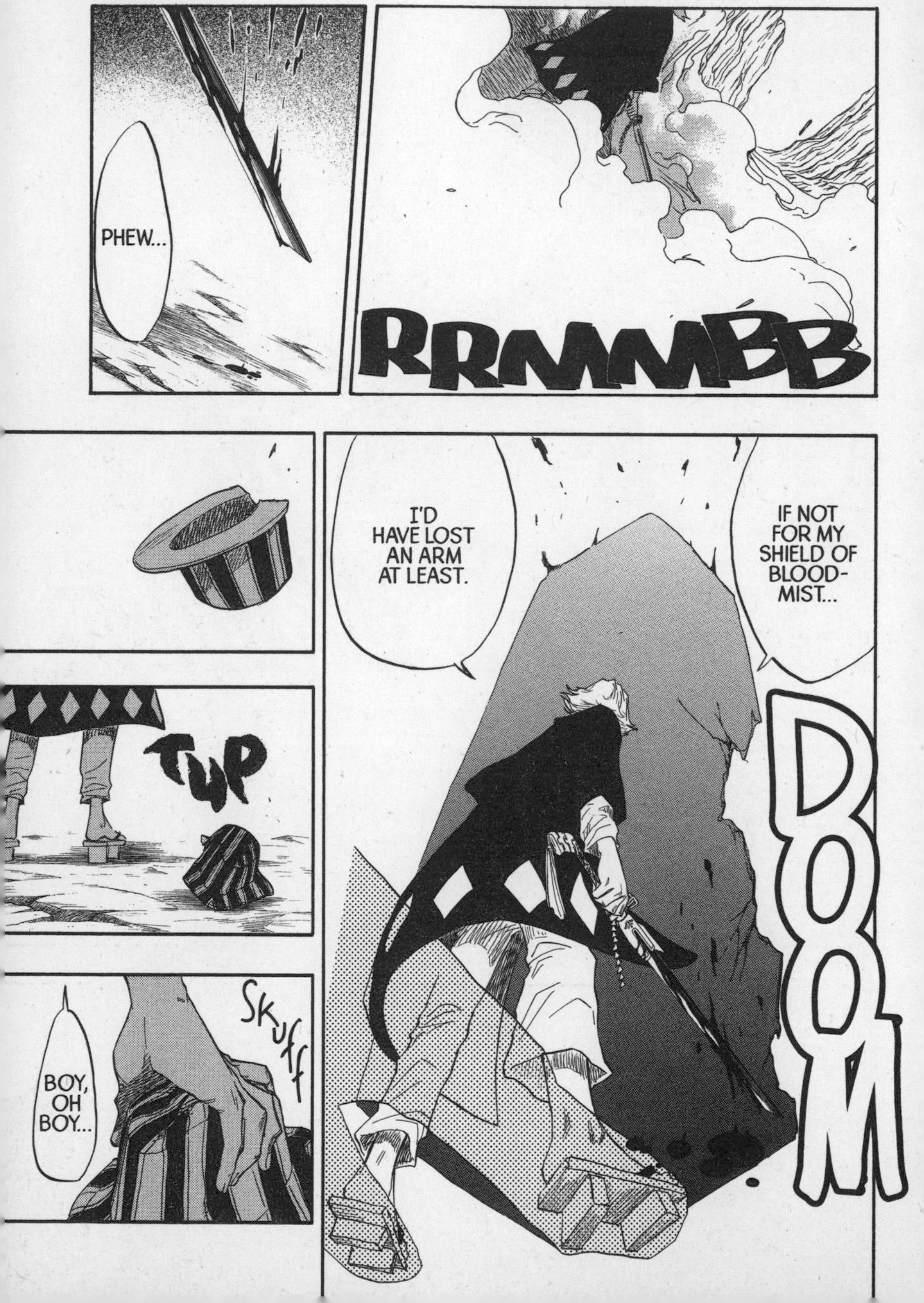
RRMMBB
PHEW...
IF NOT FOR MY SHIELD OF BLOOD-MIST...
I'D HAVE LOST AN ARM AT LEAST.
DOOM
TUP
Skuff
BOY, OH BOY...

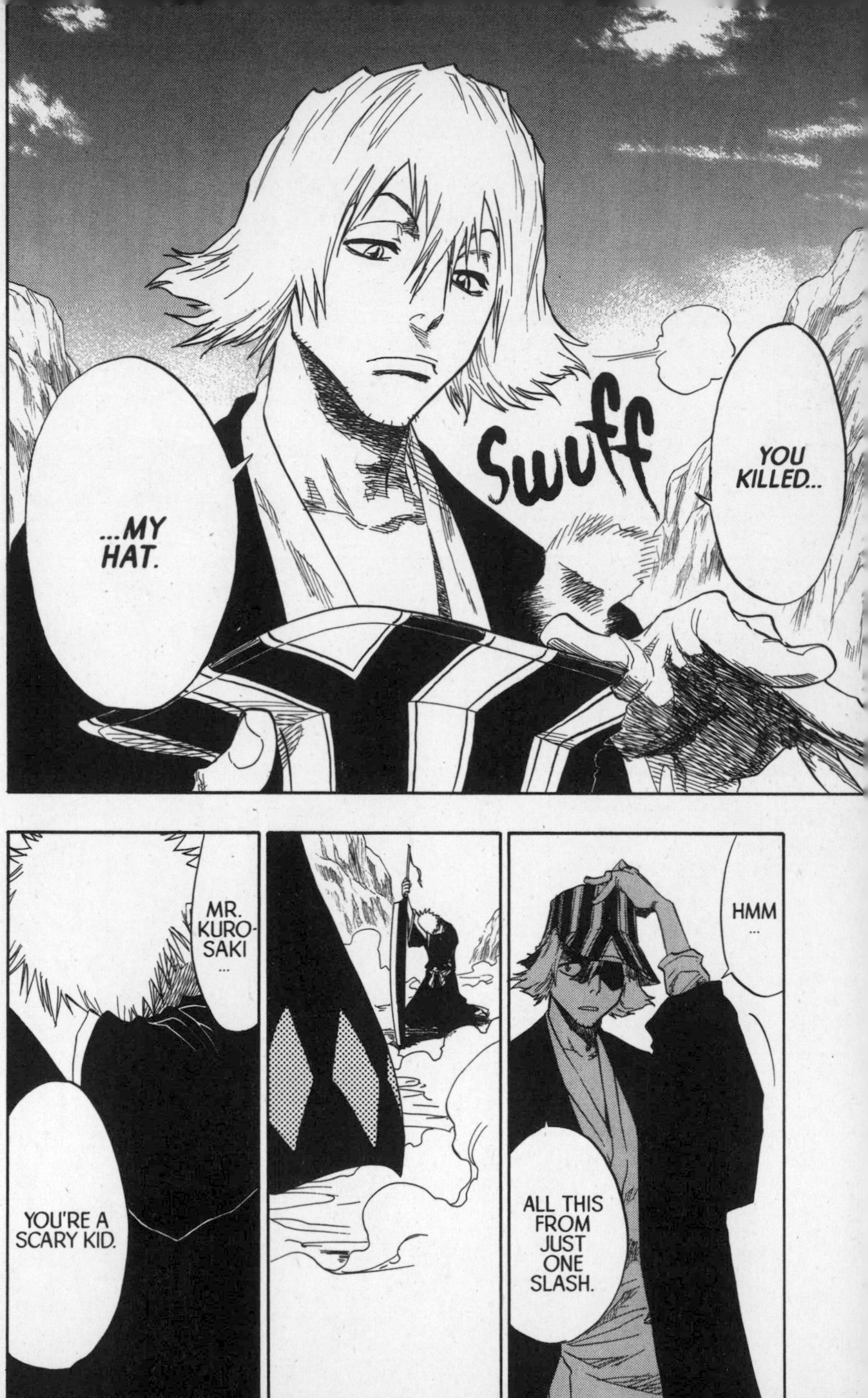
YOU KILLED...
Swuff
...MY HAT.
HMM...
ALL THIS FROM JUST ONE SLASH.
MR. KURO-SAKI...
YOU'RE A SCARY KID.

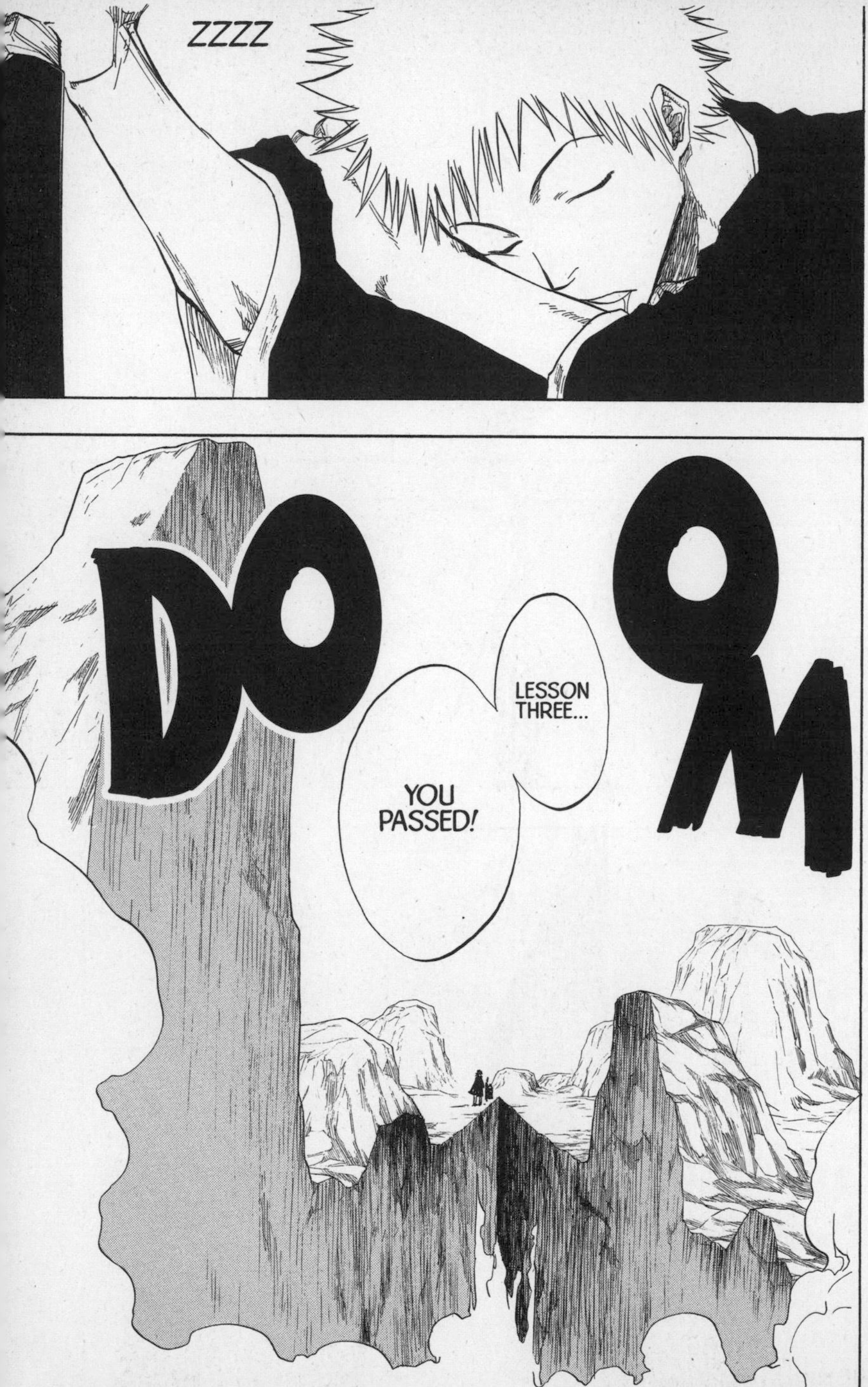
ZZZZ
DOOM
LESSON THREE...
YOU PASSED!

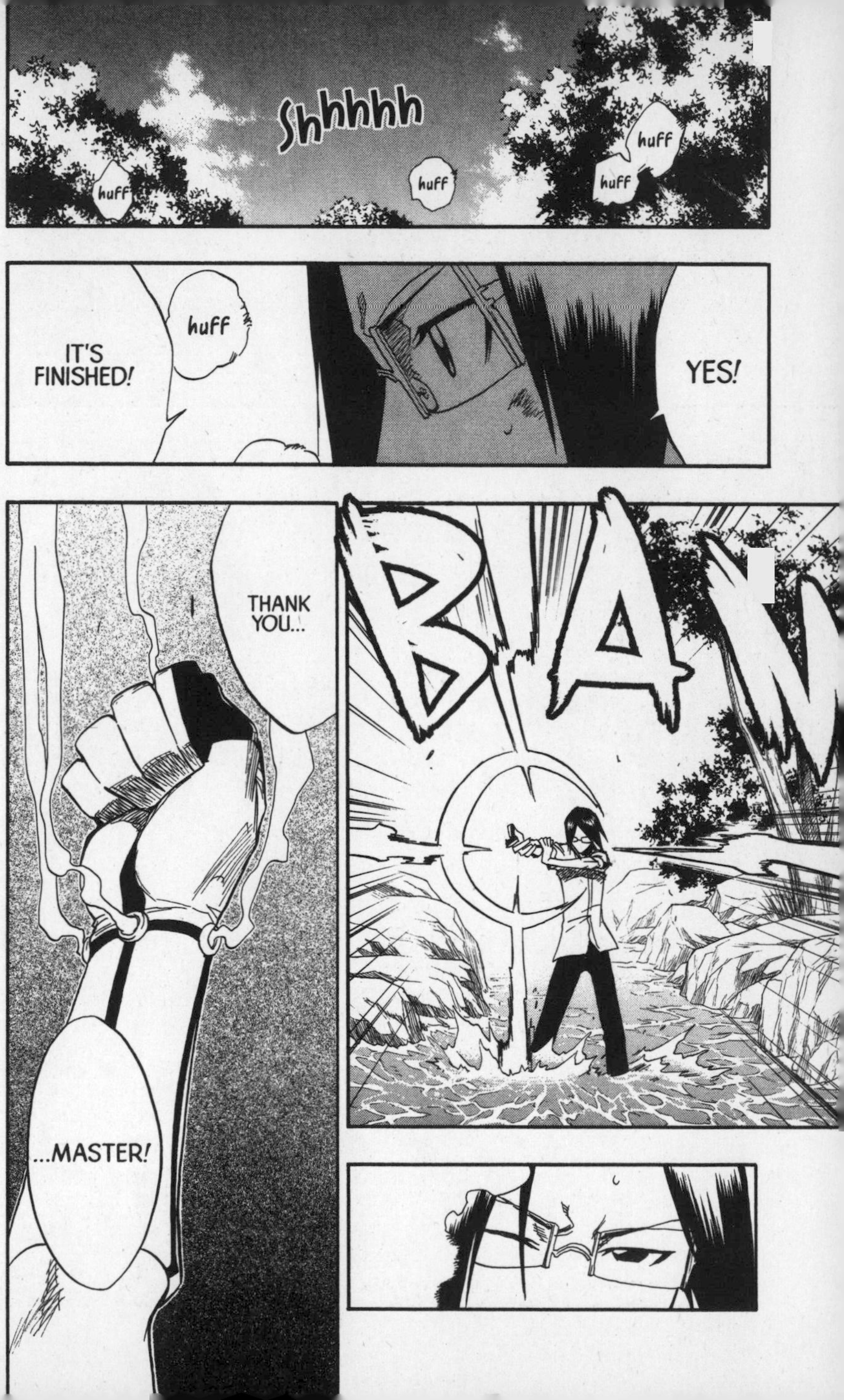

Shhhhh
huff
huff
huff
huff
YES!
huff
IT'S FINISHED!
BAM
THANK YOU...
...MASTER!

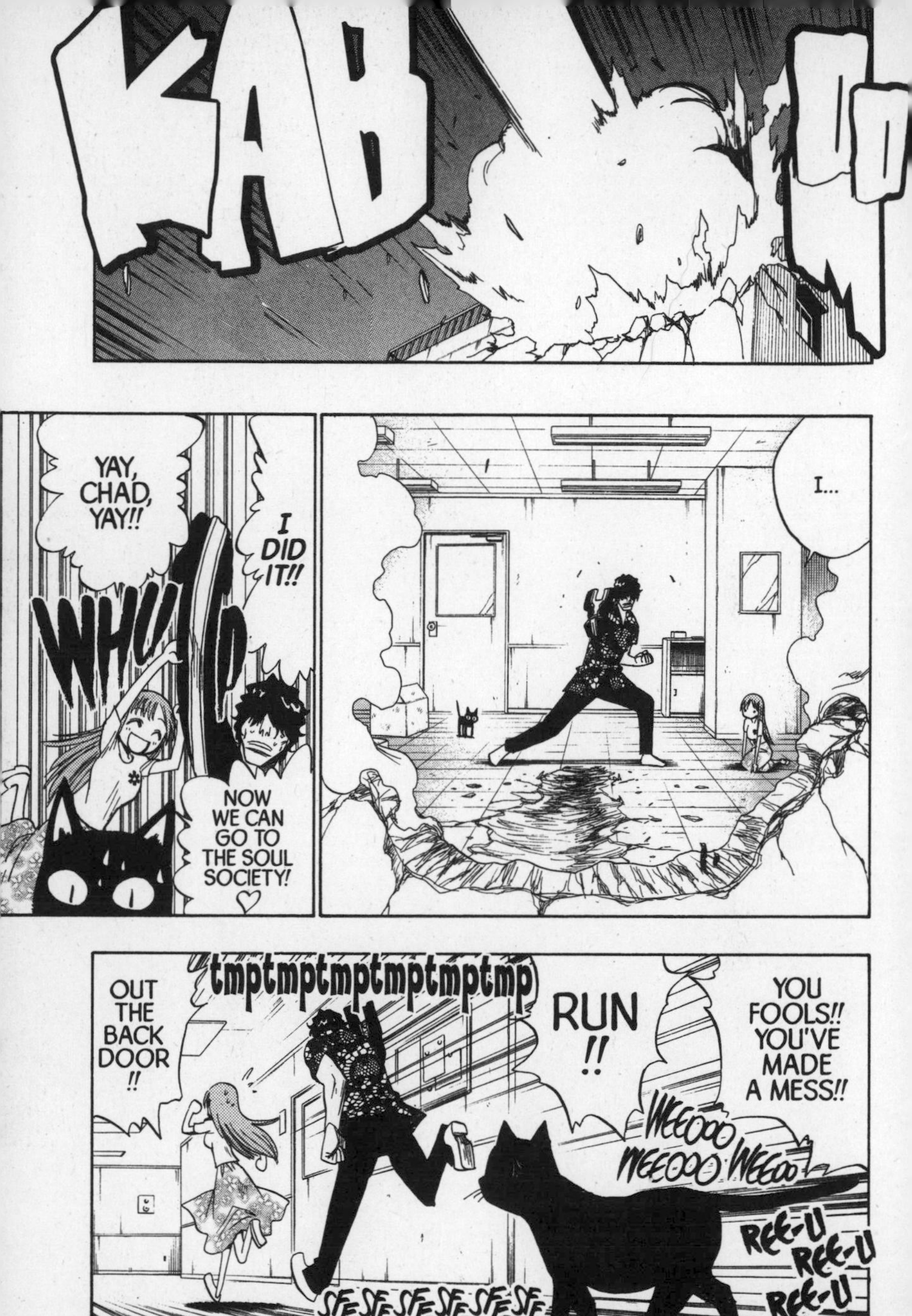
KAB
OO
I...
I DID IT!!
YAY, CHAD, YAY!!
WHUP
NOW WE CAN GO TO THE SOUL SOCIETY! ♡
YOU FOOLS!! YOU'VE MADE A MESS!!
RUN!!
tmptmptmptmptmptmp
OUT THE BACK DOOR!!
WEEOOO WEEOOO WEEOO
REE-U REE-U REE-U
SFF SFF SFF SFF SFF SFF

PEOPLE WHO ARE IN DEEP MUD IF ICHIGO IS GONE

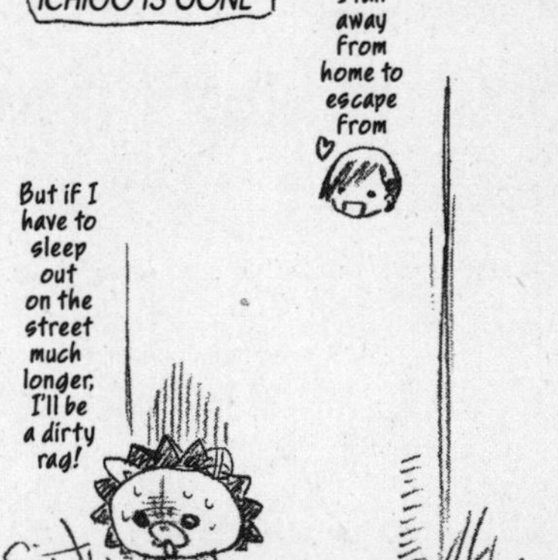
I ran away from home to escape from
But if I have to sleep out on the street much longer, I'll be a dirty rag!

68. The Last Summer Vacation

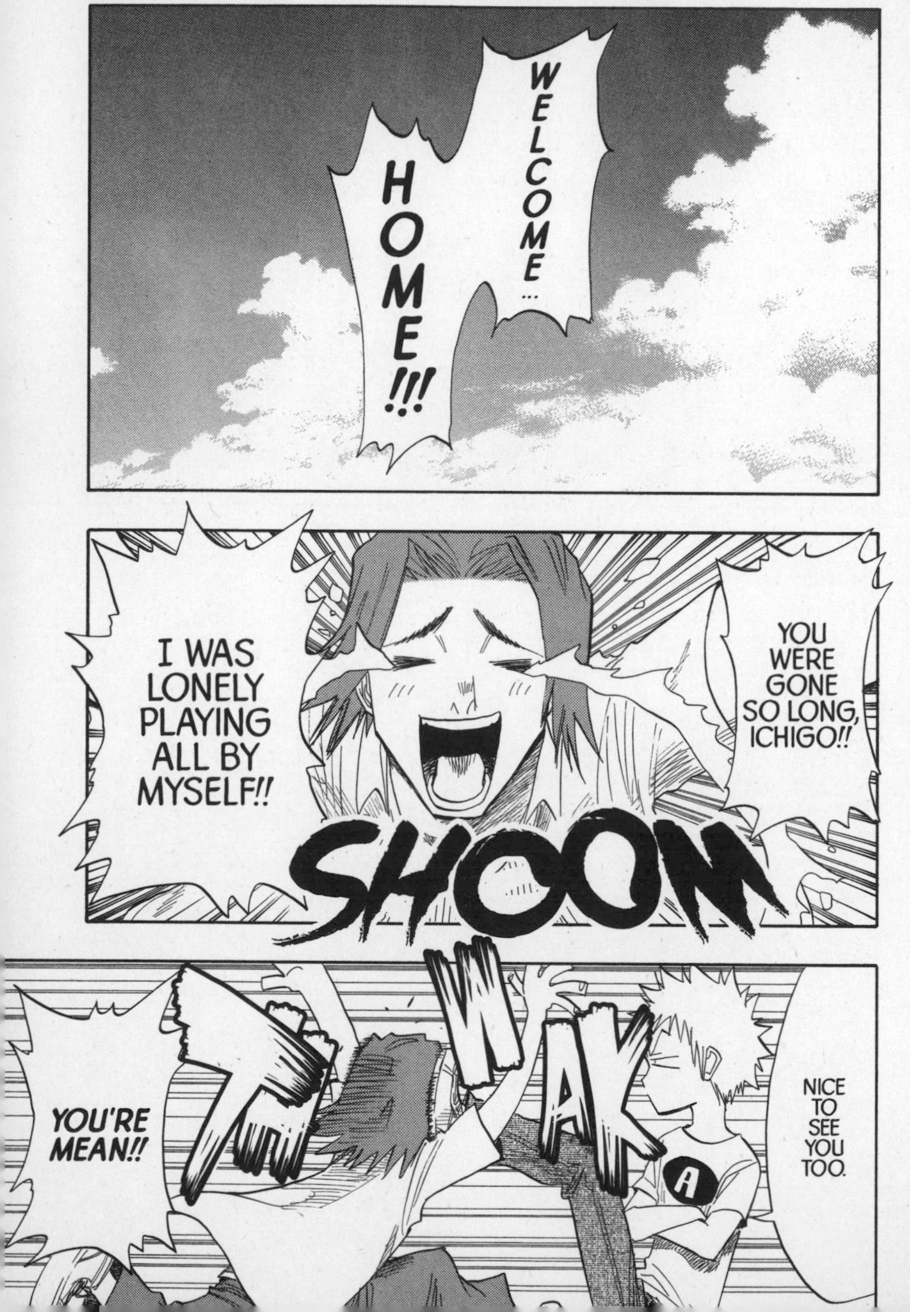
WELCOME...
HOME!!!
YOU WERE GONE SO LONG, ICHIGO!!
I WAS LONELY PLAYING ALL BY MYSELF!!
SHOOM
NICE TO SEE YOU TOO.
YOU'RE MEAN!!

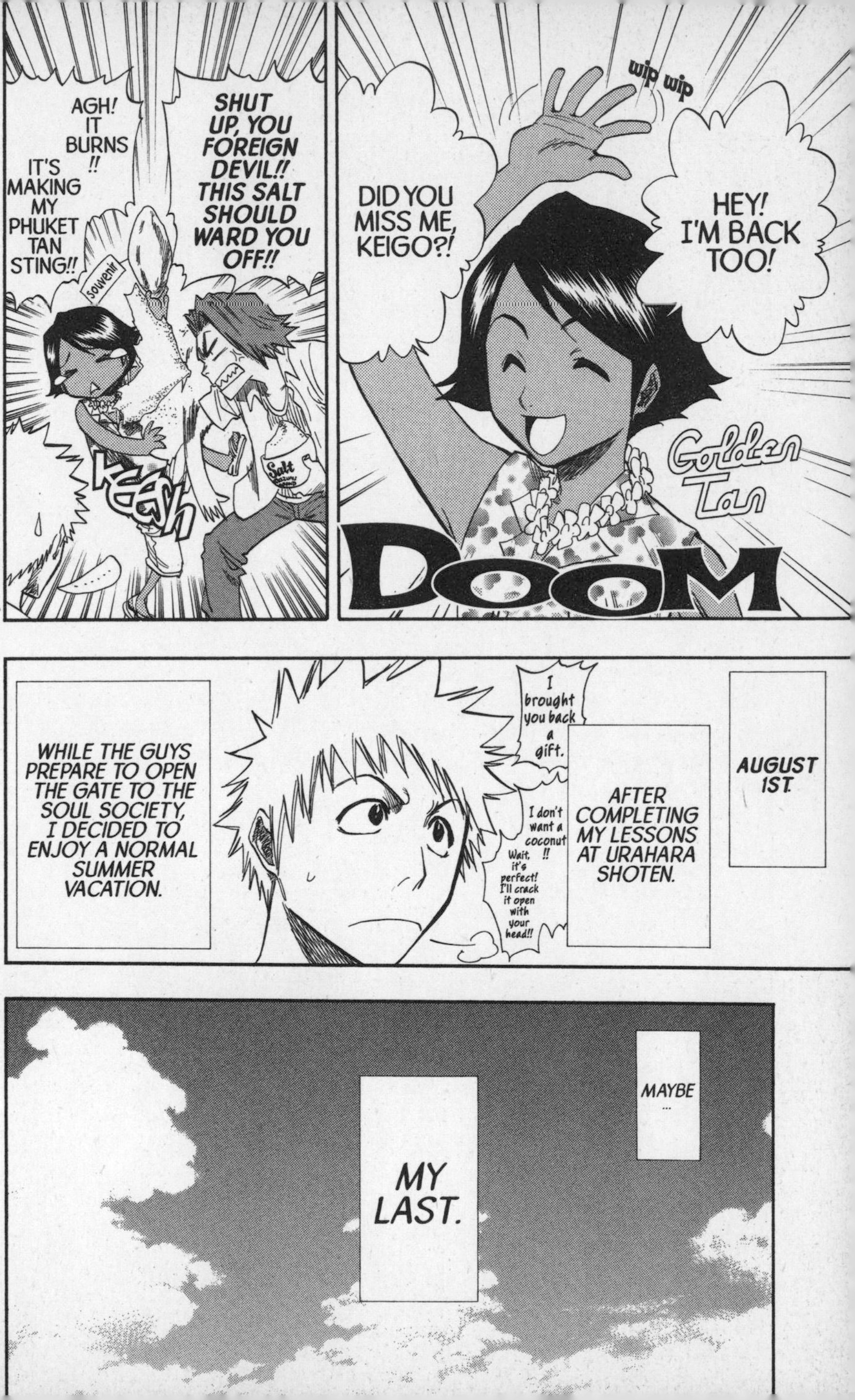
wip wip
HEY! I'M BACK TOO!
DID YOU MISS ME, KEIGO?!
Golden Tan
DOOM
SHUT UP, YOU FOREIGN DEVIL!! THIS SALT SHOULD WARD YOU OFF!!
AGH! IT BURNS!!
IT'S MAKING MY PHUKET TAN STING!!
Souvenir
Salt
KEESH
AUGUST 1ST.
AFTER COMPLETING MY LESSONS AT URAHARA SHOTEN.
I brought you back a gift.
I don't want a coconut!!
Wait, it's perfect! I'll crack it open with your head!!
WHILE THE GUYS PREPARE TO OPEN THE GATE TO THE SOUL SOCIETY, I DECIDED TO ENJOY A NORMAL SUMMER VACATION.
MAYBE...
MY LAST.

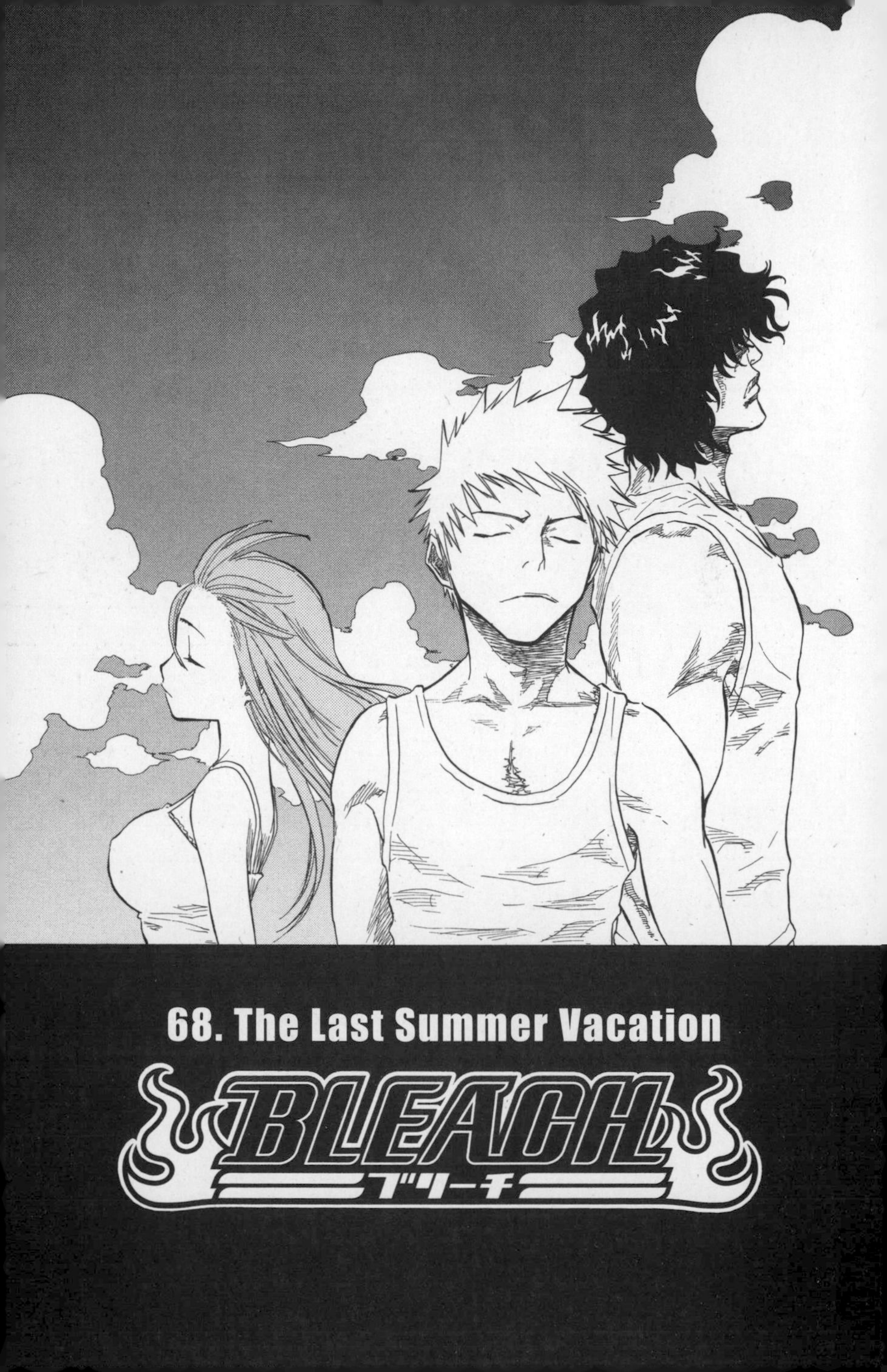

68. The Last Summer Vacation

BLEACH ブリーチ

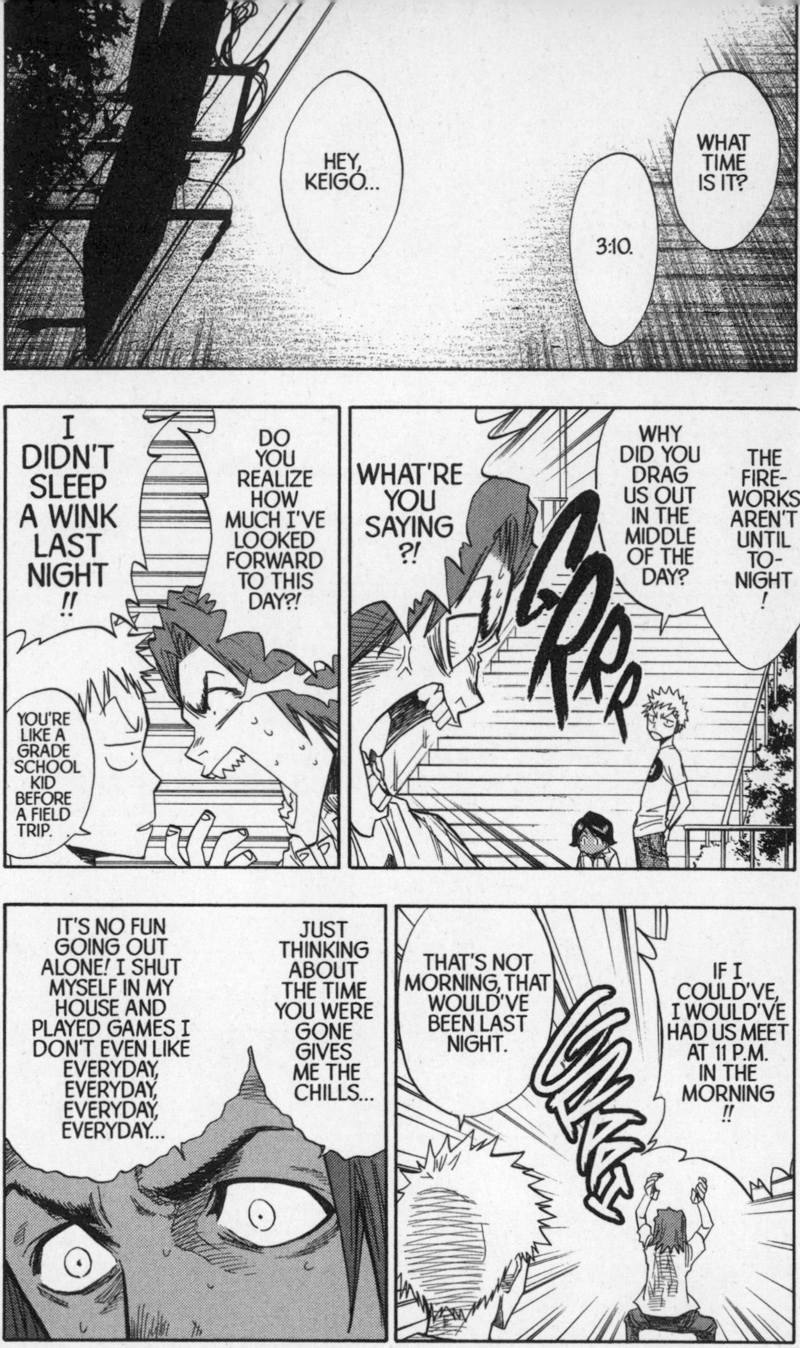
WHAT TIME IS IT?
3:10.
HEY, KEIGO...
THE FIRE-WORKS AREN'T UNTIL TO-NIGHT!
WHY DID YOU DRAG US OUT IN THE MIDDLE OF THE DAY?
GRRR
WHAT'RE YOU SAYING?!
DO YOU REALIZE HOW MUCH I'VE LOOKED FORWARD TO THIS DAY?!
I DIDN'T SLEEP A WINK LAST NIGHT!!
YOU'RE LIKE A GRADE SCHOOL KID BEFORE A FIELD TRIP.
IF I COULD'VE, I WOULD'VE HAD US MEET AT 11 P.M. IN THE MORNING!!
THAT'S NOT MORNING, THAT WOULD'VE BEEN LAST NIGHT.
JUST THINKING ABOUT THE TIME YOU WERE GONE GIVES ME THE CHILLS...
IT'S NO FUN GOING OUT ALONE! I SHUT MYSELF IN MY HOUSE AND PLAYED GAMES I DON'T EVEN LIKE EVERYDAY, EVERYDAY, EVERYDAY, EVERYDAY...

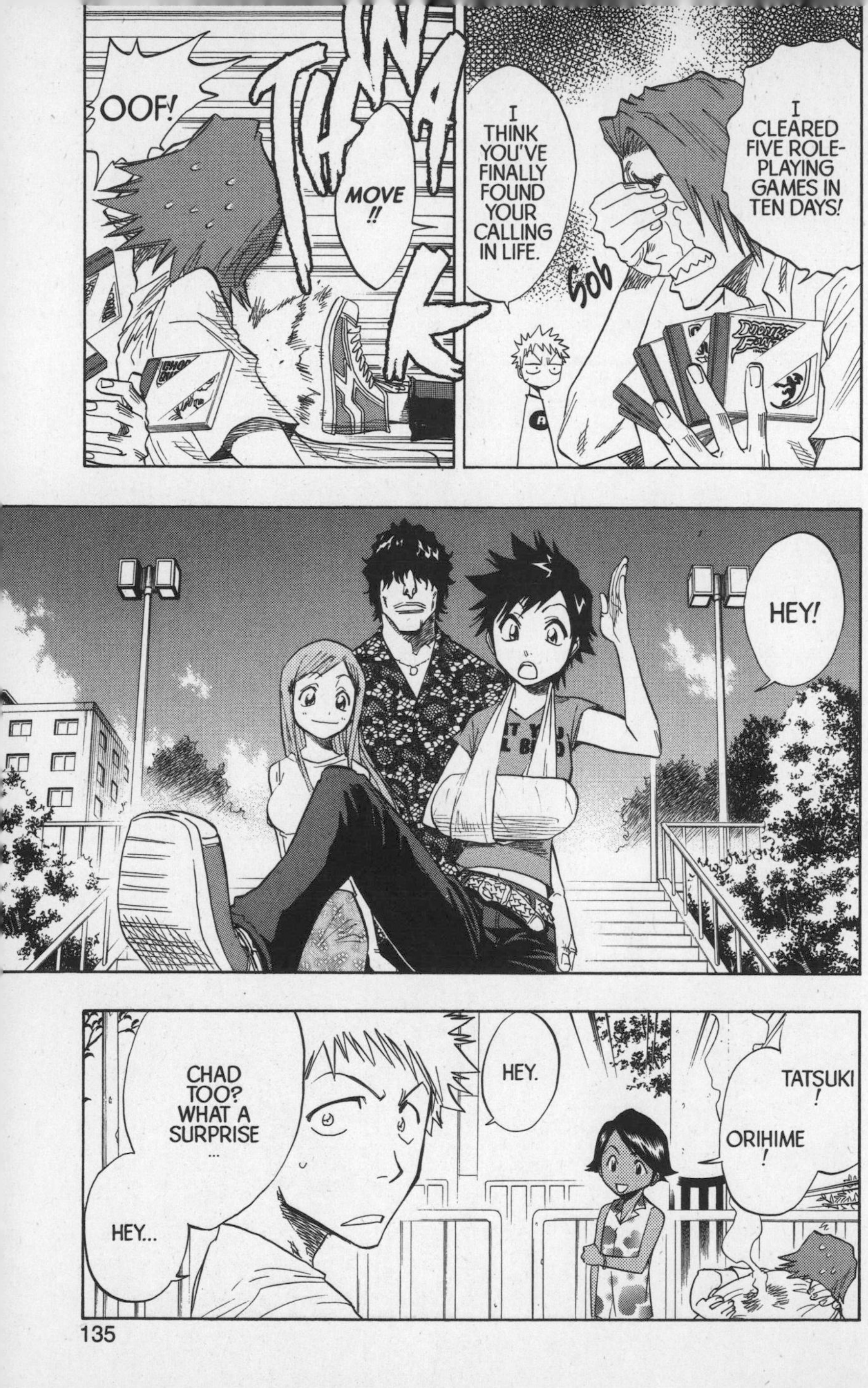
I CLEARED FIVE ROLE-PLAYING GAMES IN TEN DAYS!
Sob
I THINK YOU'VE FINALLY FOUND YOUR CALLING IN LIFE.
MOVE!!
OOF!
HEY!
TATSUKI!
ORIHIME!
HEY.
CHAD TOO? WHAT A SURPRISE...
HEY...

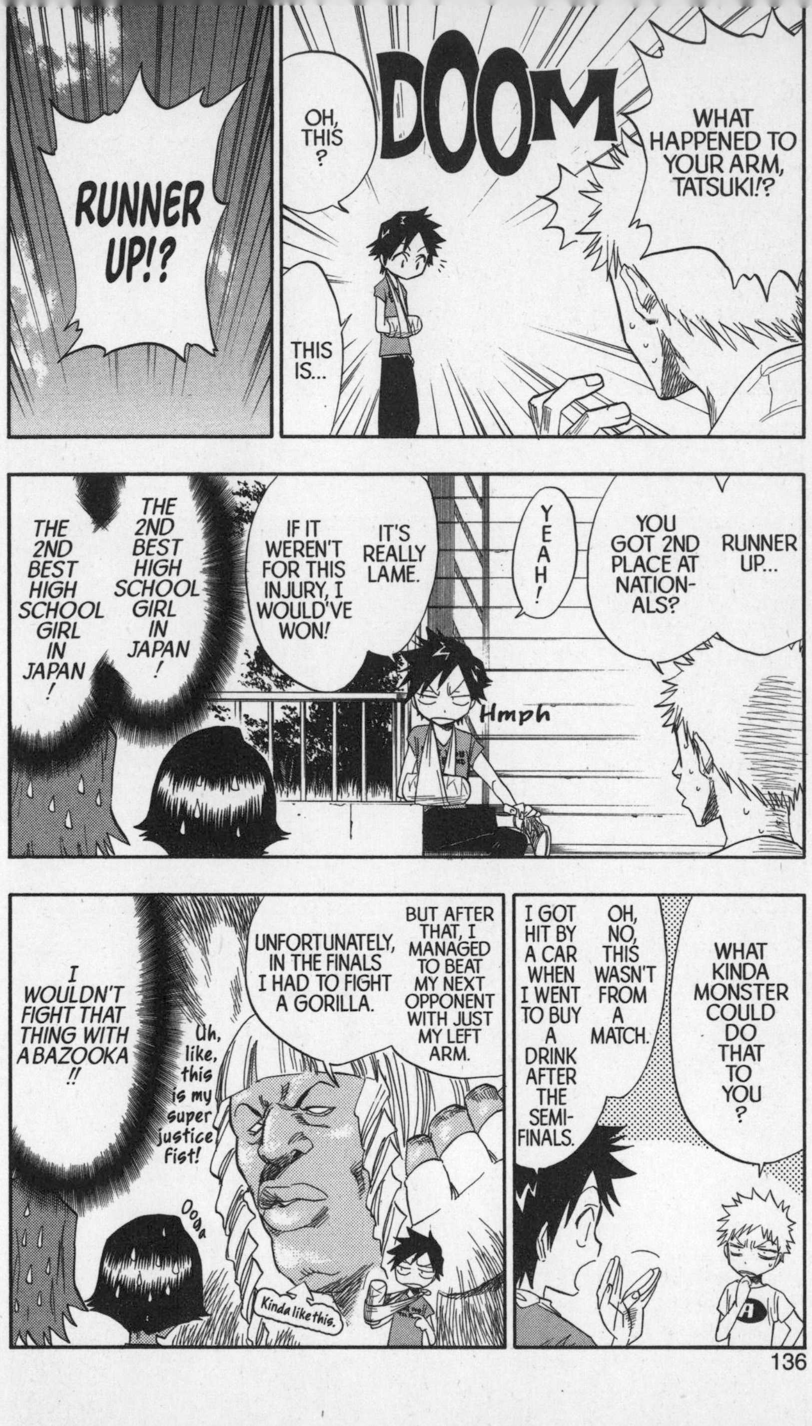
WHAT HAPPENED TO YOUR ARM, TATSUKI!?
DOOM
OH, THIS?
THIS IS...
RUNNER UP!?
RUNNER UP...
YOU GOT 2ND PLACE AT NATION-ALS?
YEAH!
IT'S REALLY LAME.
IF IT WEREN'T FOR THIS INJURY, I WOULD'VE WON!
Hmph
THE 2ND BEST HIGH SCHOOL GIRL IN JAPAN!
THE 2ND BEST HIGH SCHOOL GIRL IN JAPAN!
WHAT KINDA MONSTER COULD DO THAT TO YOU?
OH, NO, THIS WASN'T FROM A MATCH.
I GOT HIT BY A CAR WHEN I WENT TO BUY A DRINK AFTER THE SEMI-FINALS.
BUT AFTER THAT, I MANAGED TO BEAT MY NEXT OPPONENT WITH JUST MY LEFT ARM.
UNFORTUNATELY, IN THE FINALS I HAD TO FIGHT A GORILLA.
Uh, like, this is my super justice fist!
Kinda like this.
Ooga
I WOULDN'T FIGHT THAT THING WITH A BAZOOKA!!

READ THIS WAY

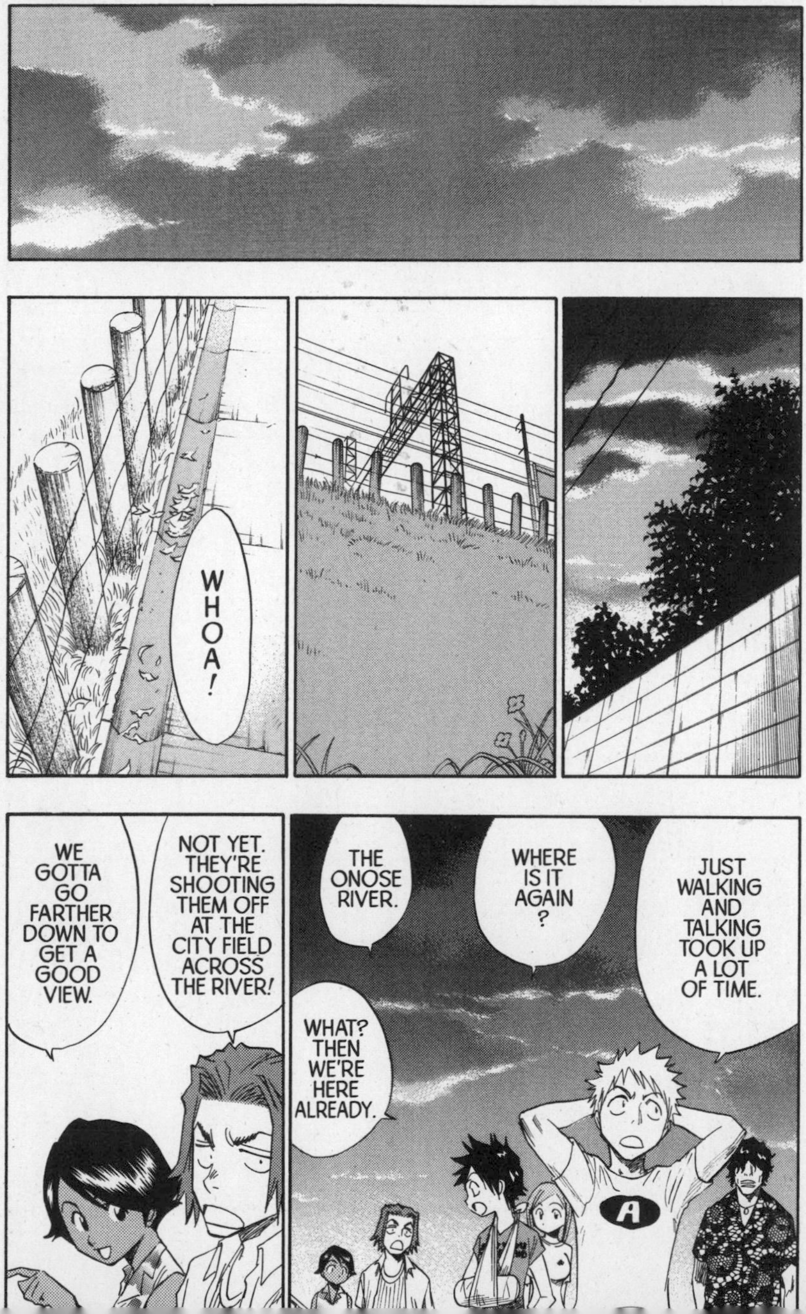
WHOA!
JUST WALKING AND TALKING TOOK UP A LOT OF TIME.
WHERE IS IT AGAIN?
THE ONOSE RIVER.
WHAT? THEN WE'RE HERE ALREADY.
NOT YET. THEY'RE SHOOTING THEM OFF AT THE CITY FIELD ACROSS THE RIVER!
WE GOTTA GO FARTHER DOWN TO GET A GOOD VIEW.

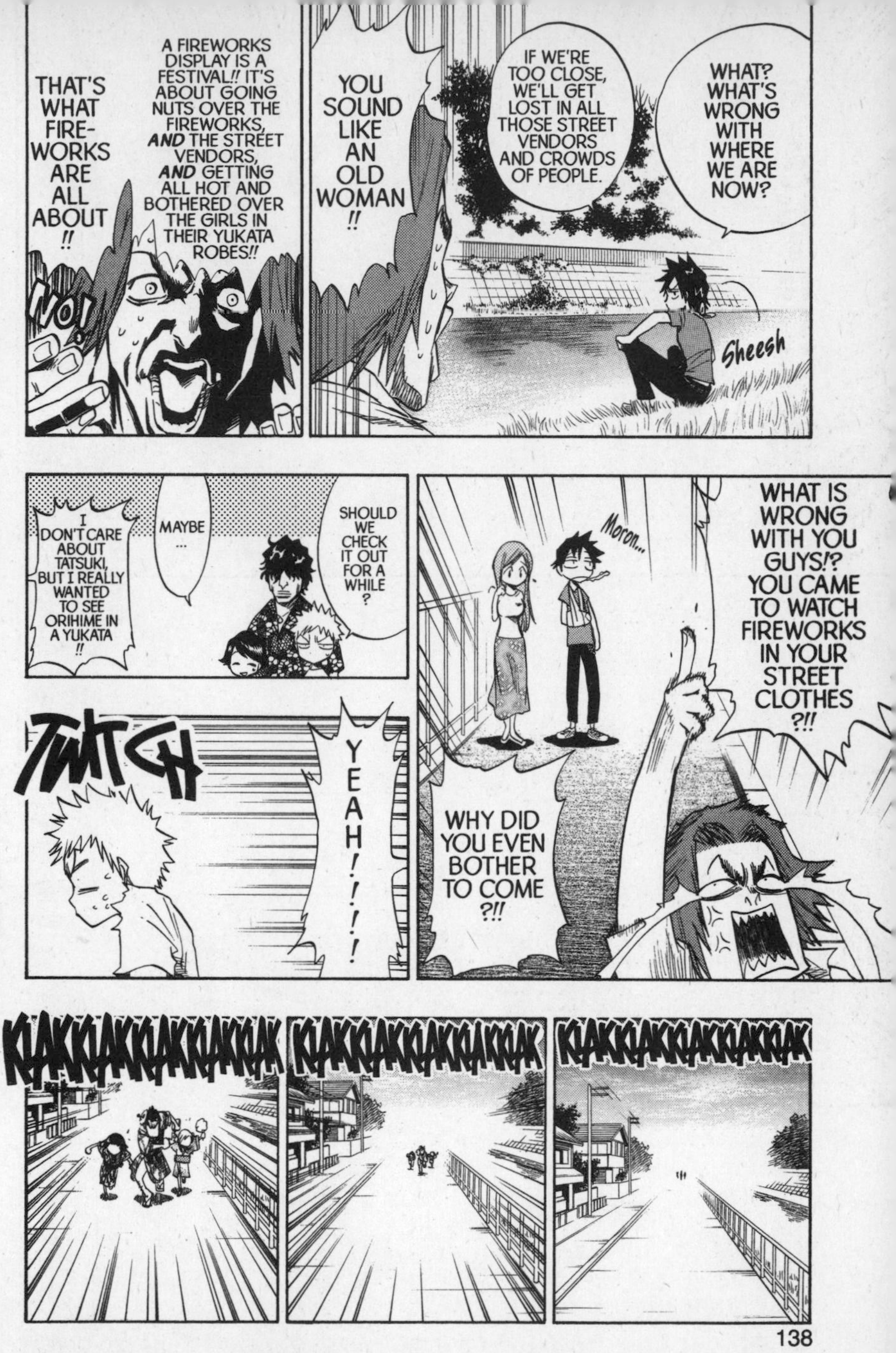
WHAT? WHAT'S WRONG WITH WHERE WE ARE NOW?
IF WE'RE TOO CLOSE, WE'LL GET LOST IN ALL THOSE STREET VENDORS AND CROWDS OF PEOPLE.
Sheesh
YOU SOUND LIKE AN OLD WOMAN!!
A FIREWORKS DISPLAY IS A FESTIVAL!! IT'S ABOUT GOING NUTS OVER THE FIREWORKS, AND THE STREET VENDORS, AND GETTING ALL HOT AND BOTHERED OVER THE GIRLS IN THEIR YUKATA ROBES!!
THAT'S WHAT FIRE-WORKS ARE ALL ABOUT!!
NO!
WHAT IS WRONG WITH YOU GUYS!? YOU CAME TO WATCH FIREWORKS IN YOUR STREET CLOTHES?!!
Moron...
WHY DID YOU EVEN BOTHER TO COME?!!
SHOULD WE CHECK IT OUT FOR A WHILE?
MAYBE...
I DON'T CARE ABOUT TATSUKI, BUT I REALLY WANTED TO SEE ORIHIME IN A YUKATA!!
YEAH!!!!
TWITCH
KLAKKLAKKLAKKLAKKLAK
KLAKKLAKKLAKKLAKKLAK
KLAKKLAKKLAKKLAKKLAK

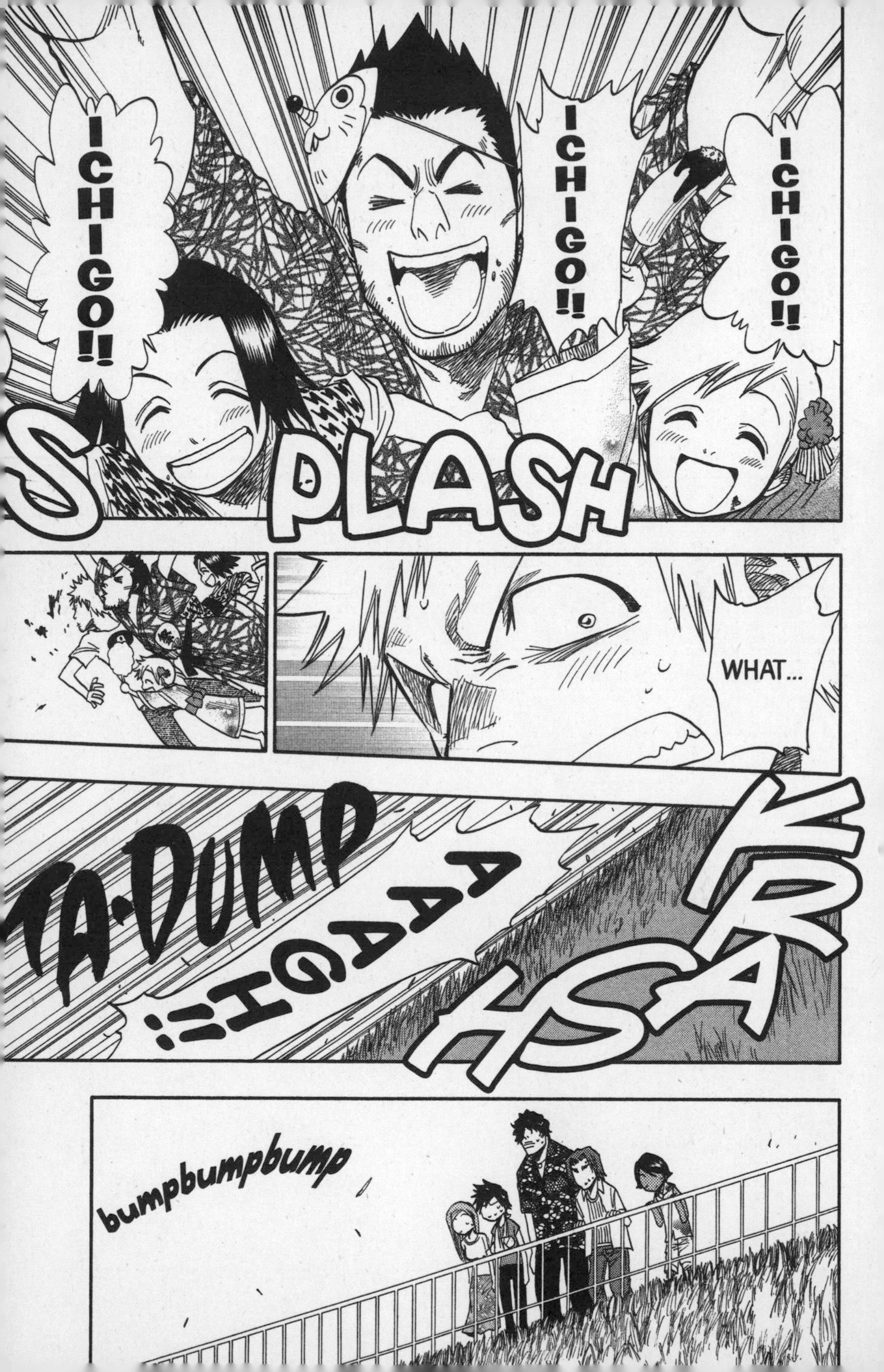
ICHIGO!!
ICHIGO!!
ICHIGO!!
SPLASH
WHAT...
KYRASH
TA-DUMP
bumpbumpbump

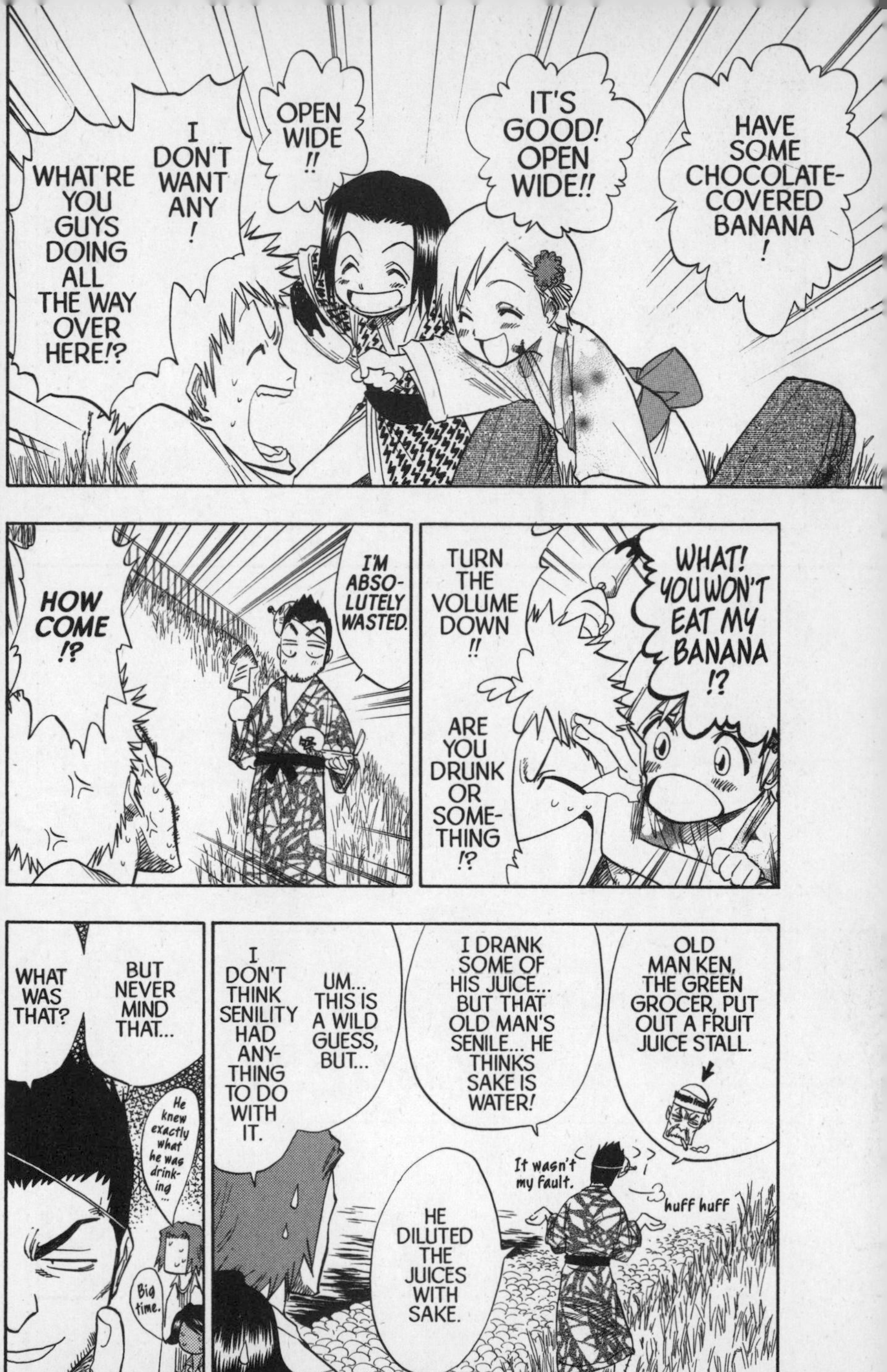
HAVE SOME CHOCOLATE-COVERED BANANA!
IT'S GOOD! OPEN WIDE!!
OPEN WIDE!!
I DON'T WANT ANY!
WHAT'RE YOU GUYS DOING ALL THE WAY OVER HERE!?
WHAT! YOU WON'T EAT MY BANANA!?
TURN THE VOLUME DOWN!!
ARE YOU DRUNK OR SOMETHING!?
I'M ABSOLUTELY WASTED.
HOW COME!?
OLD MAN KEN, THE GREEN GROCER, PUT OUT A FRUIT JUICE STALL.
huff huff
It wasn't my fault.
I DRANK SOME OF HIS JUICE... BUT THAT OLD MAN'S SENILE... HE THINKS SAKE IS WATER!
UM... THIS IS A WILD GUESS, BUT...
I DON'T THINK SENILITY HAD ANYTHING TO DO WITH IT.
HE DILUTED THE JUICES WITH SAKE.
BUT NEVER MIND THAT...
WHAT WAS THAT?
He knew exactly what he was drinking...
Big time.

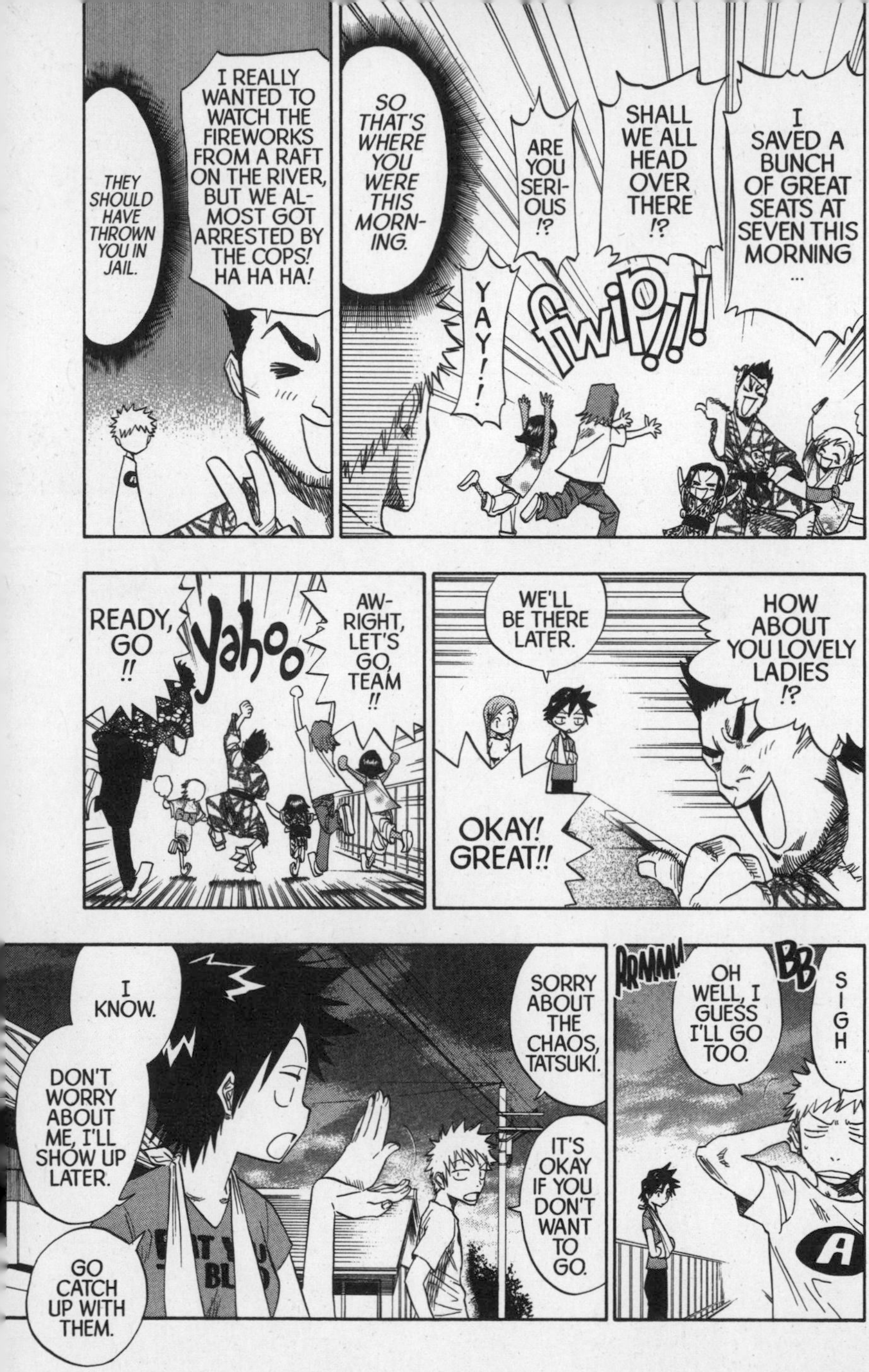
I SAVED A BUNCH OF GREAT SEATS AT SEVEN THIS MORNING ...
SHALL WE ALL HEAD OVER THERE !?
ARE YOU SERI-OUS !?
SO THAT'S WHERE YOU WERE THIS MORN-ING.
fwip!!!
YAY!!!
I REALLY WANTED TO WATCH THE FIREWORKS FROM A RAFT ON THE RIVER, BUT WE AL-MOST GOT ARRESTED BY THE COPS! HA HA HA!
THEY SHOULD HAVE THROWN YOU IN JAIL.
HOW ABOUT YOU LOVELY LADIES !?
WE'LL BE THERE LATER.
OKAY! GREAT!!
AW-RIGHT, LET'S GO, TEAM !!
yahoo
READY, GO !!
SIGH ...
RRMMMBB
OH WELL, I GUESS I'LL GO TOO.
SORRY ABOUT THE CHAOS, TATSUKI.
IT'S OKAY IF YOU DON'T WANT TO GO.
I KNOW.
DON'T WORRY ABOUT ME, I'LL SHOW UP LATER.
GO CATCH UP WITH THEM.

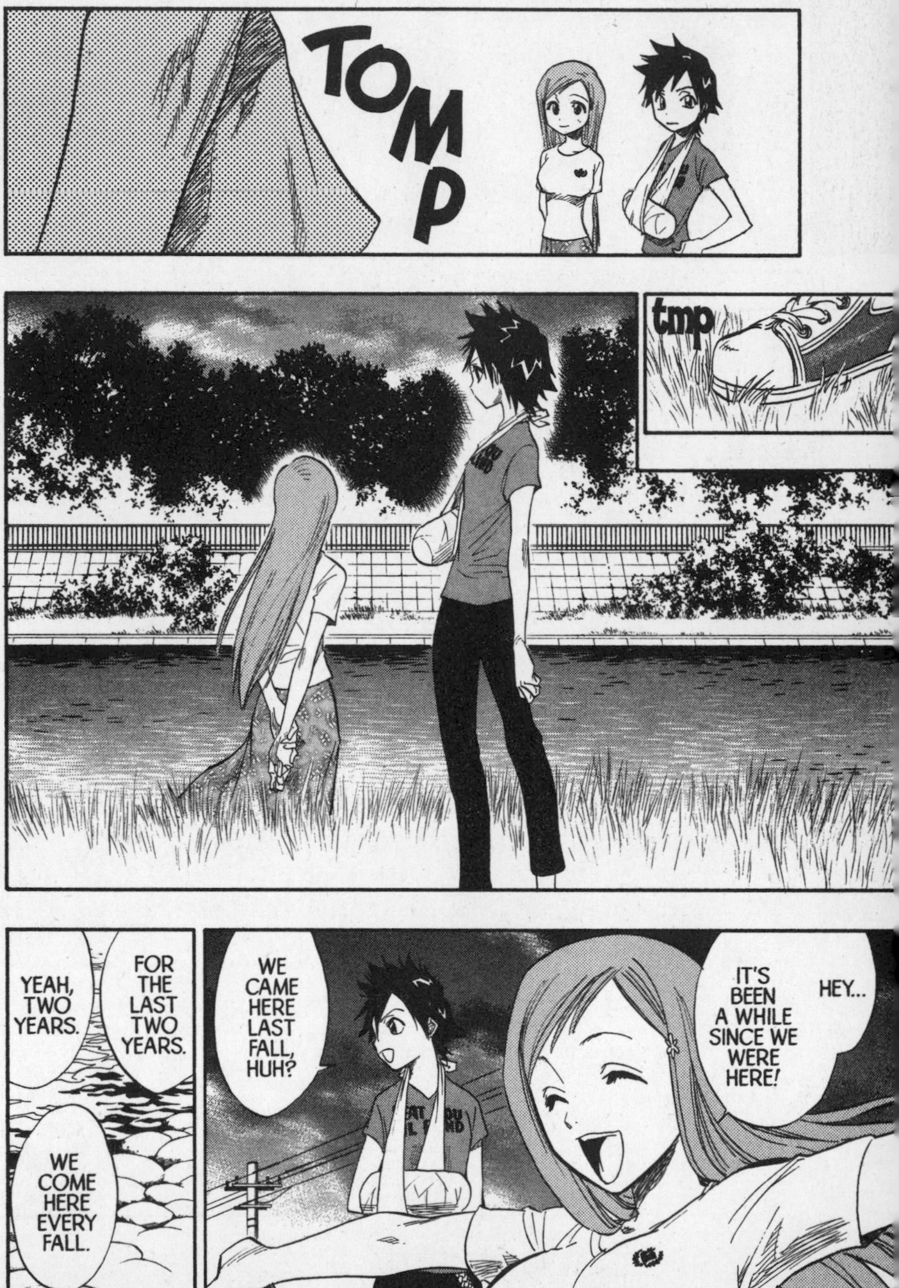
TOMP
tmp
HEY...
IT'S BEEN A WHILE SINCE WE WERE HERE!
WE CAME HERE LAST FALL, HUH?
FOR THE LAST TWO YEARS.
YEAH, TWO YEARS.
WE COME HERE EVERY FALL.

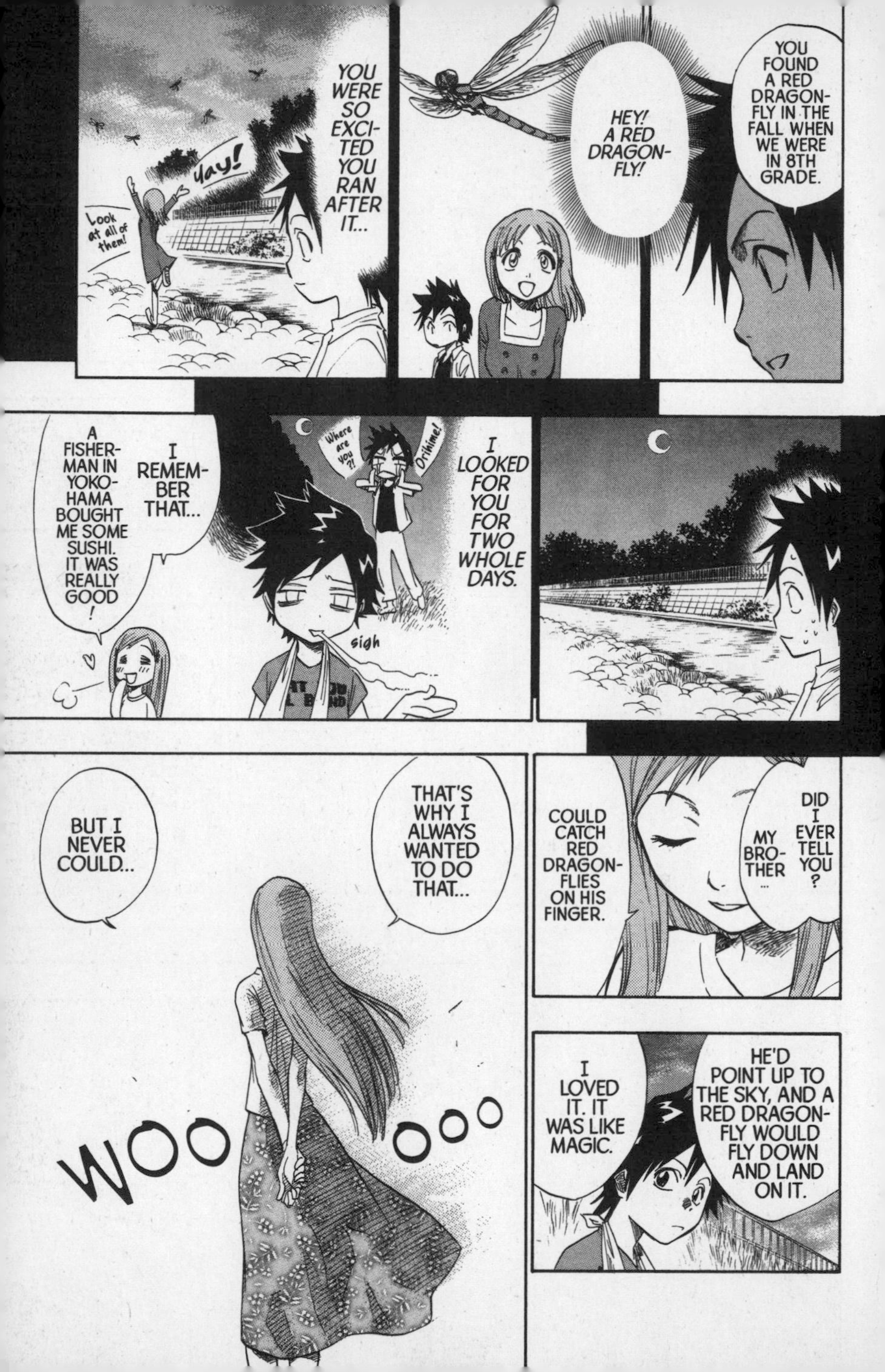
YOU FOUND A RED DRAGON-FLY IN THE FALL WHEN WE WERE IN 8TH GRADE.
HEY! A RED DRAGON-FLY!
YOU WERE SO EXCI-TED YOU RAN AFTER IT...
Yay!
Look at all of them!
I LOOKED FOR YOU FOR TWO WHOLE DAYS.
Orihime!
Where are you?!
sigh
I REMEM-BER THAT...
A FISHER-MAN IN YOKO-HAMA BOUGHT ME SOME SUSHI. IT WAS REALLY GOOD!
DID I EVER TELL YOU?
MY BRO-THER...
COULD CATCH RED DRAGON-FLIES ON HIS FINGER.
HE'D POINT UP TO THE SKY, AND A RED DRAGON-FLY WOULD FLY DOWN AND LAND ON IT.
I LOVED IT. IT WAS LIKE MAGIC.
THAT'S WHY I ALWAYS WANTED TO DO THAT...
BUT I NEVER COULD...
WOOOOO

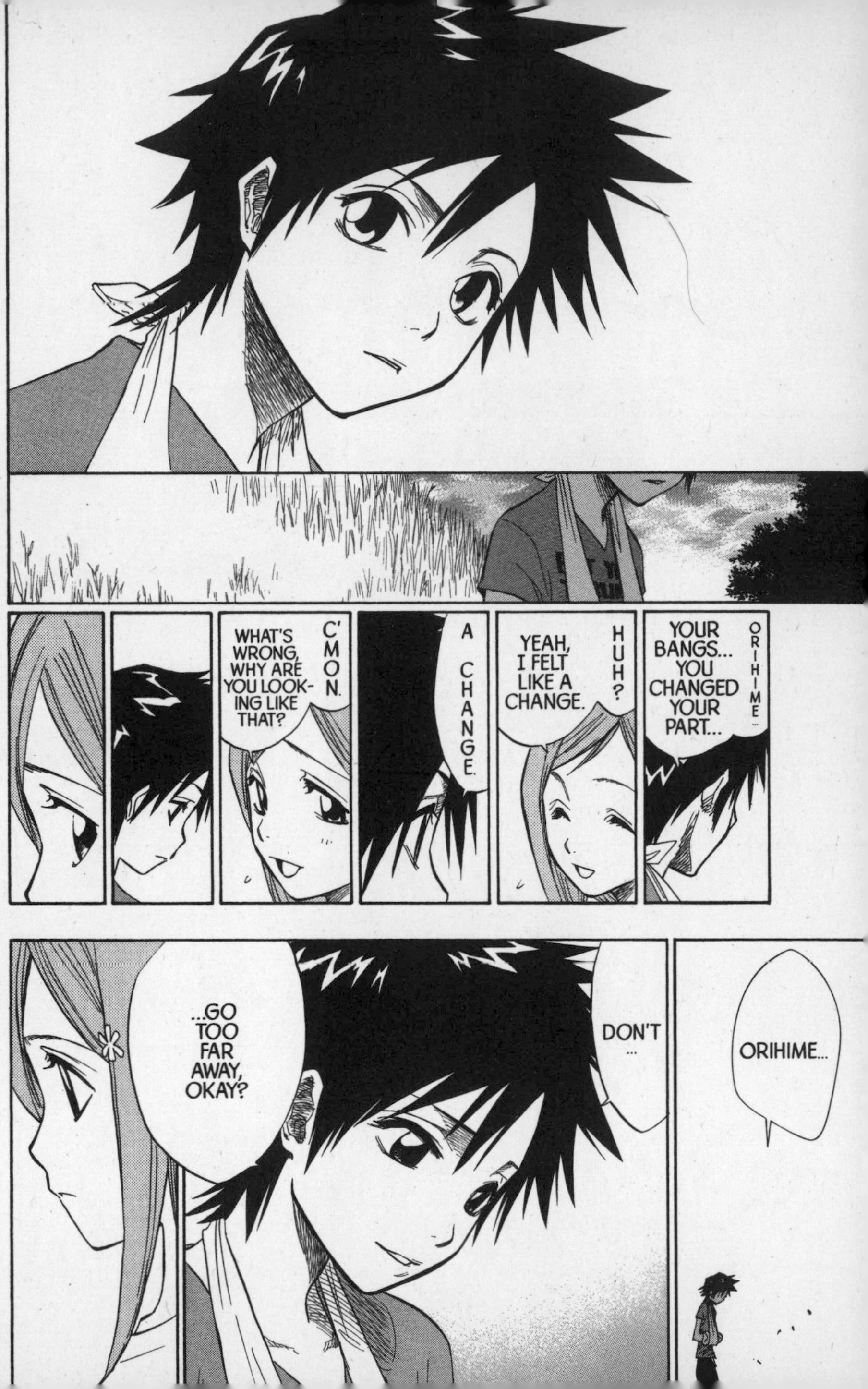
ORIHIME...
YOUR BANGS... YOU CHANGED YOUR PART...
HUH?
YEAH, I FELT LIKE A CHANGE.
A CHANGE.
C'MON.
WHAT'S WRONG, WHY ARE YOU LOOKING LIKE THAT?
ORIHIME...
DON'T...
...GO TOO FAR AWAY, OKAY?

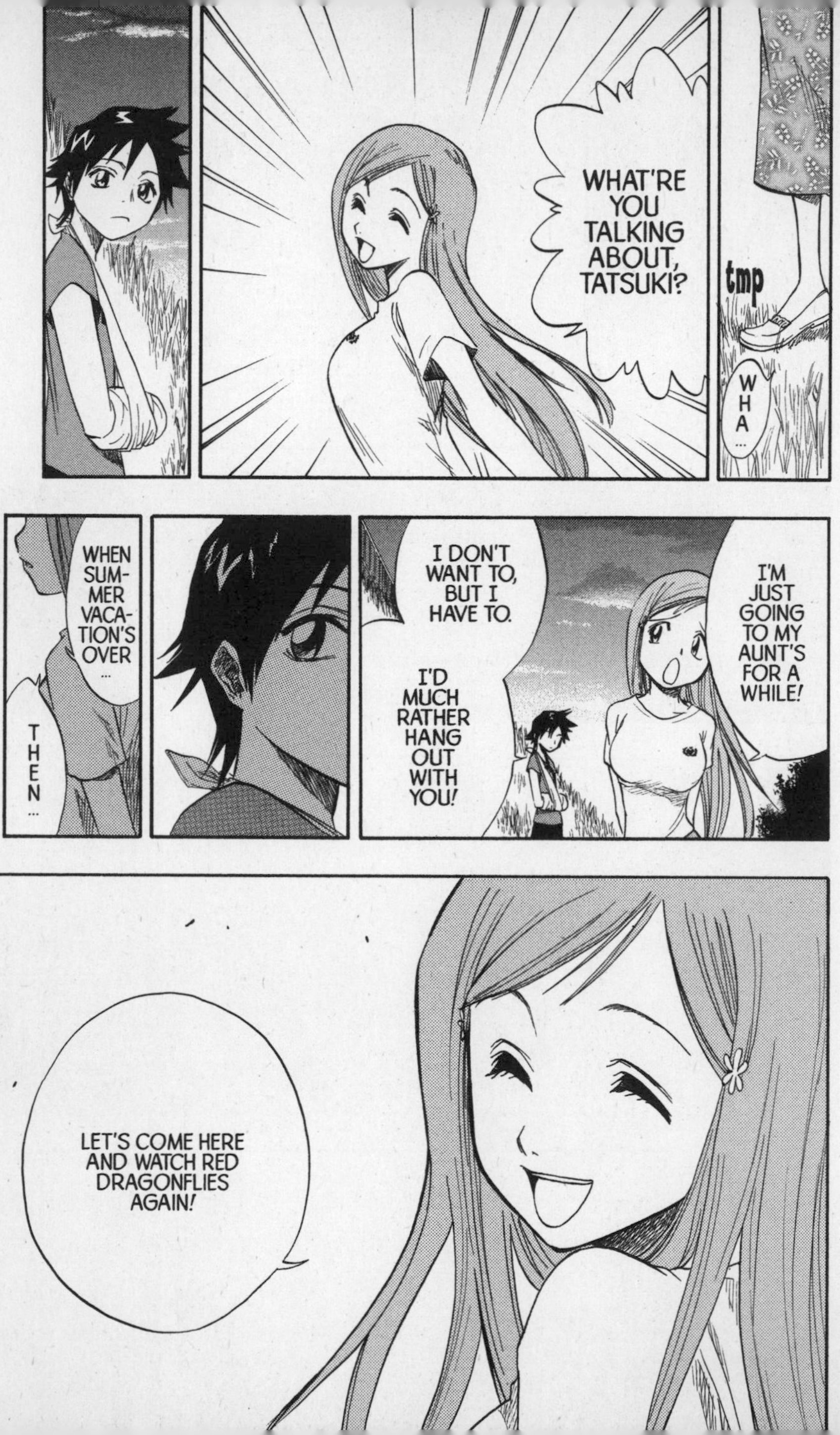
tmp
WHA...
WHAT'RE YOU TALKING ABOUT, TATSUKI?
I'M JUST GOING TO MY AUNT'S FOR A WHILE!
I DON'T WANT TO, BUT I HAVE TO.
I'D MUCH RATHER HANG OUT WITH YOU!
WHEN SUMMER VACATION'S OVER...
THEN...
LET'S COME HERE AND WATCH RED DRAGONFLIES AGAIN!

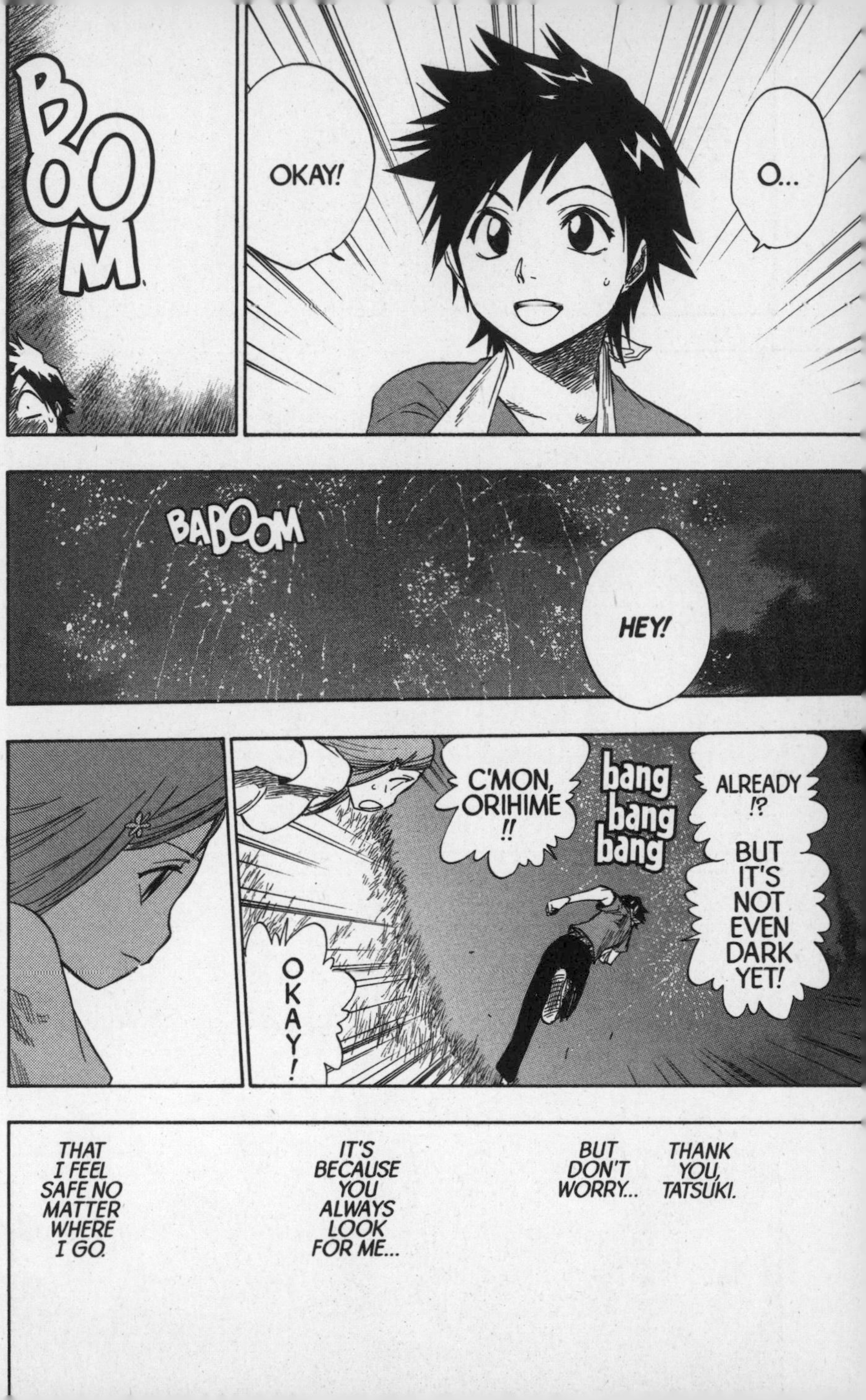
O...
OKAY!
BOOM
HEY!
BABOOM
ALREADY!? BUT IT'S NOT EVEN DARK YET!
bang bang bang
C'MON, ORIHIME!!
OKAY!
THANK YOU, TATSUKI.
BUT DON'T WORRY...
IT'S BECAUSE YOU ALWAYS LOOK FOR ME...
THAT I FEEL SAFE NO MATTER WHERE I GO.

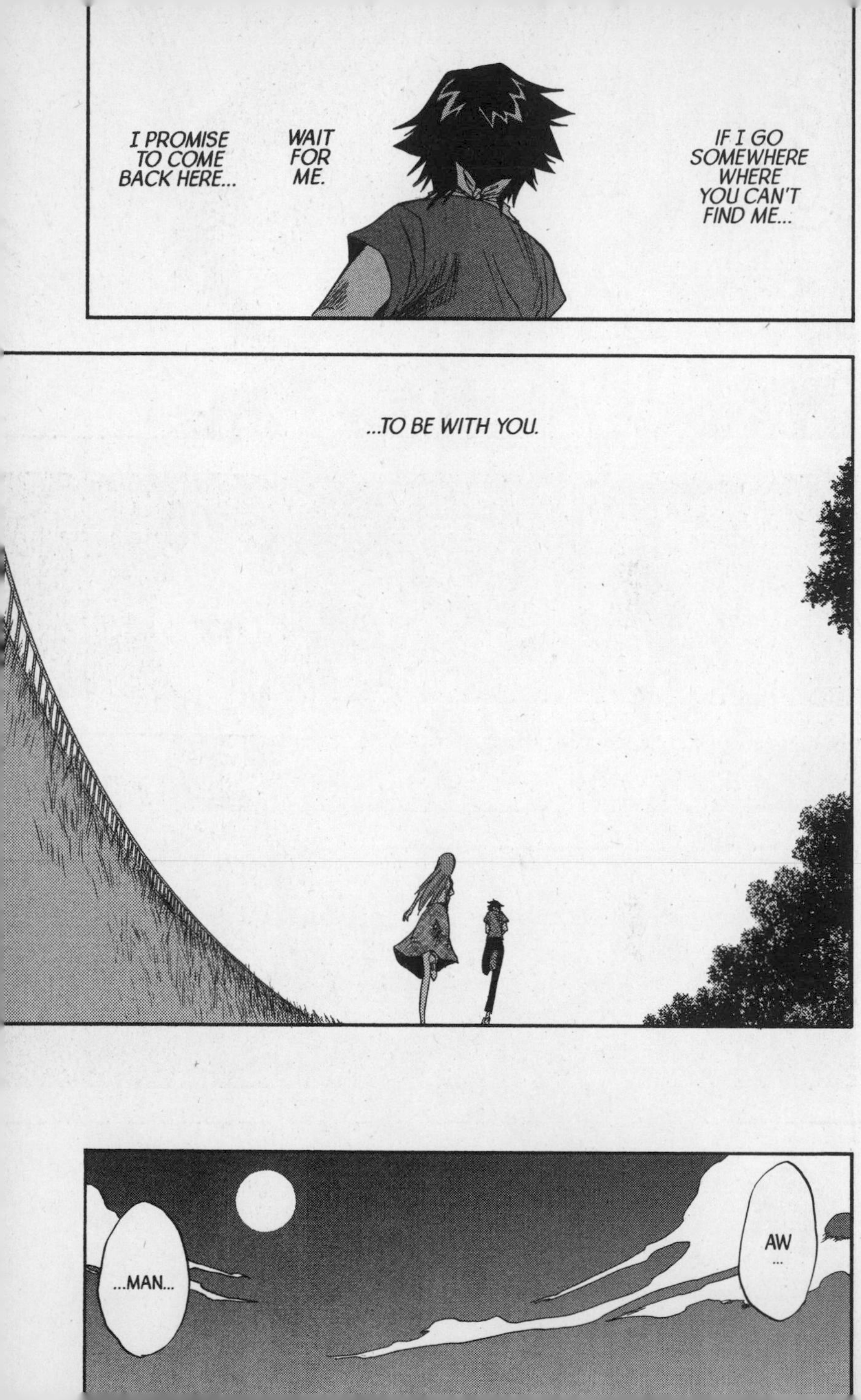
IF I GO SOMEWHERE WHERE YOU CAN'T FIND ME...
WAIT FOR ME.
I PROMISE TO COME BACK HERE...
...TO BE WITH YOU.
AW...
...MAN...

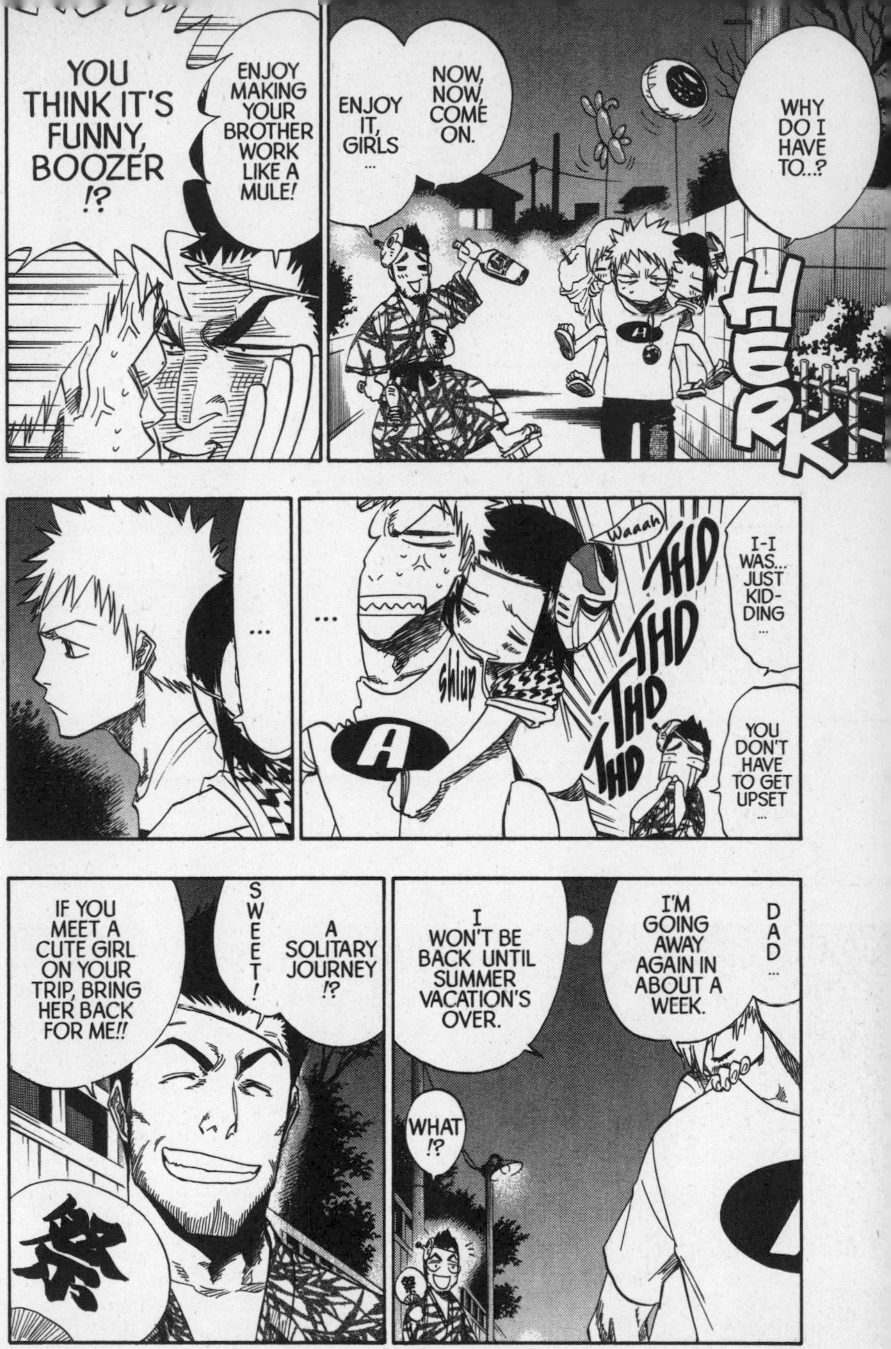
WHY DO I HAVE TO..?
HERK
NOW, NOW, COME ON.
ENJOY IT, GIRLS ...
ENJOY MAKING YOUR BROTHER WORK LIKE A MULE!
YOU THINK IT'S FUNNY, BOOZER!?
I-I WAS... JUST KID-DING ...
YOU DON'T HAVE TO GET UPSET ...
Waaah
THD THD THD THD
shlup
...
...
DAD ...
I'M GOING AWAY AGAIN IN ABOUT A WEEK.
I WON'T BE BACK UNTIL SUMMER VACATION'S OVER.
WHAT!?
A SOLITARY JOURNEY!?
SWEET!
IF YOU MEET A CUTE GIRL ON YOUR TRIP, BRING HER BACK FOR ME!!
祭

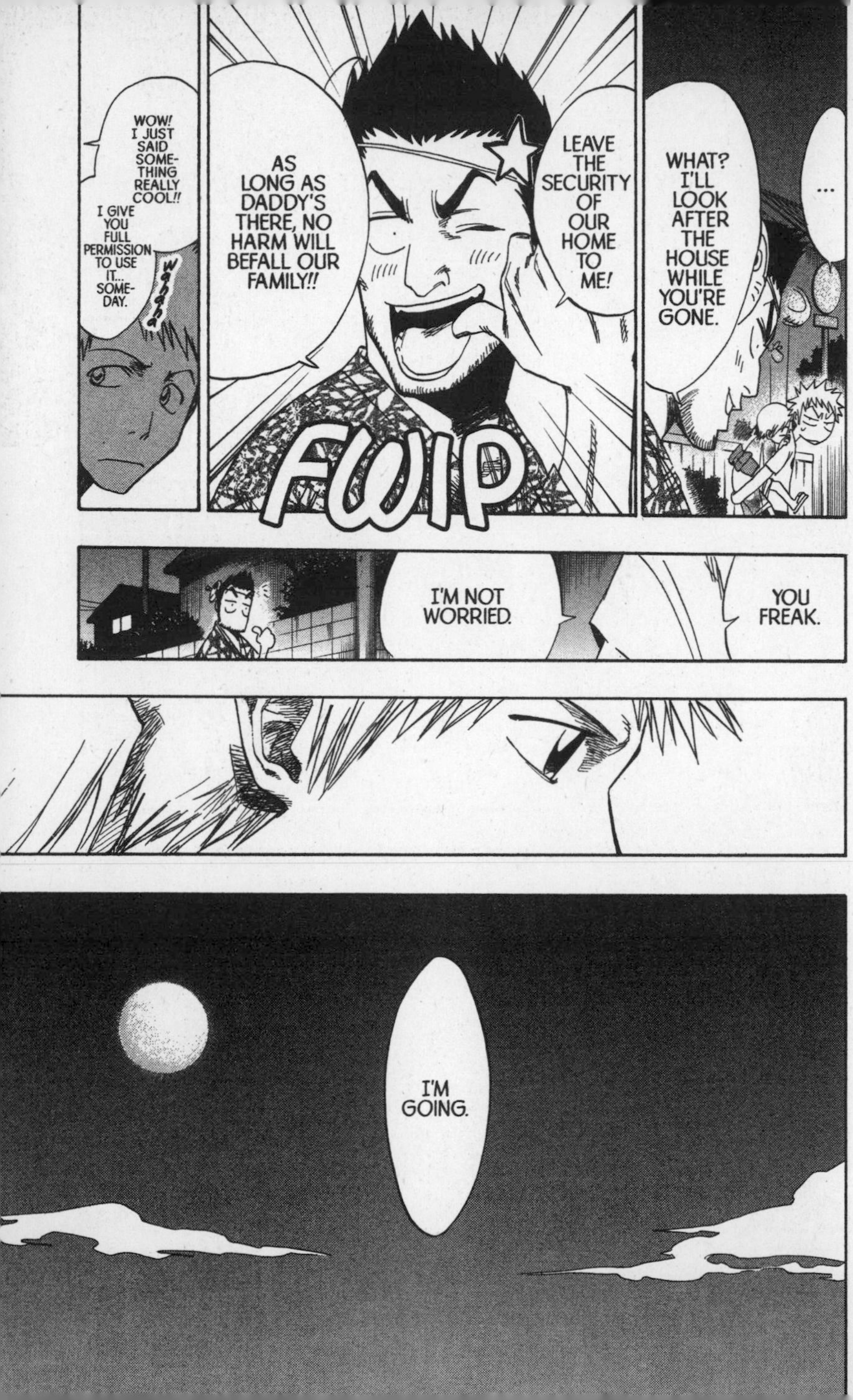
...
WHAT? I'LL LOOK AFTER THE HOUSE WHILE YOU'RE GONE.
LEAVE THE SECURITY OF OUR HOME TO ME!
AS LONG AS DADDY'S THERE, NO HARM WILL BEFALL OUR FAMILY!!
FWIP
WOW! I JUST SAID SOME-THING REALLY COOL!!
I GIVE YOU FULL PERMISSION TO USE IT... SOME-DAY.
wahaha
YOU FREAK.
I'M NOT WORRIED.
I'M GOING.

Finally collapsing from his prolonged, runaway lifestyle.

Look out, Kon!!

The owner of the black shadow approaching Kon is...

To be continued!!

69. 25:00 gathering

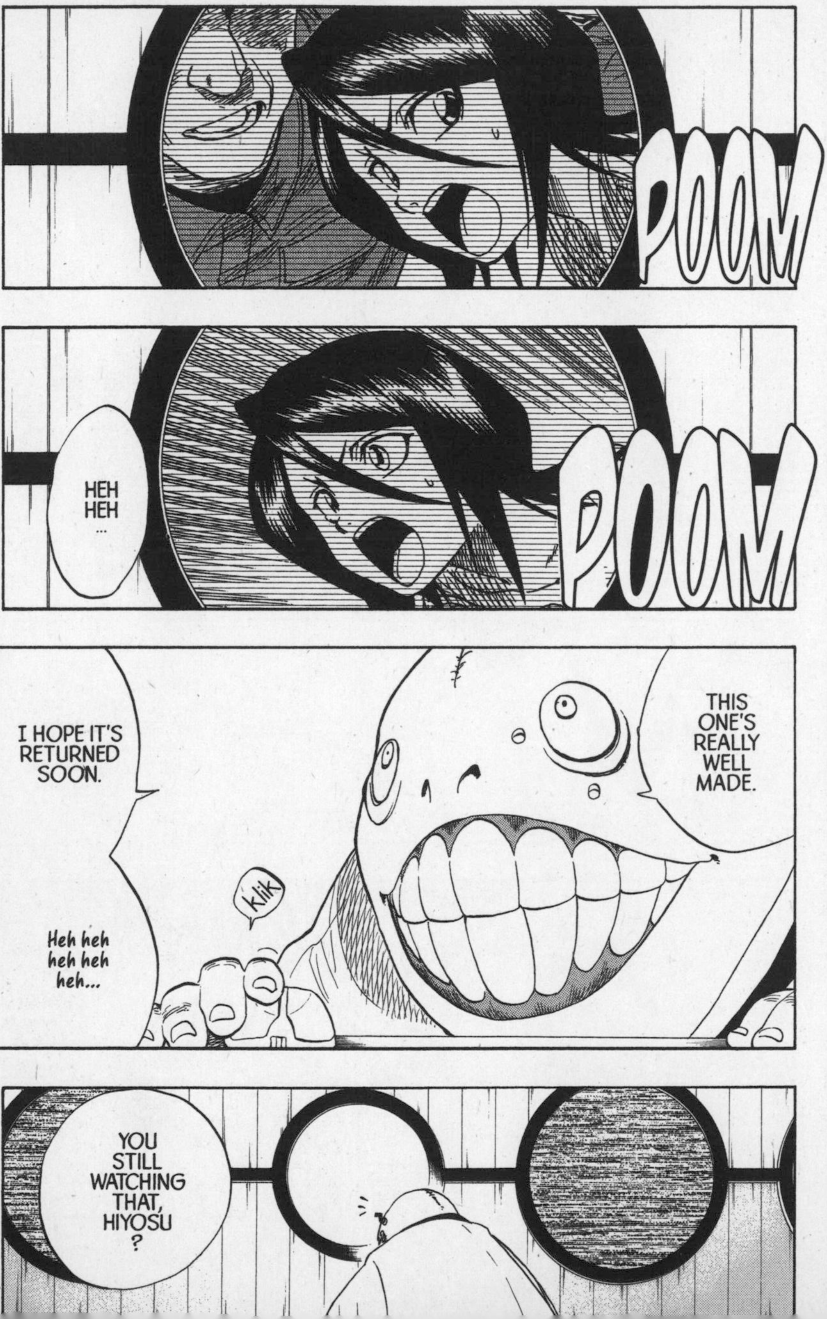
POOM
POOM
HEH HEH ...
THIS ONE'S REALLY WELL MADE.
I HOPE IT'S RETURNED SOON.
klik
Heh heh heh heh heh...
YOU STILL WATCHING THAT, HIYOSU ?

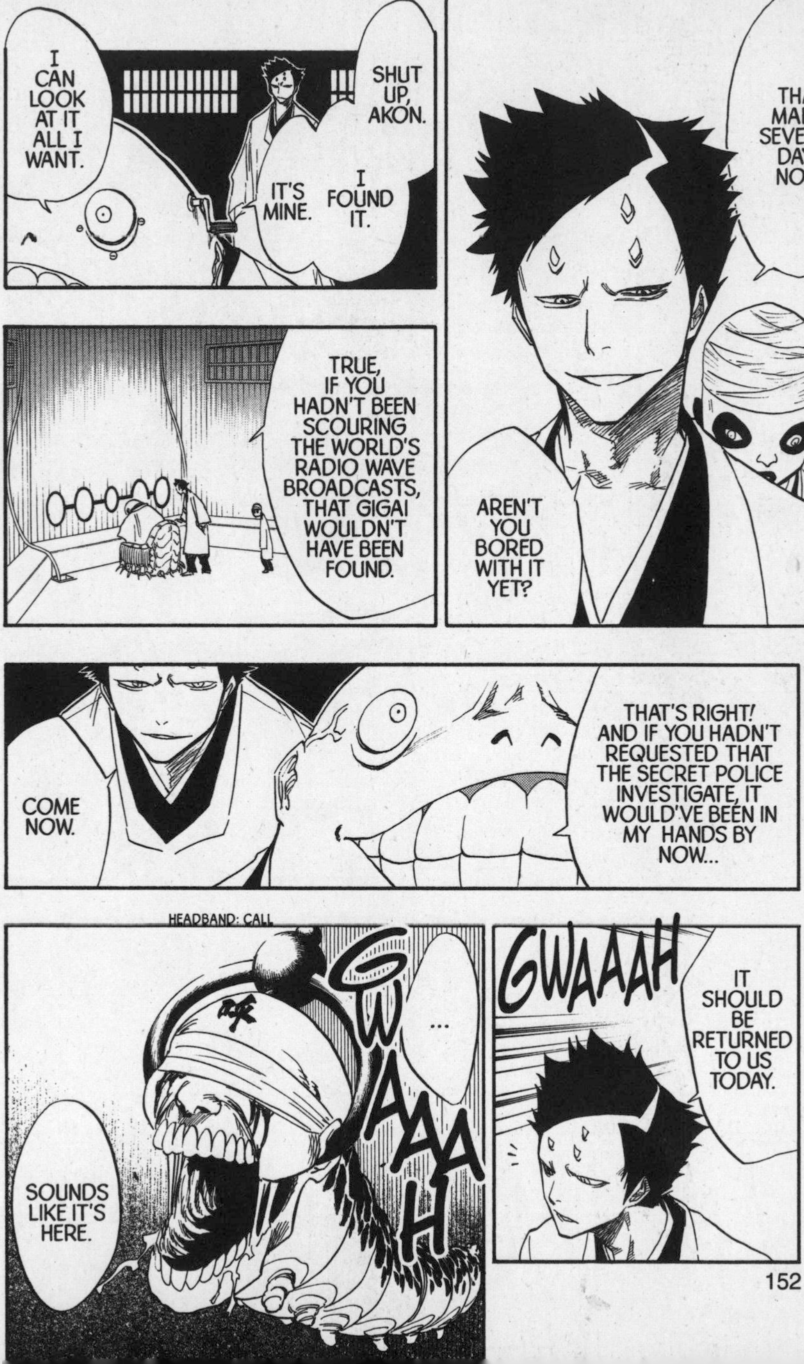

THAT MAKES SEVERAL DAYS NOW.
AREN'T YOU BORED WITH IT YET?
SHUT UP, AKON.
I FOUND IT.
IT'S MINE.
I CAN LOOK AT IT ALL I WANT.
TRUE, IF YOU HADN'T BEEN SCOURING THE WORLD'S RADIO WAVE BROADCASTS, THAT GIGAI WOULDN'T HAVE BEEN FOUND.
THAT'S RIGHT! AND IF YOU HADN'T REQUESTED THAT THE SECRET POLICE INVESTIGATE, IT WOULD'VE BEEN IN MY HANDS BY NOW...
COME NOW.
GWAAAH
IT SHOULD BE RETURNED TO US TODAY.
HEADBAND: CALL
GWAAAAH
...
SOUNDS LIKE IT'S HERE.

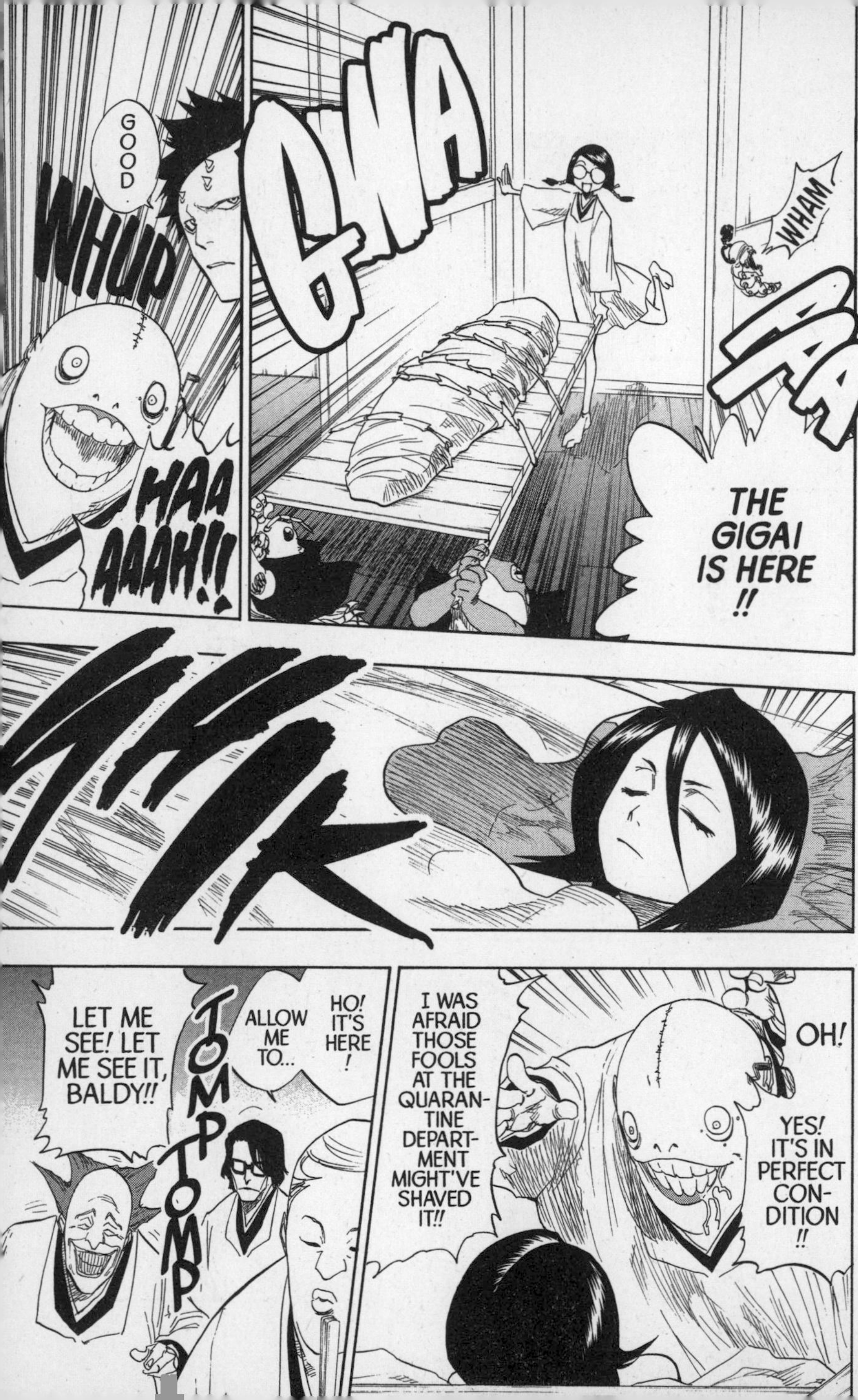
WHAM
AAA
THE GIGAI IS HERE!!
GWHA
GOOD.
WHUP
WHAA AAAH!!
OH!
YES! IT'S IN PERFECT CONDITION!!
I WAS AFRAID THOSE FOOLS AT THE QUARANTINE DEPARTMENT MIGHT'VE SHAVED IT!!
HO! IT'S HERE!
ALLOW ME TO...
TOMP TOMP
LET ME SEE! LET ME SEE IT, BALDY!!

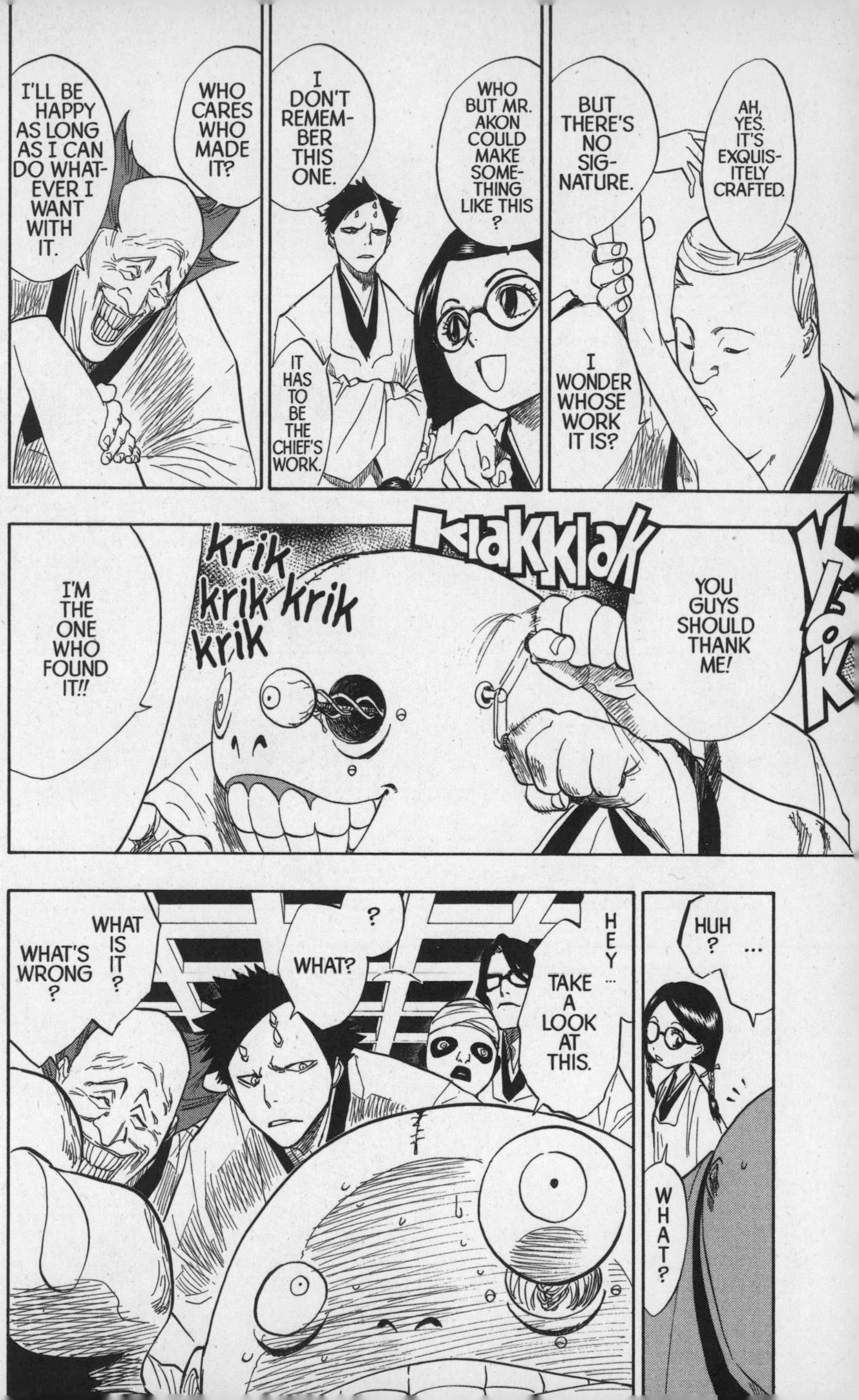
AH, YES. IT'S EXQUISITELY CRAFTED.
BUT THERE'S NO SIGNATURE.
I WONDER WHOSE WORK IT IS?
WHO BUT MR. AKON COULD MAKE SOMETHING LIKE THIS?
I DON'T REMEMBER THIS ONE.
IT HAS TO BE THE CHIEF'S WORK.
WHO CARES WHO MADE IT?
I'LL BE HAPPY AS LONG AS I CAN DO WHATEVER I WANT WITH IT.
YOU GUYS SHOULD THANK ME!
KLAKKLAK
krik krik krik krik
I'M THE ONE WHO FOUND IT!!
HUH? ...
WHAT?
HEY... TAKE A LOOK AT THIS.
?
WHAT?
WHAT IS IT?
WHAT'S WRONG?

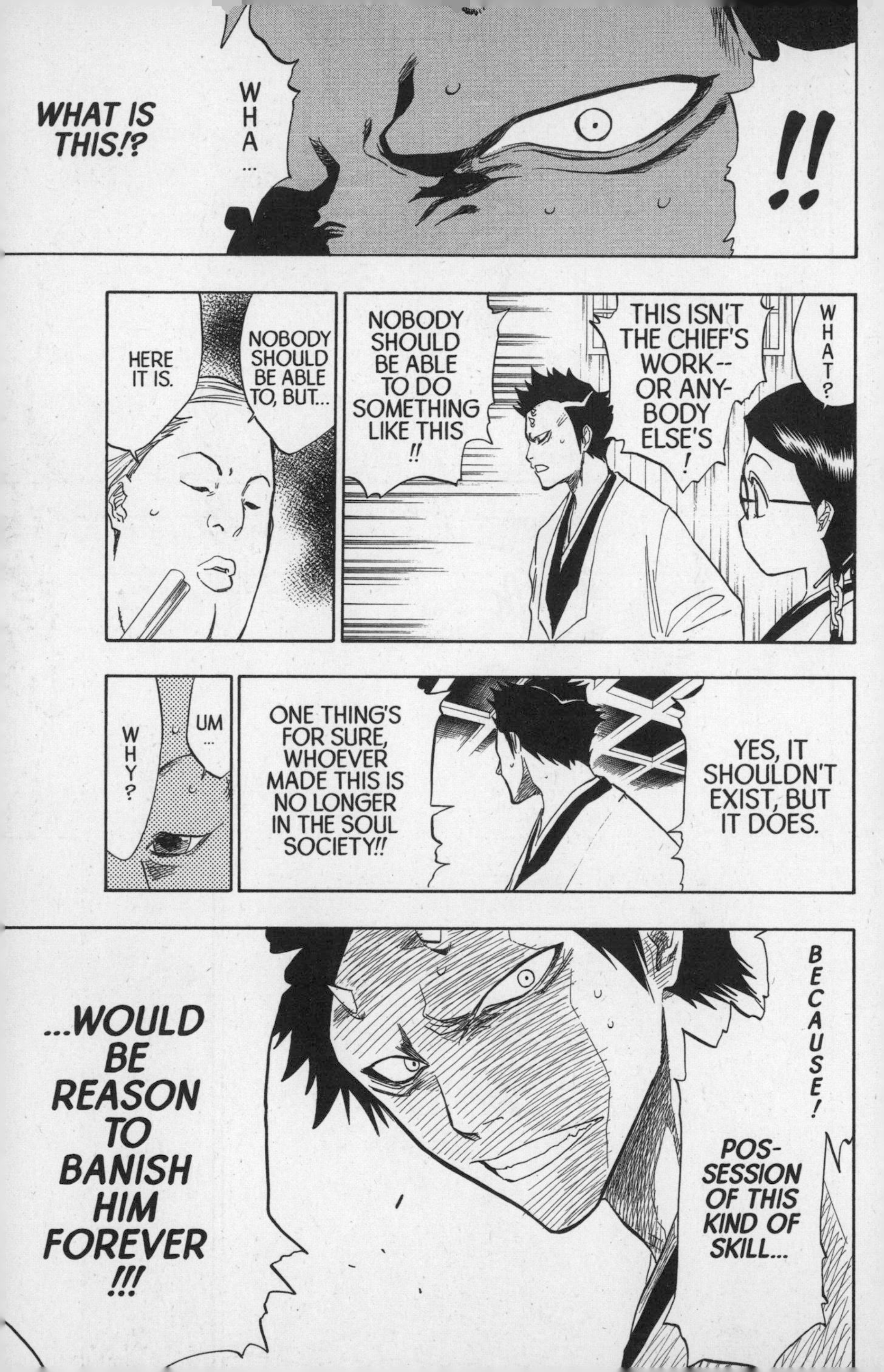
!!
WHA...
WHAT IS THIS!?
WHAT?
THIS ISN'T THE CHIEF'S WORK-- OR ANYBODY ELSE'S!
NOBODY SHOULD BE ABLE TO DO SOMETHING LIKE THIS!!
NOBODY SHOULD BE ABLE TO, BUT...
HERE IT IS.
YES, IT SHOULDN'T EXIST, BUT IT DOES.
ONE THING'S FOR SURE, WHOEVER MADE THIS IS NO LONGER IN THE SOUL SOCIETY!!
UM...
WHY?
BECAUSE!
POSSESSION OF THIS KIND OF SKILL...
...WOULD BE REASON TO BANISH HIM FOREVER!!!

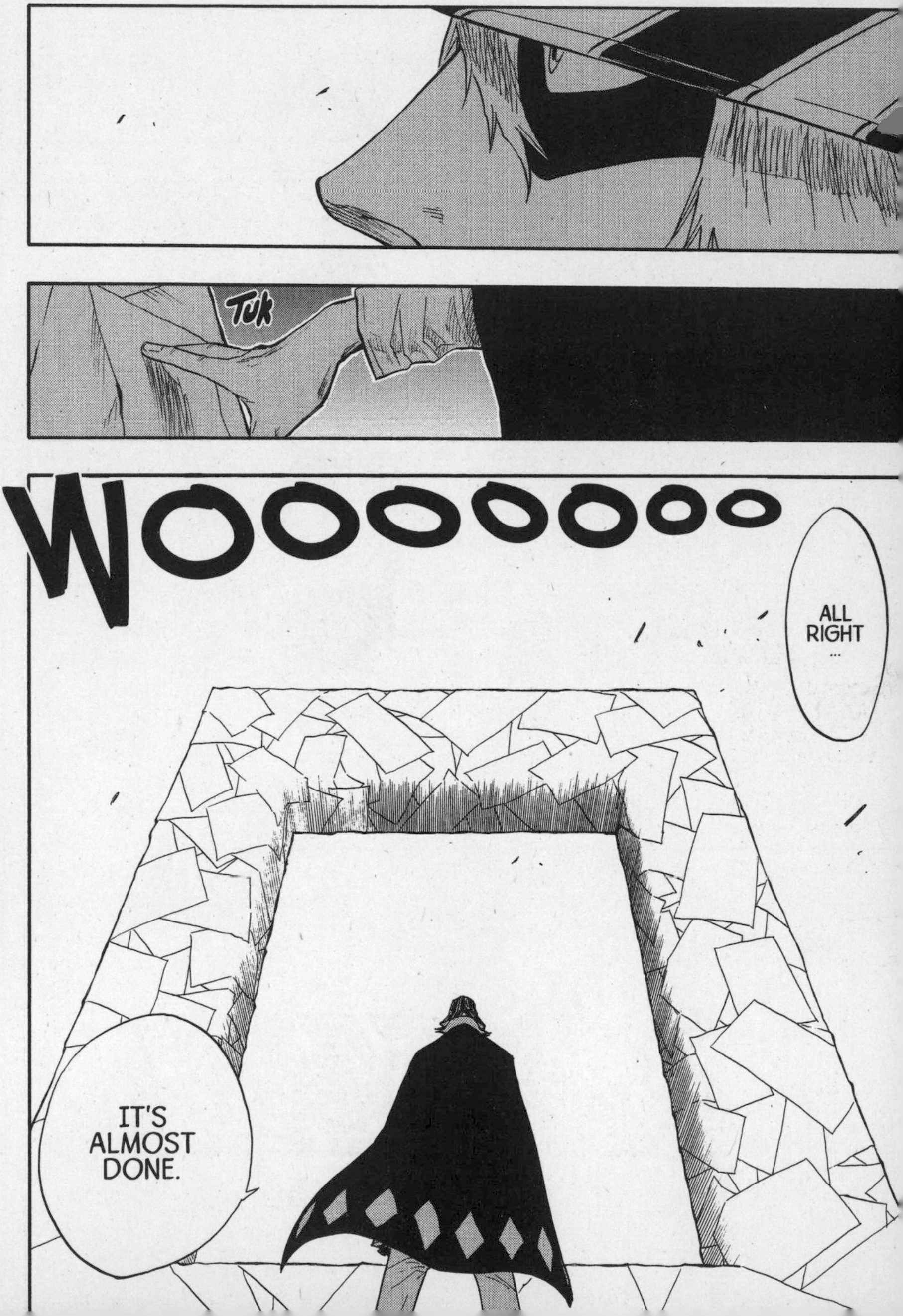
TÜK
WOOOOOOO
ALL RIGHT ...
IT'S ALMOST DONE.

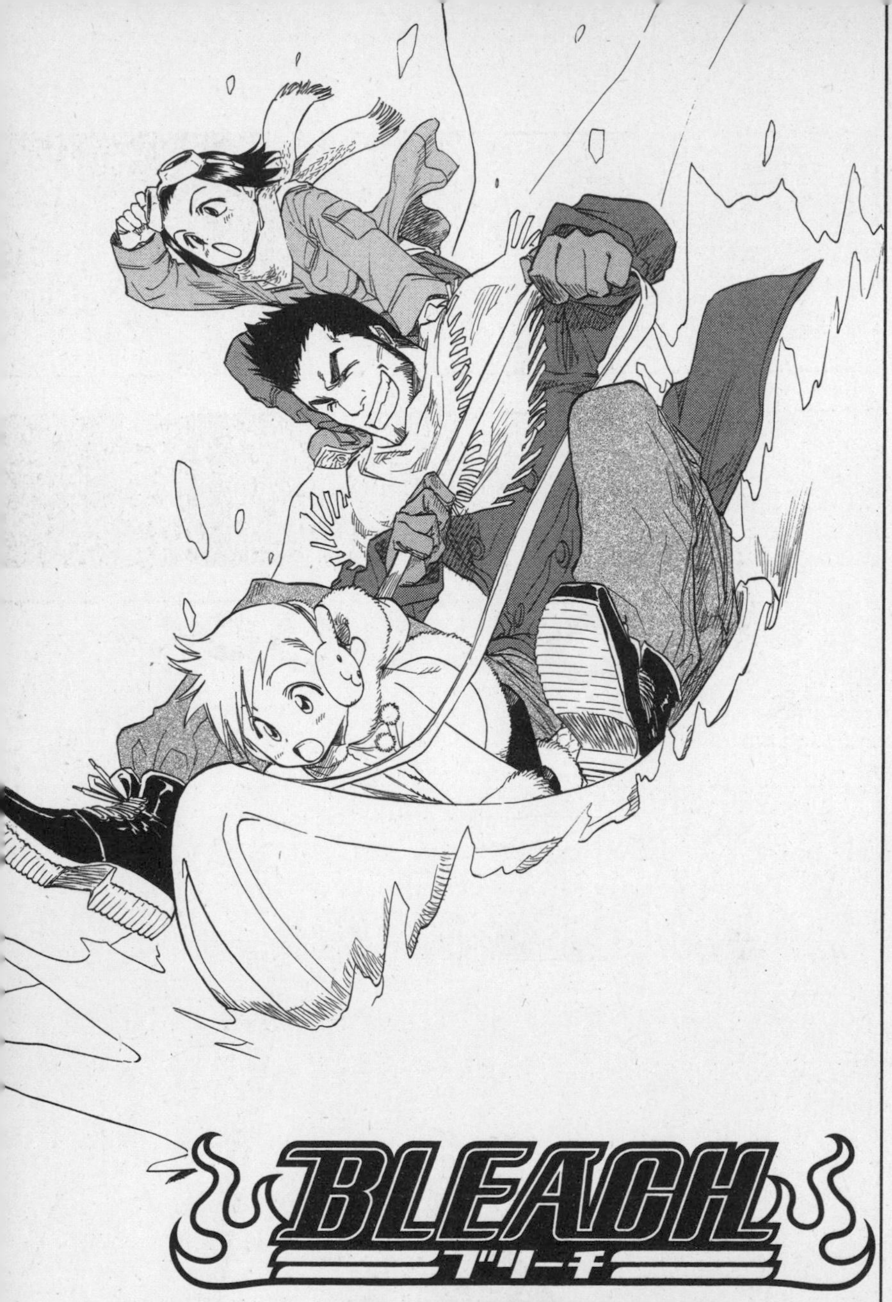

BLEACH

ブリーチ

69. 25:00 gathering

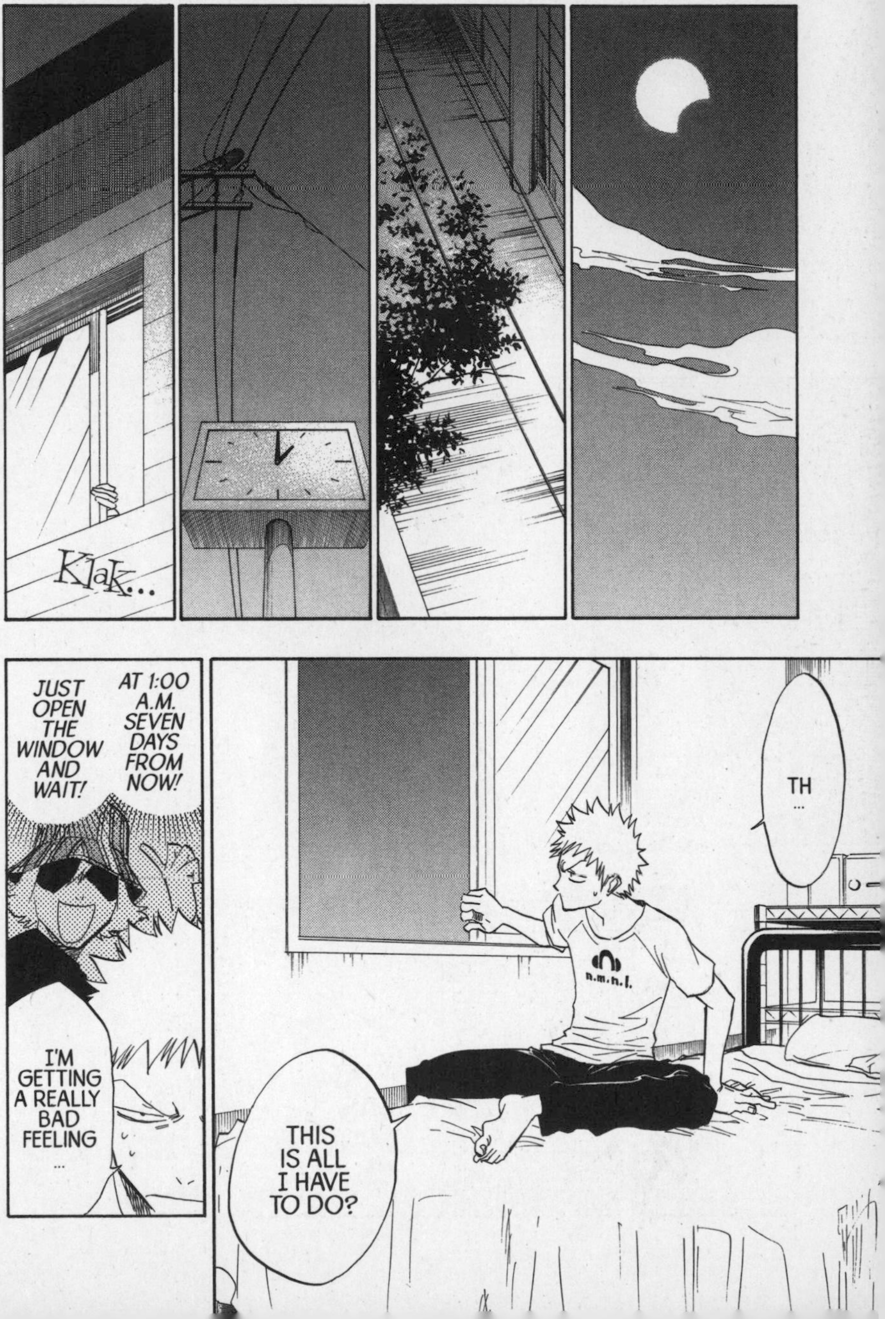
Klak...
TH ...
THIS IS ALL I HAVE TO DO?
AT 1:00 A.M. SEVEN DAYS FROM NOW!
JUST OPEN THE WINDOW AND WAIT!
I'M GETTING A REALLY BAD FEELING ...

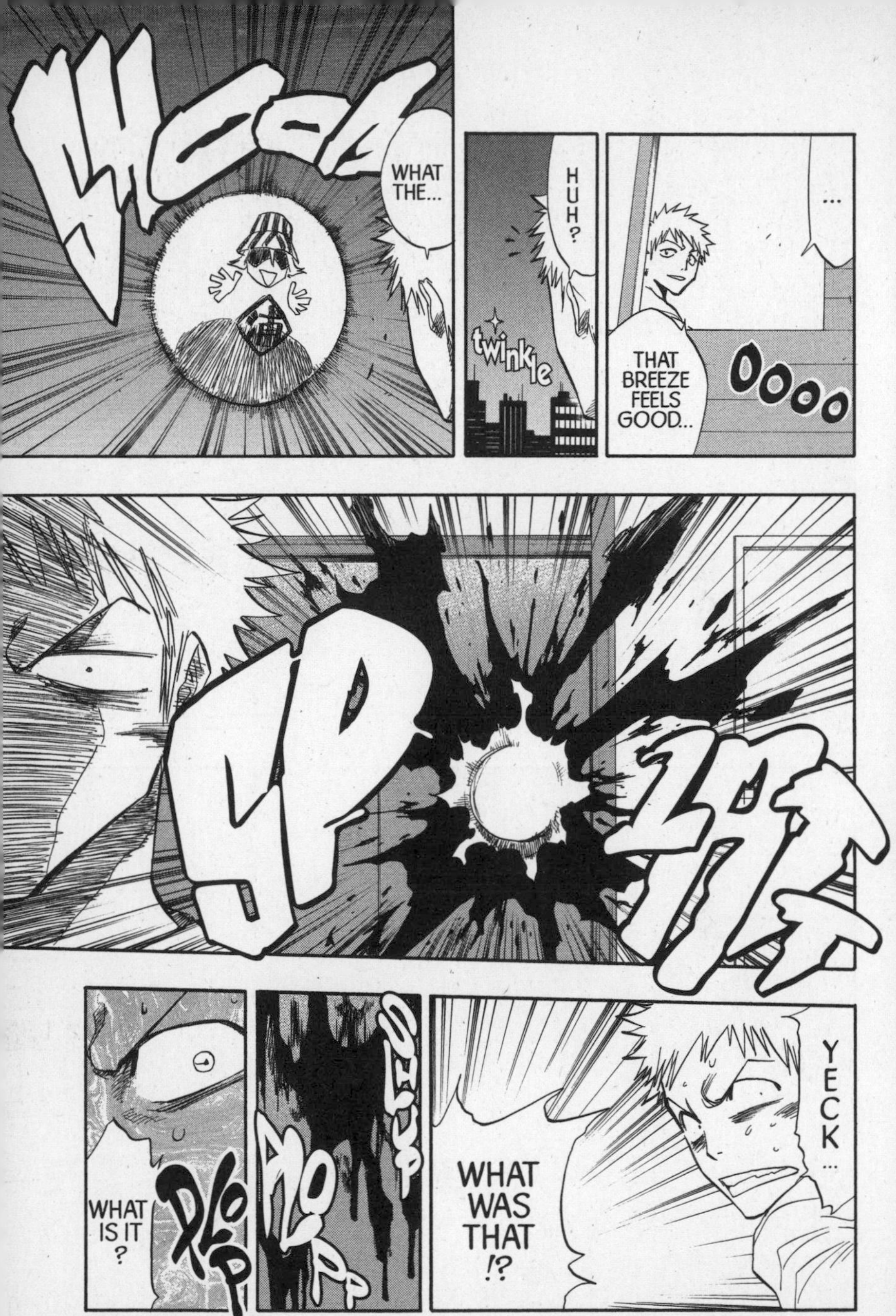
...
THAT BREEZE FEELS GOOD...
OOOO
HUH?
twinkle
WHAT THE...
SPLAT
YECK...
WHAT WAS THAT!?
SHLUP
PLOPP
PLOP
WHAT IS IT?

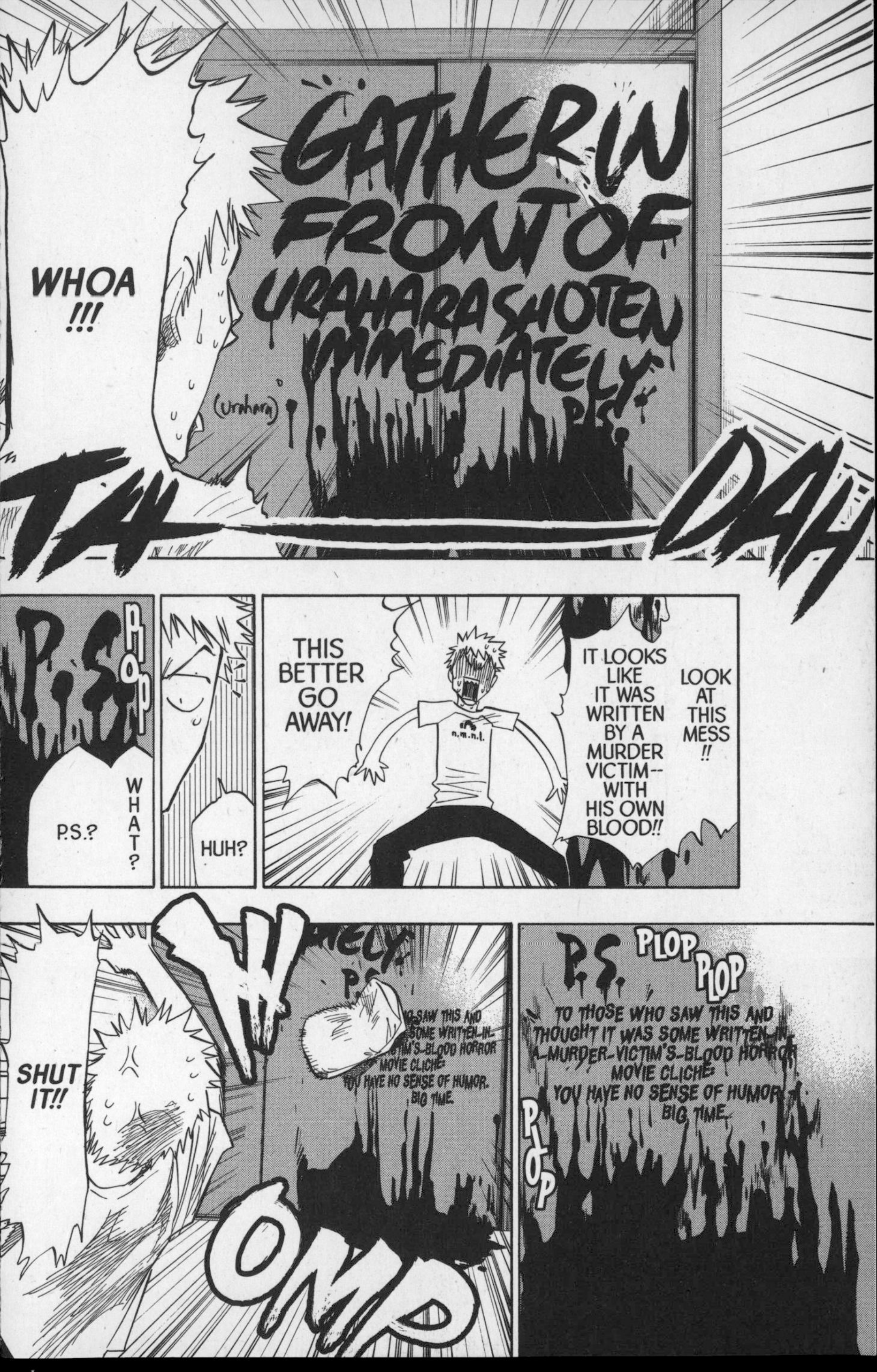

GATHER IN FRONT OF URAHARA SHOTEN IMMEDIATELY
P.S.
(Urahara)
WHOA !!!
TA
DAH
LOOK AT THIS MESS !!
IT LOOKS LIKE IT WAS WRITTEN BY A MURDER VICTIM-- WITH HIS OWN BLOOD!!
THIS BETTER GO AWAY!
HUH?
P.S.
PLOP
WHAT?
P.S.?
P.S.
PLOP
PLOP
TO THOSE WHO SAW THIS AND THOUGHT IT WAS SOME WRITTEN-IN-A-MURDER-VICTIM'S-BLOOD HORROR MOVIE CLICHE: YOU HAVE NO SENSE OF HUMOR. BIG TIME.
PLOP
SHUT IT!!
OMP

READ THIS WAY

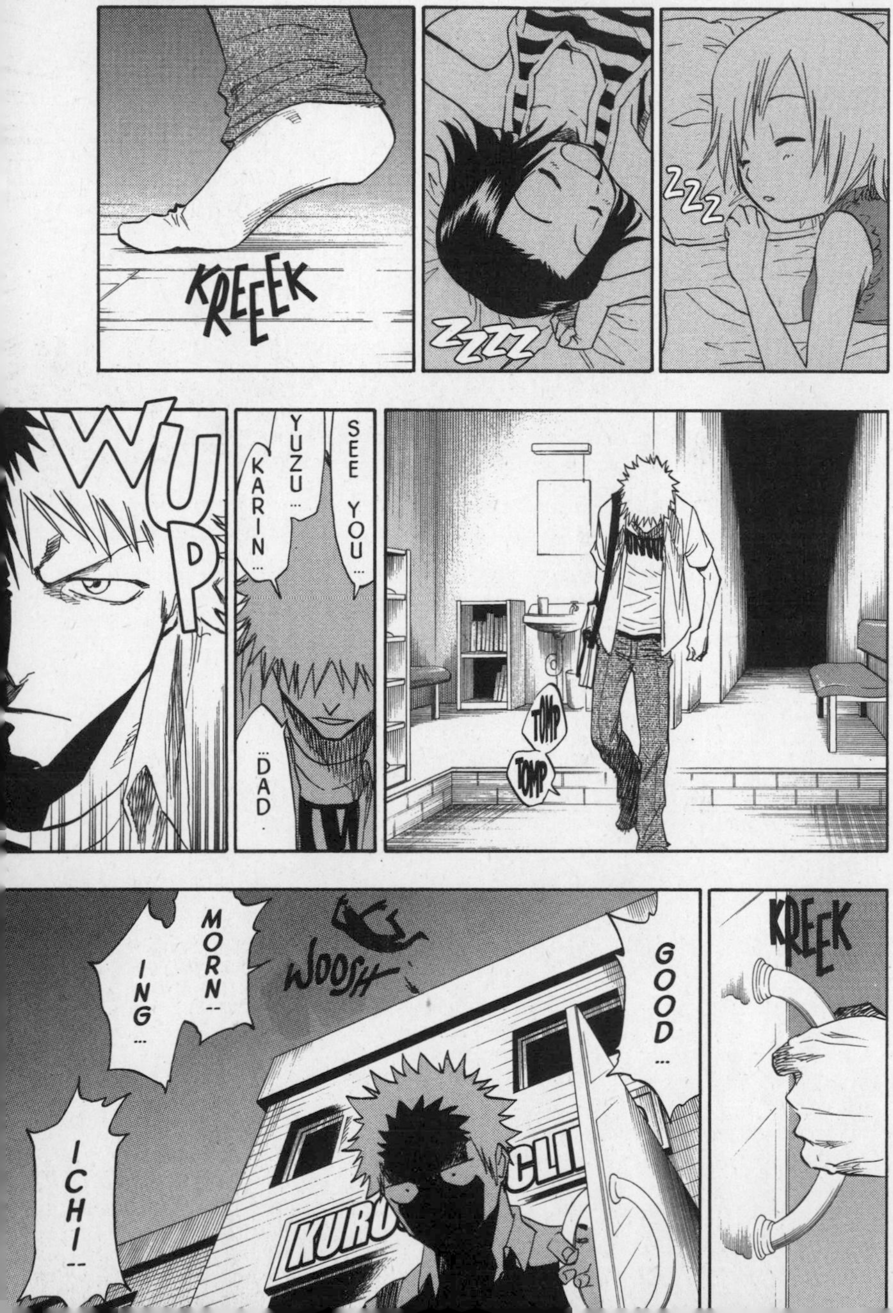
ZZZ
ZZZZ
KREEEK
TOMP
TOMP
SEE YOU...
YUZU...
KARIN...
...DAD.
WUP
KREEK
GOOD...
WOOSH
MORN--
ING...
ICHI--

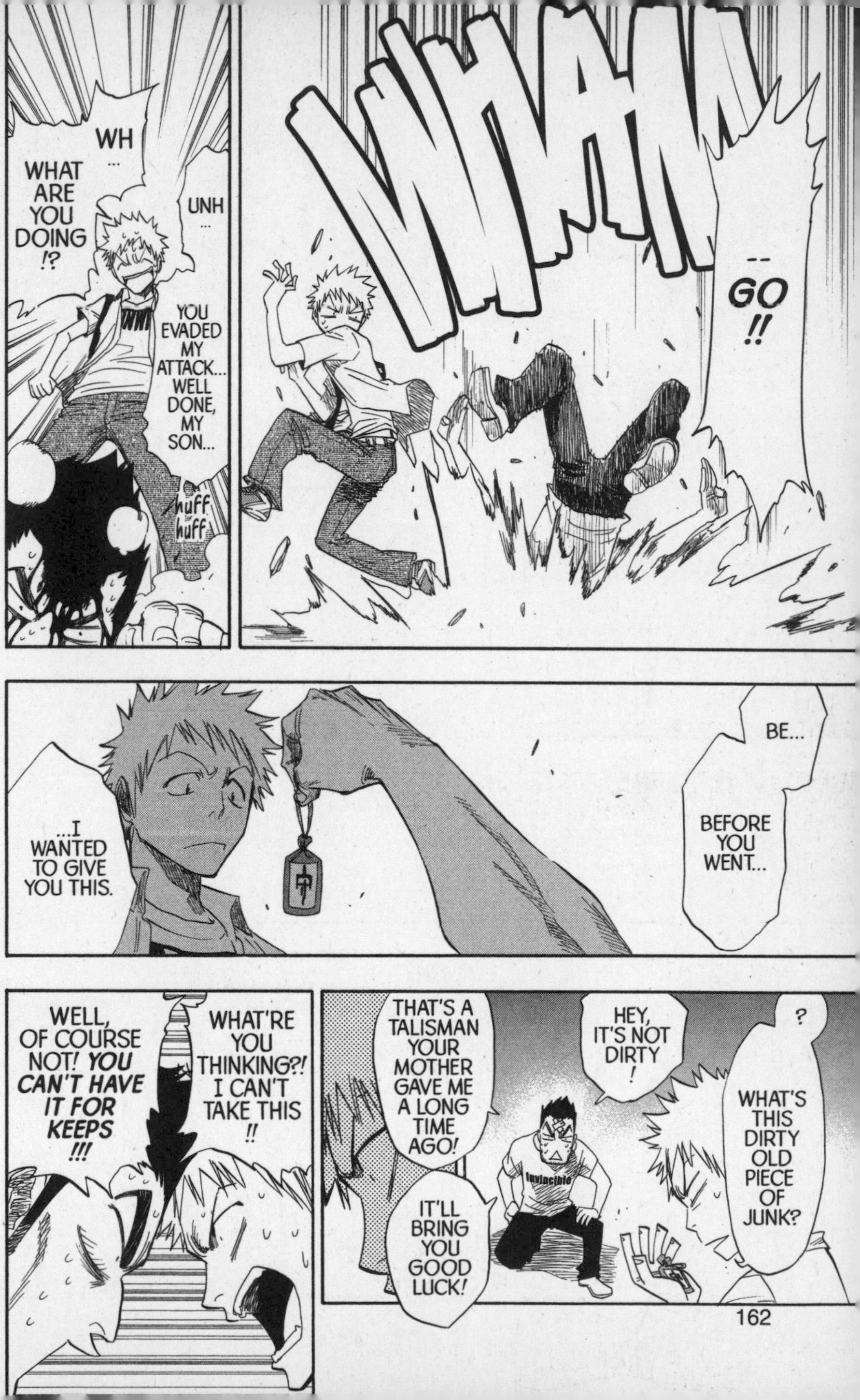
WHAM
--GO!!
WH...
WHAT ARE YOU DOING!?
UNH...
YOU EVADED MY ATTACK... WELL DONE, MY SON...
huff huff
BE...
BEFORE YOU WENT...
...I WANTED TO GIVE YOU THIS.
?
WHAT'S THIS DIRTY OLD PIECE OF JUNK?
HEY, IT'S NOT DIRTY!
THAT'S A TALISMAN YOUR MOTHER GAVE ME A LONG TIME AGO!
IT'LL BRING YOU GOOD LUCK!
Invincible
WHAT'RE YOU THINKING?! I CAN'T TAKE THIS!!
WELL, OF COURSE NOT! ***YOU CAN'T HAVE IT FOR KEEPS!!!***

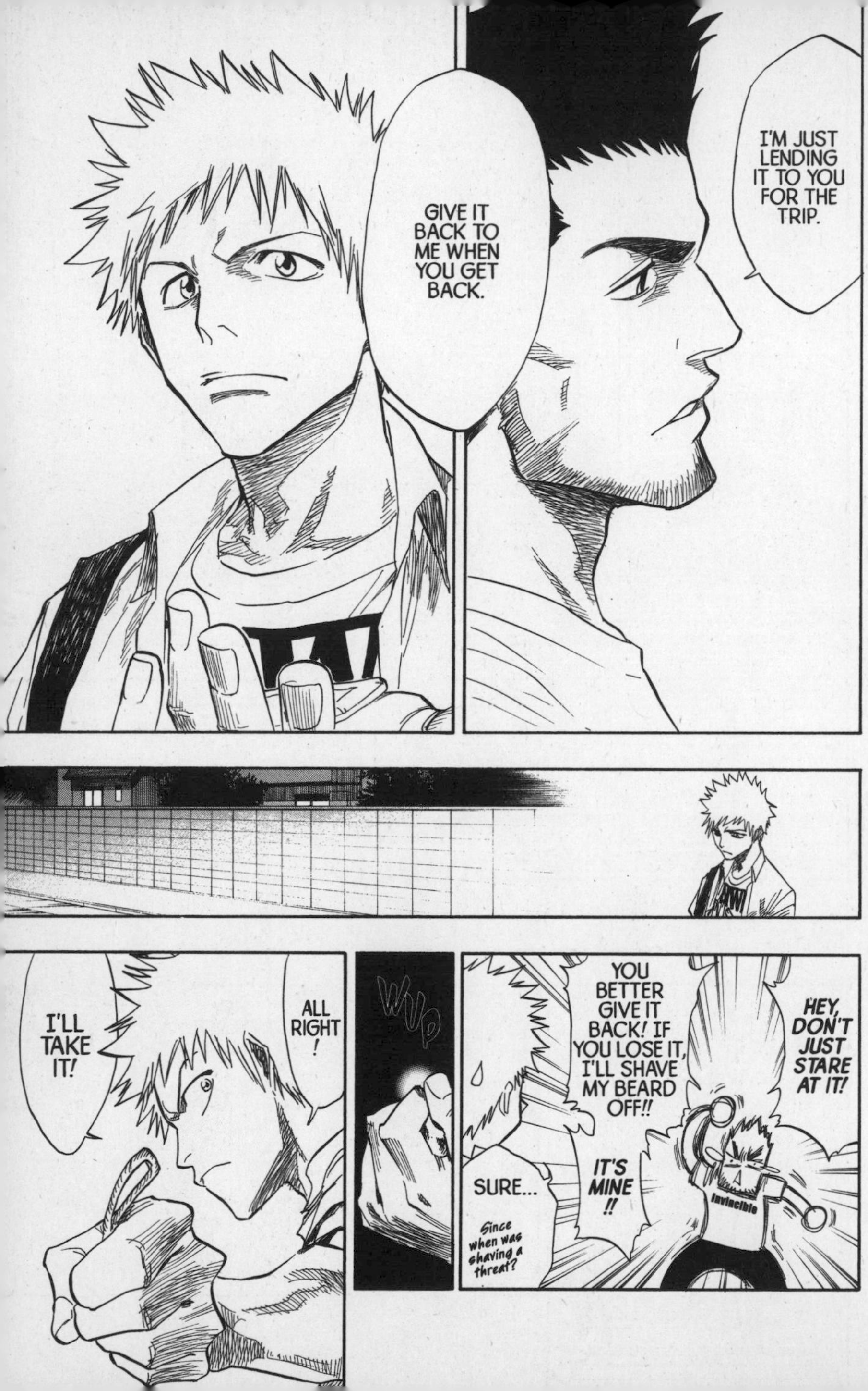
I'M JUST LENDING IT TO YOU FOR THE TRIP.
GIVE IT BACK TO ME WHEN YOU GET BACK.
HEY, DON'T JUST STARE AT IT!
YOU BETTER GIVE IT BACK! IF YOU LOSE IT, I'LL SHAVE MY BEARD OFF!!
IT'S MINE!!
SURE...
Since when was shaving a threat?
WUP
ALL RIGHT!
I'LL TAKE IT!

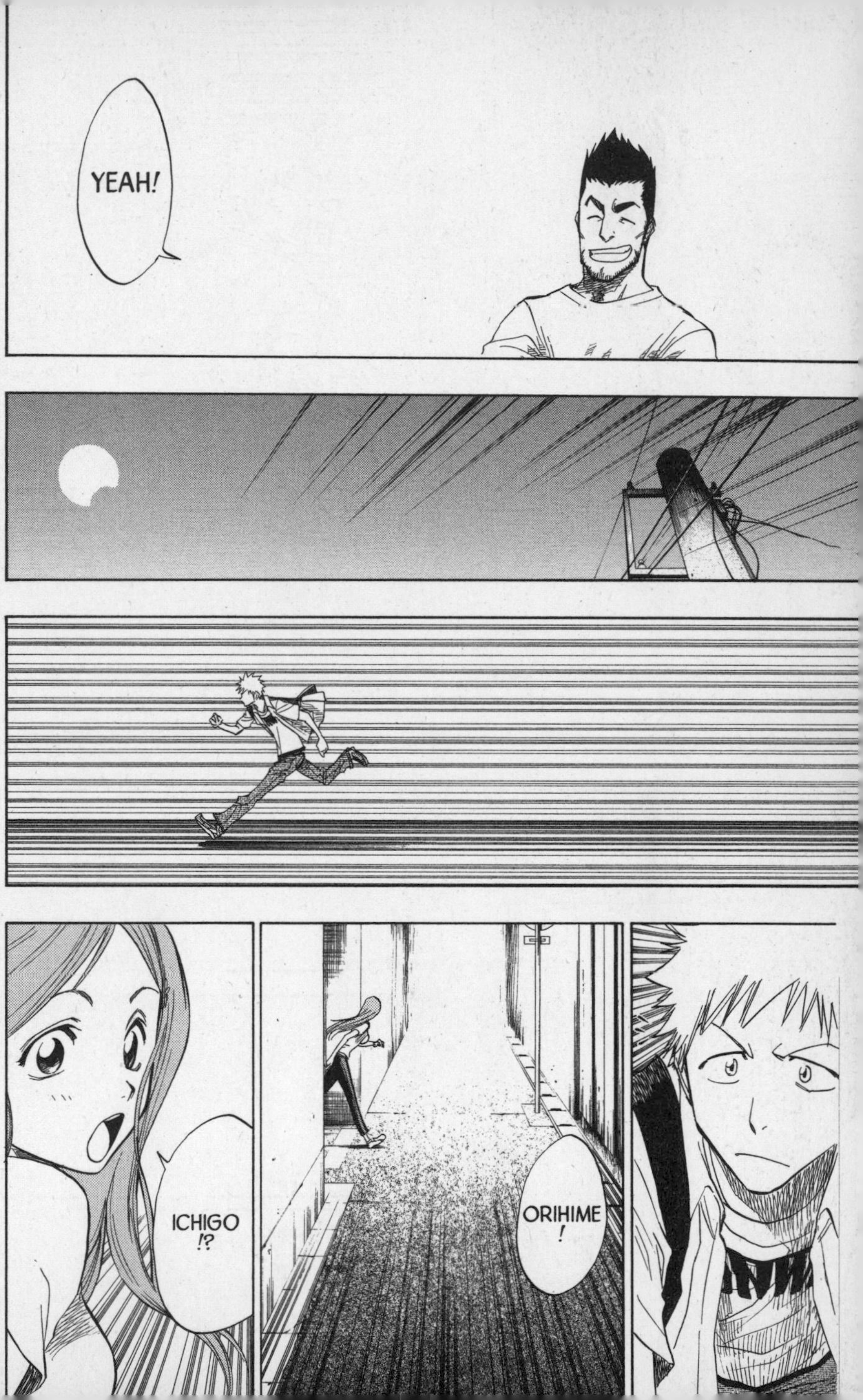
YEAH!
ORIHIME!
ICHIGO!?

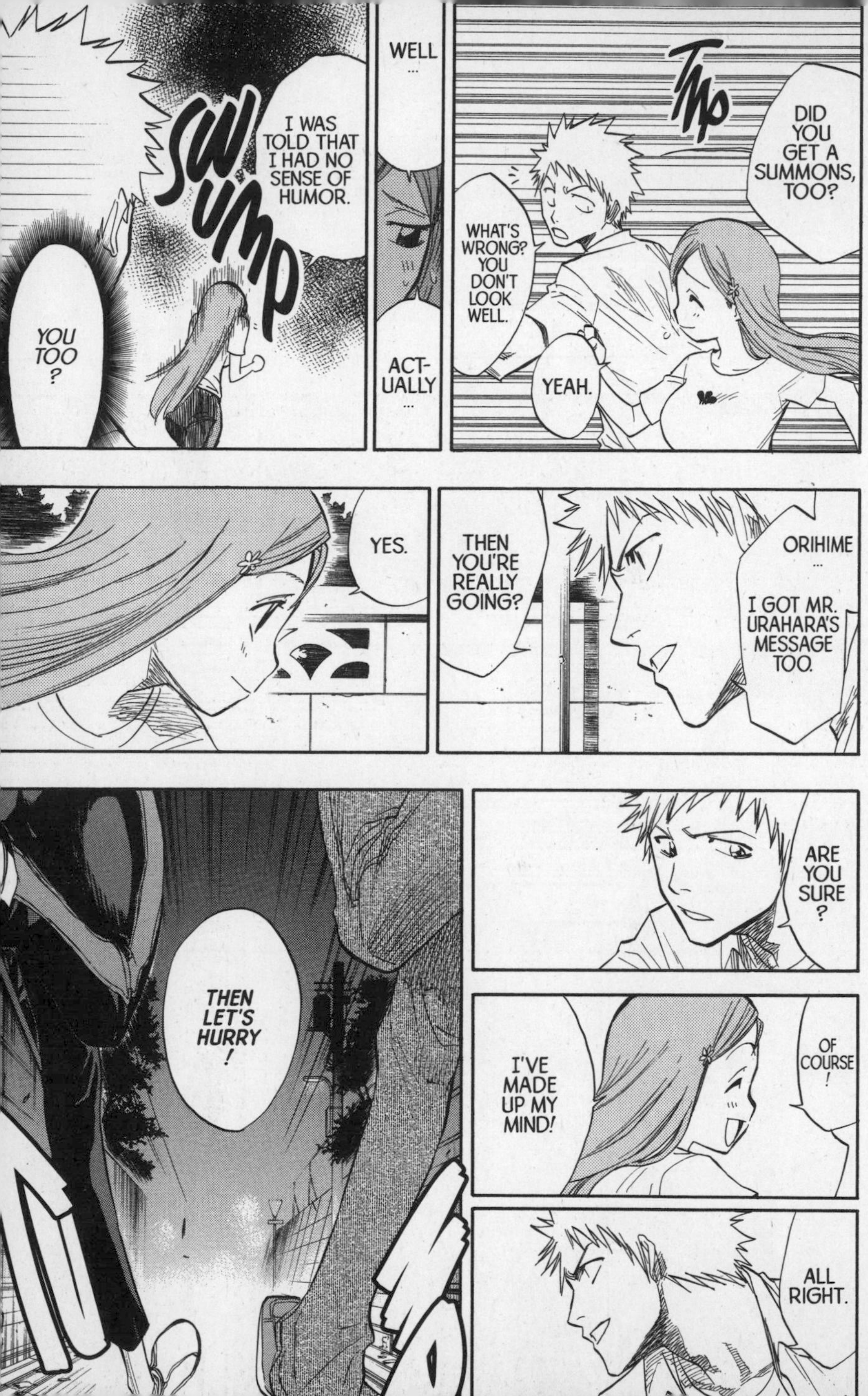
TMP
DID YOU GET A SUMMONS, TOO?
WHAT'S WRONG? YOU DON'T LOOK WELL.
YEAH.
WELL ...
ACT-UALLY ...
I WAS TOLD THAT I HAD NO SENSE OF HUMOR.
SWUMP
YOU TOO ?
ORIHIME ...
I GOT MR. URAHARA'S MESSAGE TOO.
THEN YOU'RE REALLY GOING?
YES.
ARE YOU SURE ?
OF COURSE !
I'VE MADE UP MY MIND!
ALL RIGHT.
THEN LET'S HURRY !

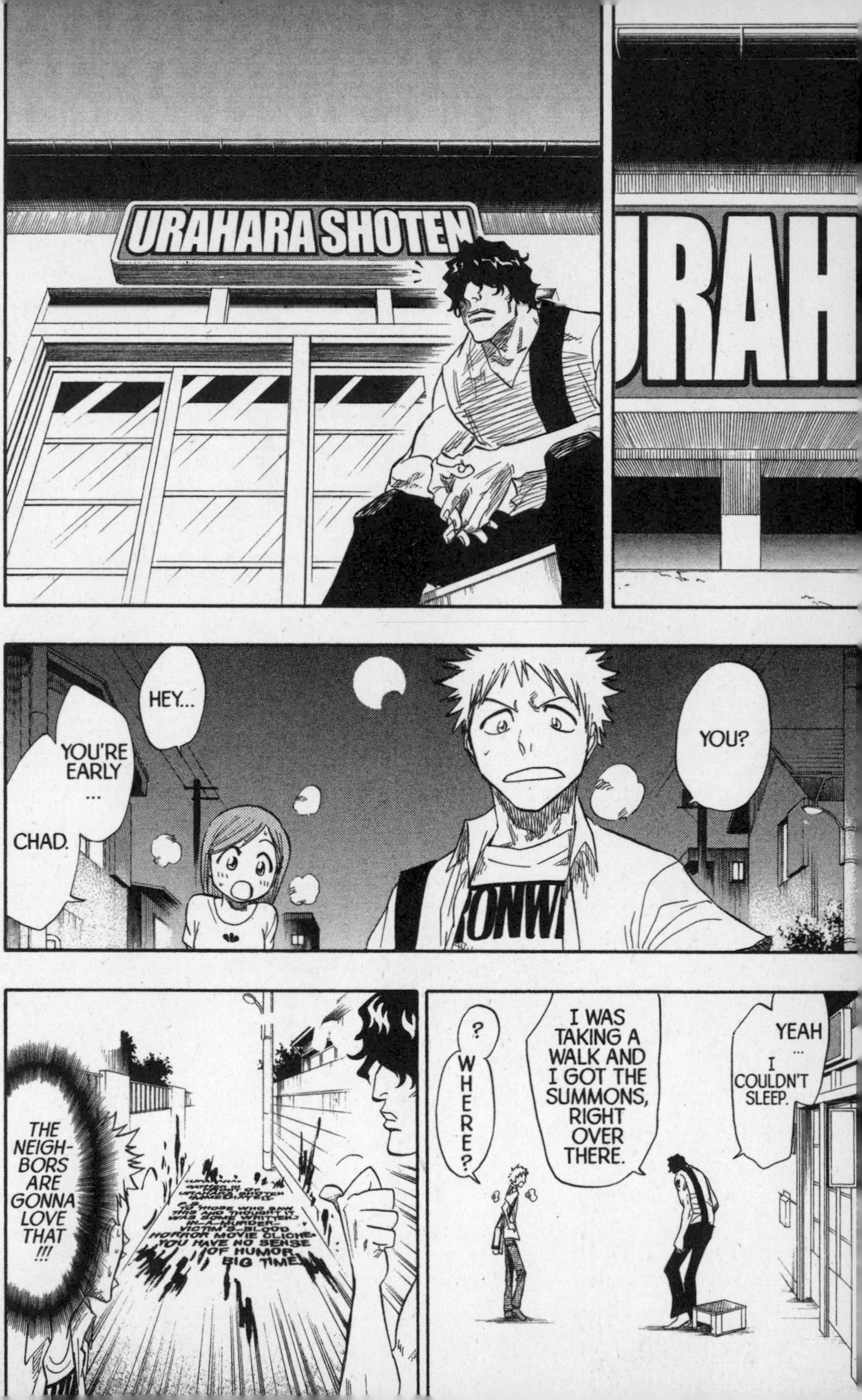
URAH
URAHARA SHOTEN
YOU?
HEY...
YOU'RE EARLY ...
CHAD.
YEAH ... I COULDN'T SLEEP.
I WAS TAKING A WALK AND I GOT THE SUMMONS, RIGHT OVER THERE.
? WHERE?
TO THOSE WHO SAW THIS AND THOUGHT IT WAS SOME WRITTEN-IN-A-MURDER-VICTIM'S-BLOOD HORROR MOVIE CLICHE YOU HAVE NO SENSE OF HUMOR BIG TIME
THE NEIGH-BORS ARE GONNA LOVE THAT !!!

READ THIS WAY

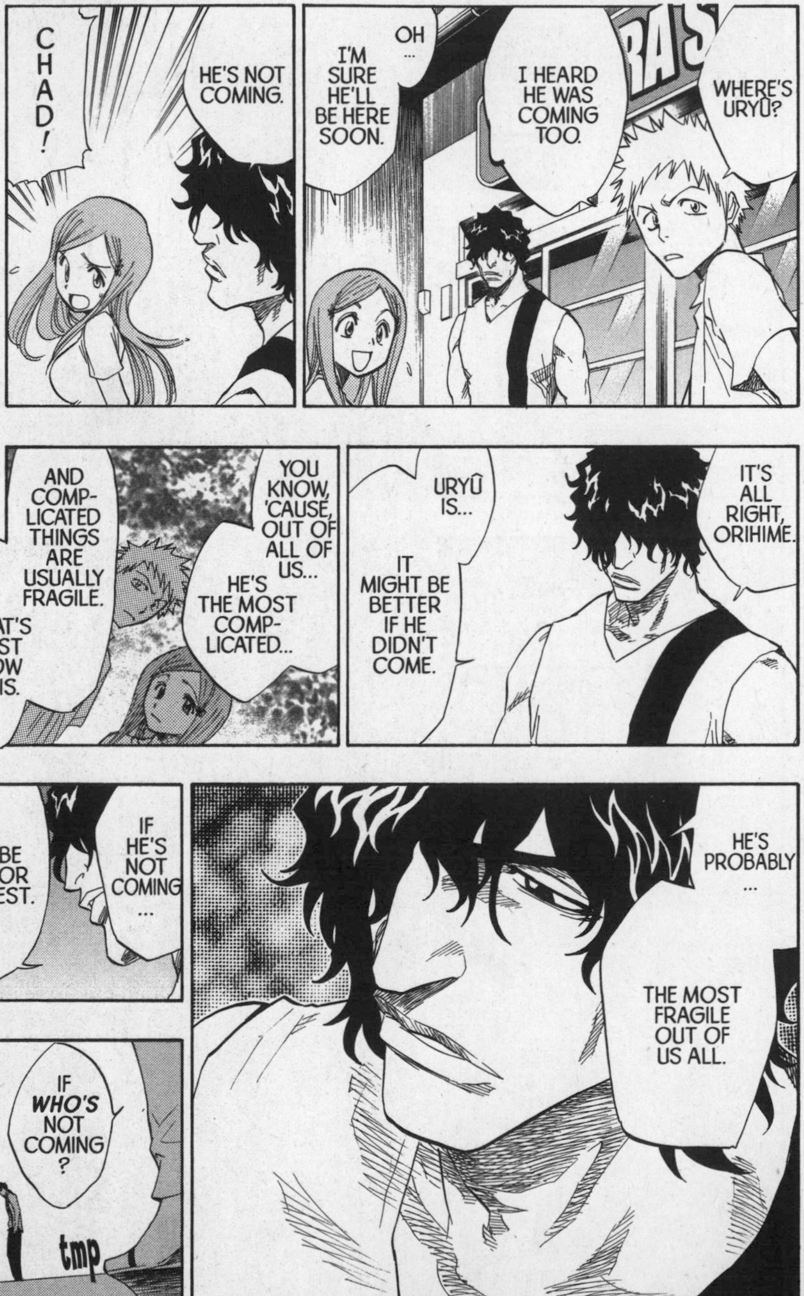
WHERE'S URYŪ?
I HEARD HE WAS COMING TOO.
OH ...
I'M SURE HE'LL BE HERE SOON.
HE'S NOT COMING.
CHAD!
IT'S ALL RIGHT, ORIHIME.
URYŪ IS...
IT MIGHT BE BETTER IF HE DIDN'T COME.
YOU KNOW, 'CAUSE, OUT OF ALL OF US...
HE'S THE MOST COMPLICATED...
AND COMPLICATED THINGS ARE USUALLY FRAGILE.
THAT'S JUST HOW IT IS.
HE'S PROBABLY ...
THE MOST FRAGILE OUT OF US ALL.
IF HE'S NOT COMING ...
MAYBE IT'S FOR THE BEST.
IF *WHO'S* NOT COMING?
tmp

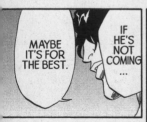

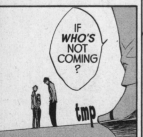

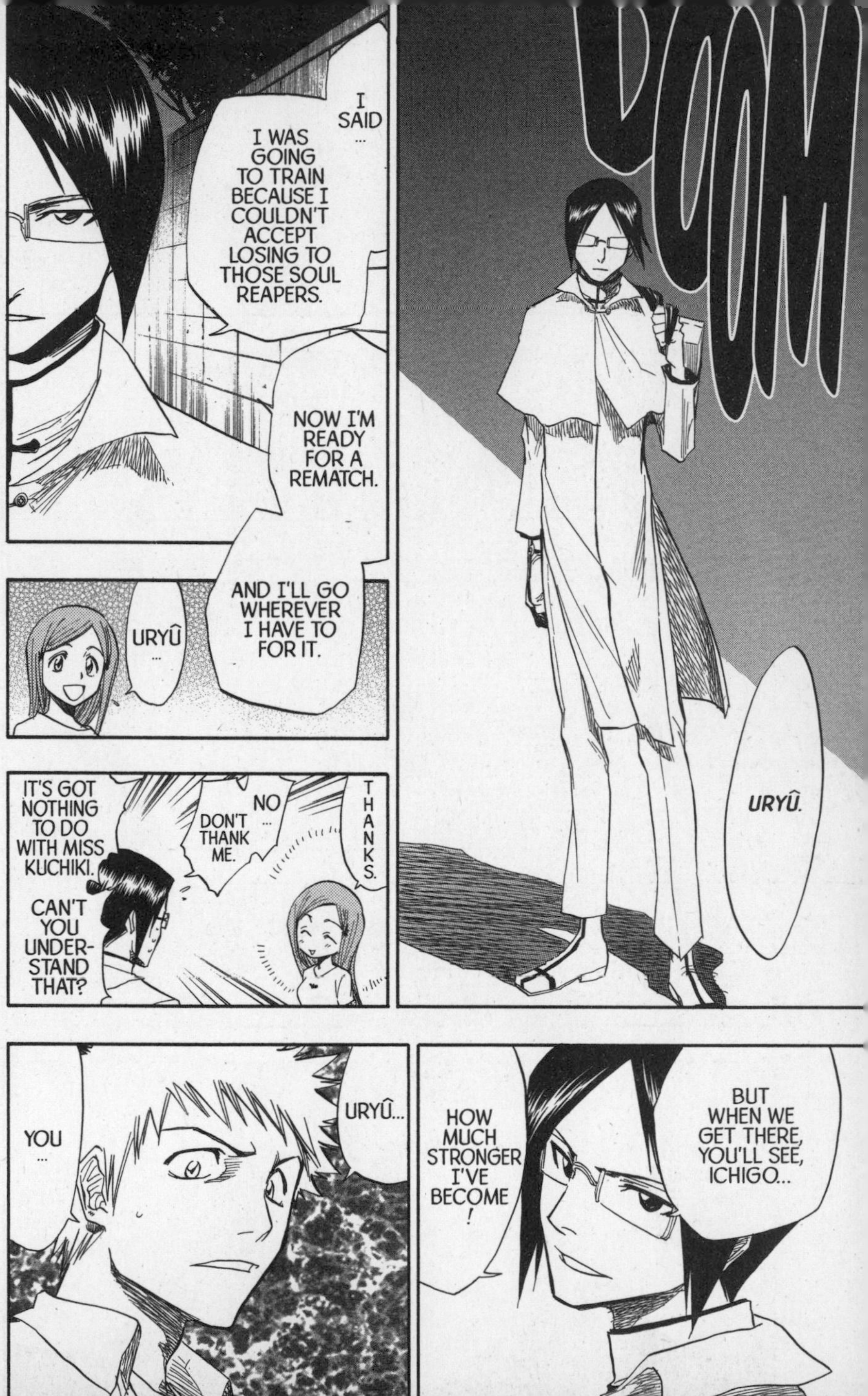

DOOM
URYÛ.
I SAID ...
I WAS GOING TO TRAIN BECAUSE I COULDN'T ACCEPT LOSING TO THOSE SOUL REAPERS.
NOW I'M READY FOR A REMATCH.
AND I'LL GO WHEREVER I HAVE TO FOR IT.
URYÛ ...
THANKS.
NO ...
DON'T THANK ME.
IT'S GOT NOTHING TO DO WITH MISS KUCHIKI.
CAN'T YOU UNDER-STAND THAT?
BUT WHEN WE GET THERE, YOU'LL SEE, ICHIGO...
HOW MUCH STRONGER I'VE BECOME!
URYÛ...
YOU ...

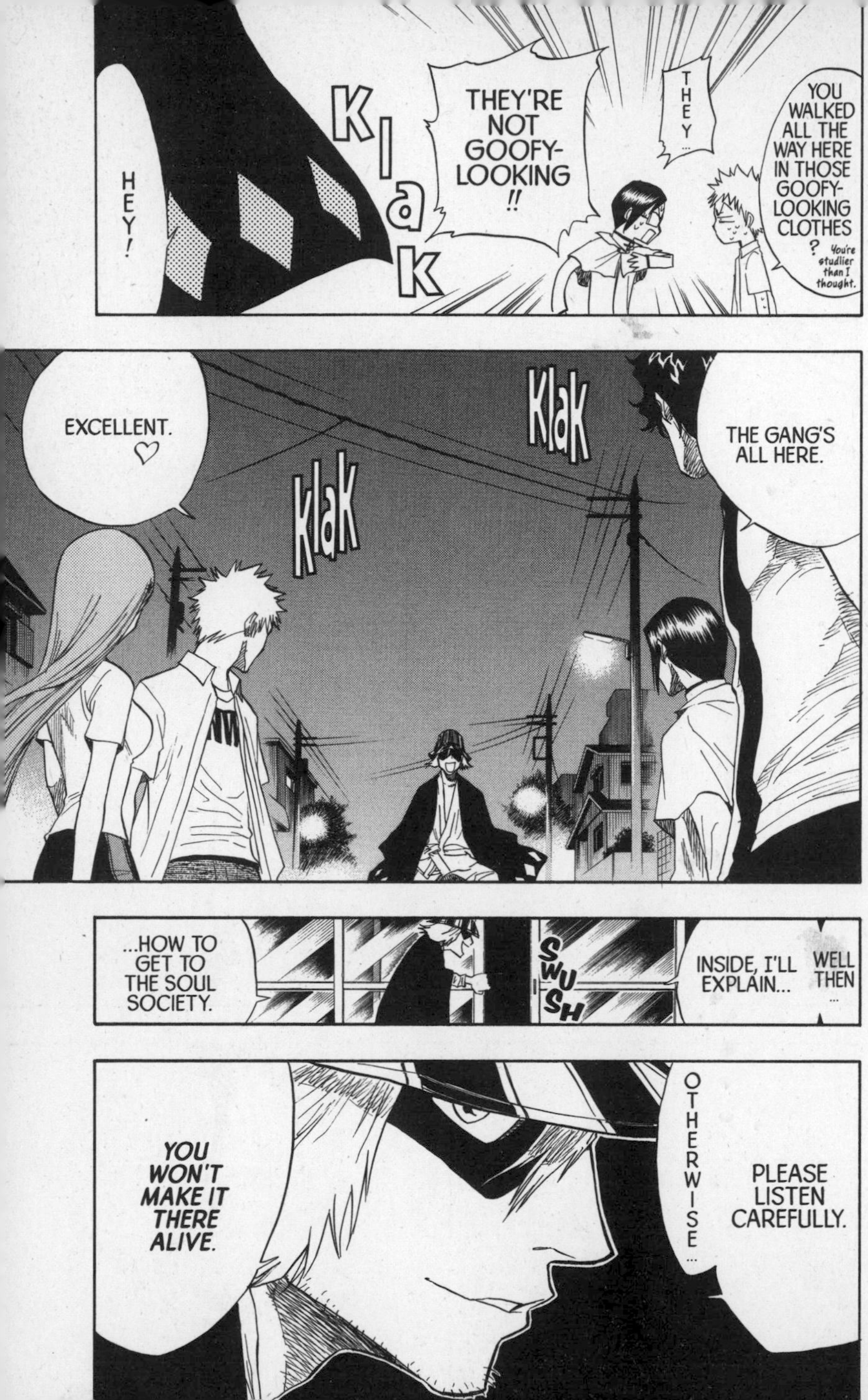
YOU WALKED ALL THE WAY HERE IN THOSE GOOFY-LOOKING CLOTHES?
You're studlier than I thought.
THEY...
THEY'RE NOT GOOFY-LOOKING!!
Klak
HEY!
THE GANG'S ALL HERE.
Klak
klak
EXCELLENT. ♡
WELL THEN...
INSIDE, I'LL EXPLAIN...
SWUSH
...HOW TO GET TO THE SOUL SOCIETY.
PLEASE LISTEN CAREFULLY.
OTHERWISE...
YOU WON'T MAKE IT THERE ALIVE.

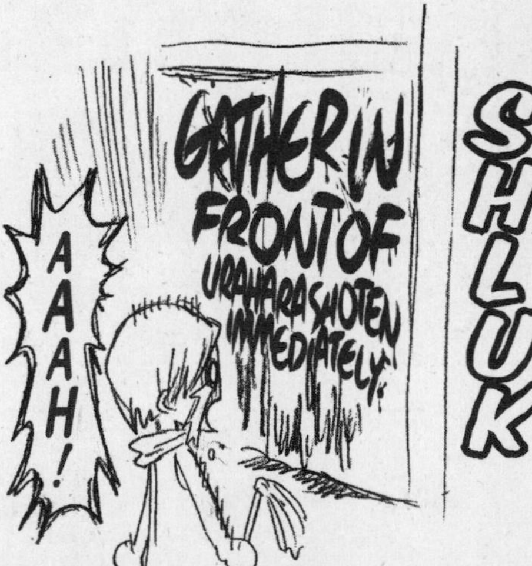
SHLUK
GATHER IN FRONT OF URAHARA SHOTEN IMMEDIATELY.
AAAAH!

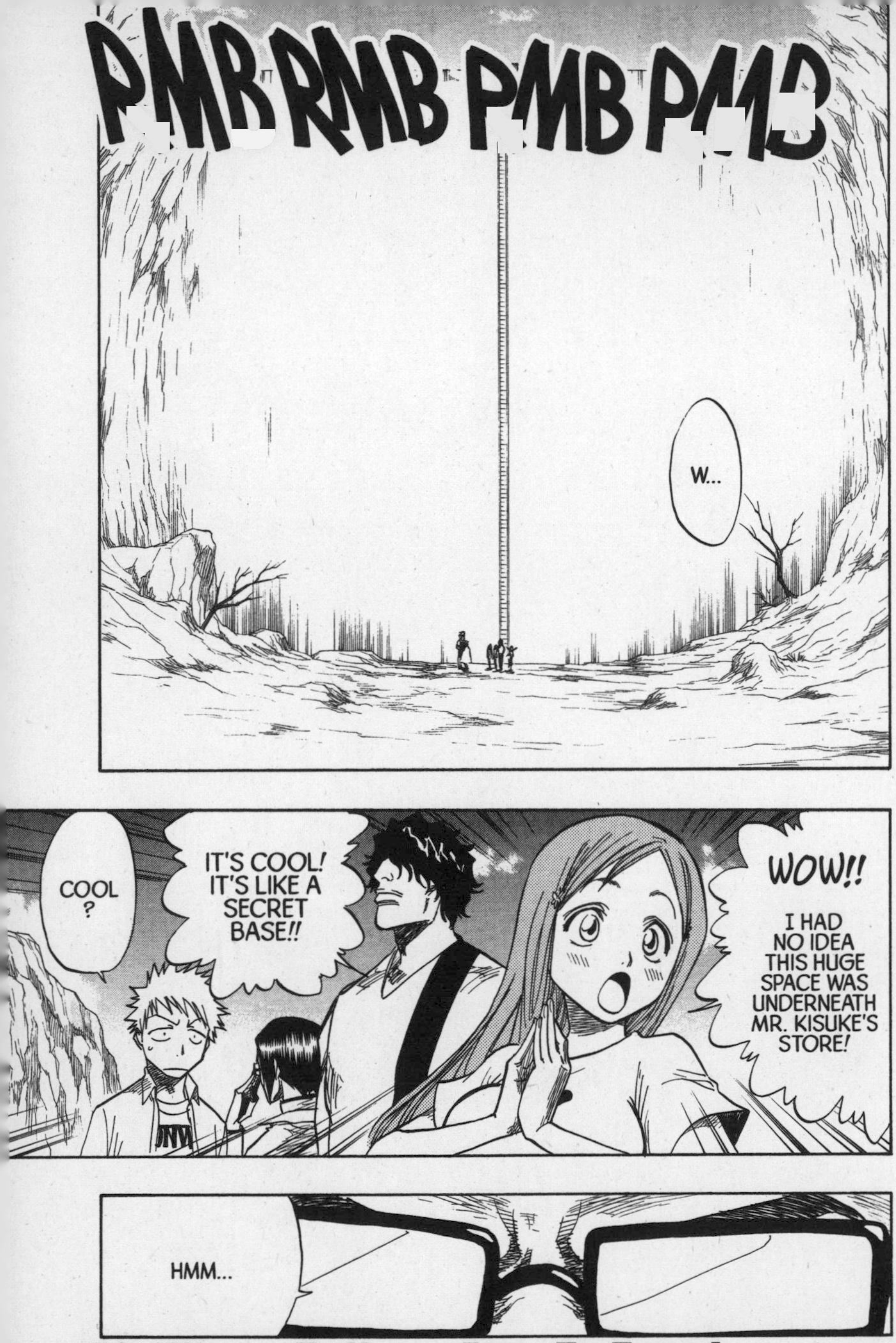
RMB RMB RMB RMB
W...
WOW!!
I HAD NO IDEA THIS HUGE SPACE WAS UNDERNEATH MR. KISUKE'S STORE!
IT'S COOL! IT'S LIKE A SECRET BASE!!
COOL?
HMM...

70. Where Hollows Fear To Tread

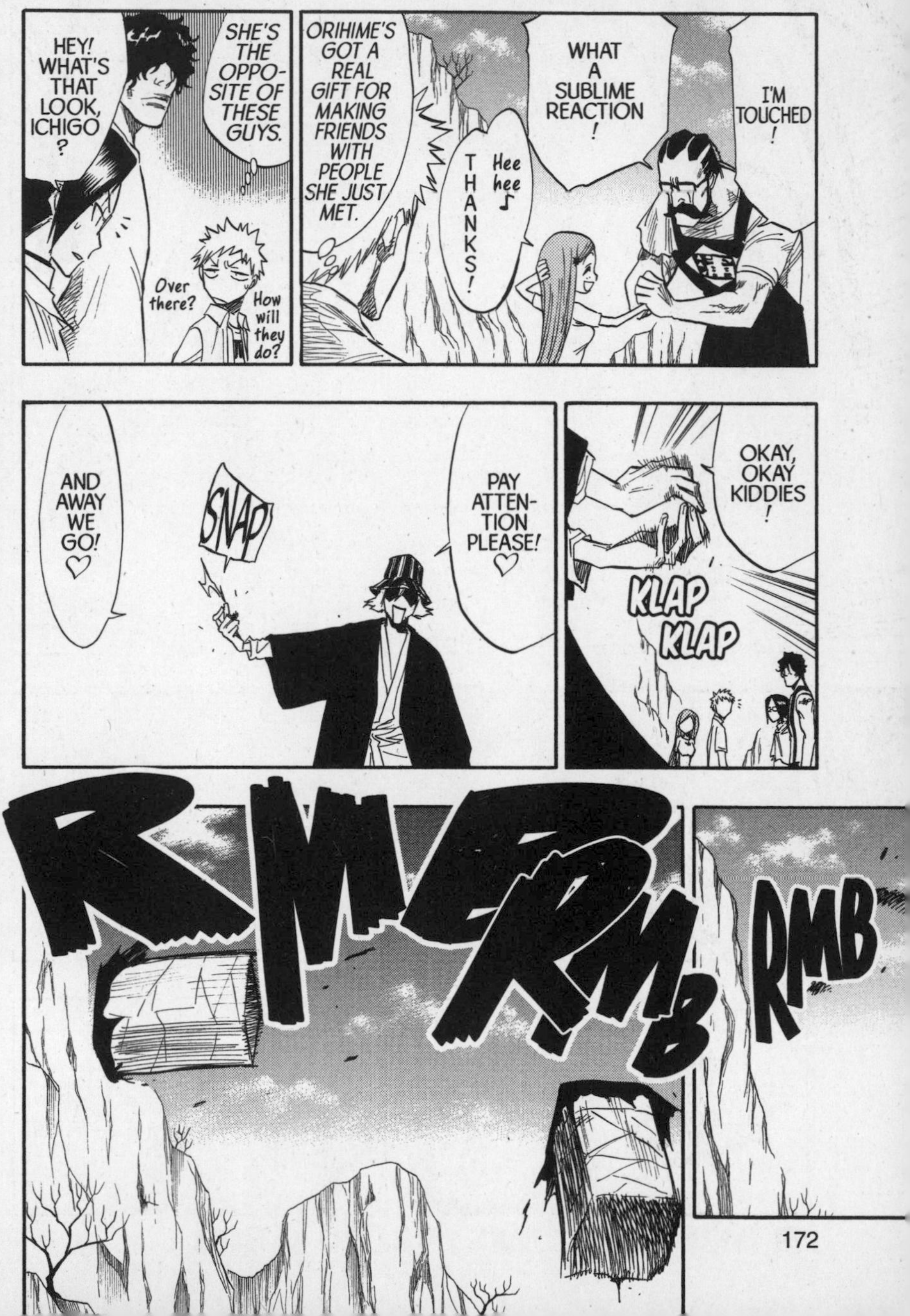
I'M TOUCHED!
WHAT A SUBLIME REACTION!
Hee hee ♪
THANKS!
ORIHIME'S GOT A REAL GIFT FOR MAKING FRIENDS WITH PEOPLE SHE JUST MET.
SHE'S THE OPPOSITE OF THESE GUYS.
HEY! WHAT'S THAT LOOK, ICHIGO?
How will they do?
Over there?
OKAY, OKAY KIDDIES!
KLAP KLAP
PAY ATTENTION PLEASE! ♡
SNAP
AND AWAY WE GO! ♡
RMB
RMMRMB

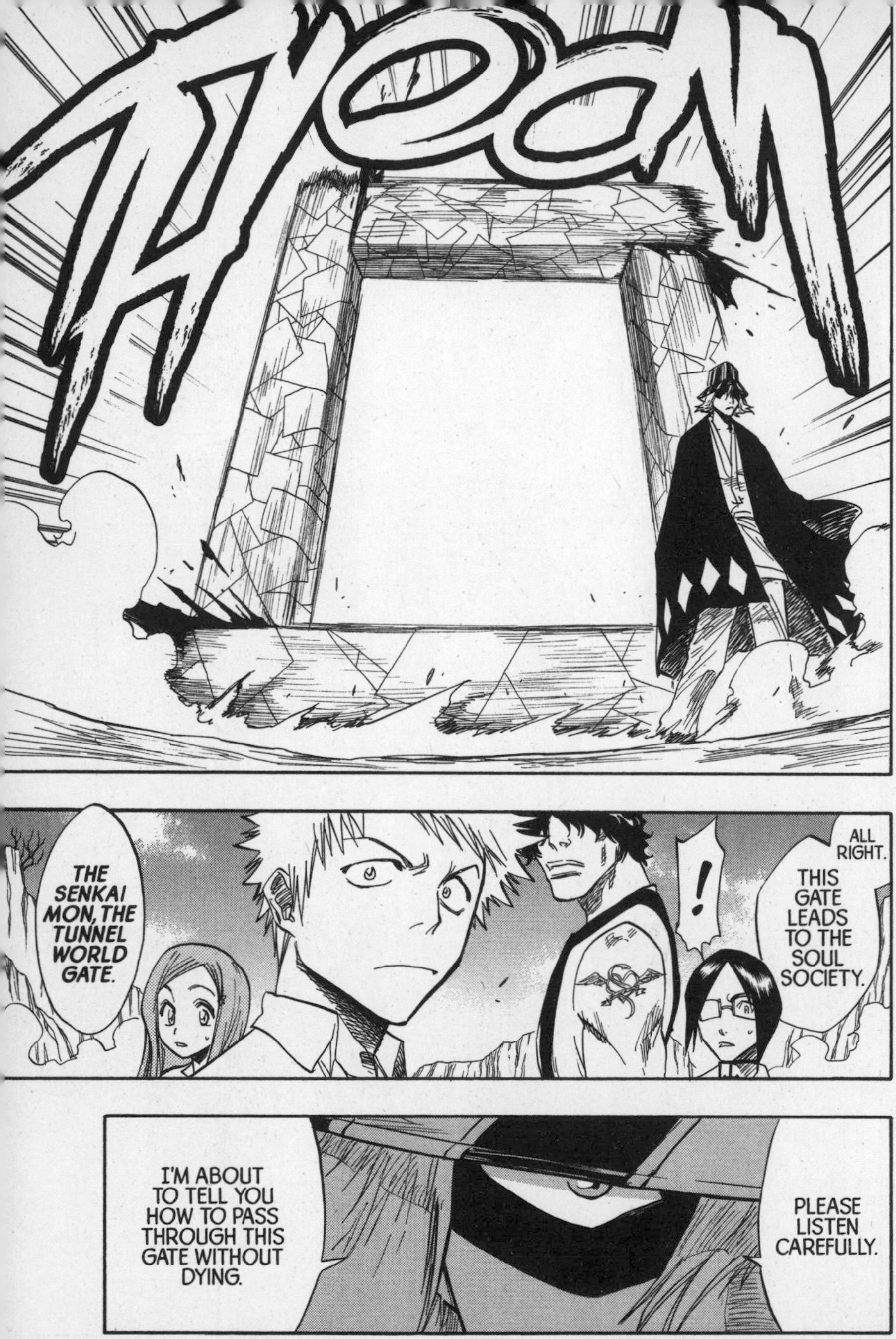
ALL RIGHT.
THIS GATE LEADS TO THE SOUL SOCIETY.
!
THE SENKAI MON, THE TUNNEL WORLD GATE.
PLEASE LISTEN CAREFULLY.
I'M ABOUT TO TELL YOU HOW TO PASS THROUGH THIS GATE WITHOUT DYING.

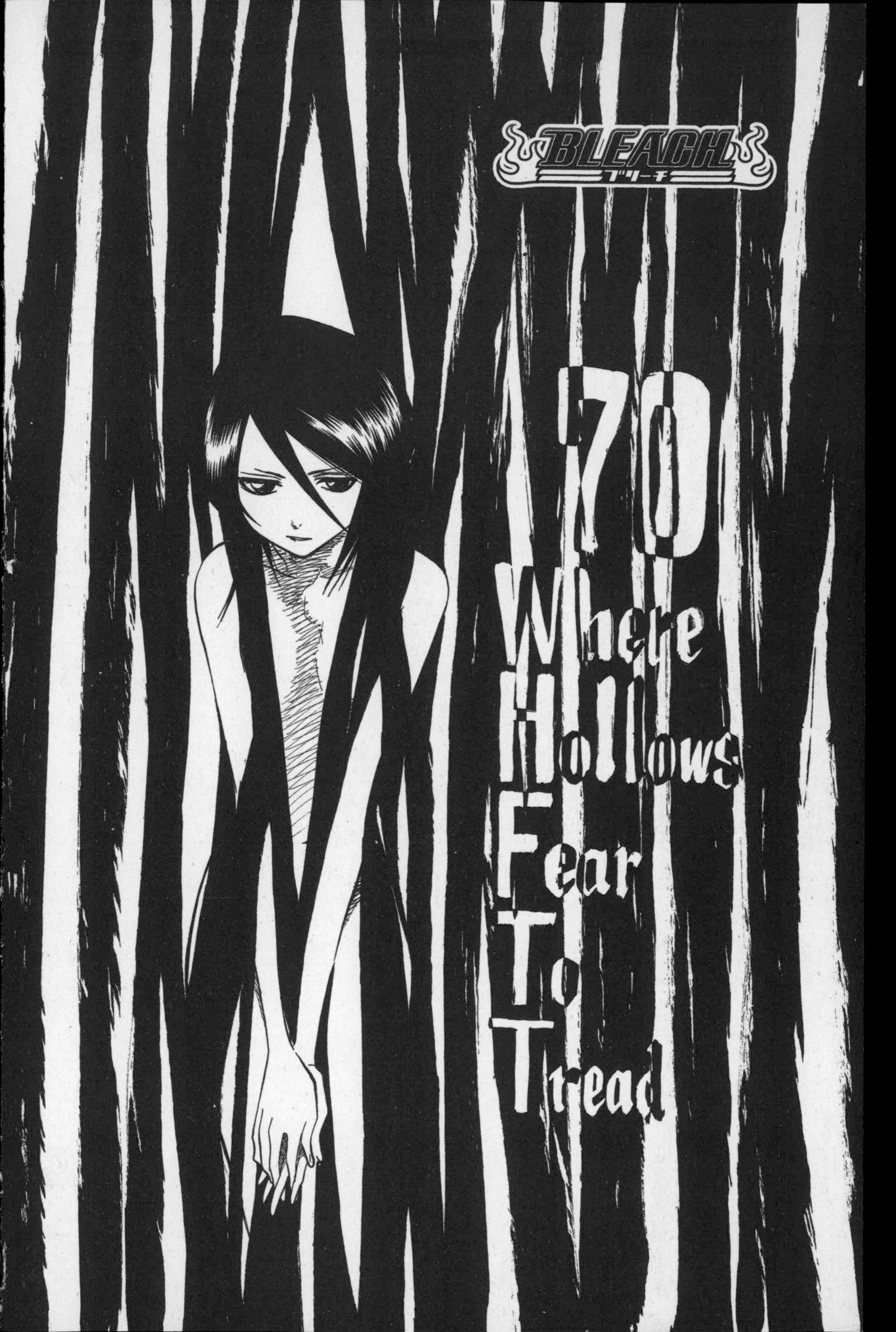
BLEACH
ブリーチ
70
Where Hollows Fear To Tread

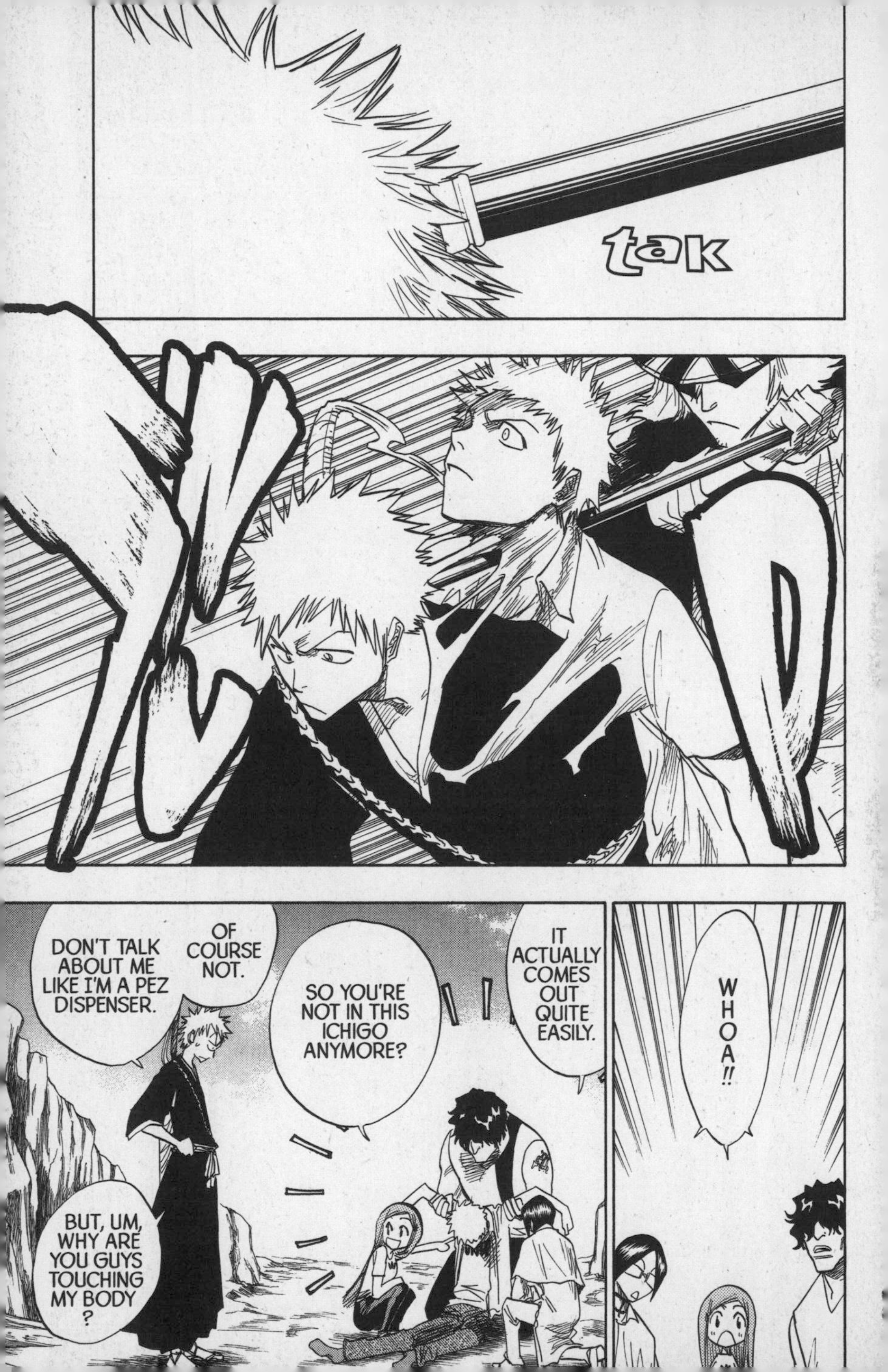
tak
WHOA!!
IT ACTUALLY COMES OUT QUITE EASILY.
SO YOU'RE NOT IN THIS ICHIGO ANYMORE?
OF COURSE NOT.
DON'T TALK ABOUT ME LIKE I'M A PEZ DISPENSER.
BUT, UM, WHY ARE YOU GUYS TOUCHING MY BODY?

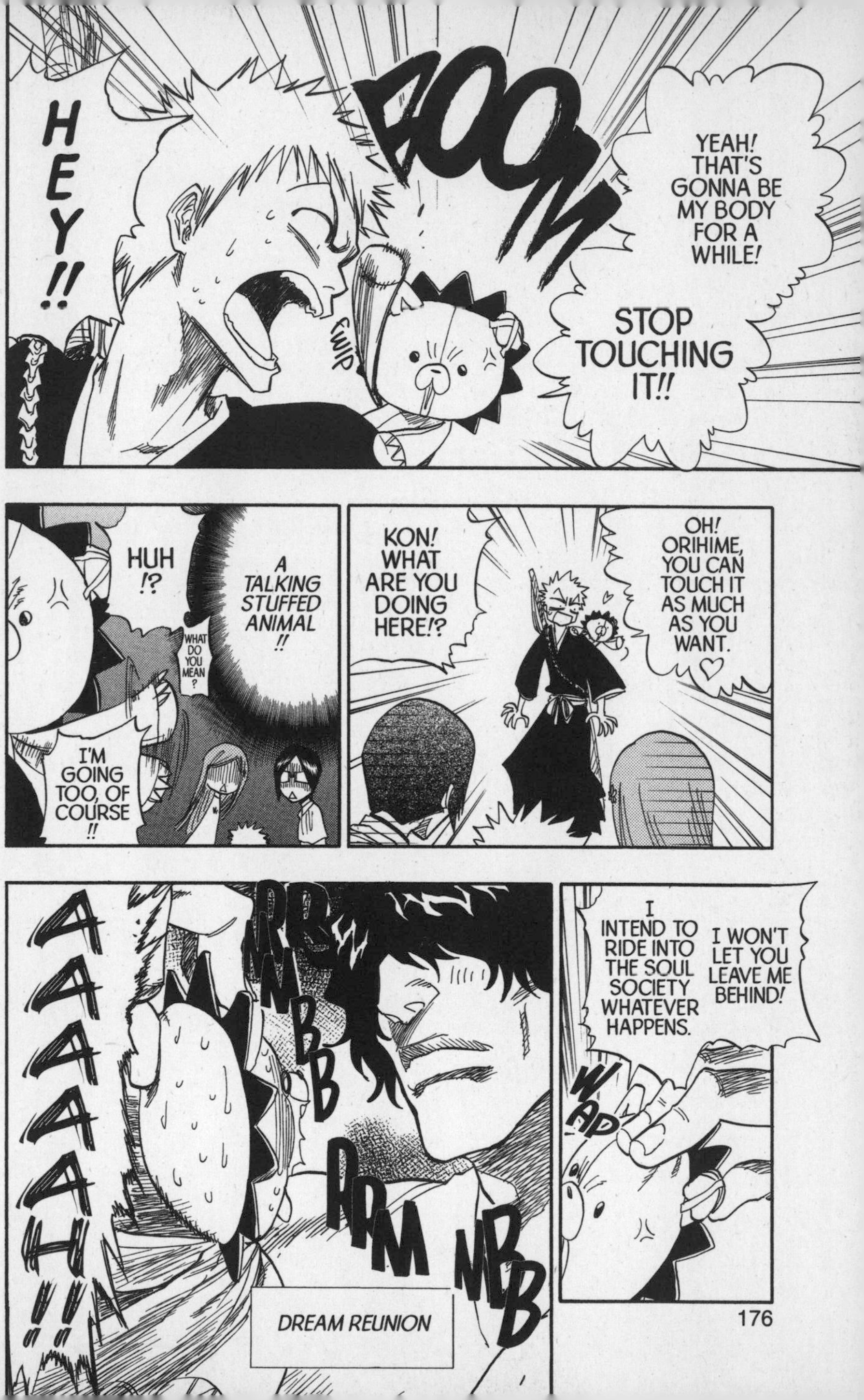
YEAH! THAT'S GONNA BE MY BODY FOR A WHILE!
STOP TOUCHING IT!!
BOOM
HEY!!
FWIP
OH! ORIHIME, YOU CAN TOUCH IT AS MUCH AS YOU WANT.
KON! WHAT ARE YOU DOING HERE!?
A TALKING STUFFED ANIMAL!!
HUH!?
WHAT DO YOU MEAN?
I'M GOING TOO, OF COURSE!!
I WON'T LET YOU LEAVE ME BEHIND!
I INTEND TO RIDE INTO THE SOUL SOCIETY WHATEVER HAPPENS.
WHAP
RRMMNBB
RRMMNBB
AAAAAH!!!
DREAM REUNION

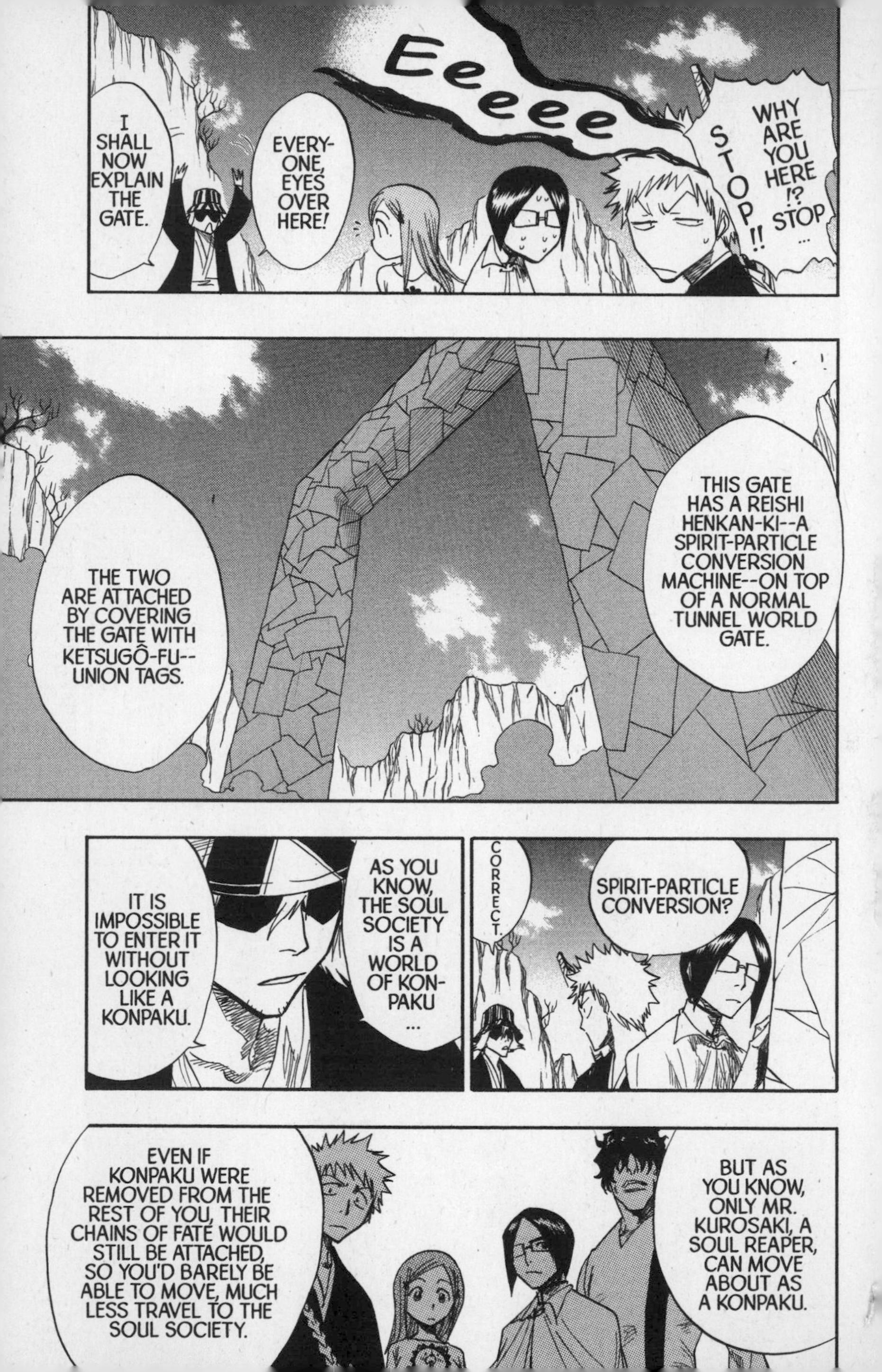
WHY ARE YOU HERE!? STOP...
STOP!!
Eeeee
EVERY-ONE, EYES OVER HERE!
I SHALL NOW EXPLAIN THE GATE.
THIS GATE HAS A REISHI HENKAN-KI--A SPIRIT-PARTICLE CONVERSION MACHINE--ON TOP OF A NORMAL TUNNEL WORLD GATE.
THE TWO ARE ATTACHED BY COVERING THE GATE WITH KETSUGÔ-FU--UNION TAGS.
SPIRIT-PARTICLE CONVERSION?
CORRECT.
AS YOU KNOW, THE SOUL SOCIETY IS A WORLD OF KON-PAKU...
IT IS IMPOSSIBLE TO ENTER IT WITHOUT LOOKING LIKE A KONPAKU.
BUT AS YOU KNOW, ONLY MR. KUROSAKI, A SOUL REAPER, CAN MOVE ABOUT AS A KONPAKU.
EVEN IF KONPAKU WERE REMOVED FROM THE REST OF YOU, THEIR CHAINS OF FATE WOULD STILL BE ATTACHED, SO YOU'D BARELY BE ABLE TO MOVE, MUCH LESS TRAVEL TO THE SOUL SOCIETY.

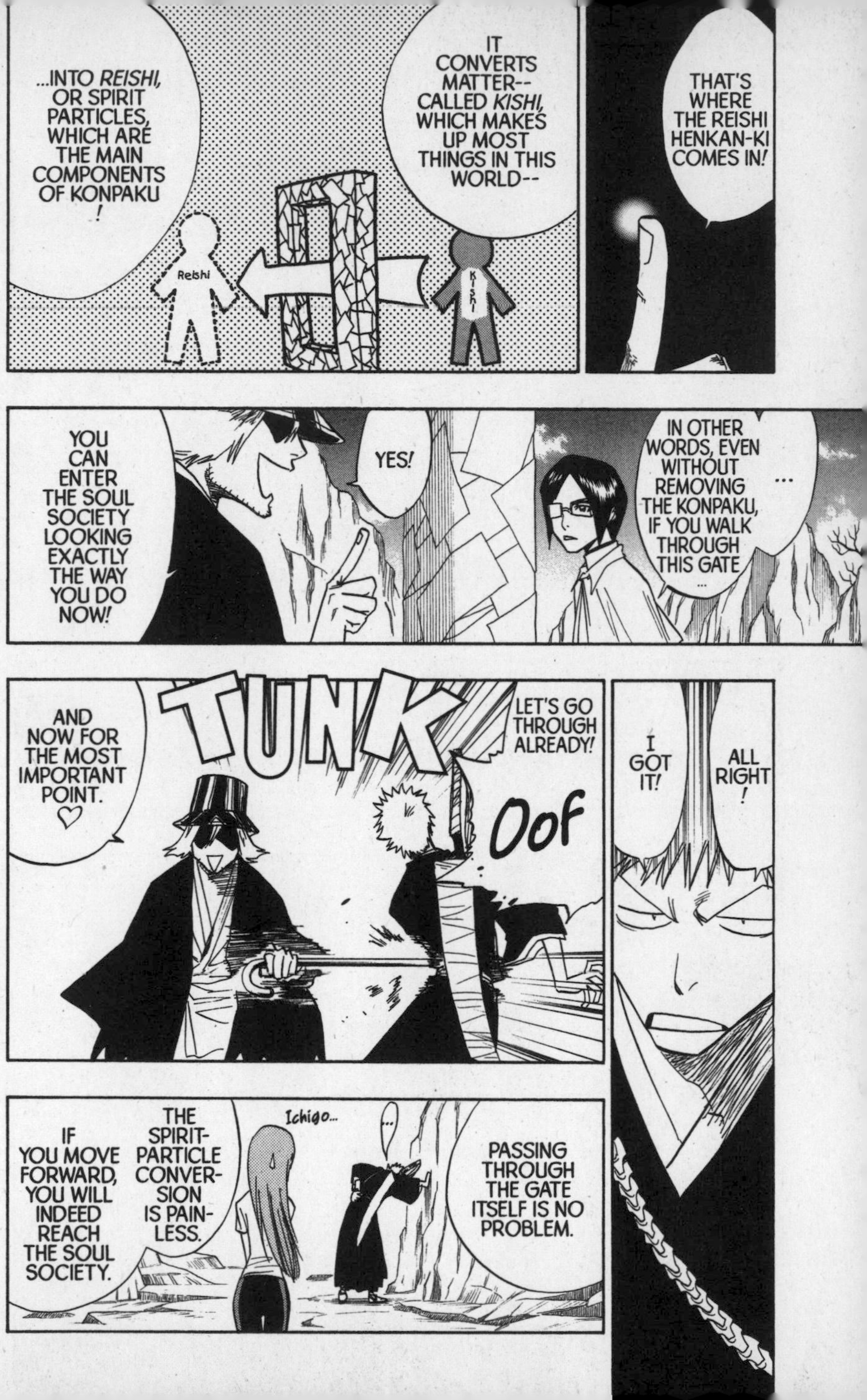
THAT'S WHERE THE REISHI HENKAN-KI COMES IN!
IT CONVERTS MATTER-- CALLED *KISHI,* WHICH MAKES UP MOST THINGS IN THIS WORLD--
Kishi
Reishi
...INTO *REISHI,* OR SPIRIT PARTICLES, WHICH ARE THE MAIN COMPONENTS OF KONPAKU!
IN OTHER WORDS, EVEN WITHOUT REMOVING THE KONPAKU, IF YOU WALK THROUGH THIS GATE...
...
YES!
YOU CAN ENTER THE SOUL SOCIETY LOOKING EXACTLY THE WAY YOU DO NOW!
ALL RIGHT!
I GOT IT!
LET'S GO THROUGH ALREADY!
Oof
TUNK
AND NOW FOR THE MOST IMPORTANT POINT. ♡
...
Ichigo...
PASSING THROUGH THE GATE ITSELF IS NO PROBLEM.
THE SPIRIT-PARTICLE CONVERSION IS PAINLESS.
IF YOU MOVE FORWARD, YOU WILL INDEED REACH THE SOUL SOCIETY.

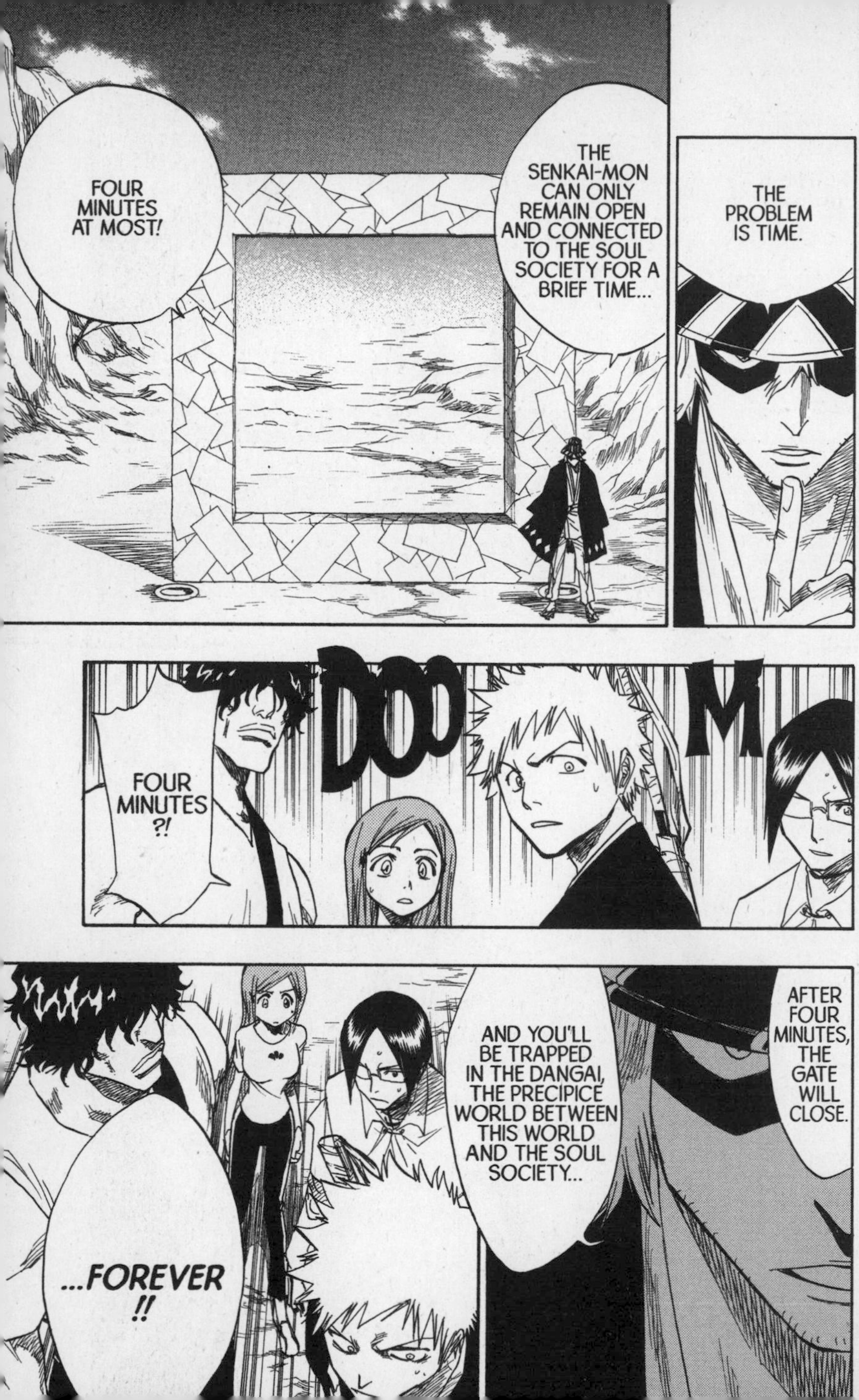
THE PROBLEM IS TIME.
THE SENKAI-MON CAN ONLY REMAIN OPEN AND CONNECTED TO THE SOUL SOCIETY FOR A BRIEF TIME...
FOUR MINUTES AT MOST!
DOOM
FOUR MINUTES ?!
AFTER FOUR MINUTES, THE GATE WILL CLOSE.
AND YOU'LL BE TRAPPED IN THE DANGAI, THE PRECIPICE WORLD BETWEEN THIS WORLD AND THE SOUL SOCIETY...
...FOREVER !!

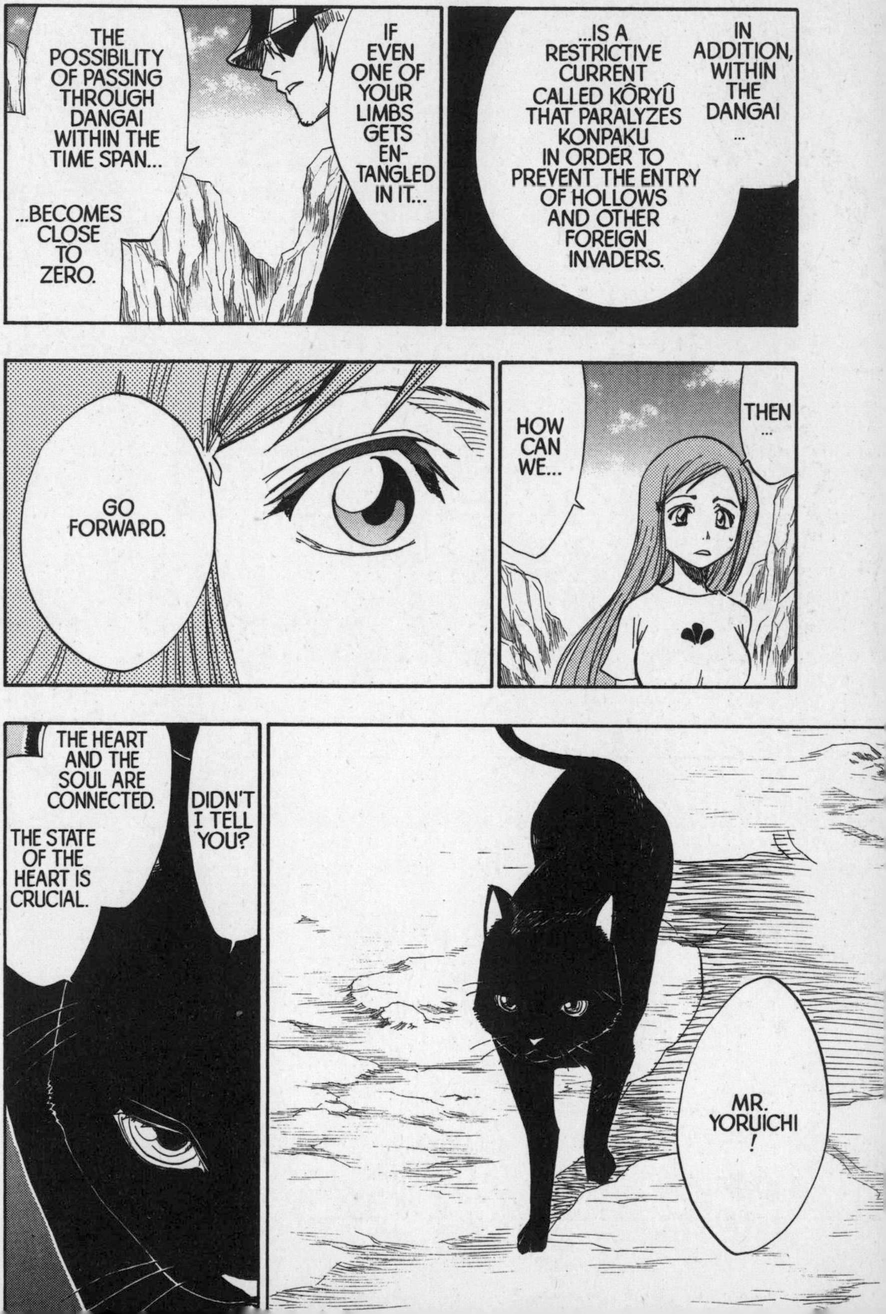
IN ADDITION, WITHIN THE DANGAI ...
...IS A RESTRICTIVE CURRENT CALLED KÔRYÛ THAT PARALYZES KONPAKU IN ORDER TO PREVENT THE ENTRY OF HOLLOWS AND OTHER FOREIGN INVADERS.
IF EVEN ONE OF YOUR LIMBS GETS EN-TANGLED IN IT...
THE POSSIBILITY OF PASSING THROUGH DANGAI WITHIN THE TIME SPAN...
...BECOMES CLOSE TO ZERO.
THEN ...
HOW CAN WE...
GO FORWARD.
MR. YORUICHI!
DIDN'T I TELL YOU?
THE HEART AND THE SOUL ARE CONNECTED.
THE STATE OF THE HEART IS CRUCIAL.

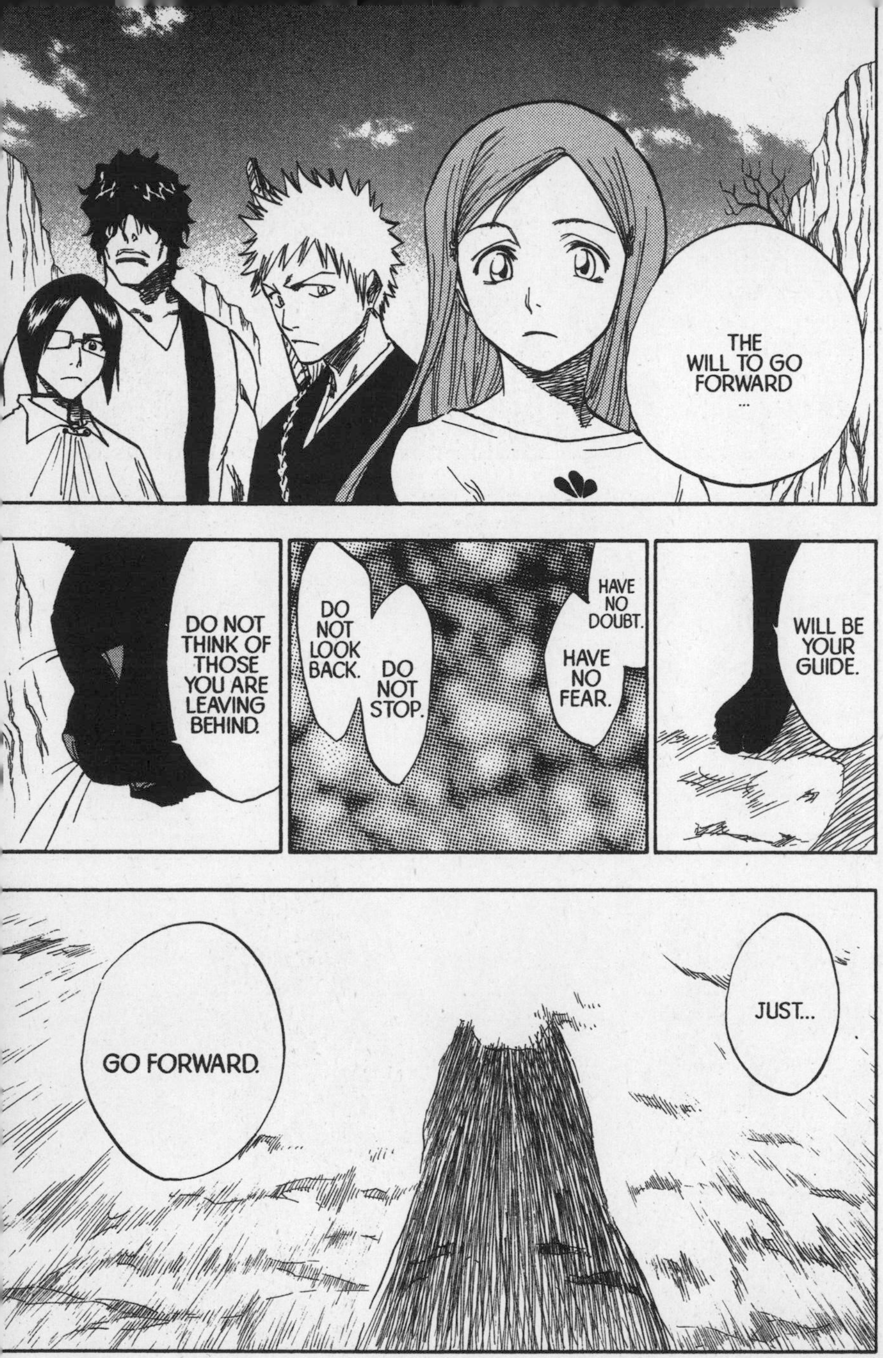
THE WILL TO GO FORWARD ...
WILL BE YOUR GUIDE.
HAVE NO DOUBT.
HAVE NO FEAR.
DO NOT LOOK BACK.
DO NOT STOP.
DO NOT THINK OF THOSE YOU ARE LEAVING BEHIND.
JUST...
GO FORWARD.

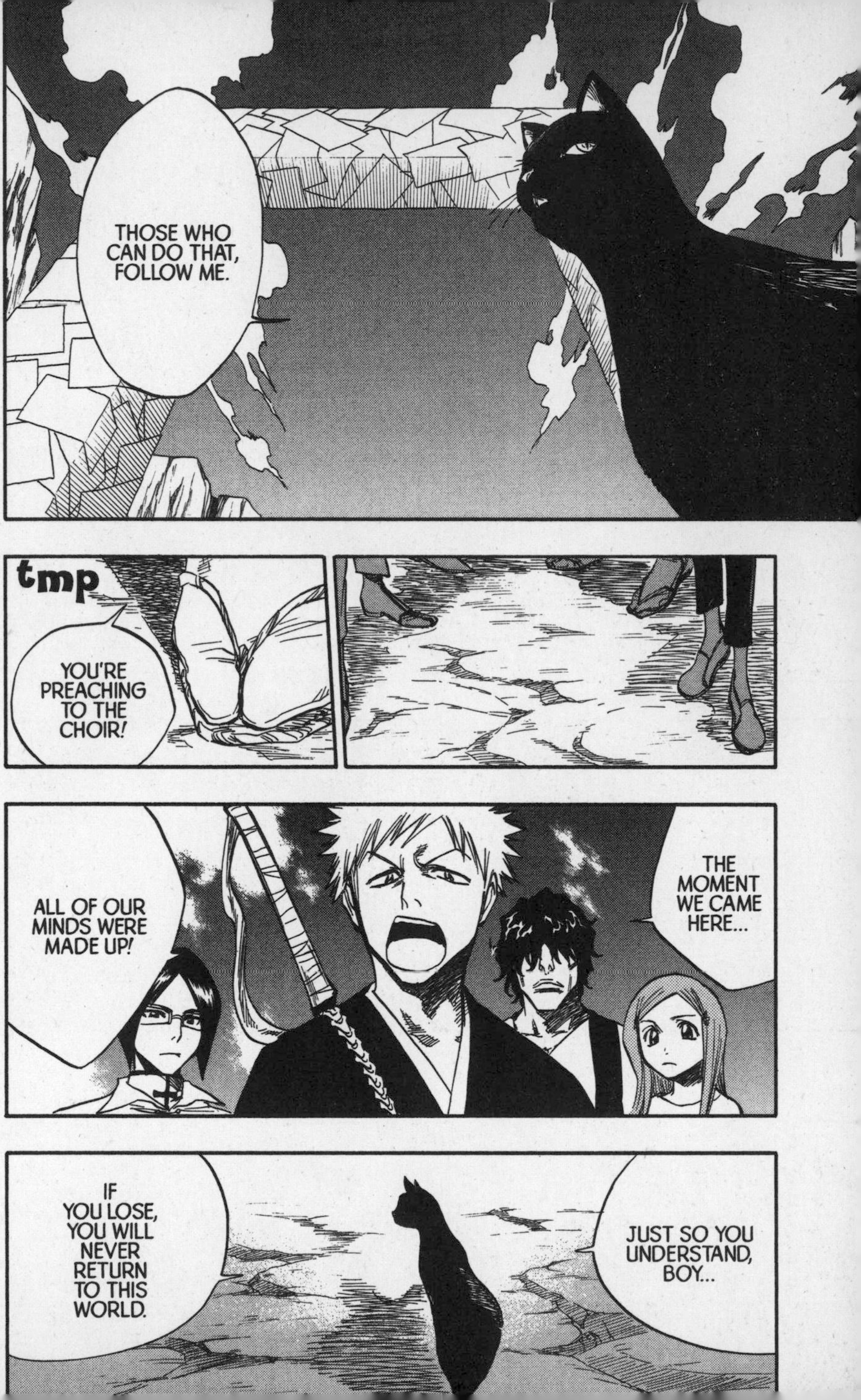
THOSE WHO CAN DO THAT, FOLLOW ME.
tmp
YOU'RE PREACHING TO THE CHOIR!
THE MOMENT WE CAME HERE...
ALL OF OUR MINDS WERE MADE UP!
JUST SO YOU UNDERSTAND, BOY...
IF YOU LOSE, YOU WILL NEVER RETURN TO THIS WORLD.

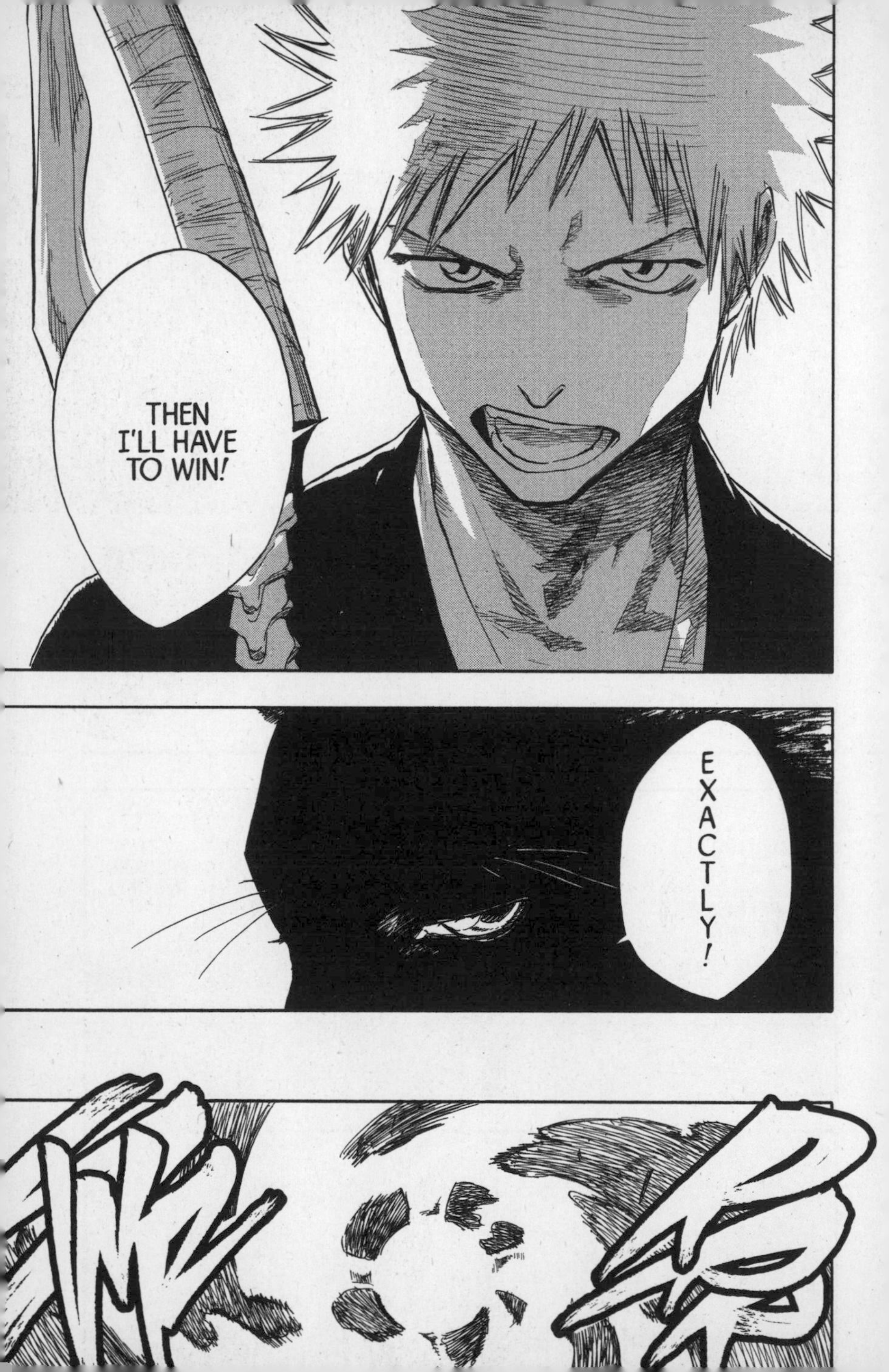
THEN I'LL HAVE TO WIN!
EXACTLY!

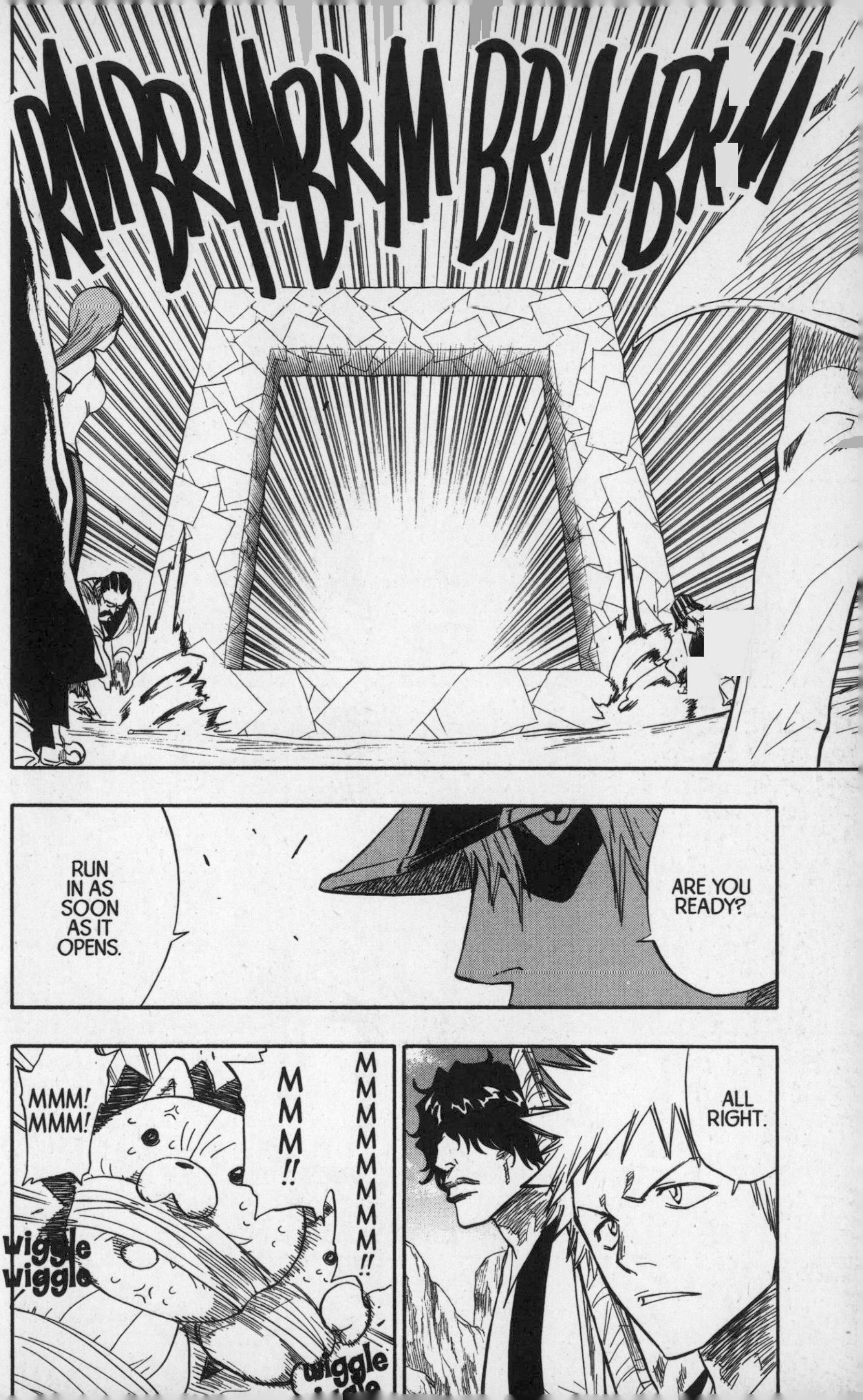
ARE YOU READY?
RUN IN AS SOON AS IT OPENS.
ALL RIGHT.
MMMMMMMMM!!
MMM!!
MMM! MMM!
wiggle wiggle
wiggle

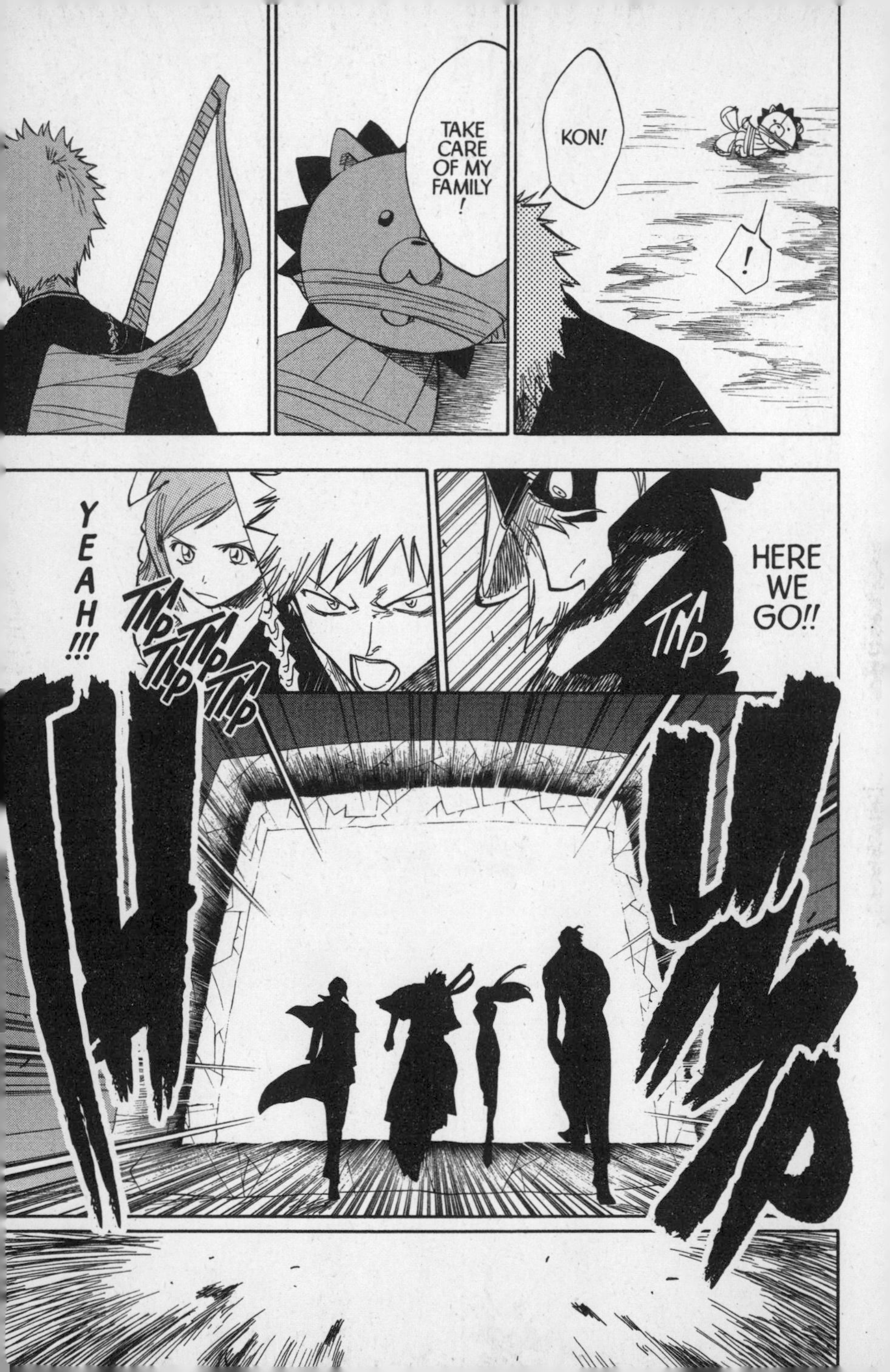
KON!
!
TAKE CARE OF MY FAMILY!
HERE WE GO!!
TMP
YEAH!!!
TMP TMP TMP TMP

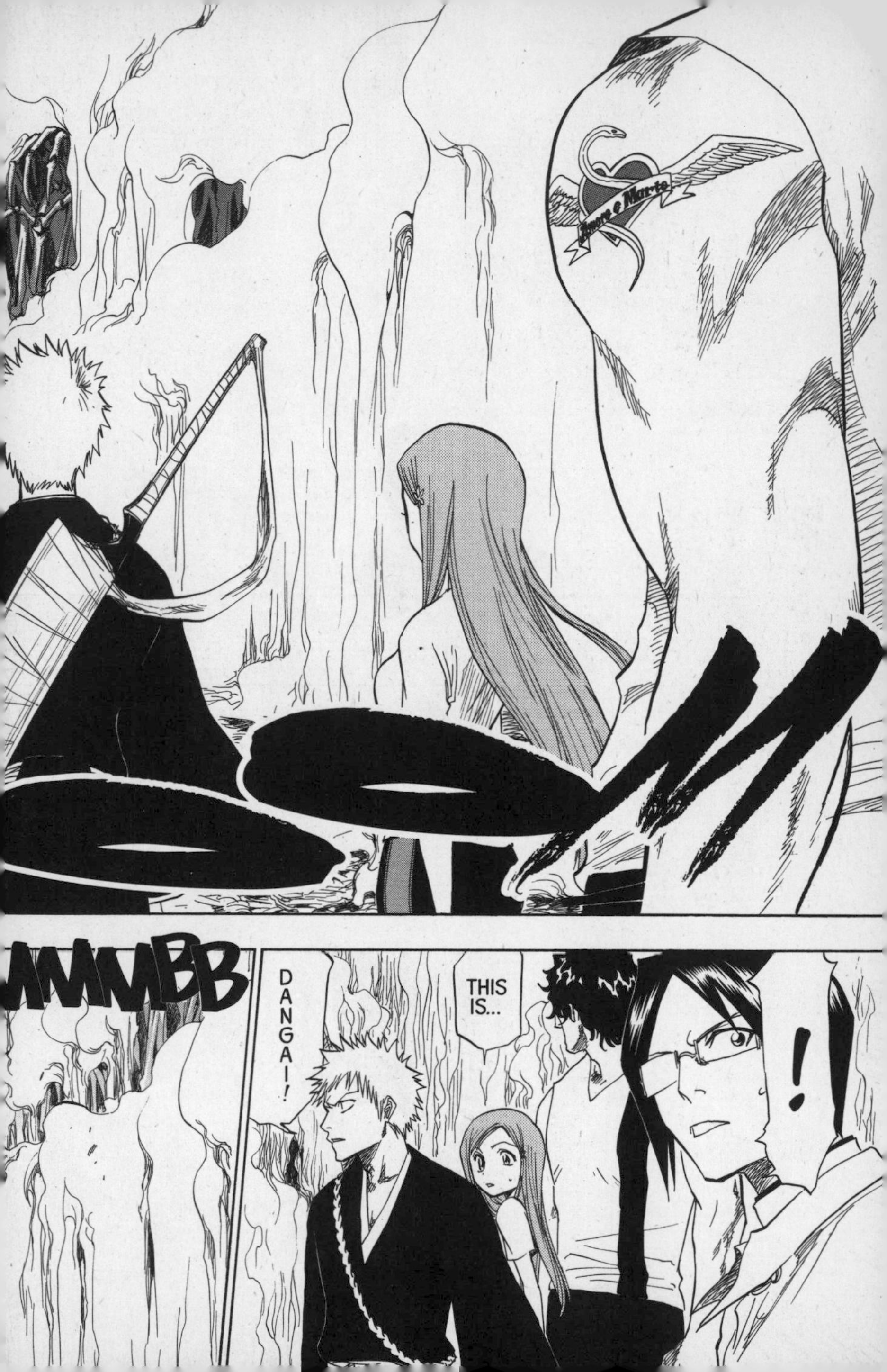
!
THIS IS...
DANGAI!
MMMBB

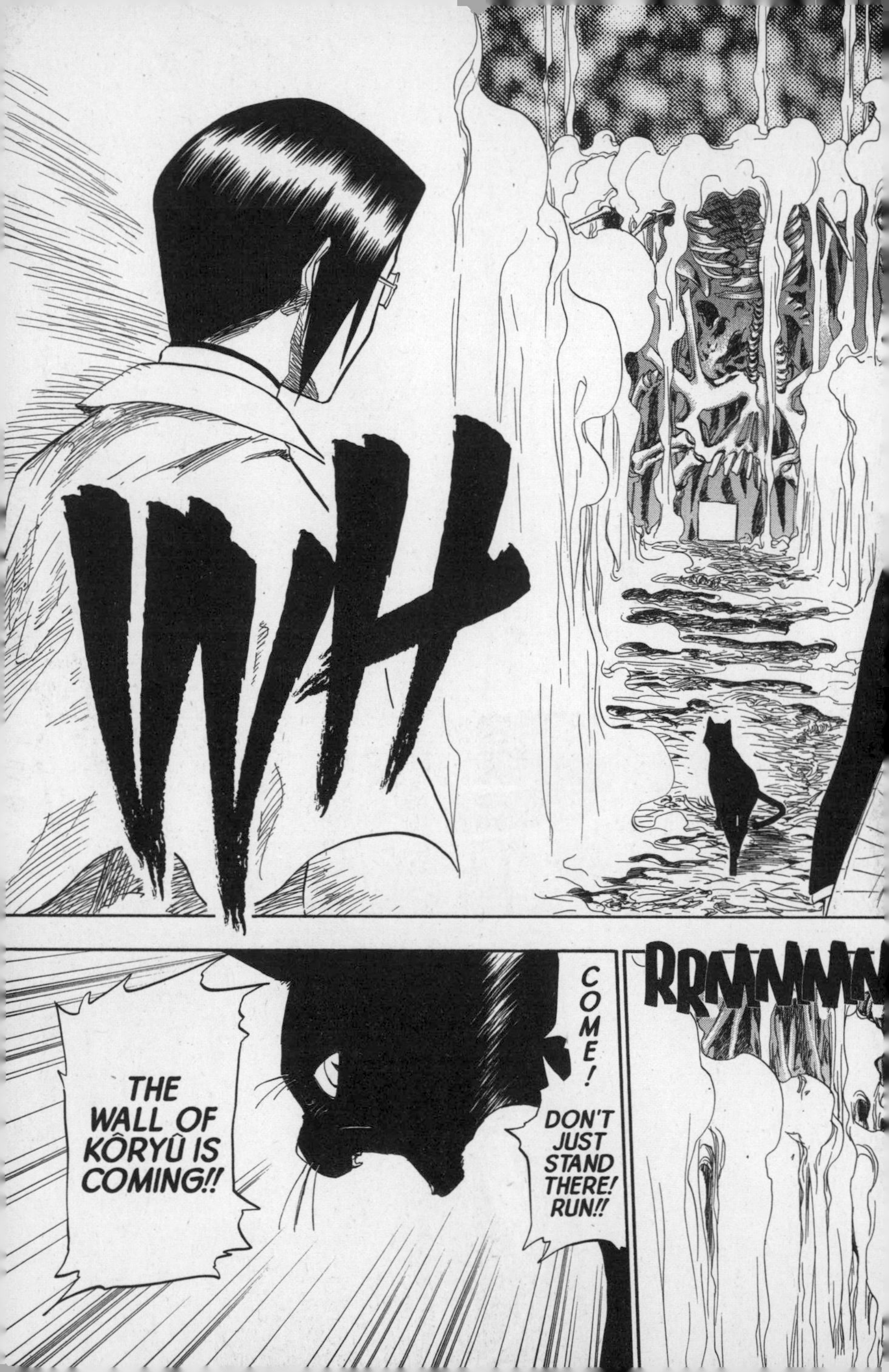
COME!
DON'T JUST STAND THERE! RUN!!
THE WALL OF KÔRYÛ IS COMING!!

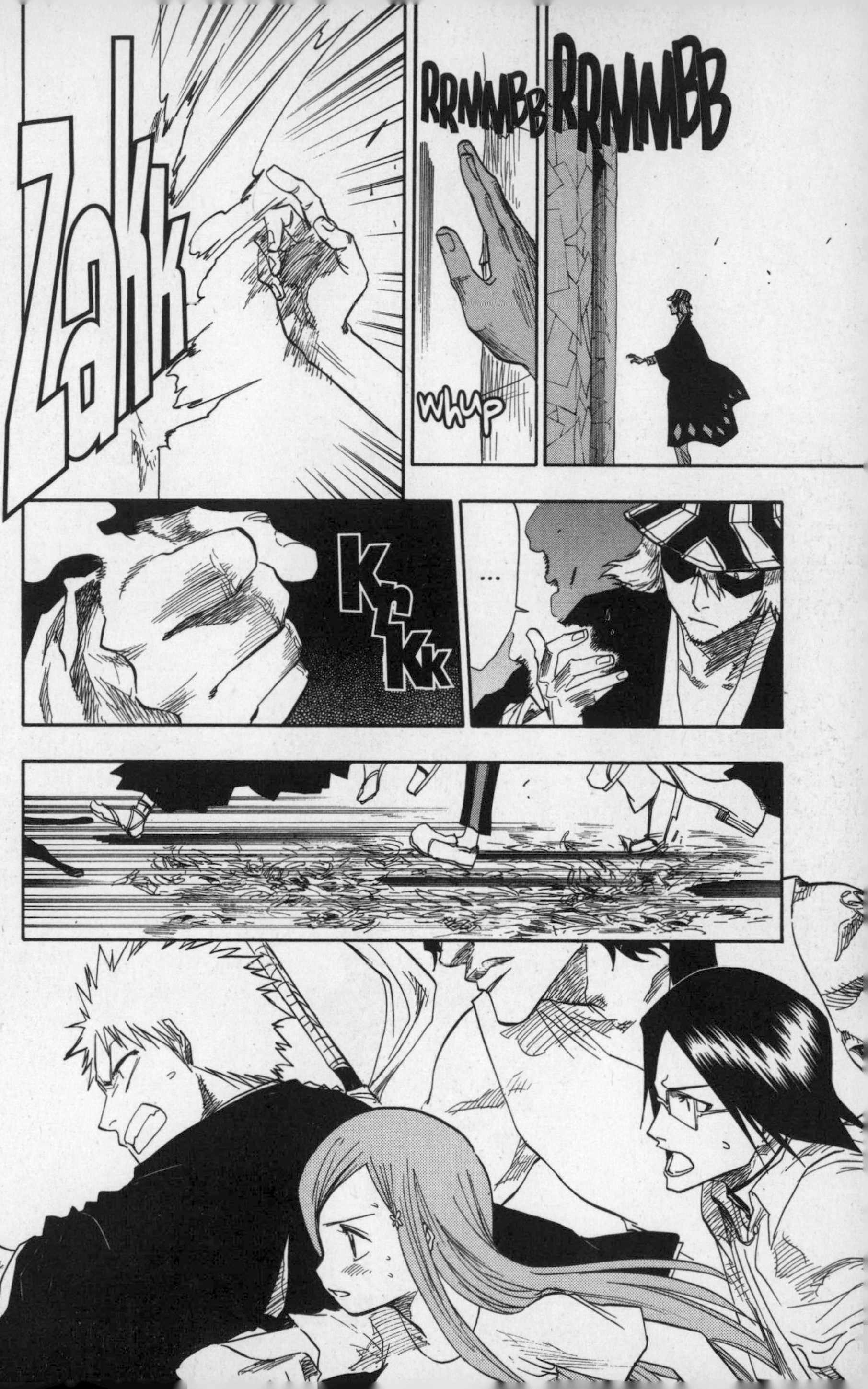
RRMMBB
RRMMBB
whup
Zakk
...
Krkk

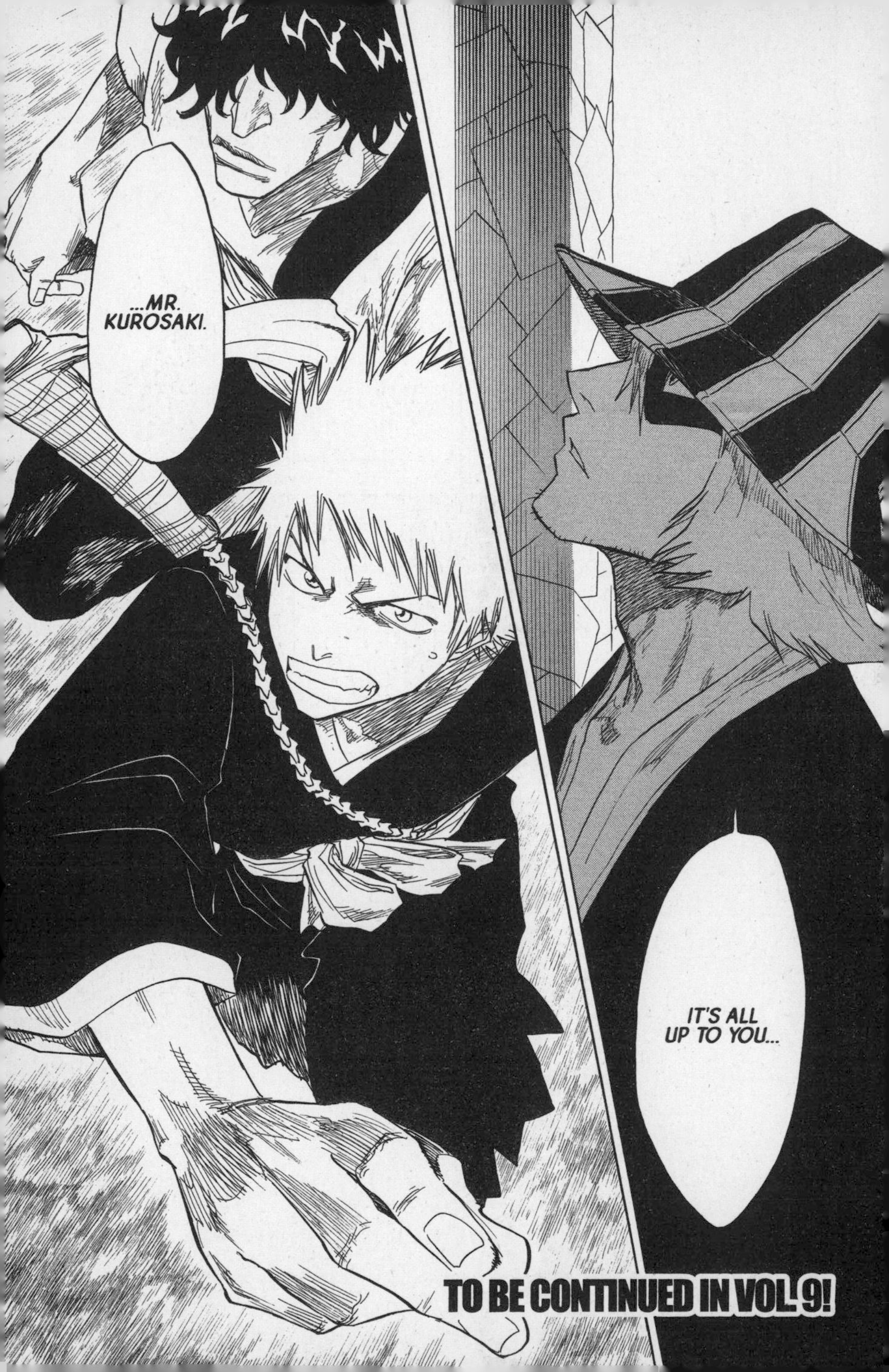
IT'S ALL UP TO YOU...
...MR. KUROSAKI.
TO BE CONTINUED IN VOL. 9!

Just when I thought he was here to stay!!

waah

Ichigo took off again!!

waah

Bleach Extra!! Radio-Kon3

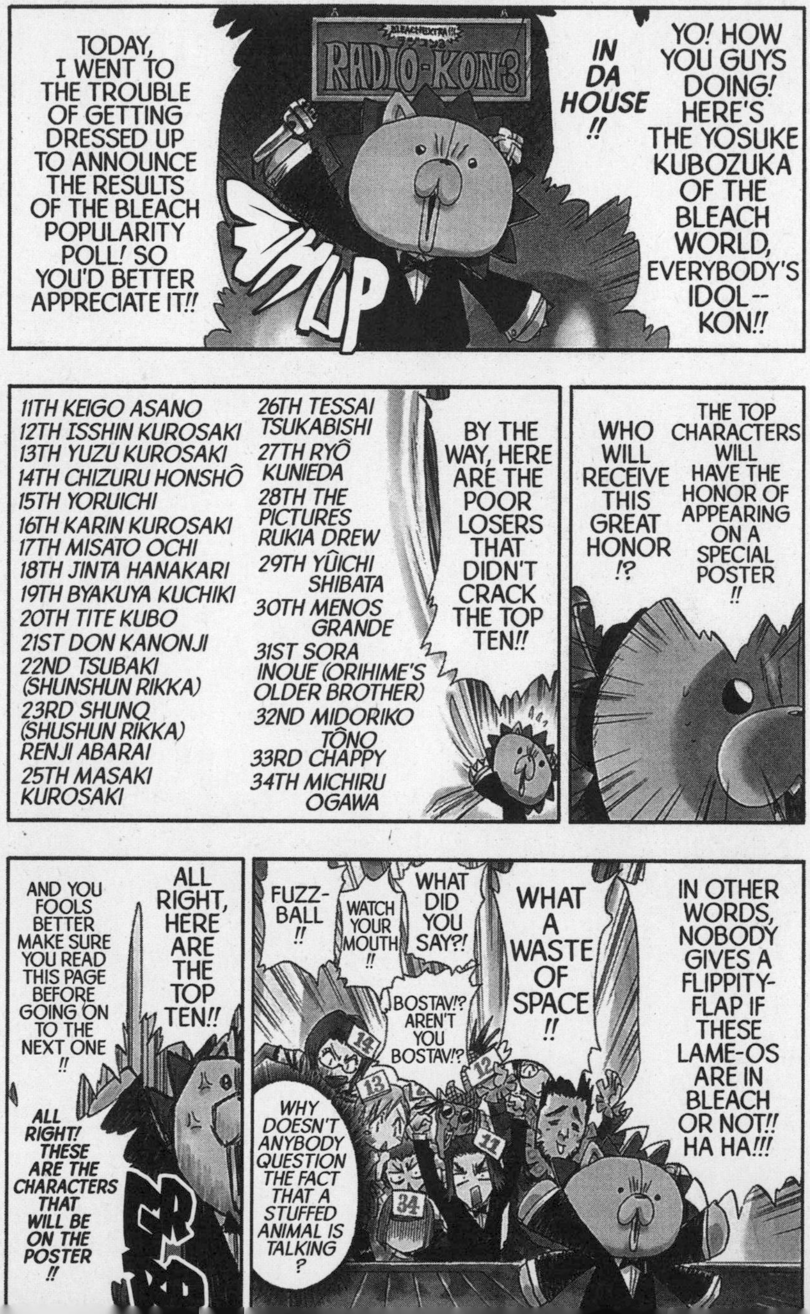

YO! HOW YOU GUYS DOING! HERE'S THE YOSUKE KUBOZUKA OF THE BLEACH WORLD, EVERYBODY'S IDOL--KON!!
IN DA HOUSE!!
RADIO-KON3
TODAY, I WENT TO THE TROUBLE OF GETTING DRESSED UP TO ANNOUNCE THE RESULTS OF THE BLEACH POPULARITY POLL! SO YOU'D BETTER APPRECIATE IT!!
THE TOP CHARACTERS WILL HAVE THE HONOR OF APPEARING ON A SPECIAL POSTER!!
WHO WILL RECEIVE THIS GREAT HONOR!?
BY THE WAY, HERE ARE THE POOR LOSERS THAT DIDN'T CRACK THE TOP TEN!!
11TH KEIGO ASANO
12TH ISSHIN KUROSAKI
13TH YUZU KUROSAKI
14TH CHIZURU HONSHÔ
15TH YORUICHI
16TH KARIN KUROSAKI
17TH MISATO OCHI
18TH JINTA HANAKARI
19TH BYAKUYA KUCHIKI
20TH TITE KUBO
21ST DON KANONJI
22ND TSUBAKI (SHUNSHUN RIKKA)
23RD SHUNO (SHUSHUN RIKKA)
RENJI ABARAI
25TH MASAKI KUROSAKI
26TH TESSAI TSUKABISHI
27TH RYÔ KUNIEDA
28TH THE PICTURES RUKIA DREW
29TH YÛICHI SHIBATA
30TH MENOS GRANDE
31ST SORA INOUE (ORIHIME'S OLDER BROTHER)
32ND MIDORIKO TÔNO
33RD CHAPPY
34TH MICHIRU OGAWA
IN OTHER WORDS, NOBODY GIVES A FLIPPITY-FLAP IF THESE LAME-OS ARE IN BLEACH OR NOT!! HA HA!!!
WHAT A WASTE OF SPACE!!
WHAT DID YOU SAY?!
WATCH YOUR MOUTH!!
FUZZ-BALL!!
BOSTAV!? AREN'T YOU BOSTAV!?
WHY DOESN'T ANYBODY QUESTION THE FACT THAT A STUFFED ANIMAL IS TALKING?
ALL RIGHT, HERE ARE THE TOP TEN!!
AND YOU FOOLS BETTER MAKE SURE YOU READ THIS PAGE BEFORE GOING ON TO THE NEXT ONE!!
ALL RIGHT! THESE ARE THE CHARACTERS THAT WILL BE ON THE POSTER!!

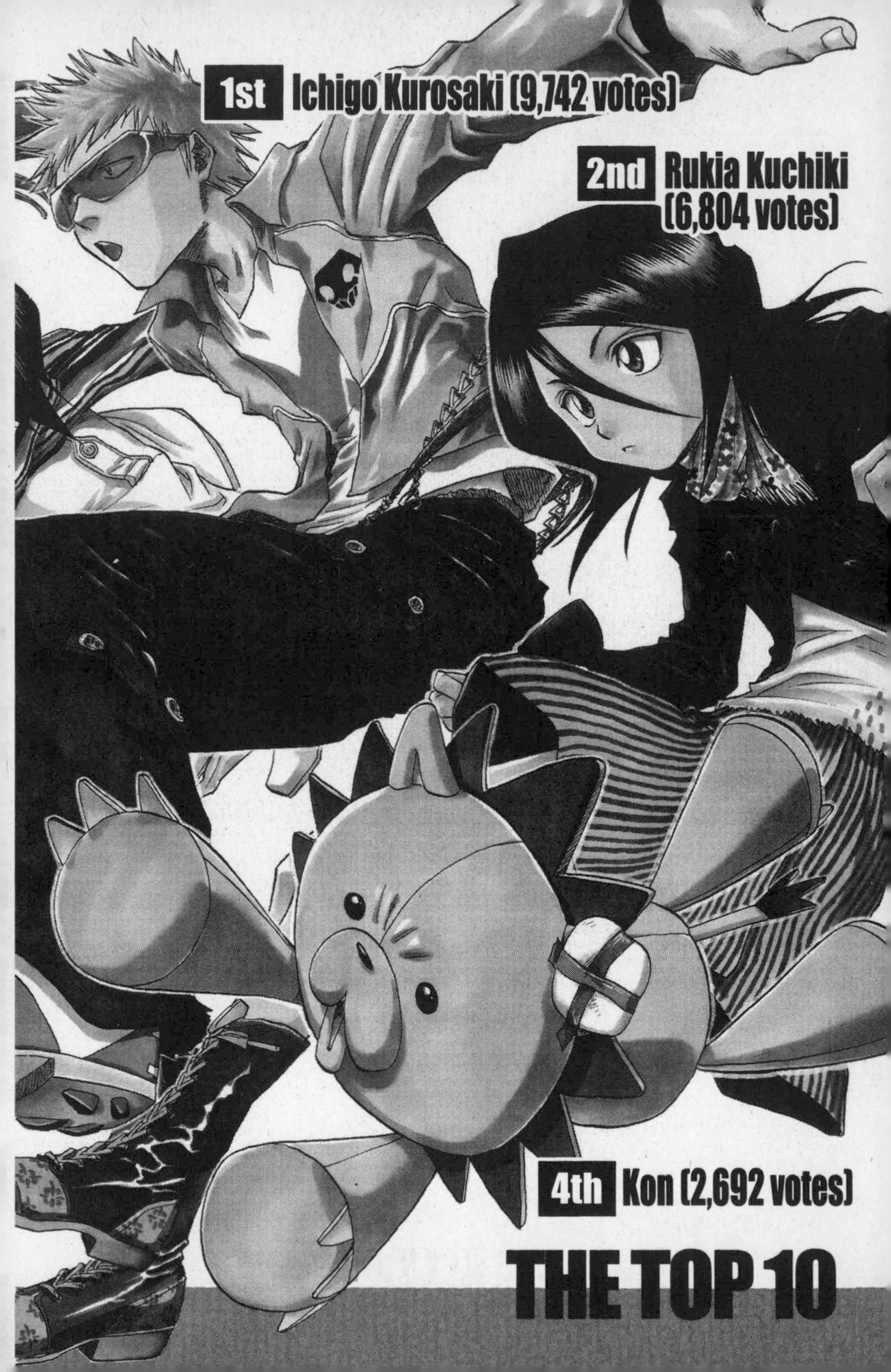
1st Ichigo Kurosaki (9,742 votes)
2nd Rukia Kuchiki (6,804 votes)
4th Kon (2,692 votes)
THE TOP 10

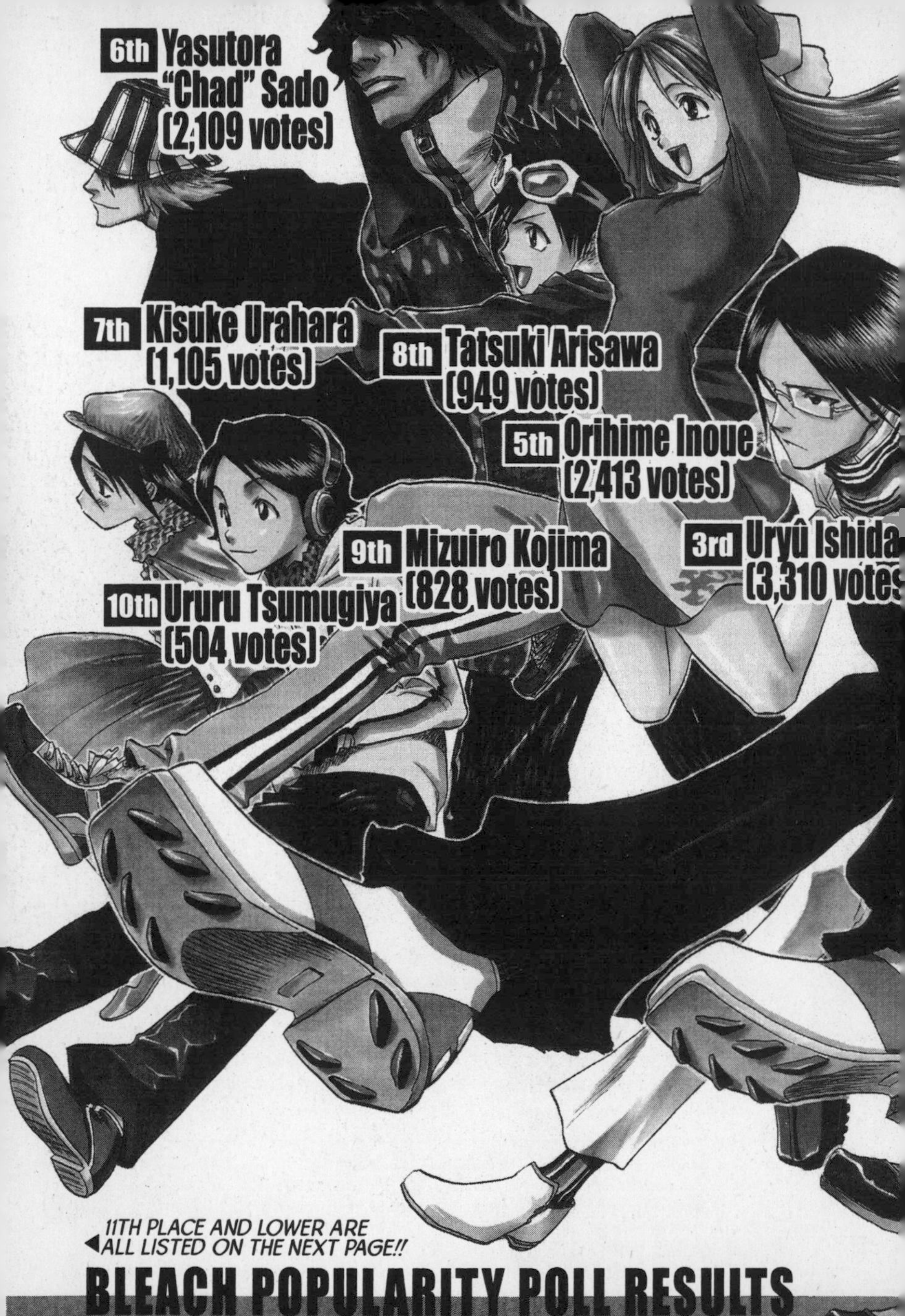
6th Yasutora "Chad" Sado (2,109 votes)
7th Kisuke Urahara (1,105 votes)
8th Tatsuki Arisawa (949 votes)
5th Orihime Inoue (2,413 votes)
3rd Uryû Ishida (3,310 votes
9th Mizuiro Kojima (828 votes)
10th Ururu Tsumugiya (504 votes)

◀ 11TH PLACE AND LOWER ARE ALL LISTED ON THE NEXT PAGE!!

BLEACH POPULARITY POLL RESULTS

These results are based on a poll conducted in the pages of WEEKLY SHONEN JUMP, Japan. Who's your favorite BLEACH character? Send your answers to: SHONEN JUMP c/o VIZ, LLC P.O. Box 77010, San Francisco, CA 94107 ATTN: BLEACH Popularity Contest

BLEACH POPULARITY POLL RESULTS

THE COMPLETE LIST
Popularity Vote Complete Results
The number of votes are in ()

11th Keigo Asano (496)
12th Isshin Kurosaki (488)
13th Yuzu Kurosaki (482)
14th Chizuru Honshō (475)
15th Yoruichi (471)
16th Karin Kurosaki (462)
17th Misato Ochi (459)
18th Jinta Hanakari (457)
19th Byakuya Kuchiki (446)
20th Tite Kubo (395)
21st Don Kanonji (390)
22nd Tsubaki
    (Shunshun Rikka) (382)
23rd Shunō
    (Shushun Rikka) (374)

Renji Abarai (374)
25th Masaki Kurosaki (351)
26th Tessai Tsukabishi (333)
27th Ryō Kunieda (292)
28th The pictures Rukia drew (281)
29th Yūichi Shibata (268)
30th Menos Grande (236)
31st Sora Inoue (203)
32nd Midori Tōno (166)
33rd Soul Candy Chappy (132)
34th Michiru Ogawa (107)
35th Shunshun Rikka (104)
36th Lilly (Shunshun Rikka) (85)
37th Ayame (Shunshun Rikka) (69)
38th The ghost girl in episode 1 (41)

39th Mahana (28)
40th Uryū's teacher (25)
41st Shigeo (22)
42nd The weirdo of the R&D
    Department (15)
43rd Grand Fisher (12)
44th Soul Candy Yuki (11)
45th Soul Candy Alfred (9)
    Ōshima (9)
47th Acidwire (8)
48th Hollow (7)
    Old man from
    vegetable store (7)
    Cookie (7)

51st Harutoki/Soul Candy Kaneshiro (6 votes each)
53rd Enraku/Soul Candy Ginosuke/Soul Candy Pupples/Principal/Micchan (5 votes each)
58th Soul Candy Schteiner/Soul Candy Gringo/Soul Candy Diana/Bostav/Teacher Kagine/Hinagiku
    (4 votes each)
64th Hitomi Victoria Odagiri/Soul Candy Blues/Soul Candy Claudia/Baigon/Spirit of the bad bear/
    The Hollow Shrieker put out/Fishbone D/Yama-chan/Melon/Hashigami
    (3 votes each)
74th Shrieker/The grandpa and son during blackout/Toshi-Rin/Marianne/Magic Girl Megalon
    (2 votes each)
79th Francois/Just Kon's doll/Snake Whistle/The parakeet that's not Yuichi/Caterpillar Hollow/
    The doll that Uryū fixed/The person who raced Orihime and Ichigo in Orihime's fantasy/
    The clerk girl at CD store/Desk used for throwing/Akutabi Ganma/Nancy/Hexapods/
    Dad's Great Whistle/Schneider/Randy Johnson/Ino/Kaneda/Kuroage-Ha/The spirit of the office
    worker Konsōed in episode one/The Inoki-like Ichigo in Orihime's fantasy/Iwao/Mikami/
    The Soul Reaper that appeared in Rukia's flashback scene/Madame Akiyama/Abuelo
    (1 vote each)

These are the results from the 1st Popularity Poll taken from August of 2002
(votes were collected beginning with episode 51). Offering the Top Ten Character
Poster to 100 people worked--we received a lot more votes than we expected.
Byakuya, Renji, Yoruichi--who are new--ranked high; one guy voted 200 times for
Miss Ochi; there was one vote for a character from my previous work (Akutabi
Gamma); and there were a lot of maniacs. Looking at all the results, I think it came
out pretty interestingly. It was fun. I hope we can do it again in the summer…

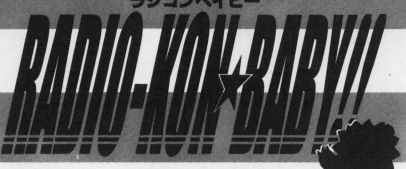

ラジコンベイビー

RADIO-KON★BABY!!

"WE ARE RADIO-KON BABY!!"

★2★

YO! WAZZUP?! THOUGH WE SAID IT WOULD BE AN INTERMITTENT FEATURE, WE GOT SUCH AN OVERWHELMING RESPONSE THAT WE COULDN'T BACK OFF EVEN IF WE WANTED TO! SO, OUR GUEST TODAY IS...UM...? TATSUKI ARISAWA!! THANK YOU VERY MUCH!

WHERE ARE WE?

OH! IT'S YOU. ORIHIME'S FRIEND, UM...I DON'T KNOW YOUR NAME! HA HA!!

WHO ARE YOU? ARE YOU, LIKE, A DOLL OR SOMETHING? WHY ARE YOU MOVING AND TALKING? IS IT BECAUSE YOU'RE RADIO-KON-TROLLED?

WHAT ARE YOU BABBLING ABOUT? C'MON, LET'S JUST DO THIS!!

I DON'T KNOW WHAT YOU ARE, BUT OKAY.

Is the accent in Tatsuki on the ta or ki? I've gotten into a lot of arguments over this...

Kappa King -- Hokkaido

WHAT? THESE QUESTIONS ARE ABOUT ME?

WELL, YOU'RE THE FREAKIN' GUEST! JUST SHUT UP AND ANSWER IT!

YOU'RE A RUDE TALKING DOLL. WELL, THE ACCENT IN TATSUKI IS ON THE TA! IT'S LIKE HAZUKI.

THAT WOULD BE THE FIRST SYLLABLE, FOLKS!

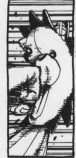

Ichigo's room has a bed, so why is his closet filled with futons?

Tatsuki, you're good friends with Ichigo, so you must know this one, right?

Asuka Koizumi-- Kanagawa

WHAT ABOUT IT, TATSUKI?

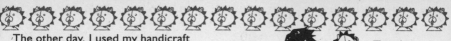

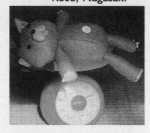

ICHIGO'S HOUSE DOESN'T HAVE MUCH STORAGE SPACE, SO YUZU'S AND KARIN'S AND BEARD MAN'S WINTER BEDDING ARE STORED IN ICHIGO'S ROOM. BUT HOW DOES THIS GIRL KNOW ABOUT THE KUROSAKI FAMILY'S CLOSETS? ARE YOU A FRIEND OF ICHIGO'S?

The other day, I used my handicraft skills to full effect and made a Kon (see photo). But without the insides, it's not a genuine Kon. Will you please tell me how to make Soul Candy or where I can buy some?
-- Rose, Nagasaki

SOUL CANDY CAN ONLY BE FOUND AT MR. URAHARA'S SHOP. IS THIS FOR REAL!? YOU DID A GOOD JOB!!! EVEN THE WEIGHT AND SIZE ARE PERFECT!! THAT'S AWESOME!! YOU CAN SELL THIS!! IT'S SURE TO BE A BIG HIT!! THANKS!! THANK YOU FOR MAKING SOMETHING SO GOOD!!!

YOU'RE RIGHT, THIS IS AMAZING. YOU'D BE CUTE IF YOU DIDN'T MOVE AROUND LIKE THAT.

...

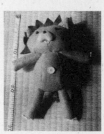

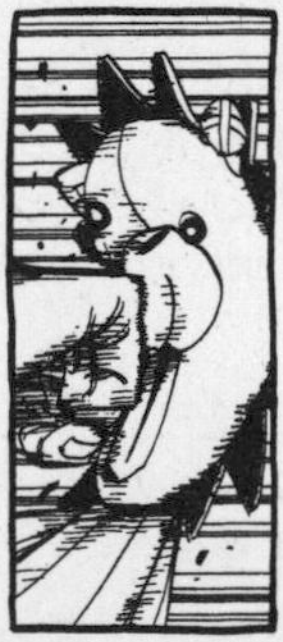

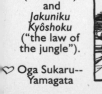

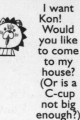

I want Kon! Would you like to come to my house? (Or is a C-cup not big enough?)

Yumiko-- Saitama

YAHOO!!! C!? HA HA!! THAT'LL DO NICELY!! I LOVE ANY SIZE SERVINGS THOUGH! THANK YOU VERY MUCH!! BUT IF YOU HAD REALLY SMALL BREASTS, LIKE TODAY'S GUEST, THAT WOULD BE A DIFFERENT STORY!!

I'M ALSO A C, BY THE WAY...

NO !!!?

What four-character idiom do you like? (My favorites are *Shiri Metsuretsu* ("chaotic") and *Jakuniku Kyôshoku* ("the law of the jungle").

♡ Oga Sukaru-- Yamagata

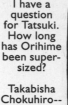

ICHIGEKI HISSATSU ("ONE SHOT, ONE KILL").
I-IN-RAN KYO-NYÛ ("BIG BOOBIE NYMPHO").
I have a question for Tatsuki. How long has Orihime been super-sized?
Takabisha Chokuhiro--Ishikawa
HOW LONG? I SAW HER ON THE FIELD BACK IN 7TH GRADE AND I THOUGHT SHE WAS AVERAGE, BUT THEN WE WERE IN THE SAME CLASS IN 8TH GRADE AND THEY WERE ALREADY PRETTY BIG.
UNLIKE YOURS...

UM, THERE'S SOMETHING ELSE WRITTEN ON THE SAME LETTER... LET'S SEE... "PLEASE, TRY TO TAKE OFF KON'S MANE. I THINK THAT WOULD TURN HIM INTO A BEAR." HMM.
HA HA! NO WAY THAT'S WRITTEN ON THERE...
IT *IS* WRITTEN ON THERE!!!
ALL RIGHT, HERE I GO...
S-STOP... STOP...
IYAAAAAAAAAAA!!!!

Single: "Good night! Radio-Kon Baby!"

Ending theme music: LION "Never Surrender" Play one chorus and fade out.

Now accepting letters!!

Any kind of question is fine!! Questions are chosen at random, but the acceptance rate for postcards is probably higher than for letters!! The third guest will be Uryû Ishida!! Include your question, name, address, age, and telephone number and send it all to the address below!

SHONEN JUMP c/o VIZ, LLC
P.O. Box 77010, San Francisco, CA 94107
ATTN: "Bleach" Radio-Kon Baby!!

Extra

URYÛ ON AUGUST 1st

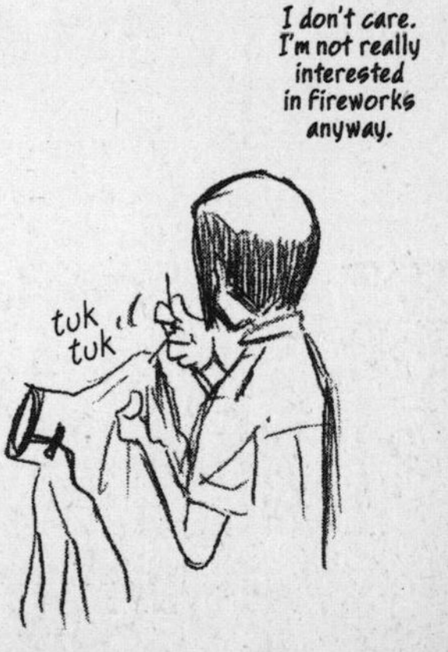
I don't care. I'm not really interested in fireworks anyway.
tuk tuk

Next Volume Preview

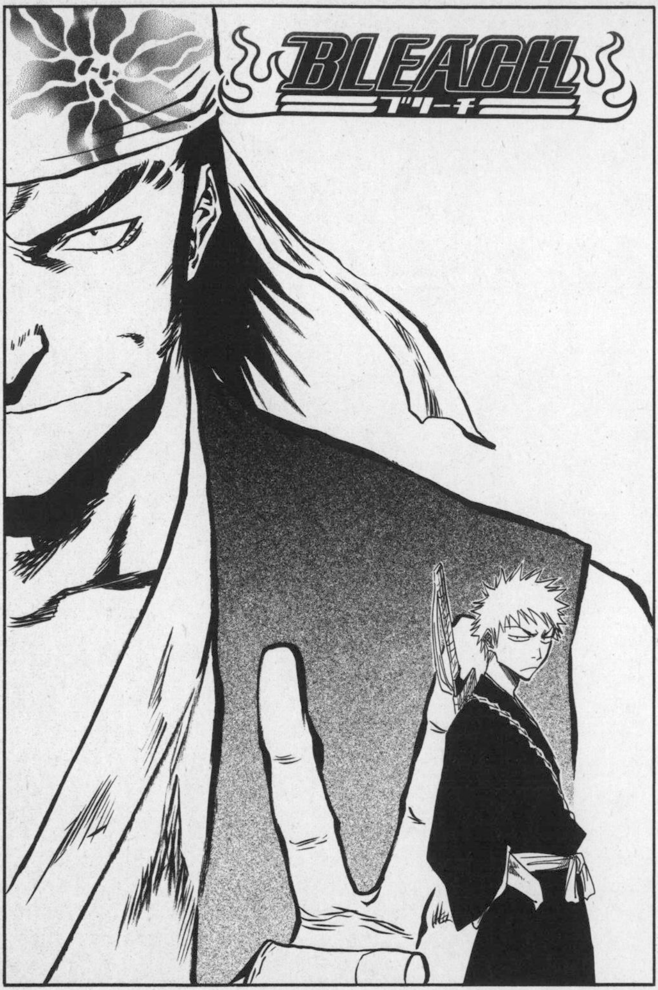
BLEACH
ブリーチ

Ichigo, Chad, Orihime, and Uryû have risked their lives trying to bust into the Soul Society, and now they're confronted with (yet another) gargantuan obstacle to their progress. Jidanbô, the enormously imposing bouncer/gatekeeper of the western gate, has defended his post for nigh on three centuries, and it doesn't look like he'll just step aside and let Ichigo's crew through without a super-sized fight. Let the gate-crashing commence!

12 rings to raise the dead... one man to find them

... HAPPY?

ONLY $7.99

Manga series on sale now!

ZOMBIEPOWDER.

SHONEN JUMP MANGA

VIZ media
www.viz.com
ZOMBIEPOWDER. © 1999 by Tite Kubo/SHUEISHA Inc.

RATED T+ FOR OLDER TEEN

ST

On sale at:
www.shonenjump.com
Also available at your local
bookstore and comic store.

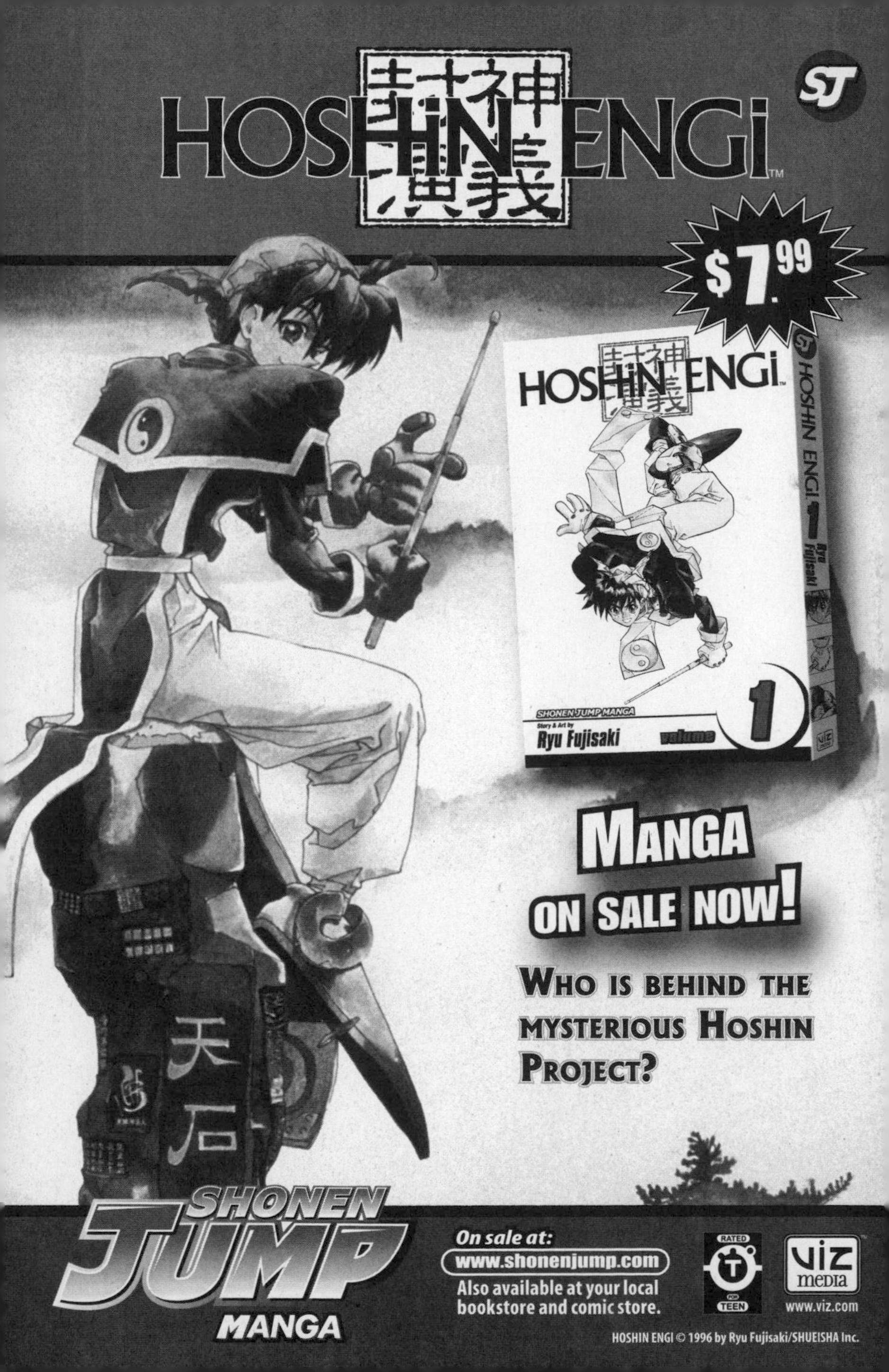

HOSHIN ENGI™
SJ
$7.99
HOSHIN ENGI
SHONEN JUMP MANGA
Story & Art by
Ryu Fujisaki
volume 1
MANGA
ON SALE NOW!
WHO IS BEHIND THE MYSTERIOUS HOSHIN PROJECT?
SHONEN JUMP MANGA
On sale at:
www.shonenjump.com
Also available at your local bookstore and comic store.
RATED T FOR TEEN
viz media
www.viz.com
HOSHIN ENGI © 1996 by Ryu Fujisaki/SHUEISHA Inc.

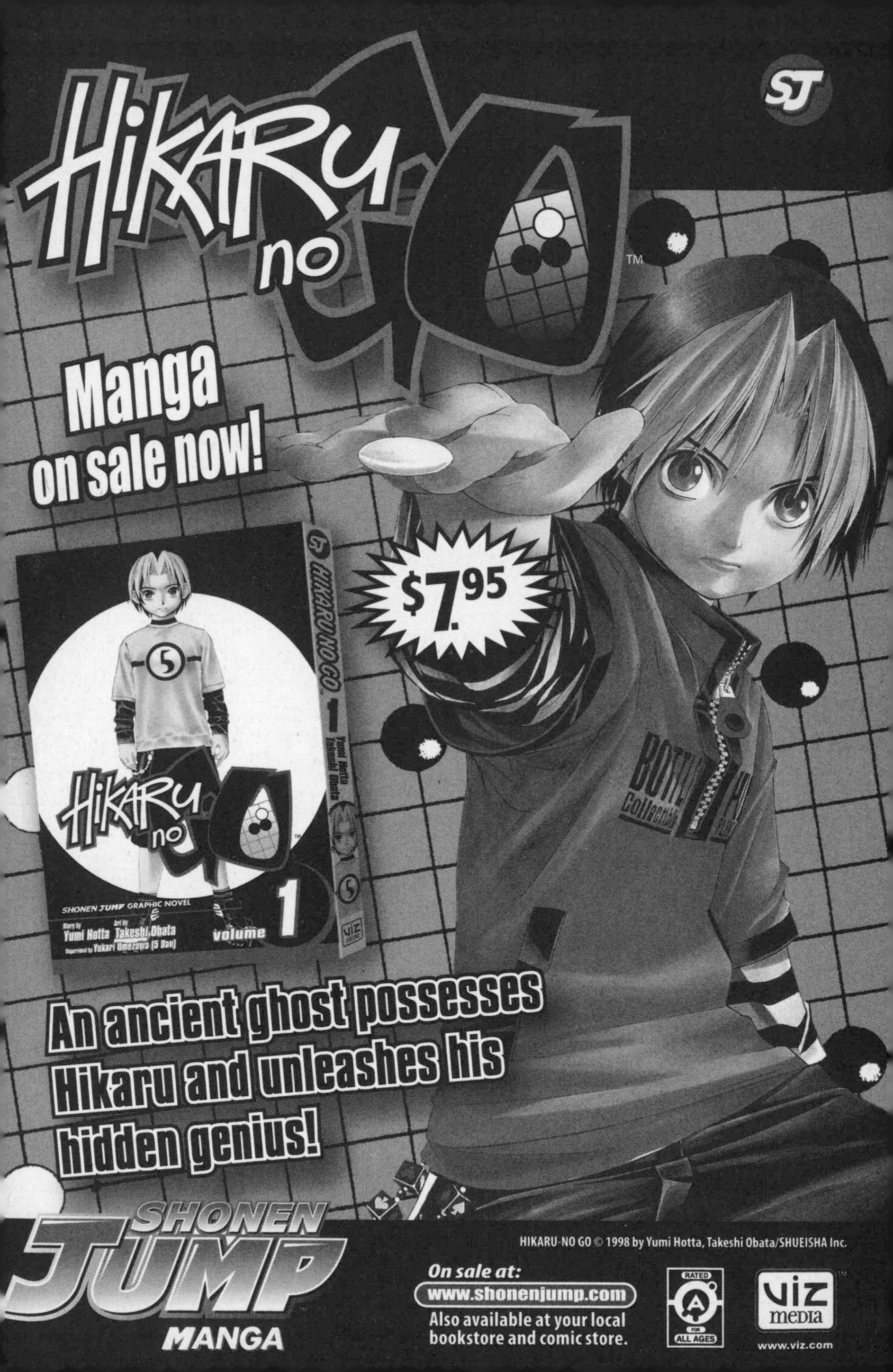

SJ
HIKARU no GO™
Manga on sale now!
$7.95
SJ HIKARU NO GO 1 Yumi Hotta Takeshi Obata
HIKARU no GO™
SHONEN JUMP GRAPHIC NOVEL
Story by Yumi Hotta Art by Takeshi Obata
Supervised by Yukari Umezawa (5 Dan)
volume 1
An ancient ghost possesses Hikaru and unleashes his hidden genius!
SHONEN JUMP MANGA
HIKARU-NO GO © 1998 by Yumi Hotta, Takeshi Obata/SHUEISHA Inc.
On sale at:
www.shonenjump.com
Also available at your local bookstore and comic store.
RATED A FOR ALL AGES
VIZ media
www.viz.com

THE START OF GOKU'S LEGENDARY QUEST!

DRAGON BALL™

BY AKIRA TORIYAMA

MANGA SERIES ON SALE NOW

On sale at:
www.shonenjump.com
Also available at your local
bookstore and comic store.

DRAGON BALL © 1984 by BIRD STUDIO/SHUEISHA Inc.

SHONEN JUMP
THE WORLD'S MOST POPULAR MANGA™

RATED
TEEN
ratings.viz.com

www.viz.com

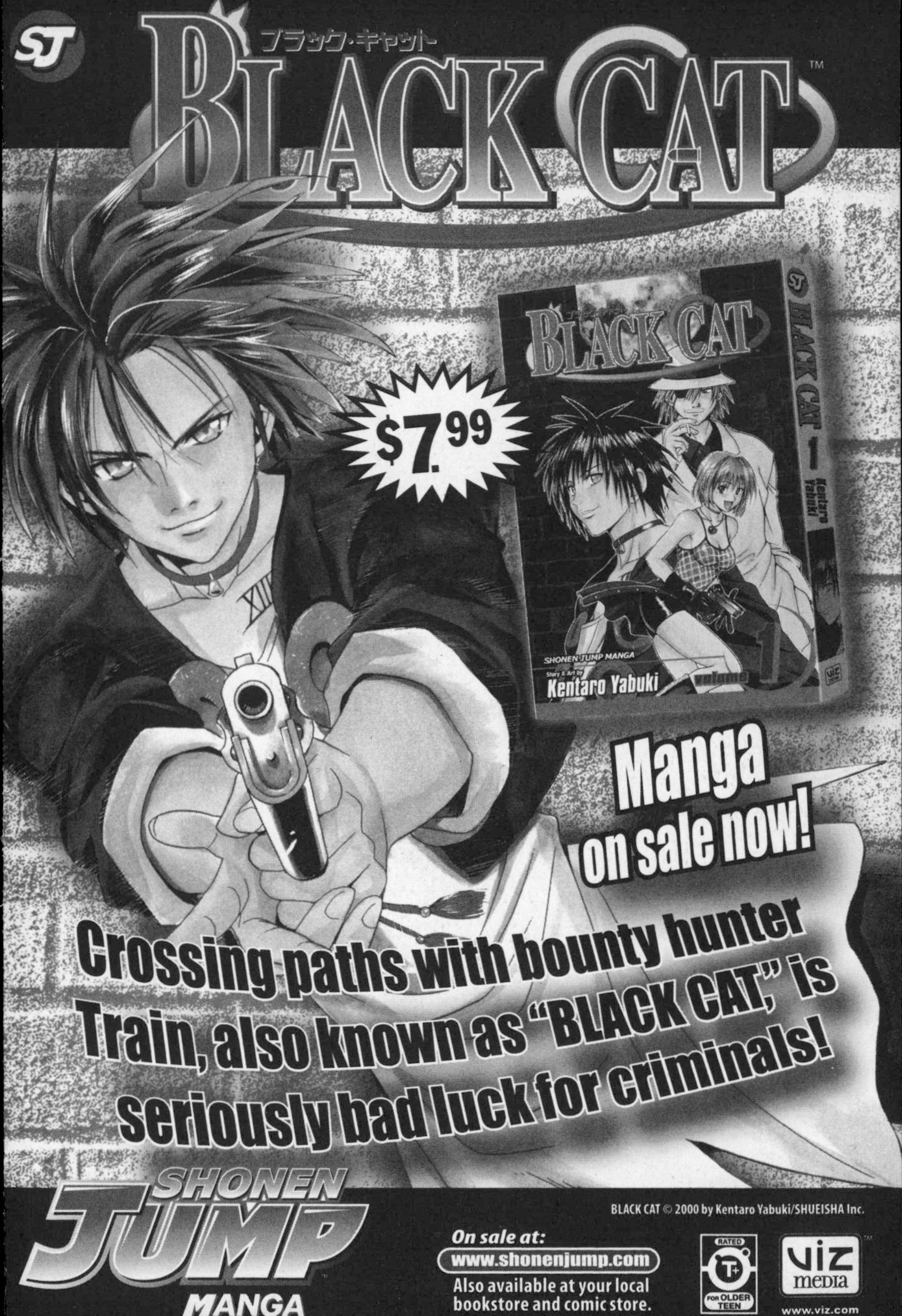
SJ
ブラック・キャット
BLACK CAT™
$7.99
SJ BLACK CAT 1 Kentaro Yabuki
SHONEN JUMP MANGA
Story & Art by
Kentaro Yabuki
volume
Manga on sale now!
Crossing paths with bounty hunter Train, also known as "BLACK CAT," is seriously bad luck for criminals!
SHONEN JUMP MANGA
BLACK CAT © 2000 by Kentaro Yabuki/SHUEISHA Inc.
On sale at:
www.shonenjump.com
Also available at your local bookstore and comic store.
RATED T+ FOR OLDER TEEN
VIZ media
www.viz.com

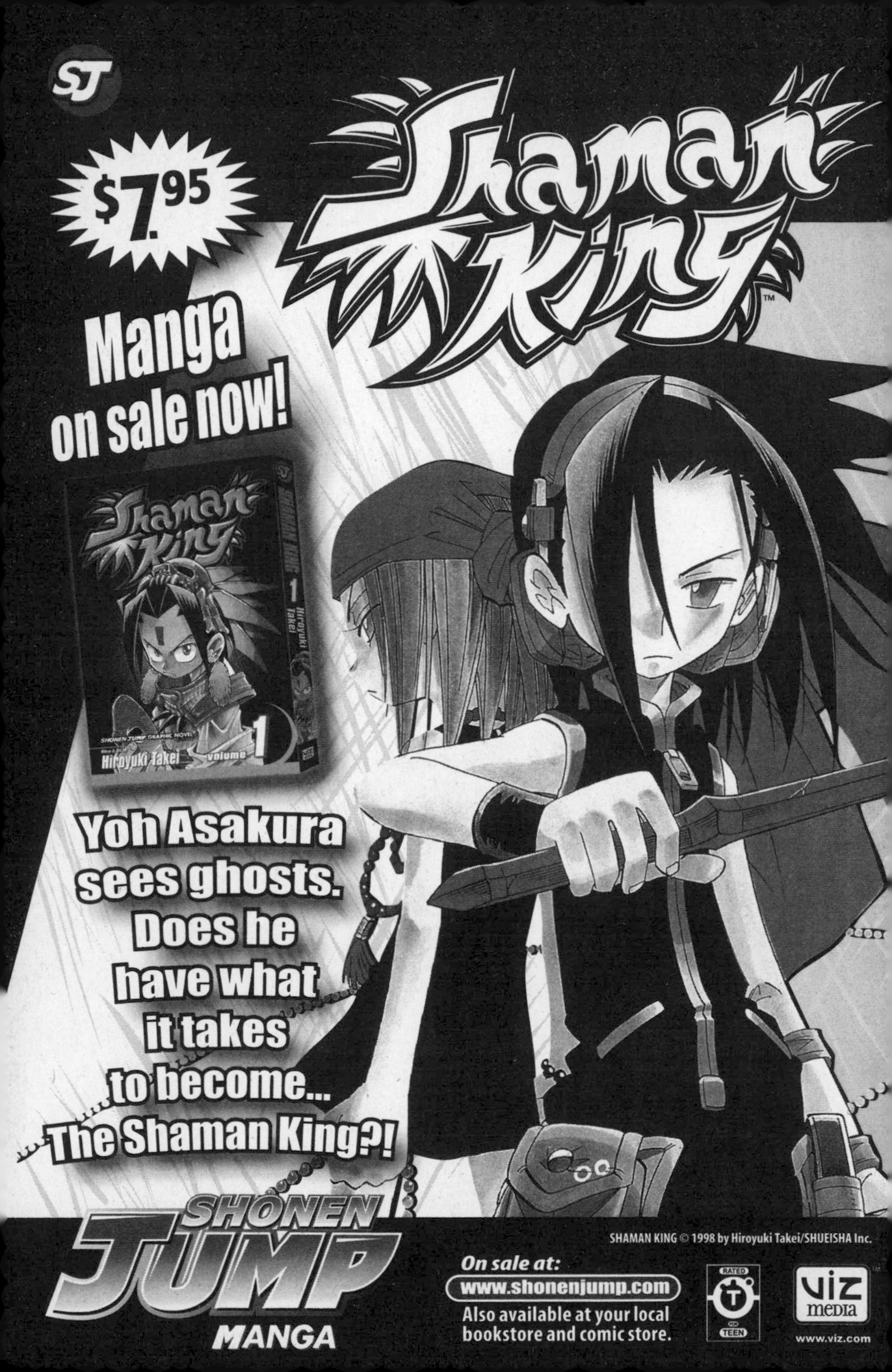
SJ
$7.95
Shaman King™
Manga on sale now!
Shaman King
1
Hiroyuki Takei
SHONEN JUMP GRAPHIC NOVEL
Hiroyuki Takei volume 1
Yoh Asakura sees ghosts. Does he have what it takes to become... The Shaman King?!
SHONEN JUMP MANGA
SHAMAN KING © 1998 by Hiroyuki Takei/SHUEISHA Inc.
On sale at:
www.shonenjump.com
Also available at your local bookstore and comic store.
RATED T FOR TEEN
VIZ media
www.viz.com

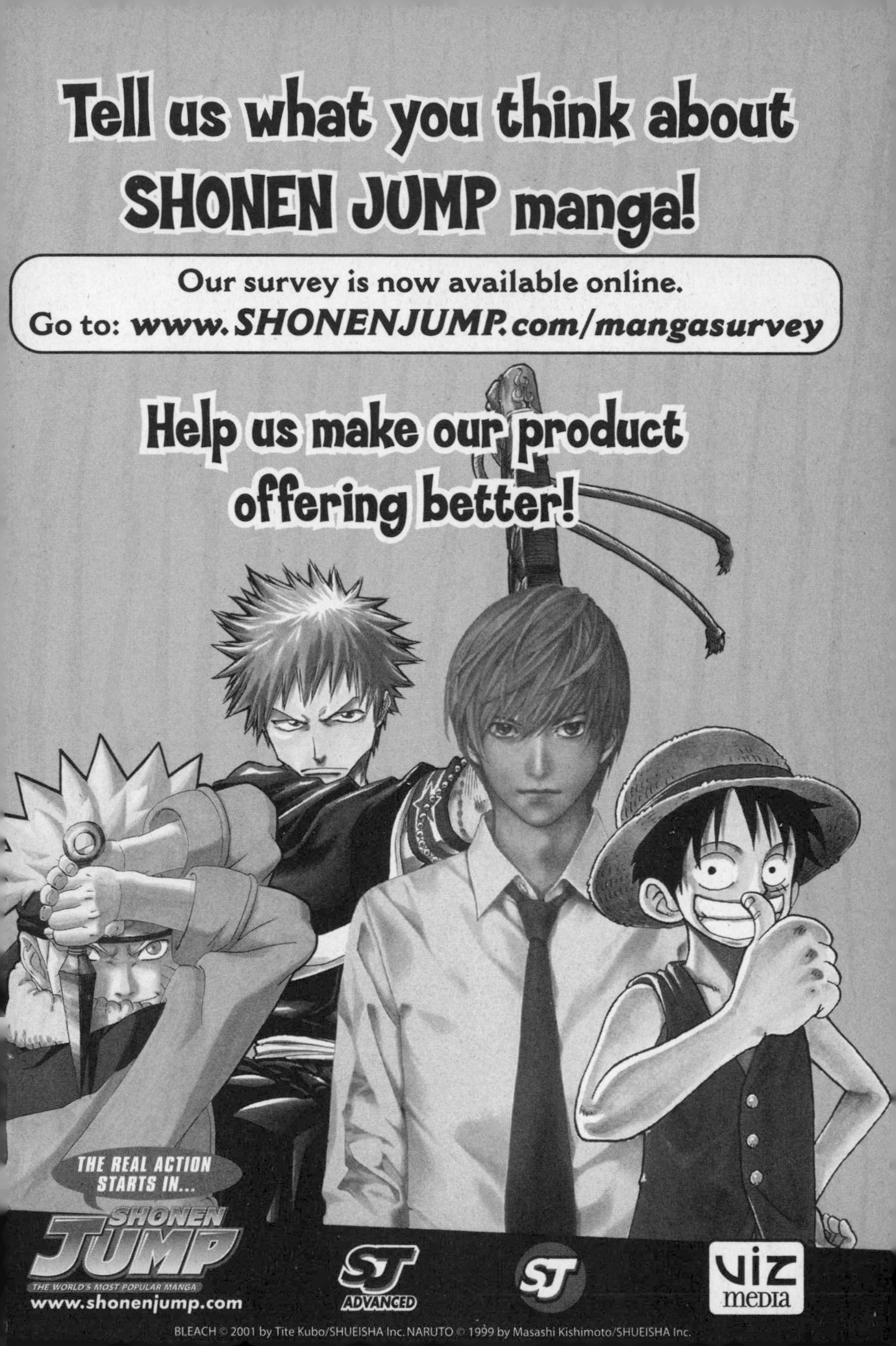
Tell us what you think about
SHONEN JUMP manga!
Our survey is now available online.
Go to: www.SHONENJUMP.com/mangasurvey
Help us make our product
offering better!
THE REAL ACTION STARTS IN...
SHONEN JUMP
THE WORLD'S MOST POPULAR MANGA
www.shonenjump.com
SJ ADVANCED
SJ
VIZ media
BLEACH © 2001 by Tite Kubo/SHUEISHA Inc. NARUTO © 1999 by Masashi Kishimoto/SHUEISHA Inc.

SHONEN JUMP

THE WORLD'S MOST POPULAR MANGA

12 ISSUES FOR ONLY $29.95*

THAT'S 50% OFF THE NEWSSTAND PRICE!

Each issue of SHONEN JUMP contains the coolest manga available in the U.S., anime news, and info on video & card games, toys AND more!

SUBSCRIBE TODAY and Become a Member of the SJ Sub Club!

- **ENJOY** 12 HUGE action-packed issues
- **SAVE** 50% OFF the cover price
- **ACCESS** exclusive areas of www.shonenjump.com
- **RECEIVE** FREE members-only gifts

Available ONLY to Subscribers!

RATED T FOR TEEN
ratings.viz.com

www.viz.com

3 EASY WAYS TO SUBSCRIBE!

1) Send in the subscription order form from this book **OR**
2) Log on to: www.shonenjump.com **OR**
3) Call 1-800-541-7919

*Canada price for 12 issues: $41.95 USD, including GST, HST, and QST. US/CAN orders only. Allow 6-8 weeks for delivery.
BLEACH © 2001 by Tite Kubo/SHUEISHA Inc. NARUTO © 1999 by Masashi Kishimoto/SHUEISHA Inc.
GINTAMA © 2003 by Hideaki Sorachi/SHUEISHA Inc. ONE PIECE © 1997 by Eiichiro Oda/SHUEISHA Inc.

Save **50% OFF** the cover price!

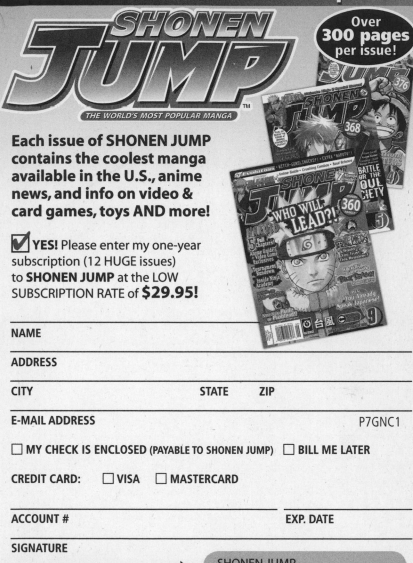

SHONEN JUMP™

THE WORLD'S MOST POPULAR MANGA

Over 300 pages per issue!

Each issue of SHONEN JUMP contains the coolest manga available in the U.S., anime news, and info on video & card games, toys AND more!

☑ **YES!** Please enter my one-year subscription (12 HUGE issues) to **SHONEN JUMP** at the LOW SUBSCRIPTION RATE of **$29.95!**

NAME _____

ADDRESS _____

CITY _____ STATE _____ ZIP _____

E-MAIL ADDRESS _____ P7GNC1

☐ MY CHECK IS ENCLOSED (PAYABLE TO SHONEN JUMP)   ☐ BILL ME LATER

CREDIT CARD: ☐ VISA   ☐ MASTERCARD

ACCOUNT # _____ EXP. DATE _____

SIGNATURE _____

CLIP AND MAIL TO ➤

SHONEN JUMP
Subscriptions Service Dept.
P.O. Box 515
Mount Morris, IL 61054-0515

Make checks payable to: **SHONEN JUMP**. Canada price for 12 issues: $41.95 USD, including GST, HST and QST. US/CAN orders only. Allow 6-8 weeks for delivery.

BLEACH © 2001 by Tite Kubo/SHUEISHA Inc. NARUTO © 1999 by Masashi Kishimoto/SHUEISHA Inc.
ONE PIECE © 1997 by Eiichiro Oda/SHUEISHA Inc.

RATED **T** TEEN

ratings.viz.com